Hayate the combat butler 18

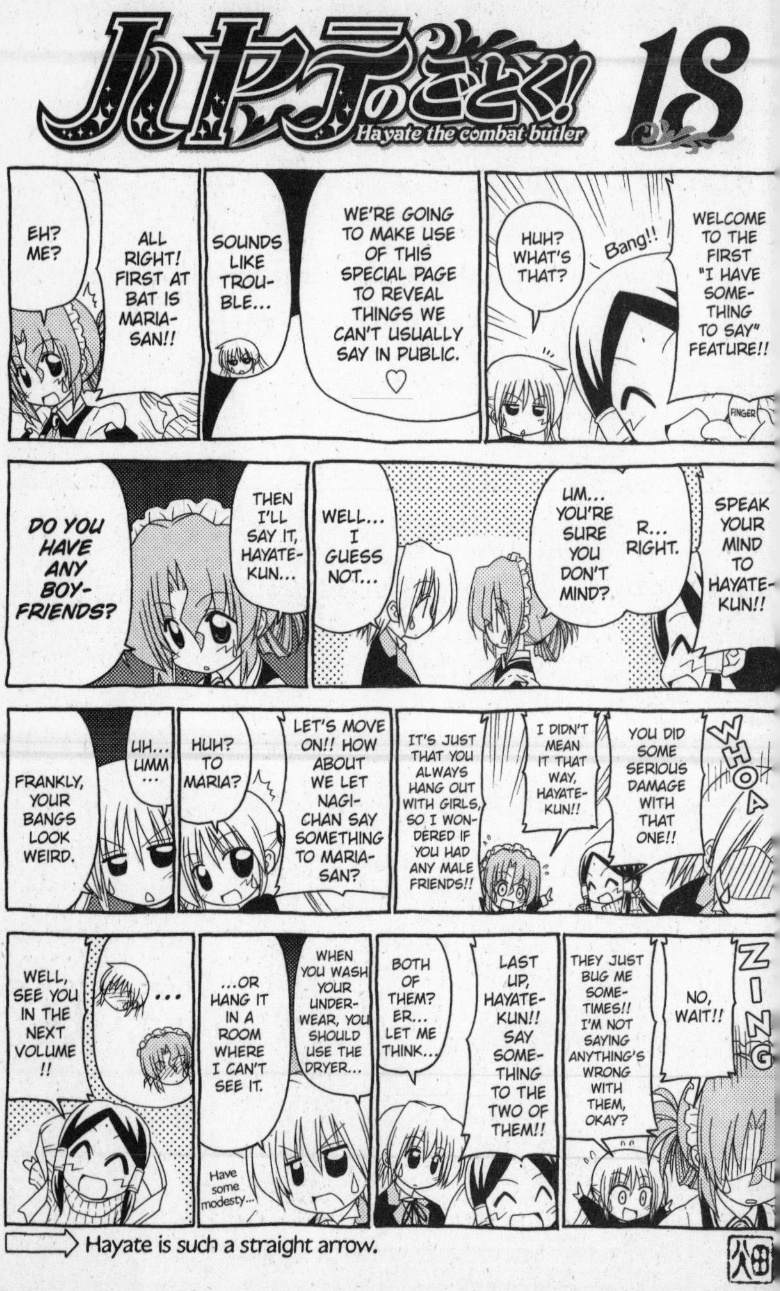
WELCOME TO THE FIRST "I HAVE SOMETHING TO SAY" FEATURE!!
Bang!!
HUH? WHAT'S THAT?
FINGER
WE'RE GOING TO MAKE USE OF THIS SPECIAL PAGE TO REVEAL THINGS WE CAN'T USUALLY SAY IN PUBLIC. ♡
SOUNDS LIKE TROUBLE...
ALL RIGHT! FIRST AT BAT IS MARIA-SAN!!
EH? ME?
SPEAK YOUR MIND TO HAYATE-KUN!!
R... RIGHT.
UM... YOU'RE SURE YOU DON'T MIND?
WELL... I GUESS NOT...
THEN I'LL SAY IT, HAYATE-KUN...
DO YOU HAVE ANY BOYFRIENDS?
WHOA
YOU DID SOME SERIOUS DAMAGE WITH THAT ONE!!
I DIDN'T MEAN IT THAT WAY, HAYATE-KUN!!
IT'S JUST THAT YOU ALWAYS HANG OUT WITH GIRLS, SO I WONDERED IF YOU HAD ANY MALE FRIENDS!!
LET'S MOVE ON!! HOW ABOUT WE LET NAGI-CHAN SAY SOMETHING TO MARIA-SAN?
HUH? TO MARIA?
UH... UMM ...
FRANKLY, YOUR BANGS LOOK WEIRD.
ZING
NO, WAIT!!
THEY JUST BUG ME SOMETIMES!! I'M NOT SAYING ANYTHING'S WRONG WITH THEM, OKAY?
LAST UP, HAYATE-KUN!! SAY SOMETHING TO THE TWO OF THEM!!
BOTH OF THEM? ER... LET ME THINK...
WHEN YOU WASH YOUR UNDERWEAR, YOU SHOULD USE THE DRYER...
...OR HANG IT IN A ROOM WHERE I CAN'T SEE IT.
Have some modesty...
...
WELL, SEE YOU IN THE NEXT VOLUME!!

Hayate is such a straight arrow.

HAYATE THE COMBAT BUTLER
VOL. 18
Shonen Sunday Edition

STORY AND ART BY
KENJIRO HATA

Original Japanese edition "HAYATE NO GOTOKU!" published by SHOGAKUKAN Inc.

English Adaptation/Mark Giambruno
Translation/Yuki Yoshioka and Cindy H. Yamauchi
Touch-up Art & Lettering/HudsonYards
Design/Yukiko Whitley
Editor/Shaenon K. Garrity

The rights of the author(s) of the work(s) in this publication to be so identified have been asserted in accordance with the Copyright, Designs and Patents Act 1988. A CIP catalogue record for this book is available from the British Library.

Printed in Canada

Published by VIZ Media, LLC
P.O. Box 77010
San Francisco, CA 94107

10 9 8 7 6 5 4 3 2 1
First printing, September 2011

www.viz.com

WWW.SHONENSUNDAY.COM

PARENTAL ADVISORY
HAYATE THE COMBAT BUTLER is rated T+ for Older Teen and is recommended for ages 16 and up. This volume contains fantasy violence and crude humor.

T+ FOR OLDER TEEN

ratings.viz.com

Hayate the Combat Butler

18

TOY STORE
RAINBOW BRIDGE
PART-TIMER
WANTED

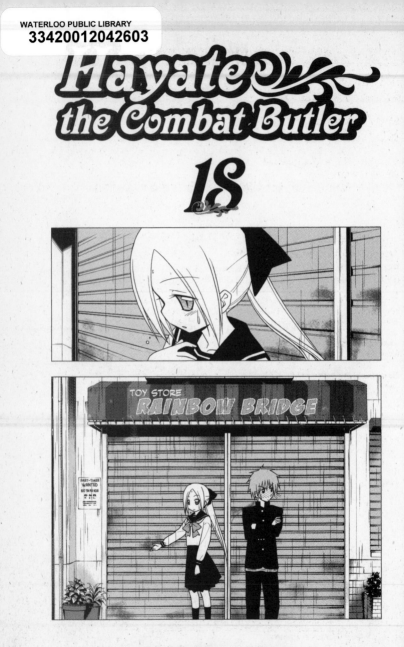

KENJIRO HATA

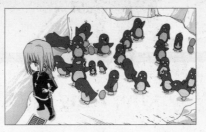

*The penguins spell out "Table of Contents."

Episode 1: "THE END OF THE WORLD ⑧ The Birth of the King of Hatred"

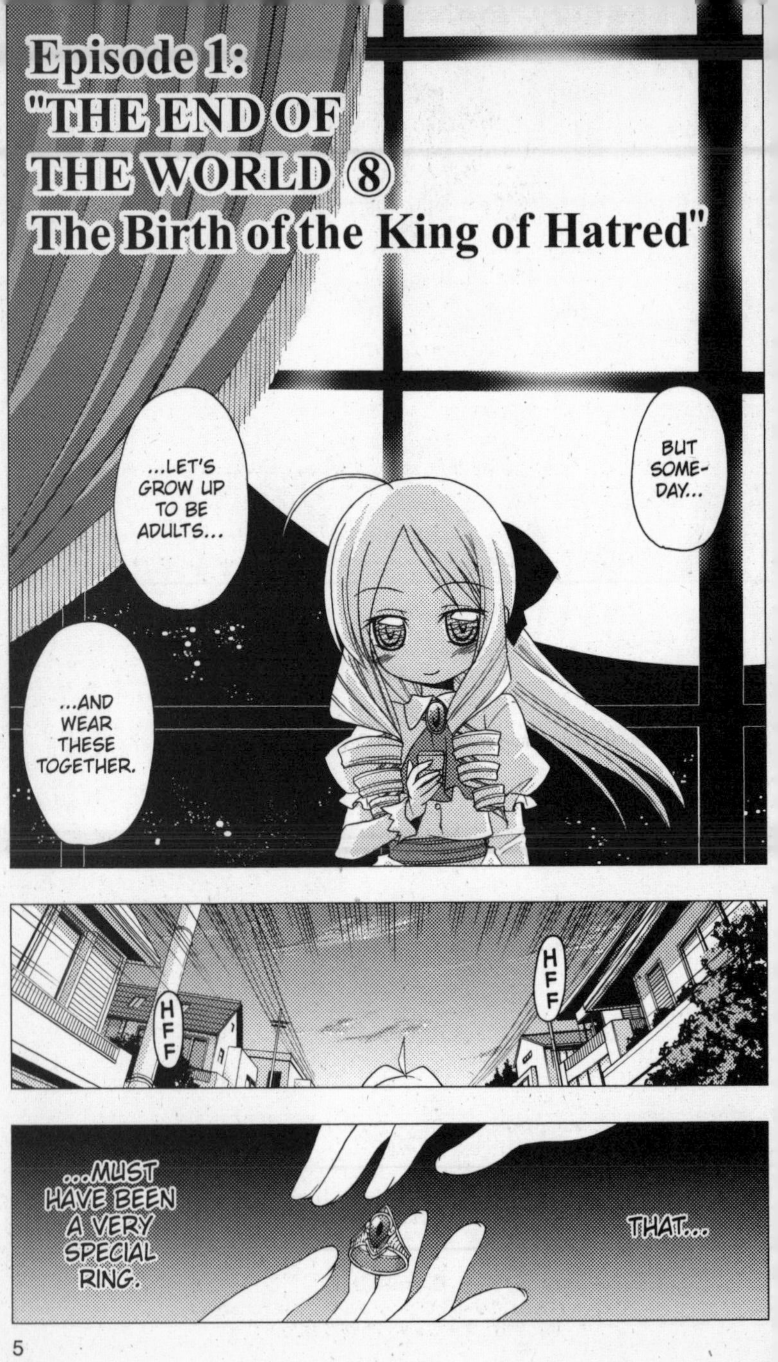
BUT SOME-DAY...
...LET'S GROW UP TO BE ADULTS...
...AND WEAR THESE TOGETHER.
HFF
HFF
THAT...
...MUST HAVE BEEN A VERY SPECIAL RING.

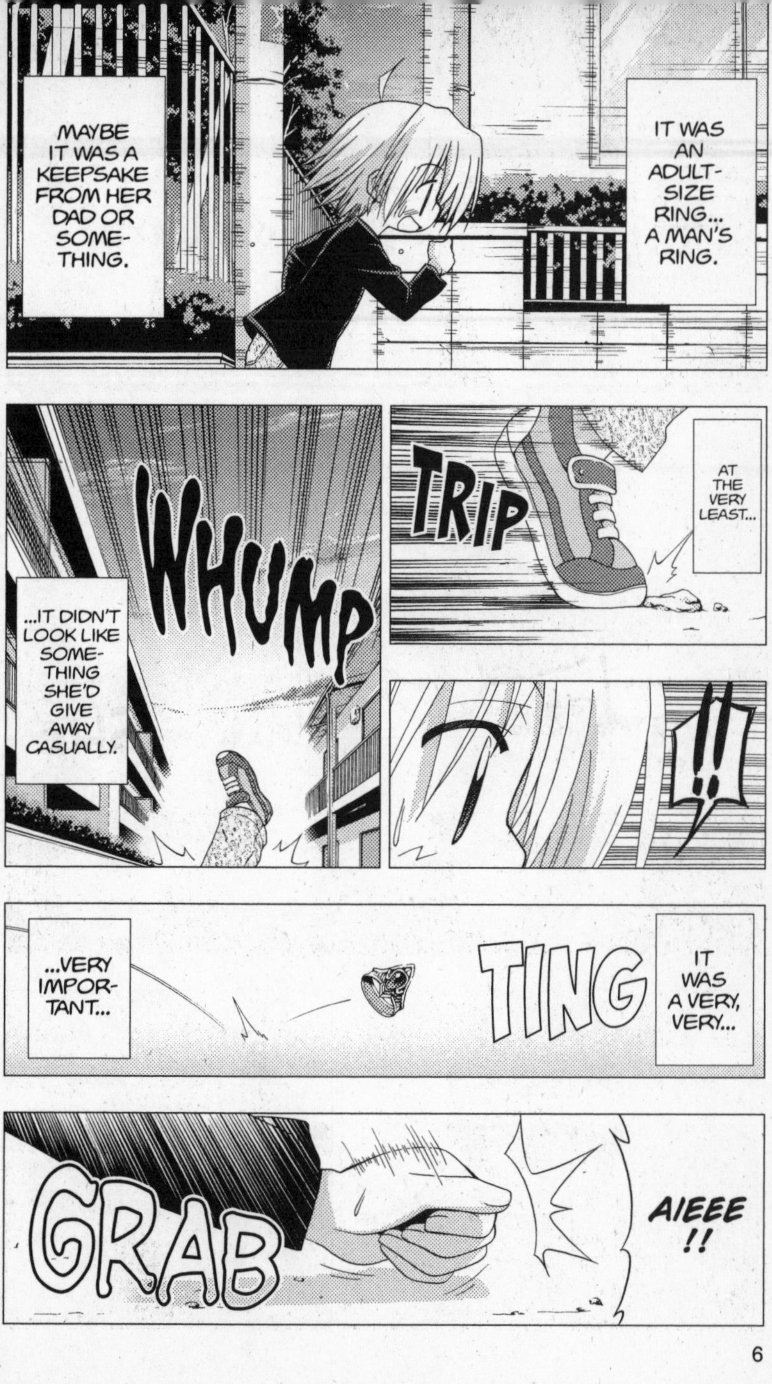
IT WAS AN ADULT-SIZE RING... A MAN'S RING.
MAYBE IT WAS A KEEPSAKE FROM HER DAD OR SOMETHING.
AT THE VERY LEAST...
TRIP
!!
WHUMP
...IT DIDN'T LOOK LIKE SOMETHING SHE'D GIVE AWAY CASUALLY.
IT WAS A VERY, VERY...
TING
...VERY IMPORTANT...
AIEEE !!
GRAB

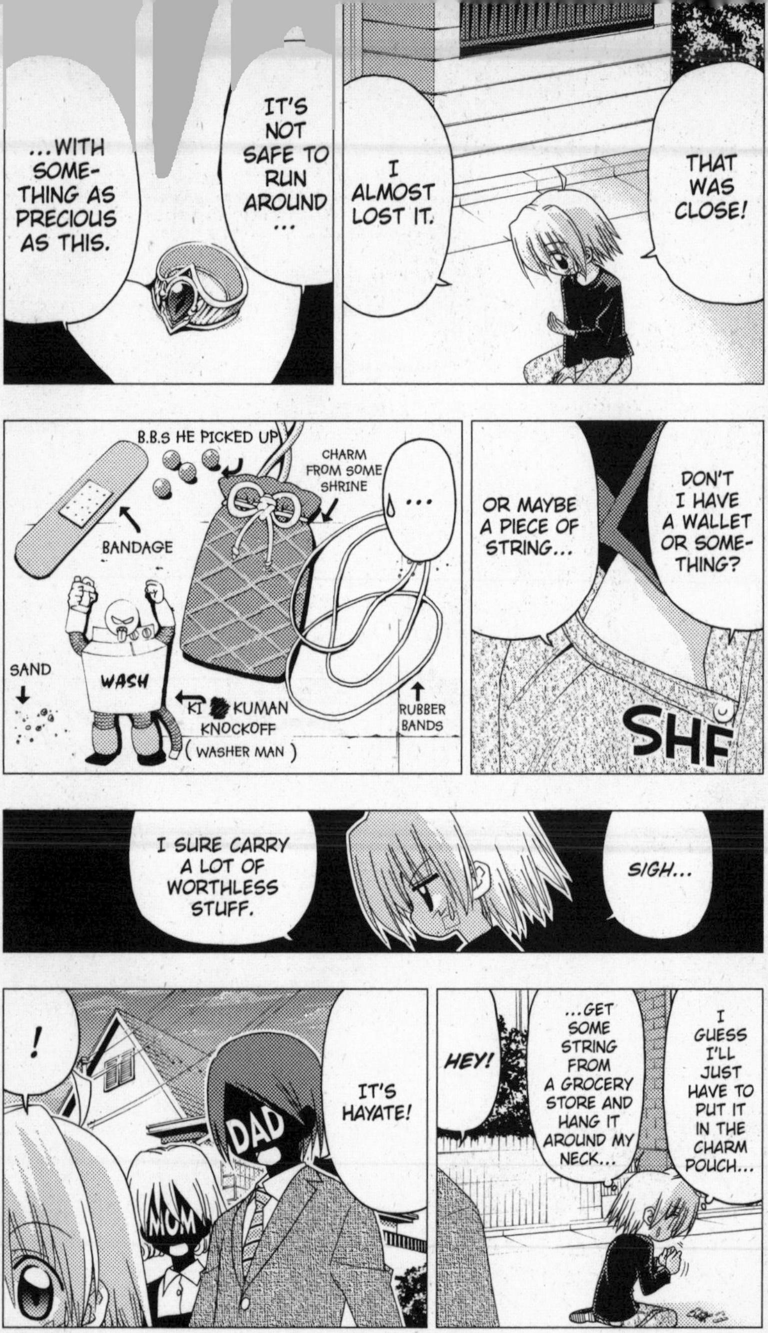
THAT WAS CLOSE!
I ALMOST LOST IT.
IT'S NOT SAFE TO RUN AROUND...
...WITH SOME-THING AS PRECIOUS AS THIS.
DON'T I HAVE A WALLET OR SOME-THING?
OR MAYBE A PIECE OF STRING...
SHF
...
B.B.S HE PICKED UP
CHARM FROM SOME SHRINE
BANDAGE
WASH
SAND
KUMAN KNOCKOFF
(WASHER MAN)
RUBBER BANDS
SIGH...
I SURE CARRY A LOT OF WORTHLESS STUFF.
I GUESS I'LL JUST HAVE TO PUT IT IN THE CHARM POUCH...
...GET SOME STRING FROM A GROCERY STORE AND HANG IT AROUND MY NECK...
HEY!
IT'S HAYATE!
DAD
MOM
!

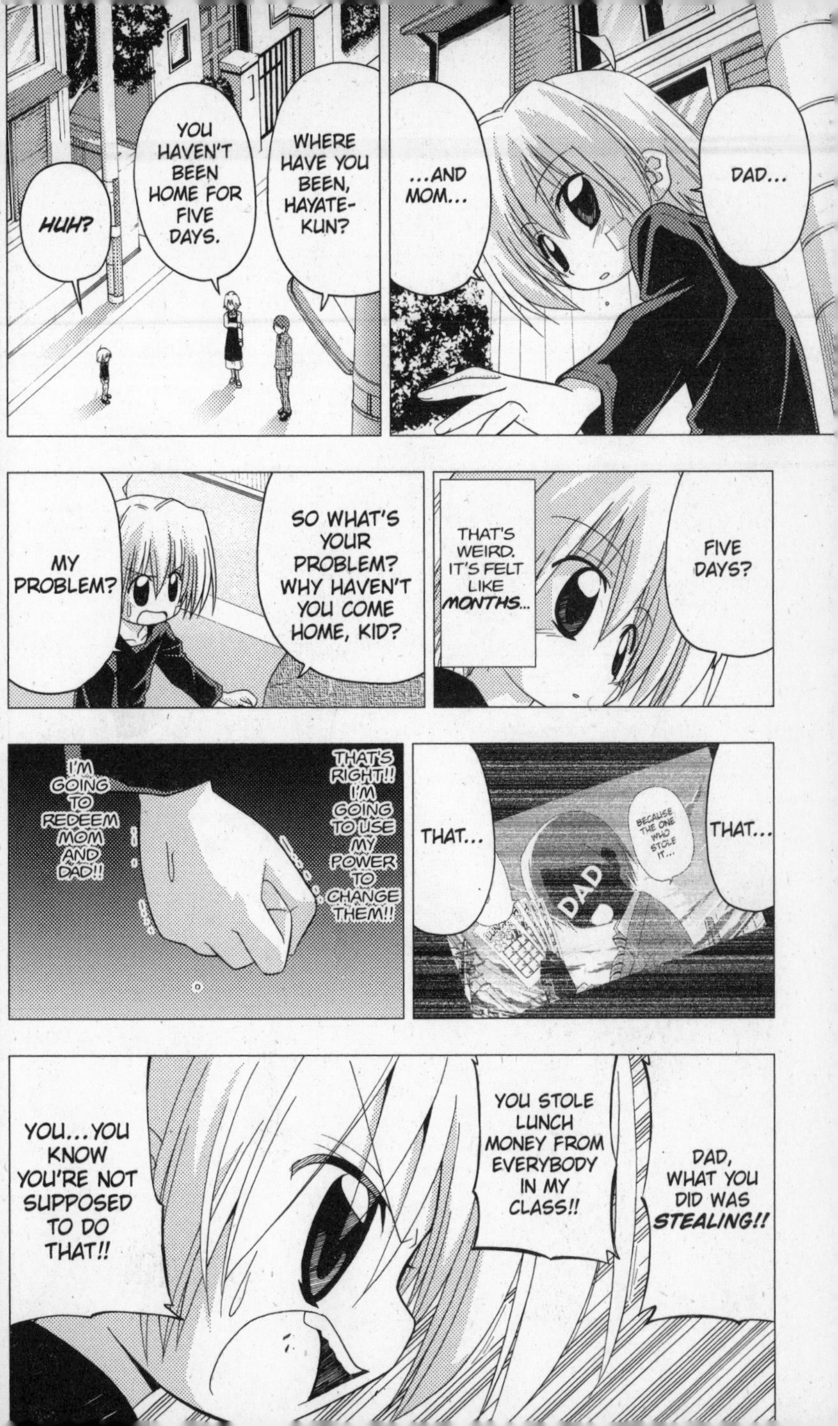
DAD...
...AND MOM...
WHERE HAVE YOU BEEN, HAYATE-KUN?
YOU HAVEN'T BEEN HOME FOR FIVE DAYS.
HUH?
FIVE DAYS?
THAT'S WEIRD. IT'S FELT LIKE MONTHS...
SO WHAT'S YOUR PROBLEM? WHY HAVEN'T YOU COME HOME, KID?
MY PROBLEM?
THAT...
BECAUSE THE ONE WHO STOLE IT...
DAD
THAT...
THAT'S RIGHT!! I'M GOING TO USE MY POWER TO CHANGE THEM!!
I'M GOING TO REDEEM MOM AND DAD!!
DAD, WHAT YOU DID WAS STEALING!!
YOU STOLE LUNCH MONEY FROM EVERYBODY IN MY CLASS!!
YOU...YOU KNOW YOU'RE NOT SUPPOSED TO DO THAT!!

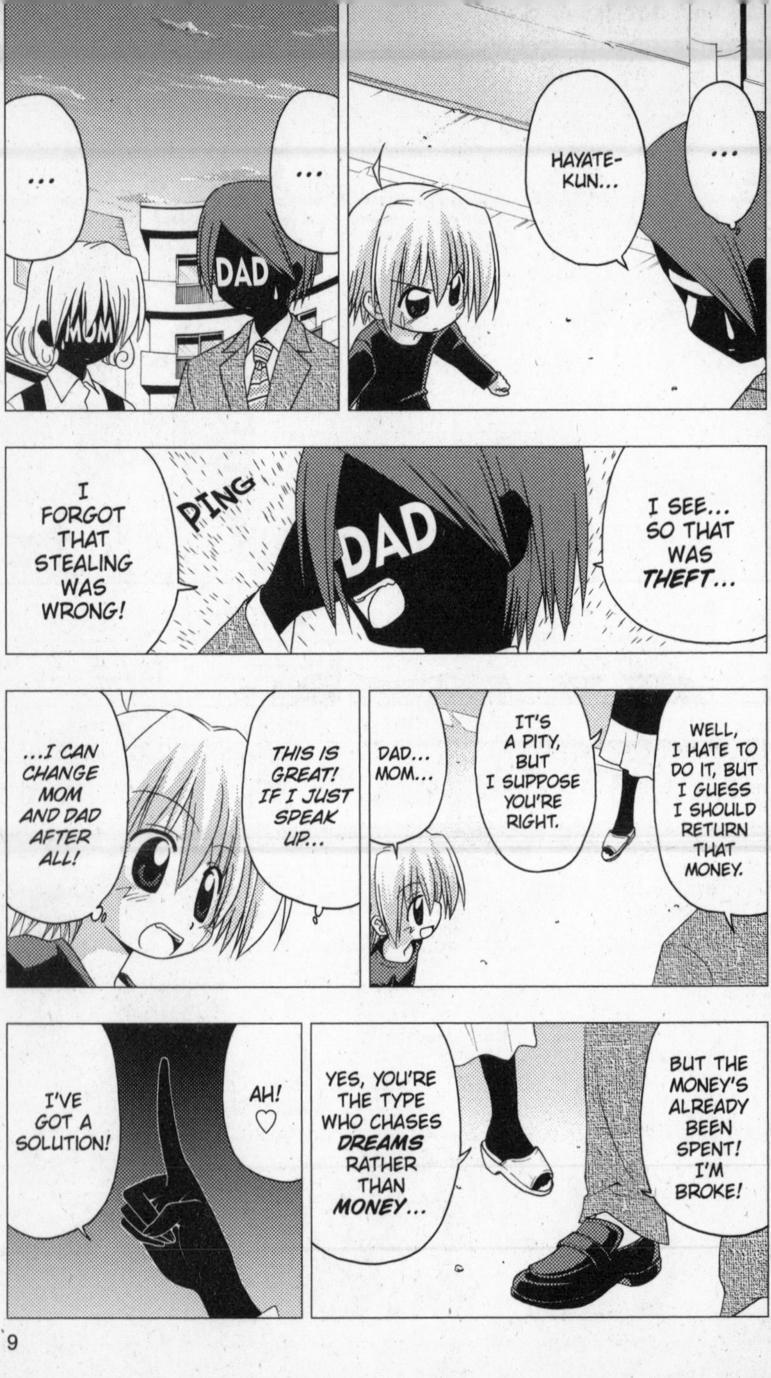

...
HAYATE-KUN...
...
DAD
...
MOM
I SEE... SO THAT WAS *THEFT*...
DAD
PING
I FORGOT THAT STEALING WAS WRONG!
WELL, I HATE TO DO IT, BUT I GUESS I SHOULD RETURN THAT MONEY.
IT'S A PITY, BUT I SUPPOSE YOU'RE RIGHT.
DAD... MOM...
THIS IS GREAT! IF I JUST SPEAK UP...
...I CAN CHANGE MOM AND DAD AFTER ALL!
BUT THE MONEY'S ALREADY BEEN SPENT! I'M BROKE!
YES, YOU'RE THE TYPE WHO CHASES ***DREAMS*** RATHER THAN ***MONEY***...
AH! ♡
I'VE GOT A SOLUTION!

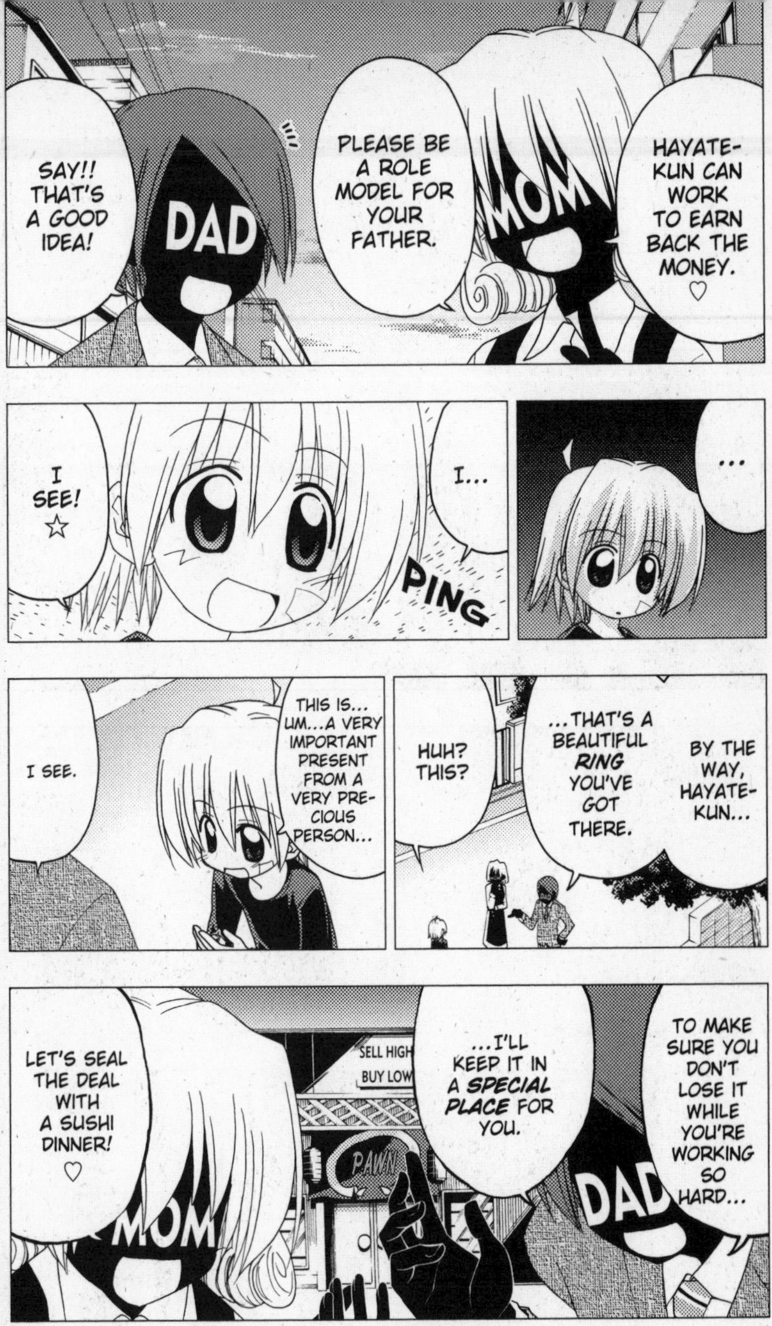
HAYATE-KUN CAN WORK TO EARN BACK THE MONEY. ♡
MOM
PLEASE BE A ROLE MODEL FOR YOUR FATHER.
DAD
SAY!! THAT'S A GOOD IDEA!
...
I...
PING
I SEE! ☆
BY THE WAY, HAYATE-KUN...
...THAT'S A BEAUTIFUL RING YOU'VE GOT THERE.
HUH? THIS?
THIS IS... UM...A VERY IMPORTANT PRESENT FROM A VERY PRECIOUS PERSON...
I SEE.
TO MAKE SURE YOU DON'T LOSE IT WHILE YOU'RE WORKING SO HARD...
DAD
...I'LL KEEP IT IN A SPECIAL PLACE FOR YOU.
SELL HIGH
BUY LOW
PAWN
LET'S SEAL THE DEAL WITH A SUSHI DINNER! ♡
MOM

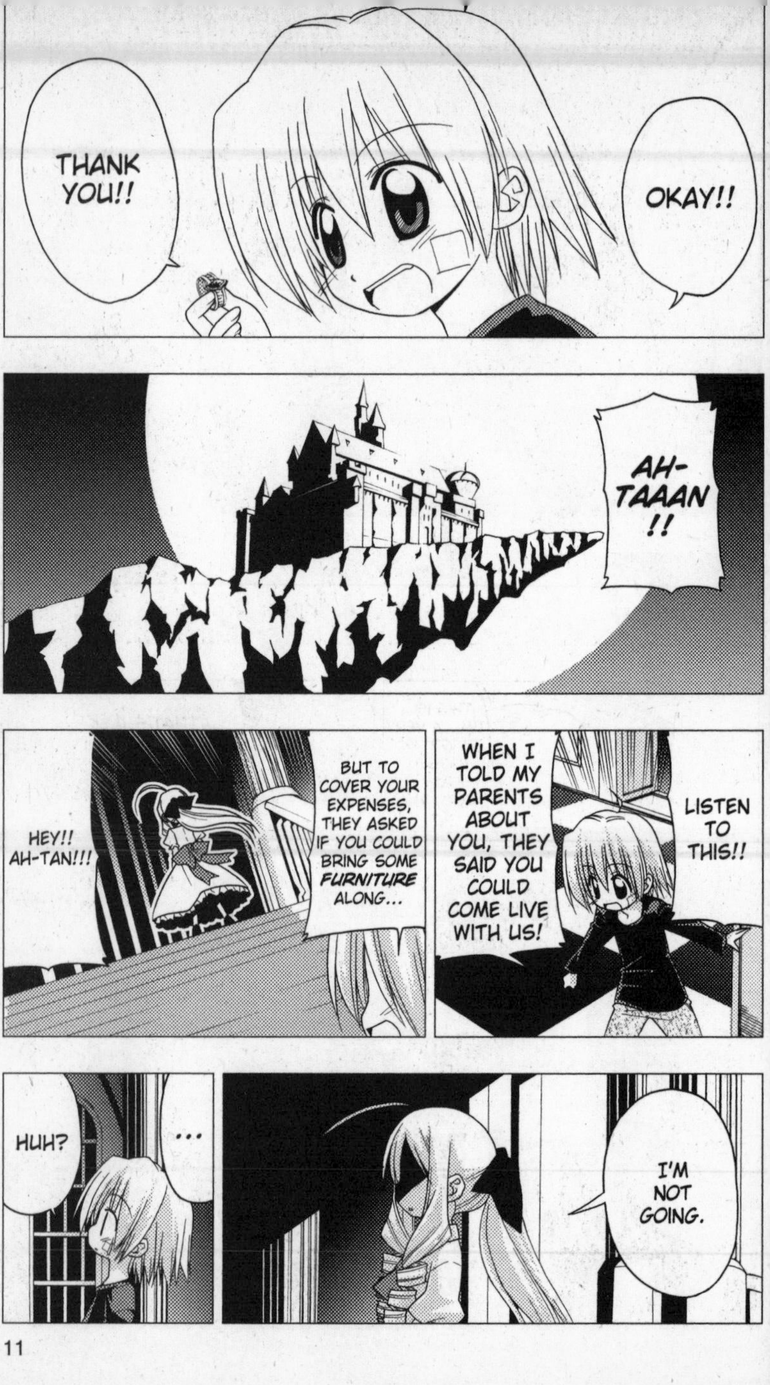
OKAY!!
THANK YOU!!
AH-TAAAN!!
LISTEN TO THIS!!
WHEN I TOLD MY PARENTS ABOUT YOU, THEY SAID YOU COULD COME LIVE WITH US!
BUT TO COVER YOUR EXPENSES, THEY ASKED IF YOU COULD BRING SOME FURNITURE ALONG...
HEY!! AH-TAN!!!
I'M NOT GOING.
...
HUH?

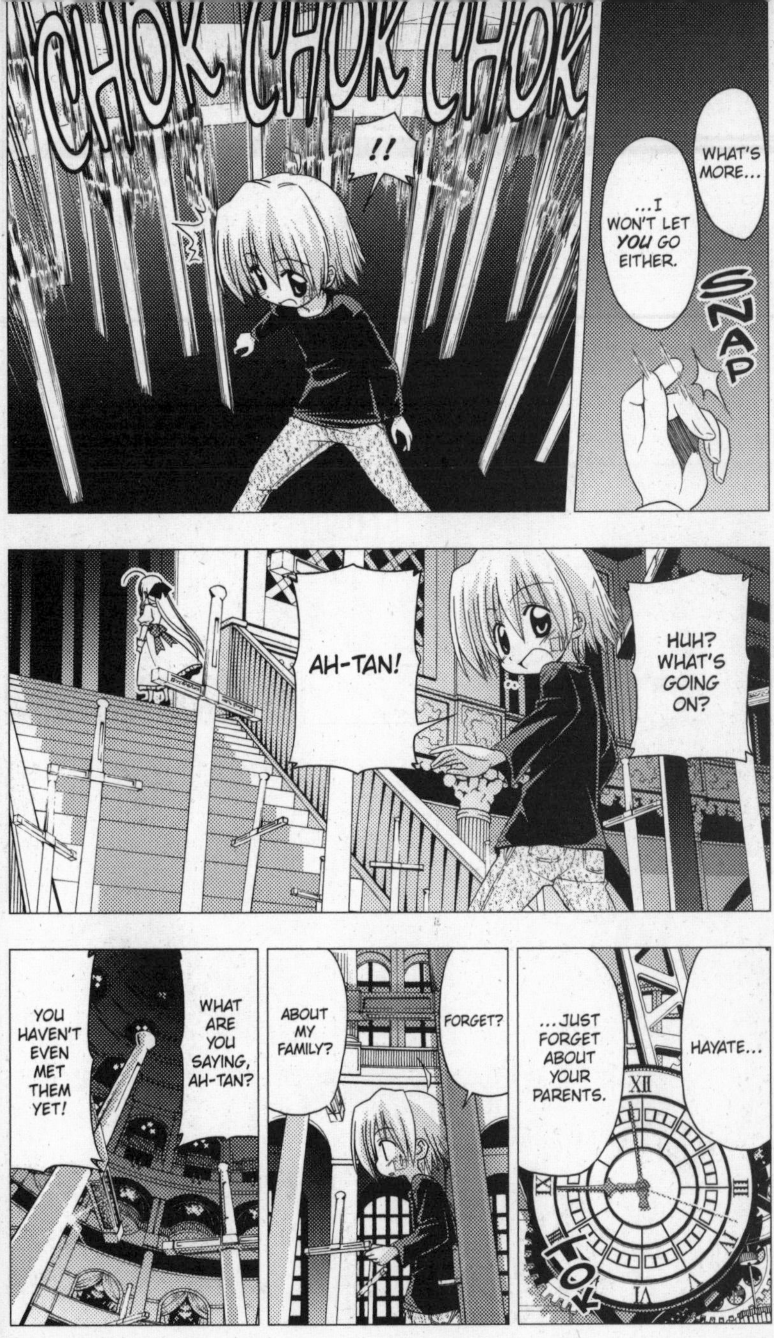
WHAT'S MORE...
...I WON'T LET YOU GO EITHER.
SNAP
CHOK CHOK CHOK
!!
HUH? WHAT'S GOING ON?
AH-TAN!
HAYATE...
...JUST FORGET ABOUT YOUR PARENTS.
TOK
FORGET?
ABOUT MY FAMILY?
WHAT ARE YOU SAYING, AH-TAN?
YOU HAVEN'T EVEN MET THEM YET!

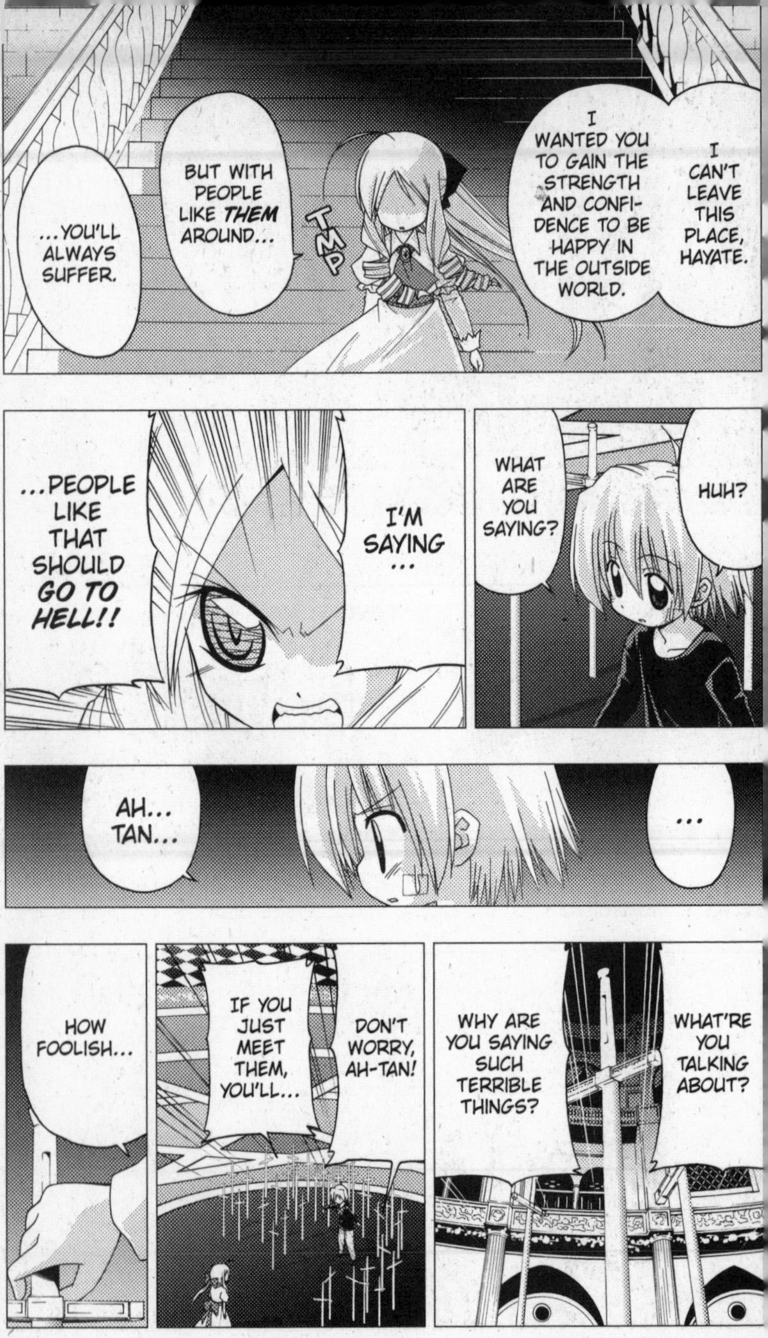
I CAN'T LEAVE THIS PLACE, HAYATE.
I WANTED YOU TO GAIN THE STRENGTH AND CONFIDENCE TO BE HAPPY IN THE OUTSIDE WORLD.
TMP
BUT WITH PEOPLE LIKE *THEM* AROUND...
...YOU'LL ALWAYS SUFFER.
HUH?
WHAT ARE YOU SAYING?
I'M SAYING...
...PEOPLE LIKE THAT SHOULD *GO TO HELL!!*
...
AH... TAN...
WHAT'RE YOU TALKING ABOUT?
WHY ARE YOU SAYING SUCH TERRIBLE THINGS?
DON'T WORRY, AH-TAN!
IF YOU JUST MEET THEM, YOU'LL...
HOW FOOLISH...

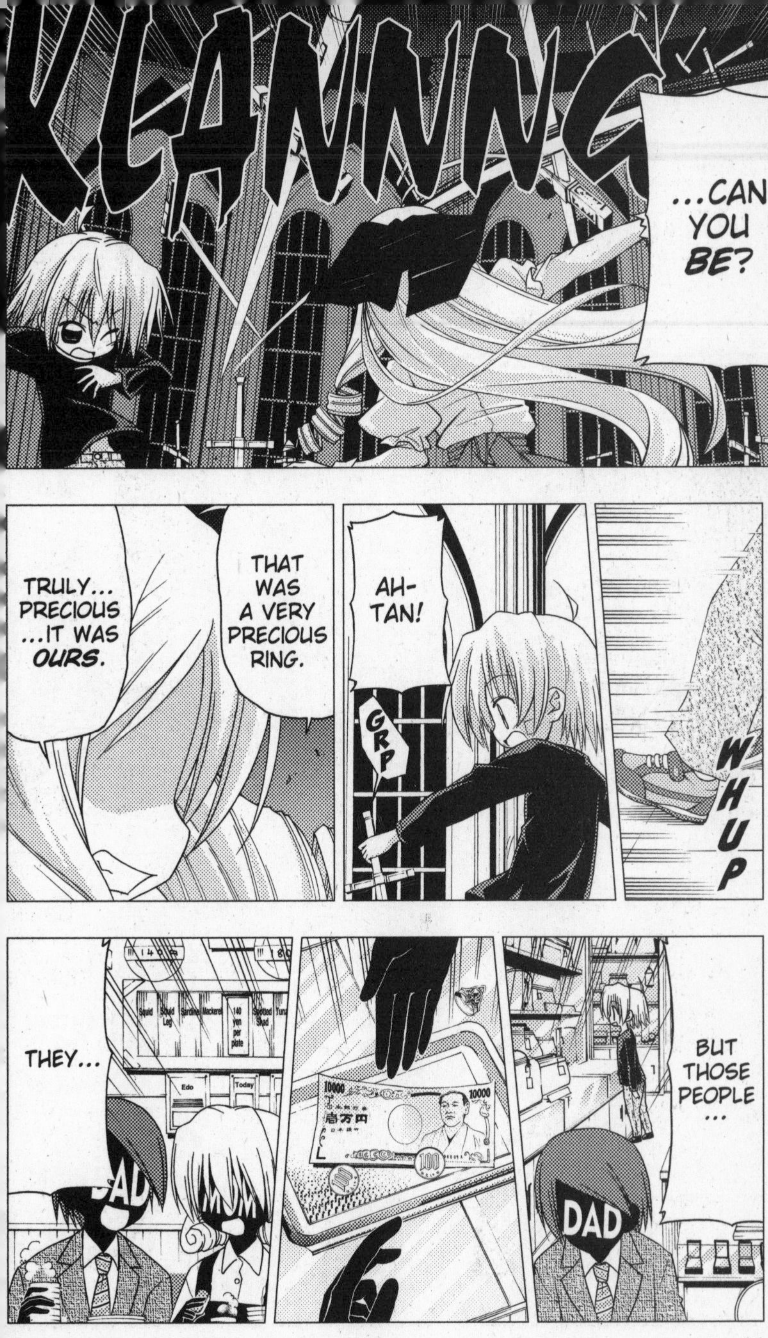
KLANNNG
...CAN YOU BE?
WHUP
AH-TAN!
GRP
THAT WAS A VERY PRECIOUS RING.
TRULY... PRECIOUS ...IT WAS OURS.
BUT THOSE PEOPLE ...
DAD
10000
THEY...
Squid
Squid Leg
Sardine
Mackerel
140 yen per plate
Spotted Shad
Tuna
Edo
Today
DAD
MUM

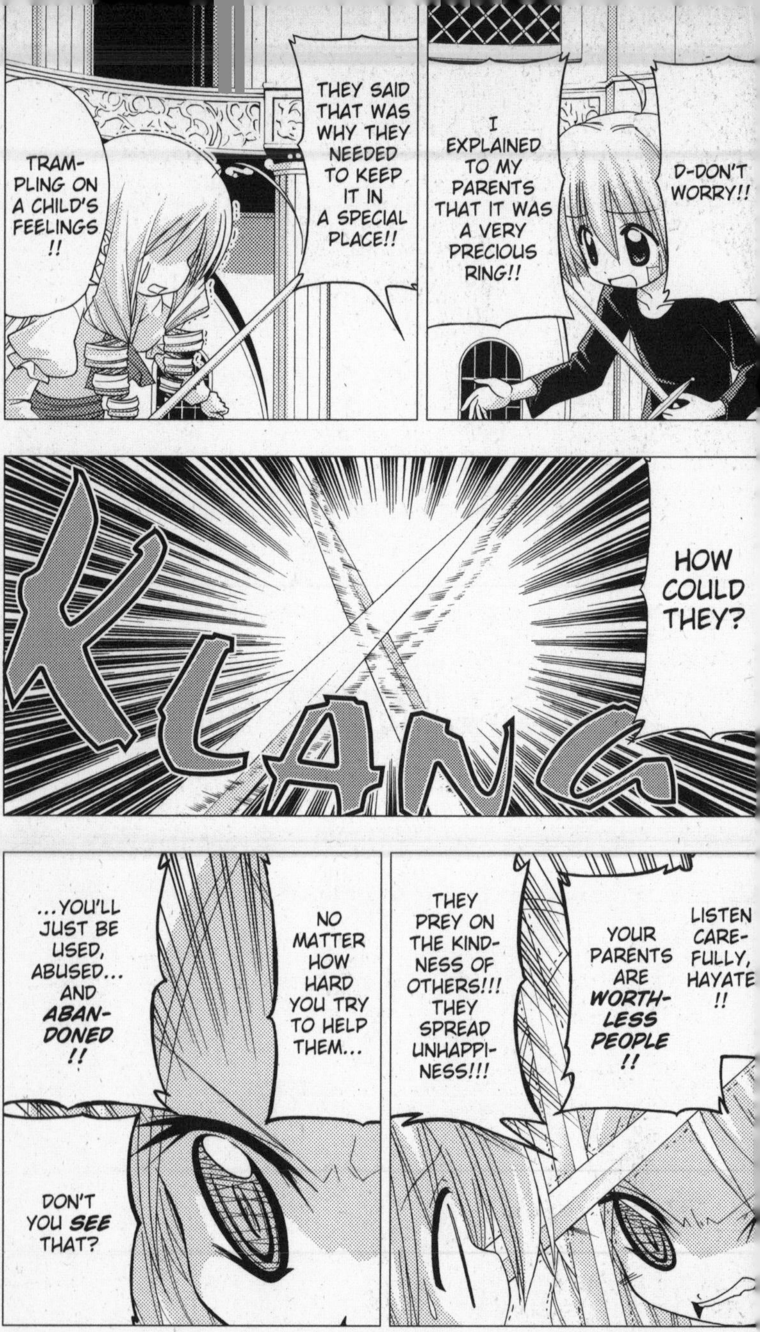
D-DON'T WORRY!!
I EXPLAINED TO MY PARENTS THAT IT WAS A VERY PRECIOUS RING!!
THEY SAID THAT WAS WHY THEY NEEDED TO KEEP IT IN A SPECIAL PLACE!!
TRAMPLING ON A CHILD'S FEELINGS!!
HOW COULD THEY?
KLANG
LISTEN CAREFULLY, HAYATE!!
YOUR PARENTS ARE *WORTHLESS PEOPLE*!!
THEY PREY ON THE KINDNESS OF OTHERS!!! THEY SPREAD UNHAPPINESS!!!
NO MATTER HOW HARD YOU TRY TO HELP THEM...
...YOU'LL JUST BE USED, ABUSED... AND *ABANDONED*!!
DON'T YOU *SEE* THAT?

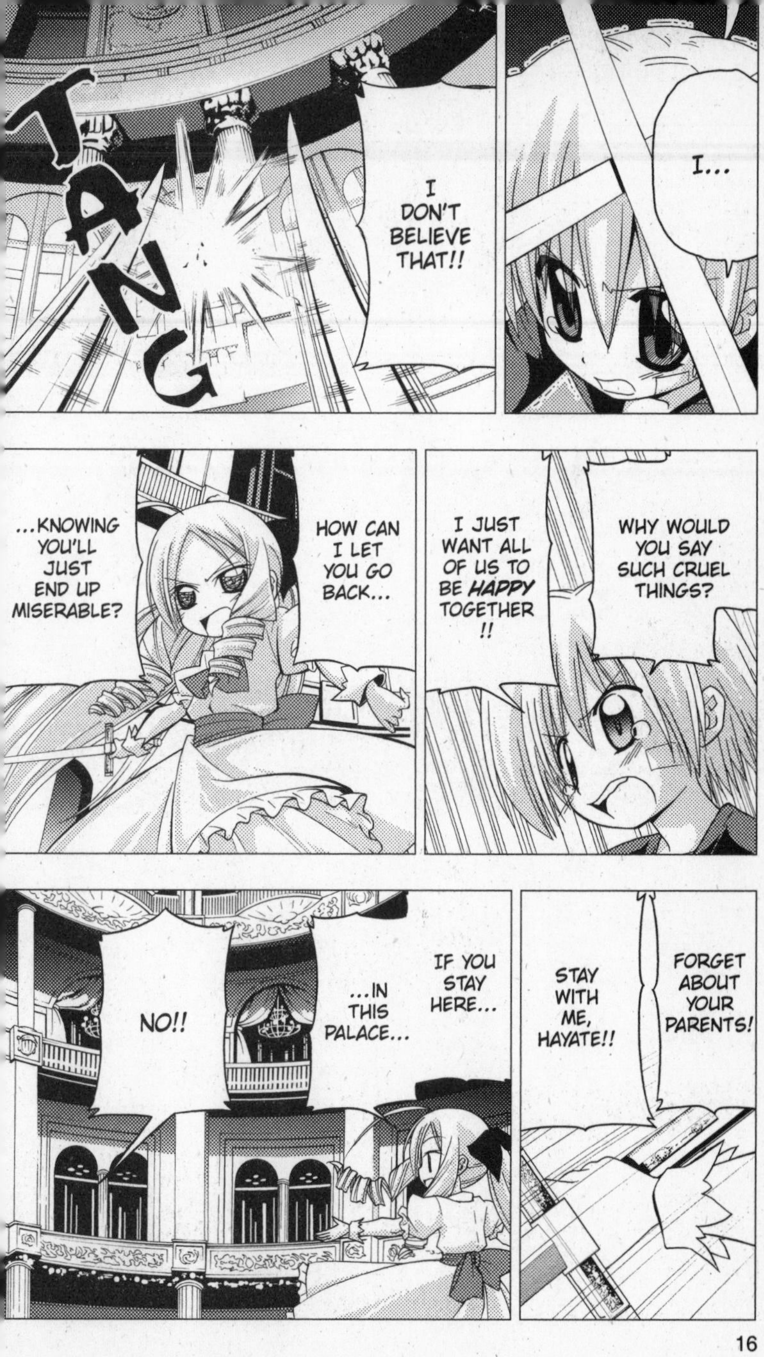
I...
I DON'T BELIEVE THAT!!
TANG
WHY WOULD YOU SAY SUCH CRUEL THINGS?
I JUST WANT ALL OF US TO BE *HAPPY* TOGETHER !!
HOW CAN I LET YOU GO BACK...
...KNOWING YOU'LL JUST END UP MISERABLE?
FORGET ABOUT YOUR PARENTS!
STAY WITH ME, HAYATE!!
IF YOU STAY HERE...
...IN THIS PALACE...
NO!!

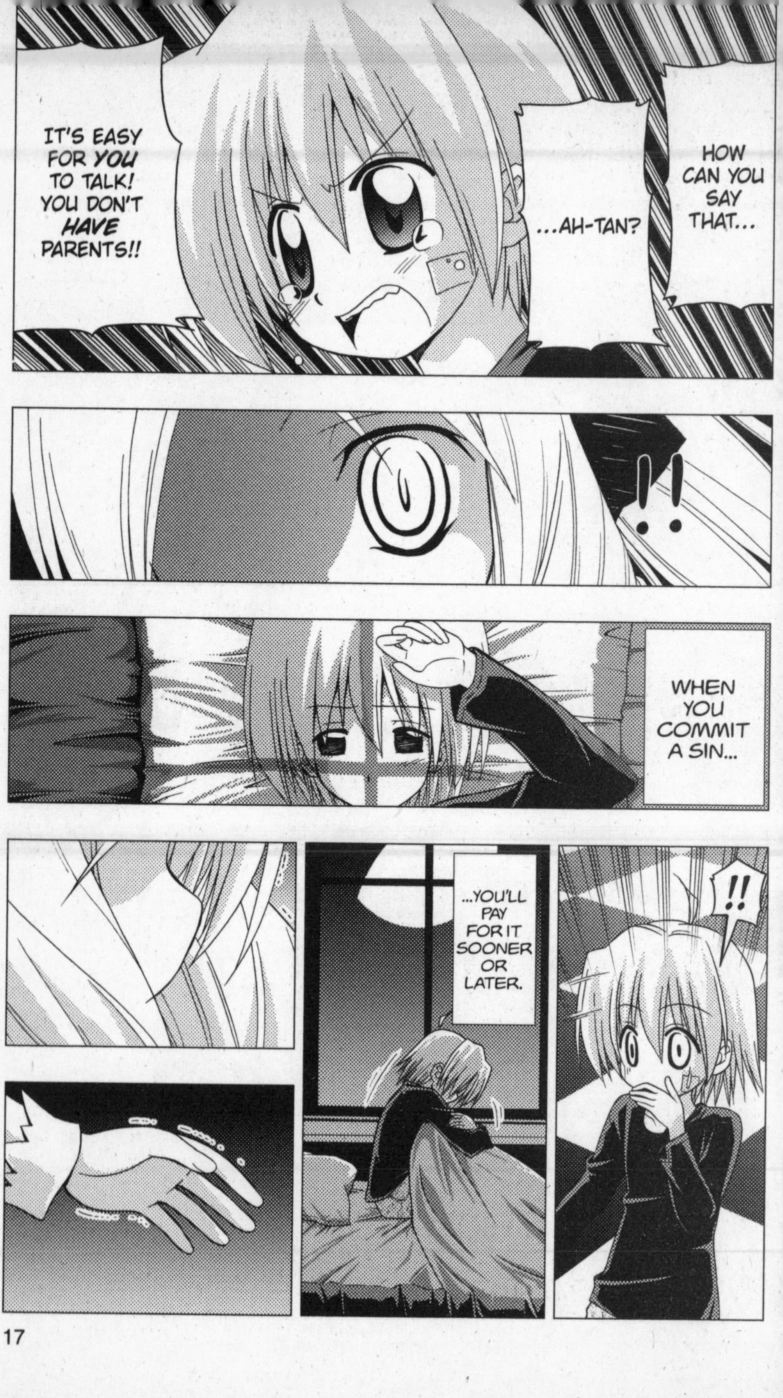
HOW CAN YOU SAY THAT...
...AH-TAN?
IT'S EASY FOR *YOU* TO TALK! YOU DON'T ***HAVE*** PARENTS!!
!!
WHEN YOU COMMIT A SIN...
!!
...YOU'LL PAY FOR IT SOONER OR LATER.

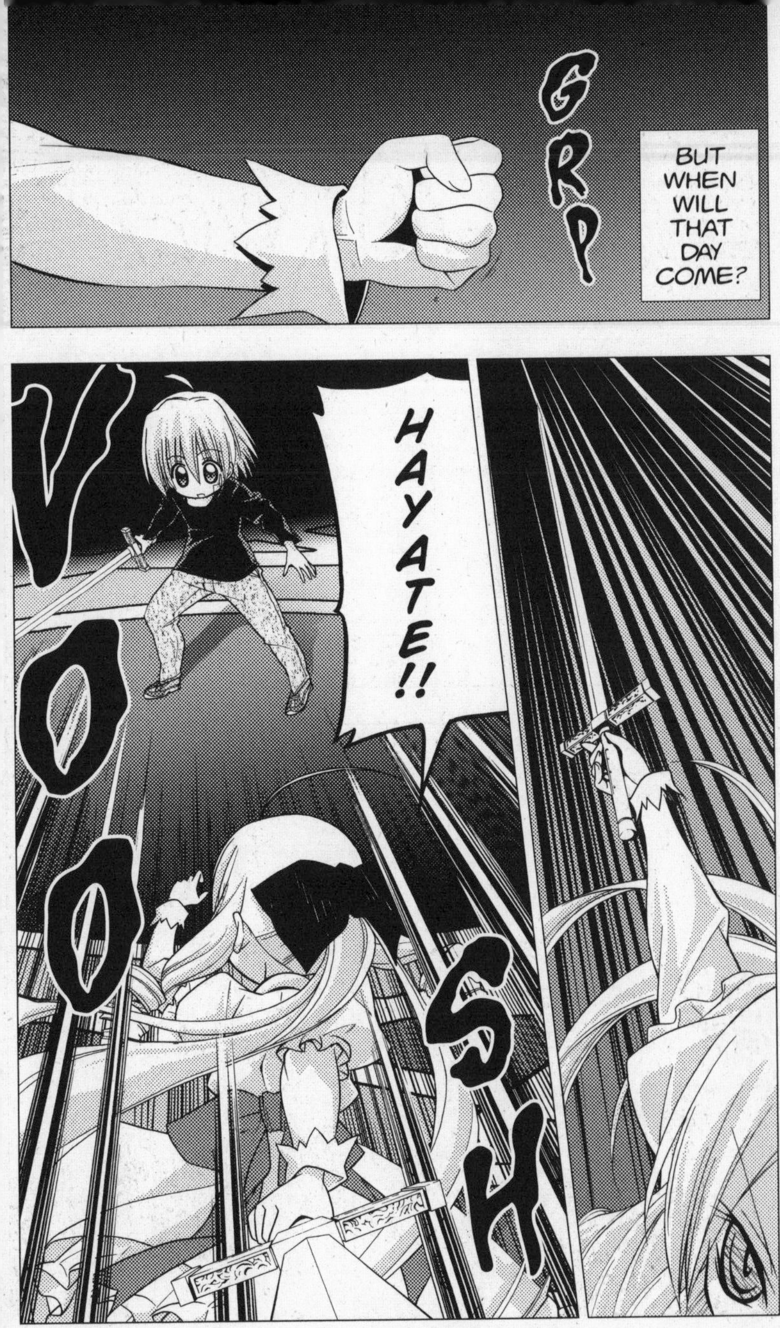
BUT WHEN WILL THAT DAY COME?
GRP
HAYATE!!
VOOSH

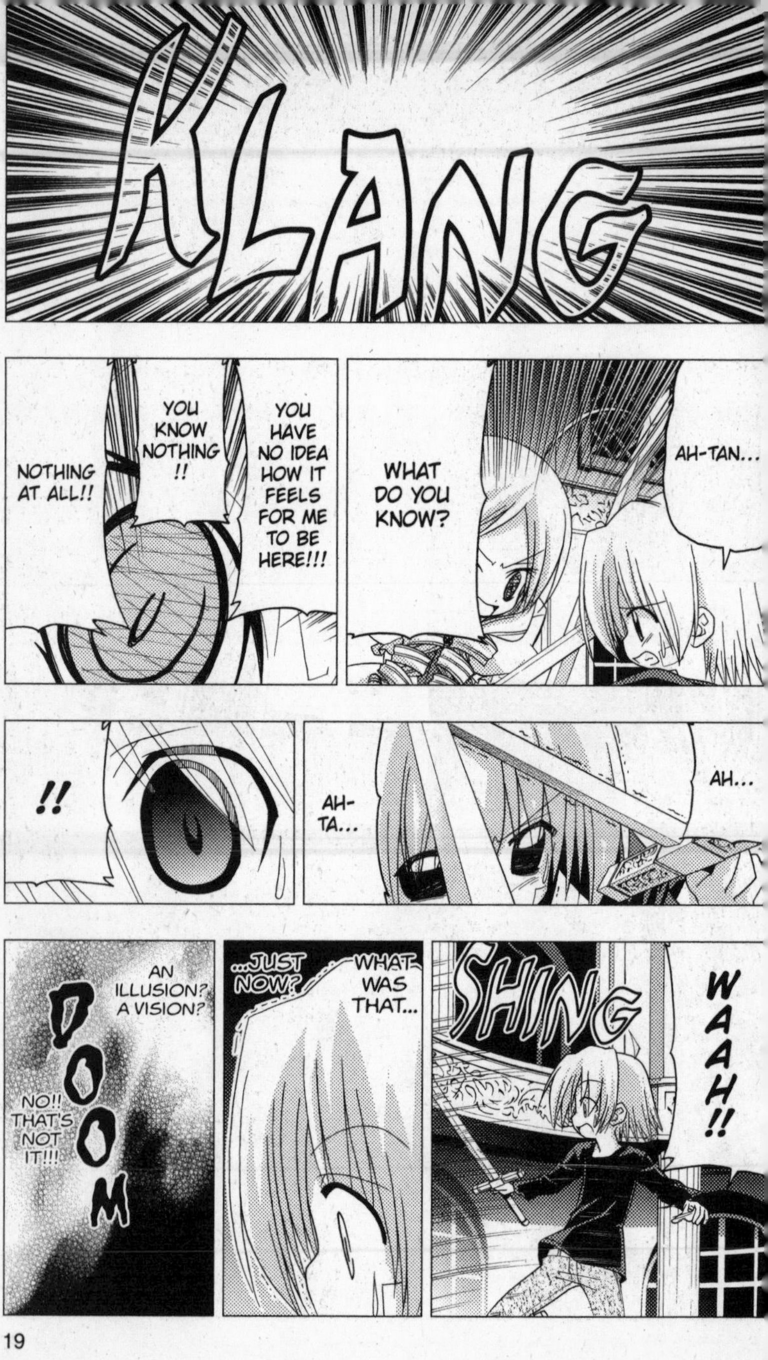
KLANG
AH-TAN...
WHAT DO YOU KNOW?
YOU HAVE NO IDEA HOW IT FEELS FOR ME TO BE HERE!!!
YOU KNOW NOTHING !!
NOTHING AT ALL!!
AH...
AH-TA...
!!
WAAAH!!
SHING
WHAT WAS THAT...
...JUST NOW?
AN ILLUSION? A VISION?
DOOOM
NO!! THAT'S NOT IT!!!

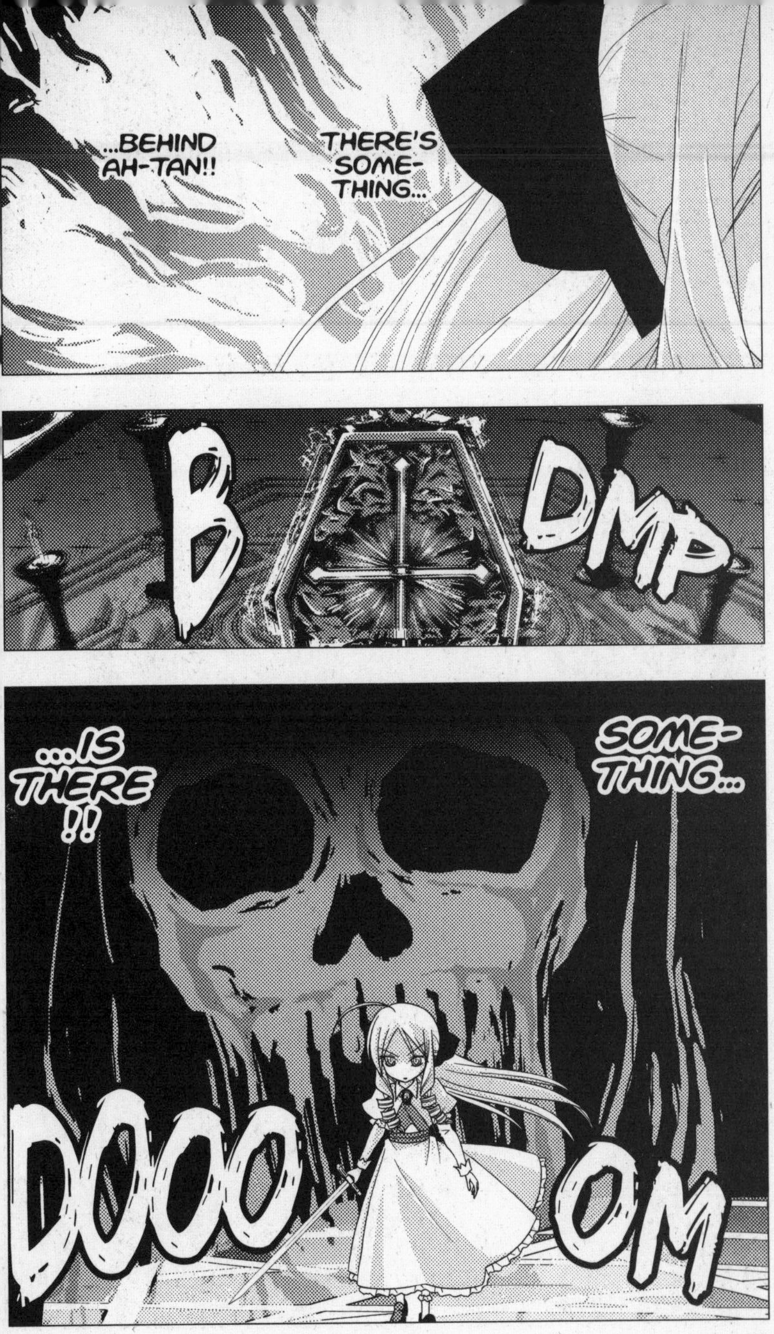
THERE'S SOME-THING...
...BEHIND AH-TAN!!
B DMP
SOME-THING...
...IS THERE!!
DOOO OM

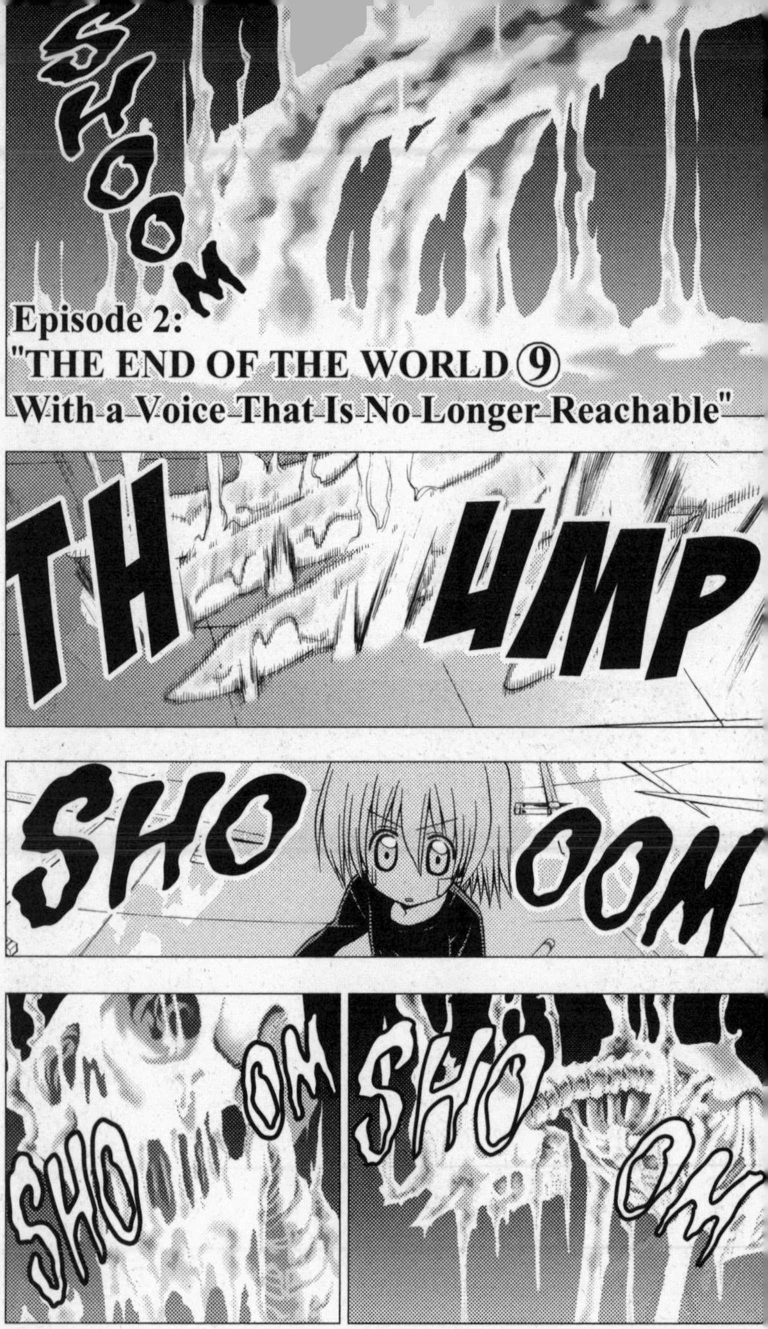
SHOOM
Episode 2:
"THE END OF THE WORLD ⑨
With a Voice That Is No Longer Reachable"
THUMP
SHOOOM
SHOOM
SHOOM

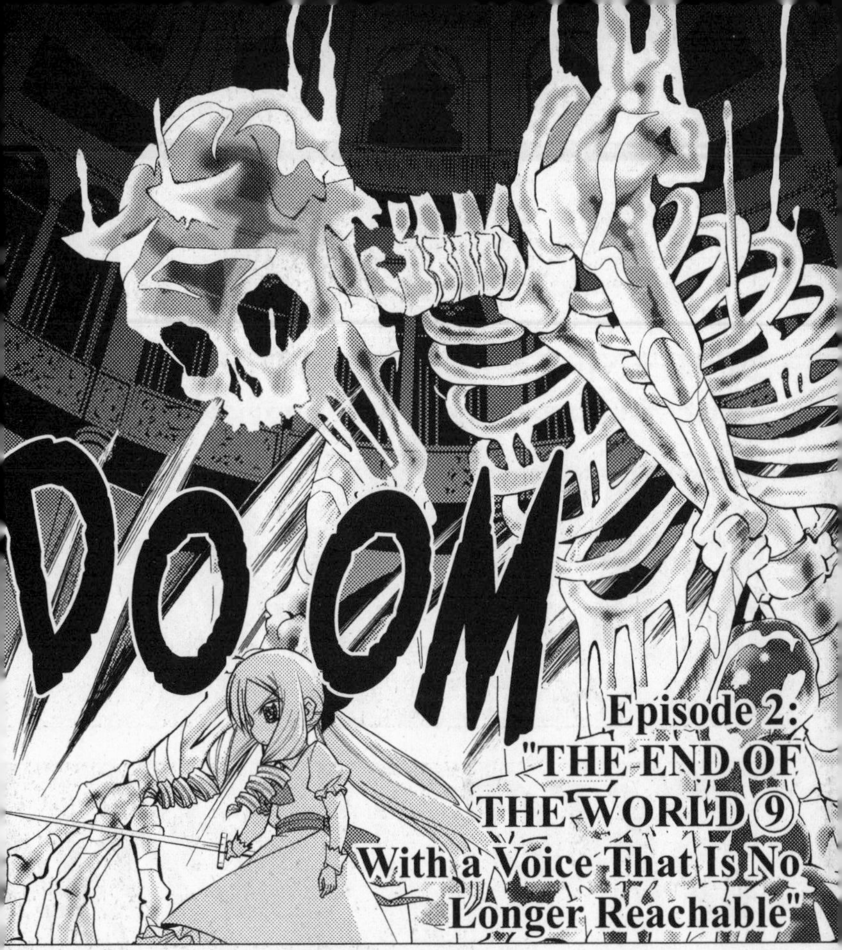
DOOM
Episode 2: "THE END OF THE WORLD ⑨ With a Voice That Is No Longer Reachable"
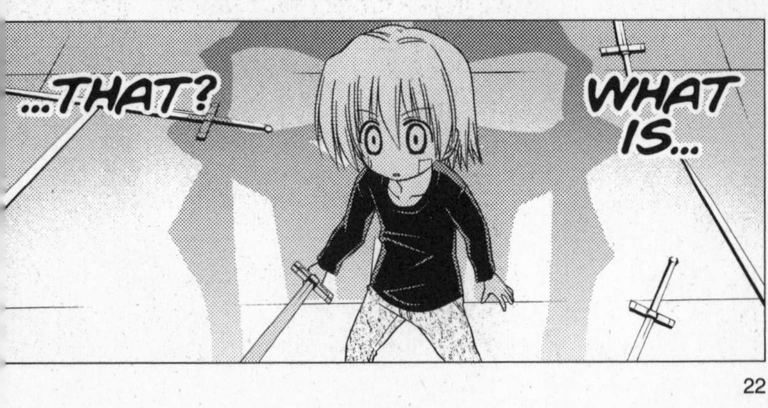
WHAT IS...
...THAT?

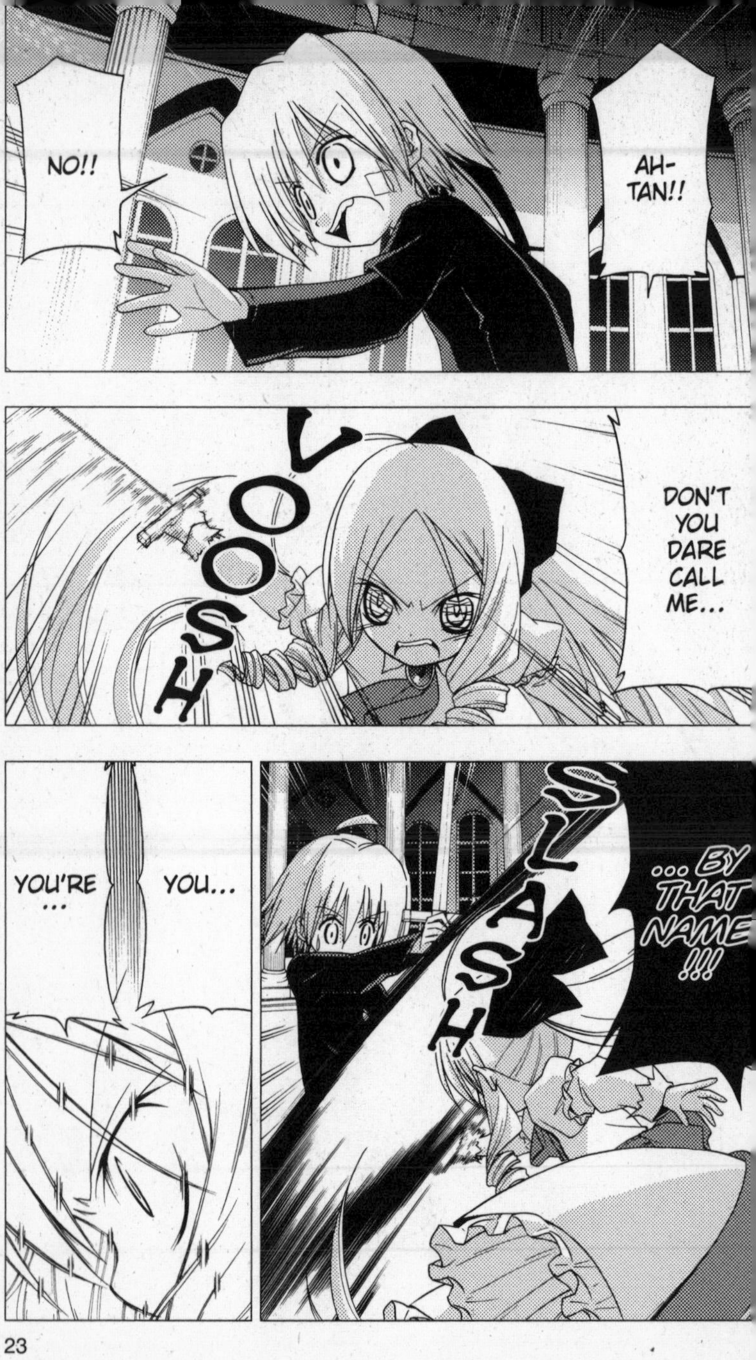
AH-TAN!!
NO!!
DON'T YOU DARE CALL ME...
VOOSH
SLASH
...BY THAT NAME!!!
YOU...
YOU'RE...

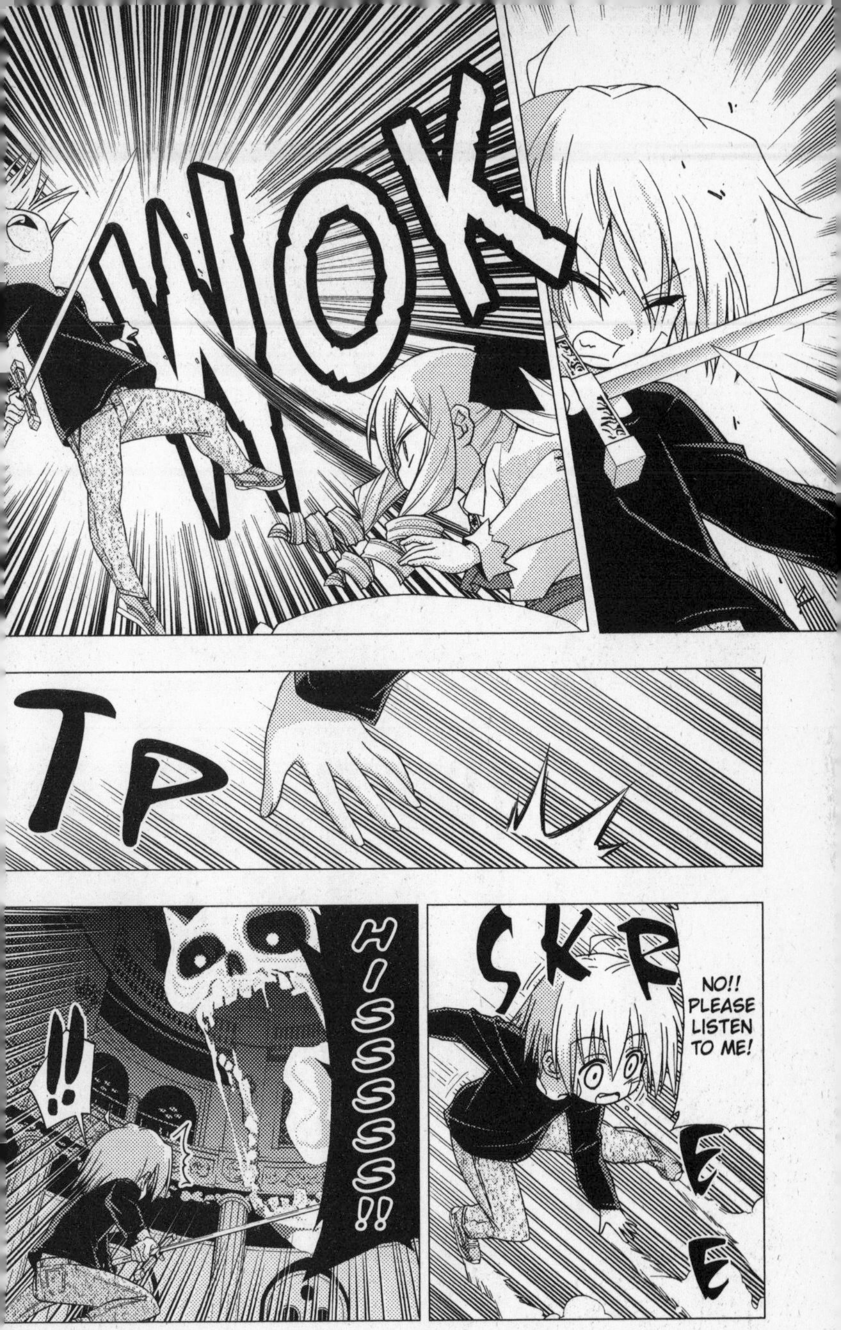
WOK
TP
SKREEE
NO!! PLEASE LISTEN TO ME!
HISSSSSS!!
!!

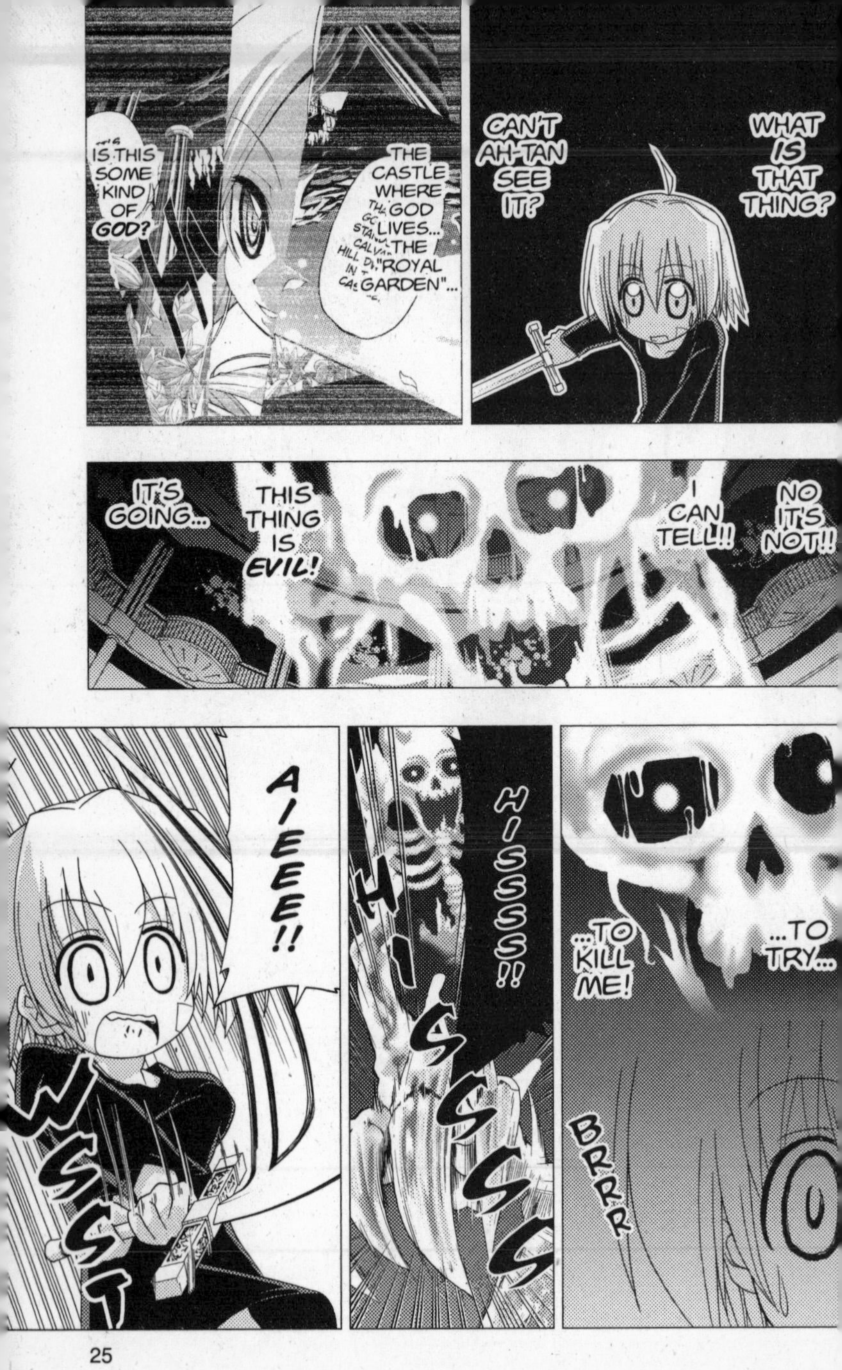

WHAT IS THAT THING?
CAN'T AH-TAN SEE IT?
THE CASTLE WHERE GOD LIVES... THE "ROYAL GARDEN"...
IS THIS SOME KIND OF GOD?
NO IT'S NOT!!
I CAN TELL!!
THIS THING IS EVIL!
IT'S GOING...
...TO TRY...
...TO KILL ME!
BRRR
HISSSS!!
SHISSSS
AIEEE!!
WSSST

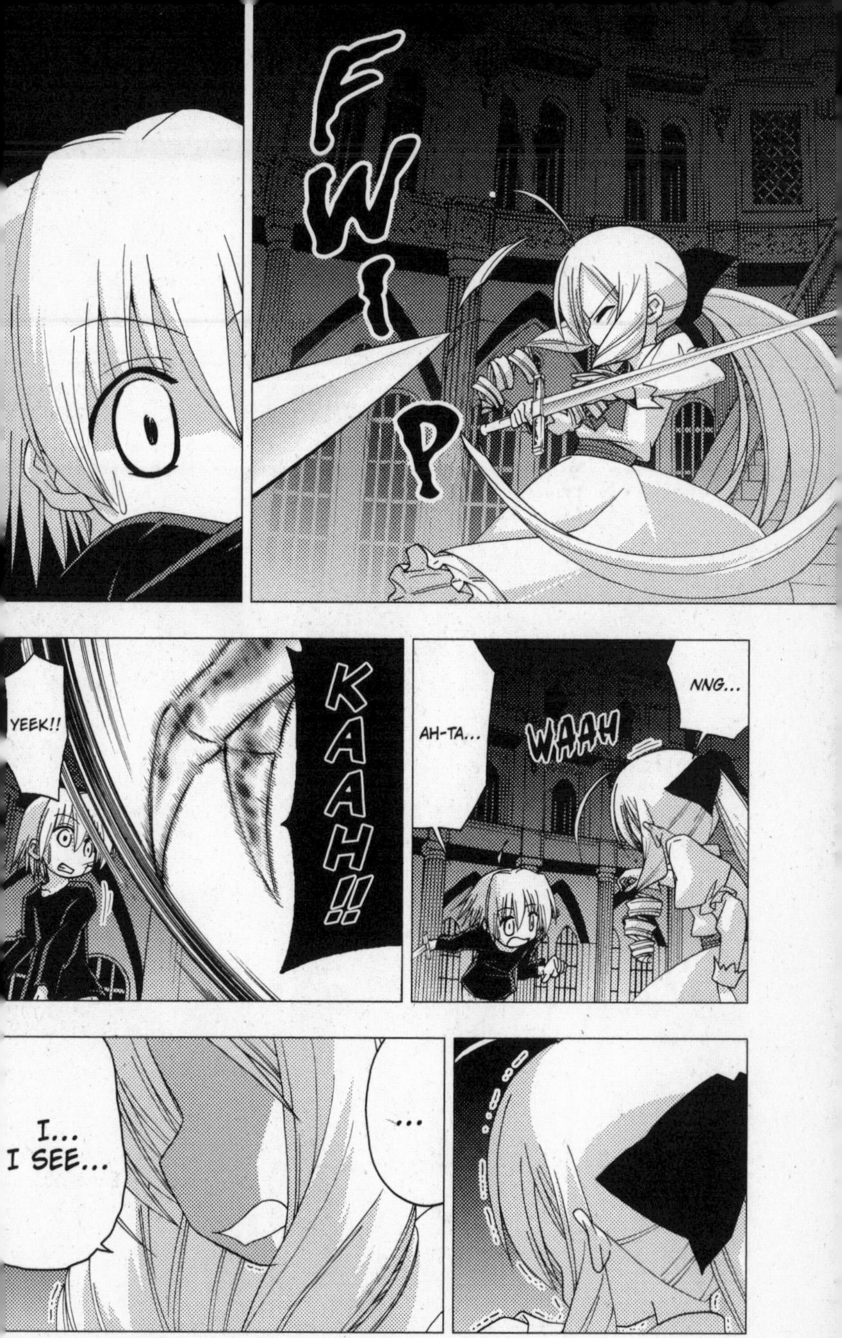
FWIP
NNG...
WAAH
AH-TA...
KAAAH!!
YEEK!!
...
I... I SEE...

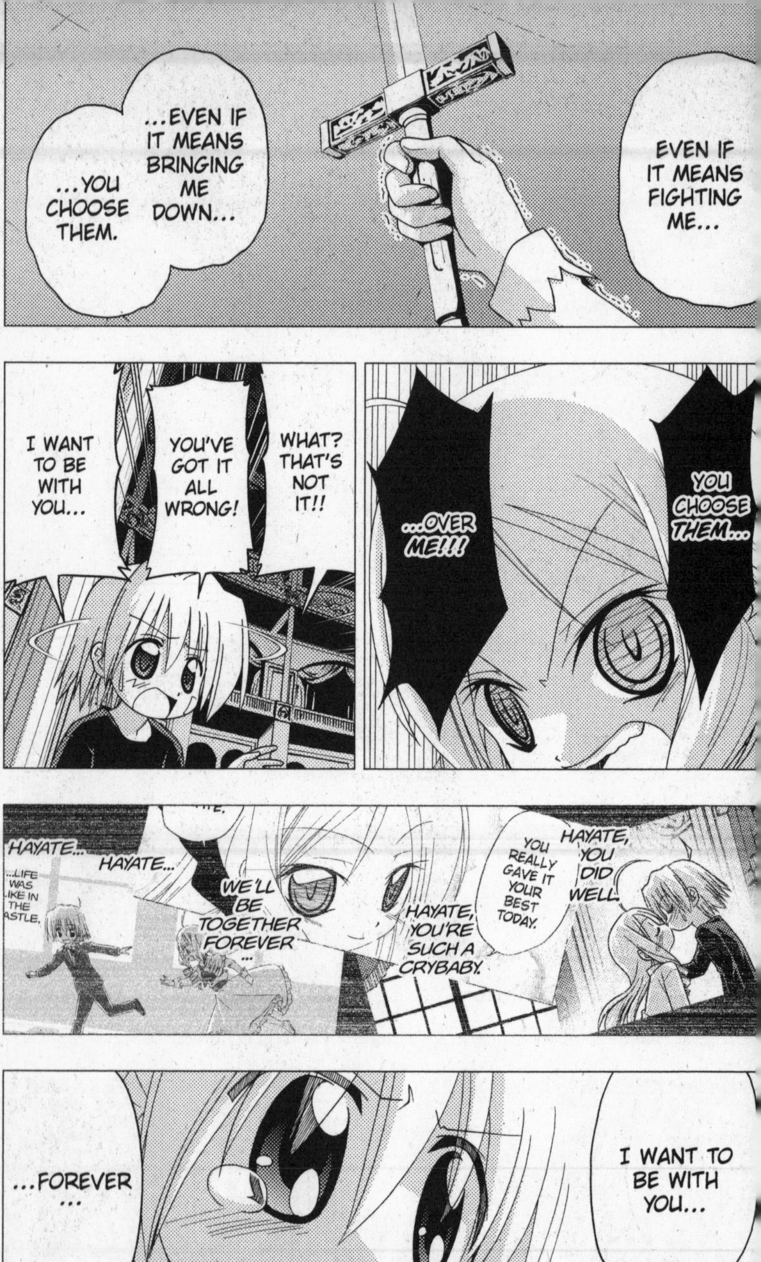
EVEN IF IT MEANS FIGHTING ME...
...EVEN IF IT MEANS BRINGING ME DOWN...
...YOU CHOOSE THEM.
YOU CHOOSE THEM...
...OVER ME!!!
WHAT? THAT'S NOT IT!!
YOU'VE GOT IT ALL WRONG!
I WANT TO BE WITH YOU...
HAYATE, YOU DID WELL.
YOU REALLY GAVE IT YOUR BEST TODAY.
HAYATE, YOU'RE SUCH A CRYBABY.
WE'LL BE TOGETHER FOREVER...
HAYATE...
HAYATE...
...LIFE WAS IKE IN THE ASTLE.
I WANT TO BE WITH YOU...
...FOREVER...

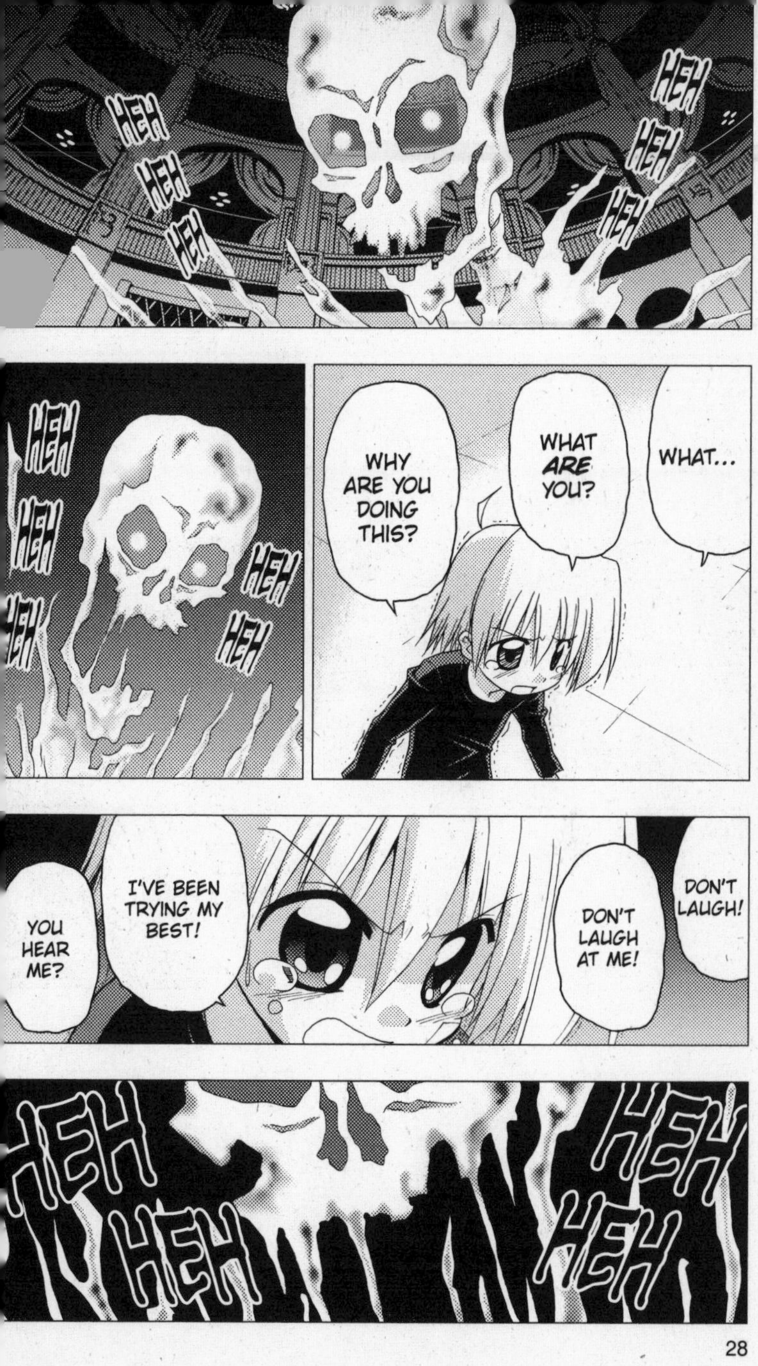
HEH HEH HEH
HEH HEH HEH
WHAT...
WHAT ARE YOU?
WHY ARE YOU DOING THIS?
HEH HEH
HEH HEH HEH
DON'T LAUGH!
DON'T LAUGH AT ME!
I'VE BEEN TRYING MY BEST!
YOU HEAR ME?
HEH HEH
HEH HEH

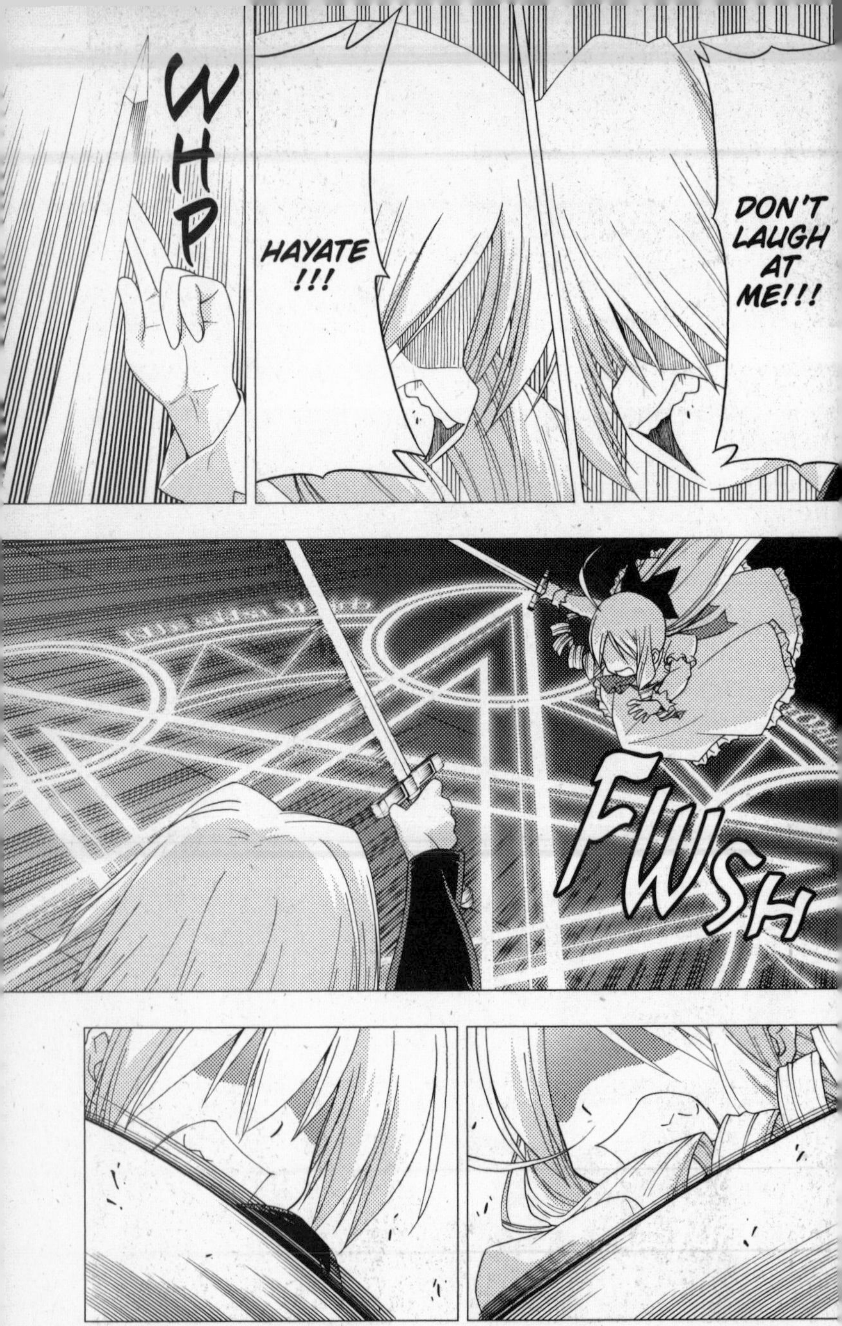
DON'T LAUGH AT ME!!!
HAYATE !!!
WHP
FWSH

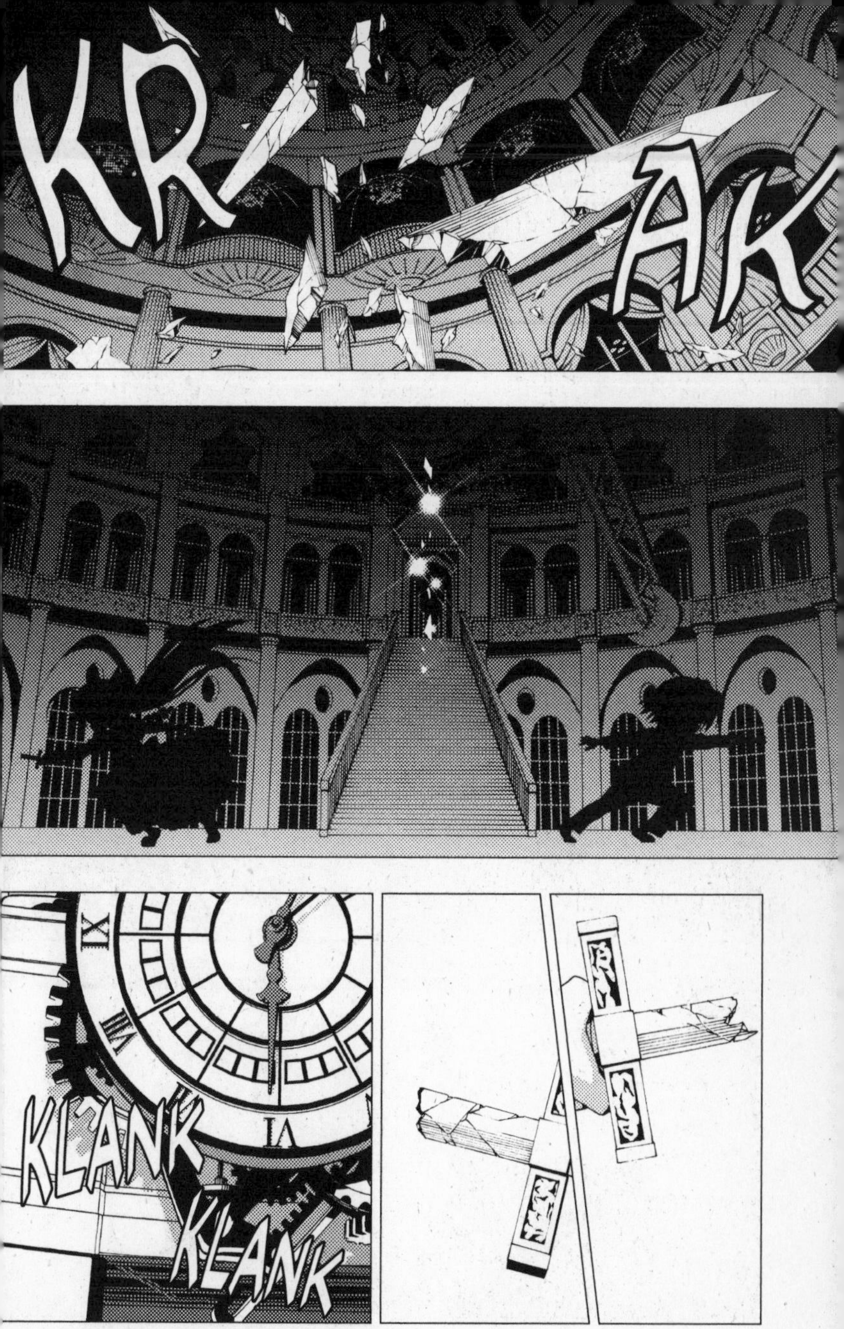
KRAK
KLANK
KLANK

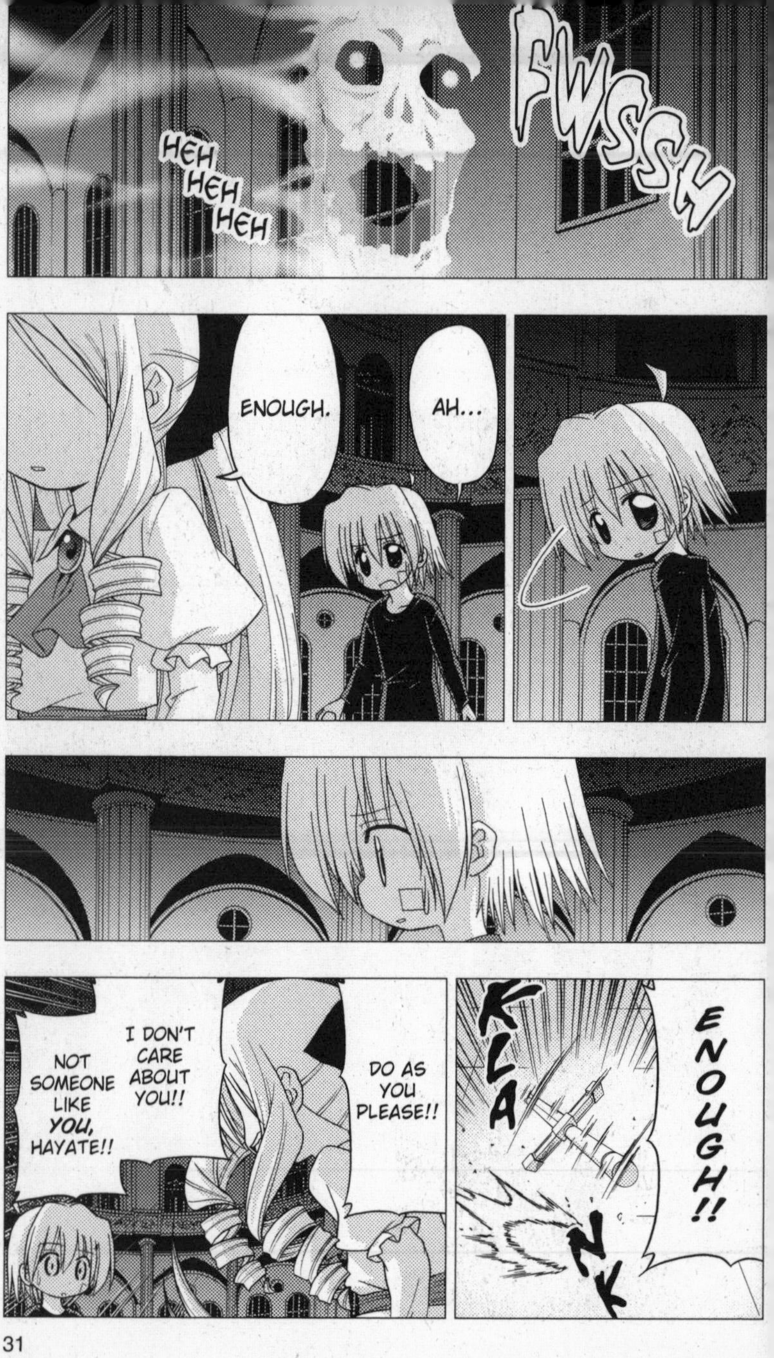
FWSSH
HEH HEH HEH
AH...
ENOUGH.
ENOUGH!!
KLANK
DO AS YOU PLEASE!!
I DON'T CARE ABOUT YOU!!
NOT SOMEONE LIKE *YOU*, HAYATE!!

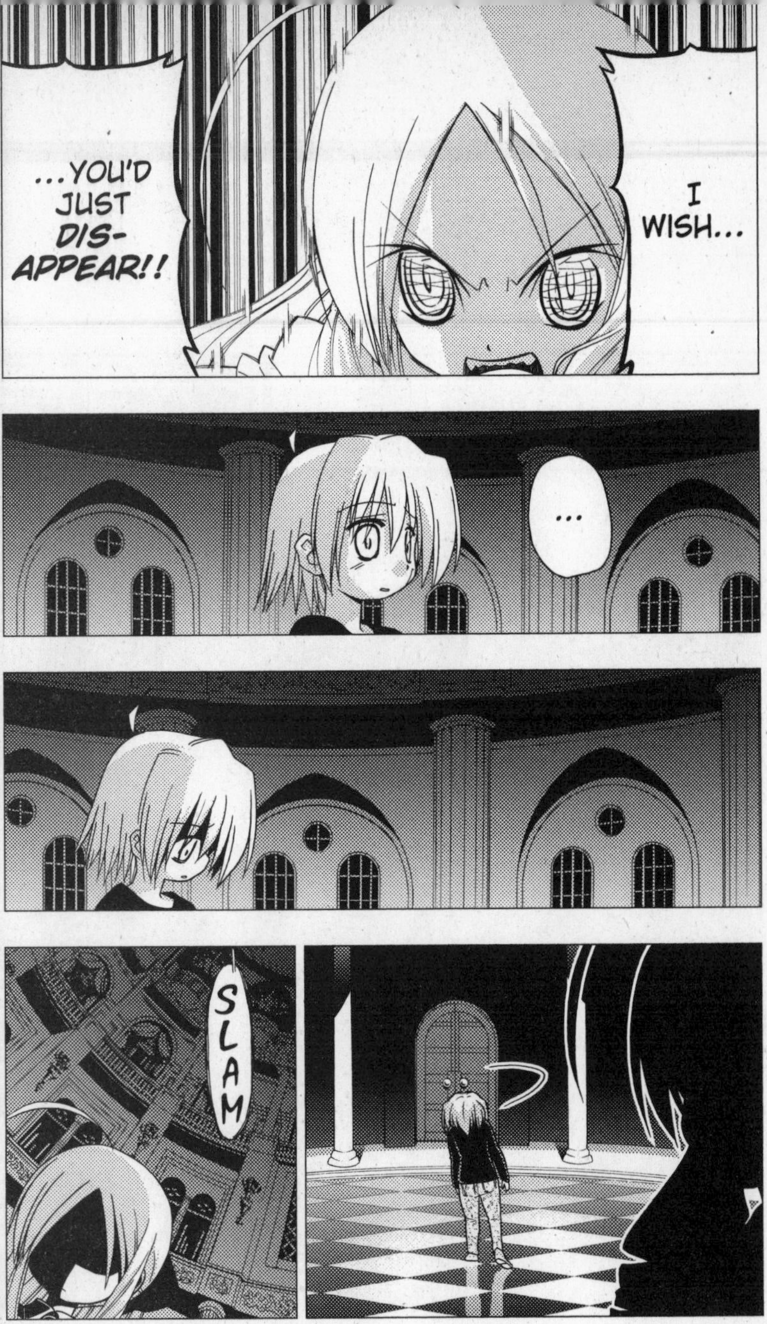
I WISH...
...YOU'D JUST DIS-APPEAR!!
...
SLAM

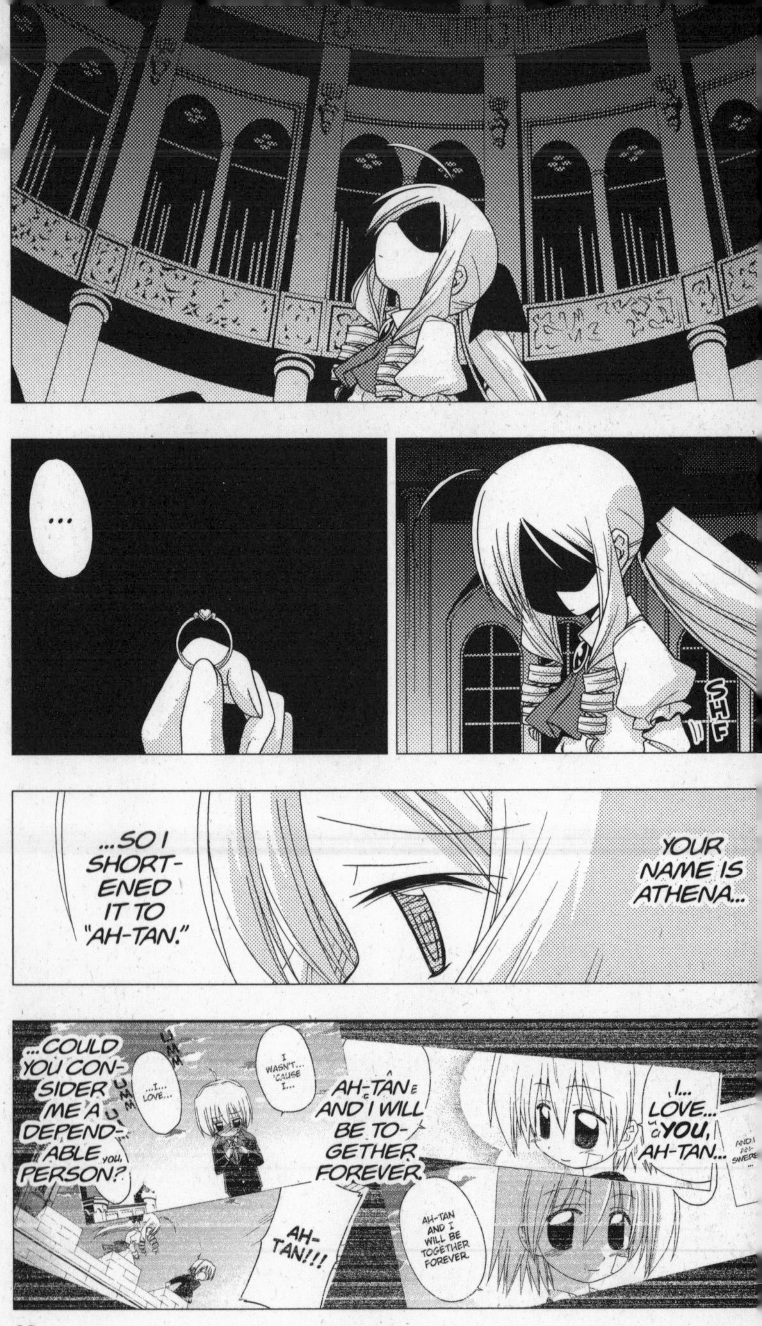
...
SHF
YOUR NAME IS ATHENA...
...SO I SHORTENED IT TO "AH-TAN."
AND I AN-SWERE...
I... LOVE... YOU, AH-TAN...
AH-TAN AND I WILL BE TOGETHER FOREVER.
AH-TAN AND I WILL BE TO-GETHER FOREVER.
I WASN'T... 'CAUSE I...
...I... LOVE...
UMM
UMM
UMM
...COULD YOU CON-SIDER ME A DEPEND-ABLE PERSON?
YOU,
AH-TAN!!!

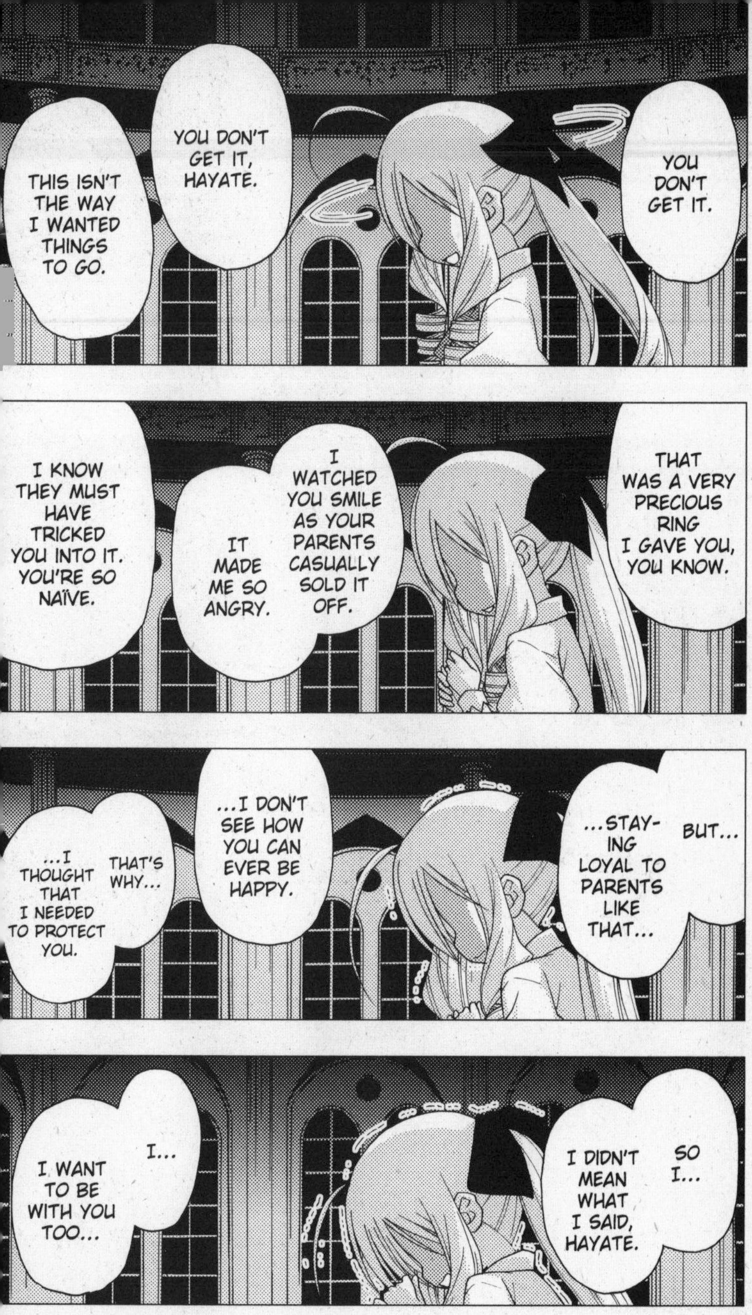
YOU DON'T GET IT.
YOU DON'T GET IT, HAYATE.
THIS ISN'T THE WAY I WANTED THINGS TO GO.
THAT WAS A VERY PRECIOUS RING I GAVE YOU, YOU KNOW.
I WATCHED YOU SMILE AS YOUR PARENTS CASUALLY SOLD IT OFF.
IT MADE ME SO ANGRY.
I KNOW THEY MUST HAVE TRICKED YOU INTO IT. YOU'RE SO NAÏVE.
BUT...
...STAY-ING LOYAL TO PARENTS LIKE THAT...
...I DON'T SEE HOW YOU CAN EVER BE HAPPY.
THAT'S WHY...
...I THOUGHT THAT I NEEDED TO PROTECT YOU.
SO I...
I DIDN'T MEAN WHAT I SAID, HAYATE.
I...
I WANT TO BE WITH YOU TOO...

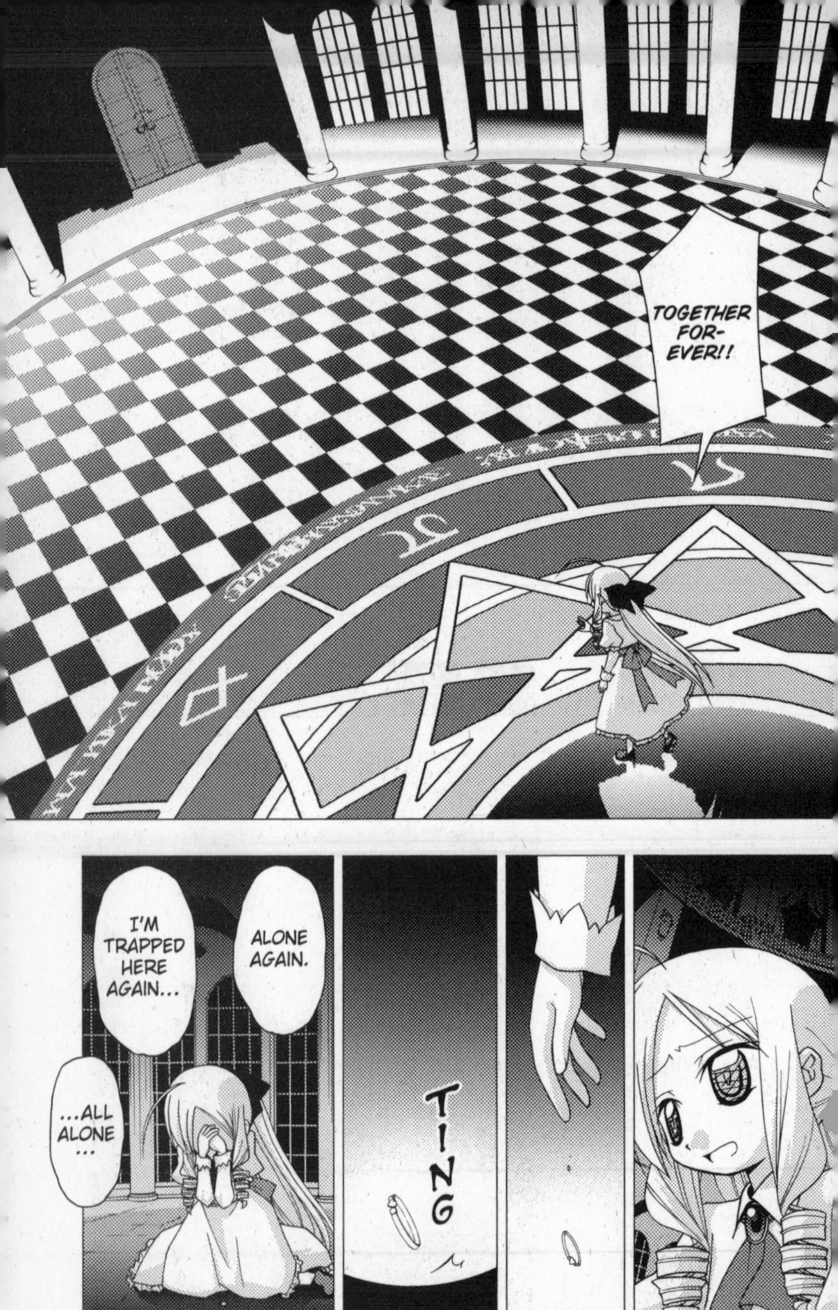
TOGETHER FOR-EVER!!
TING
ALONE AGAIN.
I'M TRAPPED HERE AGAIN...
...ALL ALONE ...

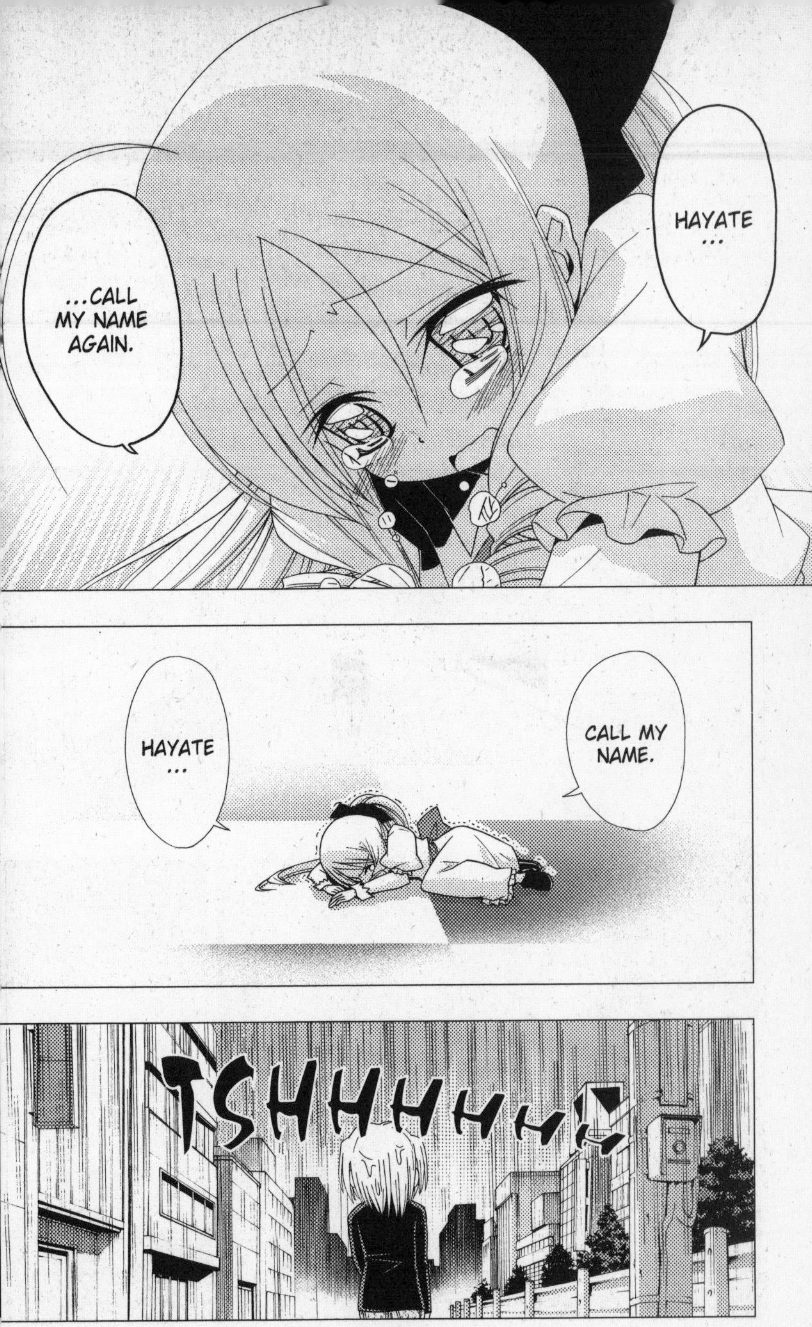
HAYATE ...
...CALL MY NAME AGAIN.
CALL MY NAME.
HAYATE ...
TSHHHHH

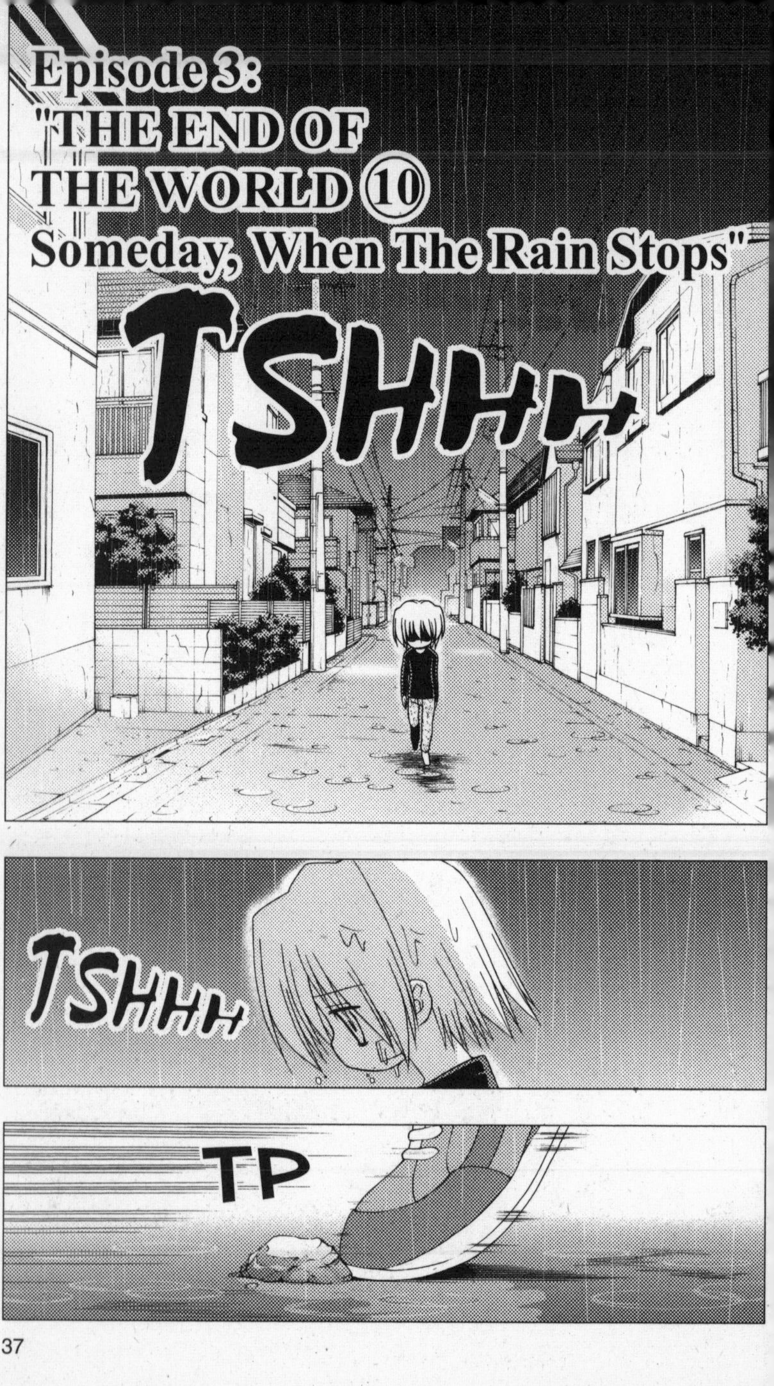
Episode 3:
"THE END OF
THE WORLD ⑩
Someday, When The Rain Stops"
TSHHH
TSHHH
TP

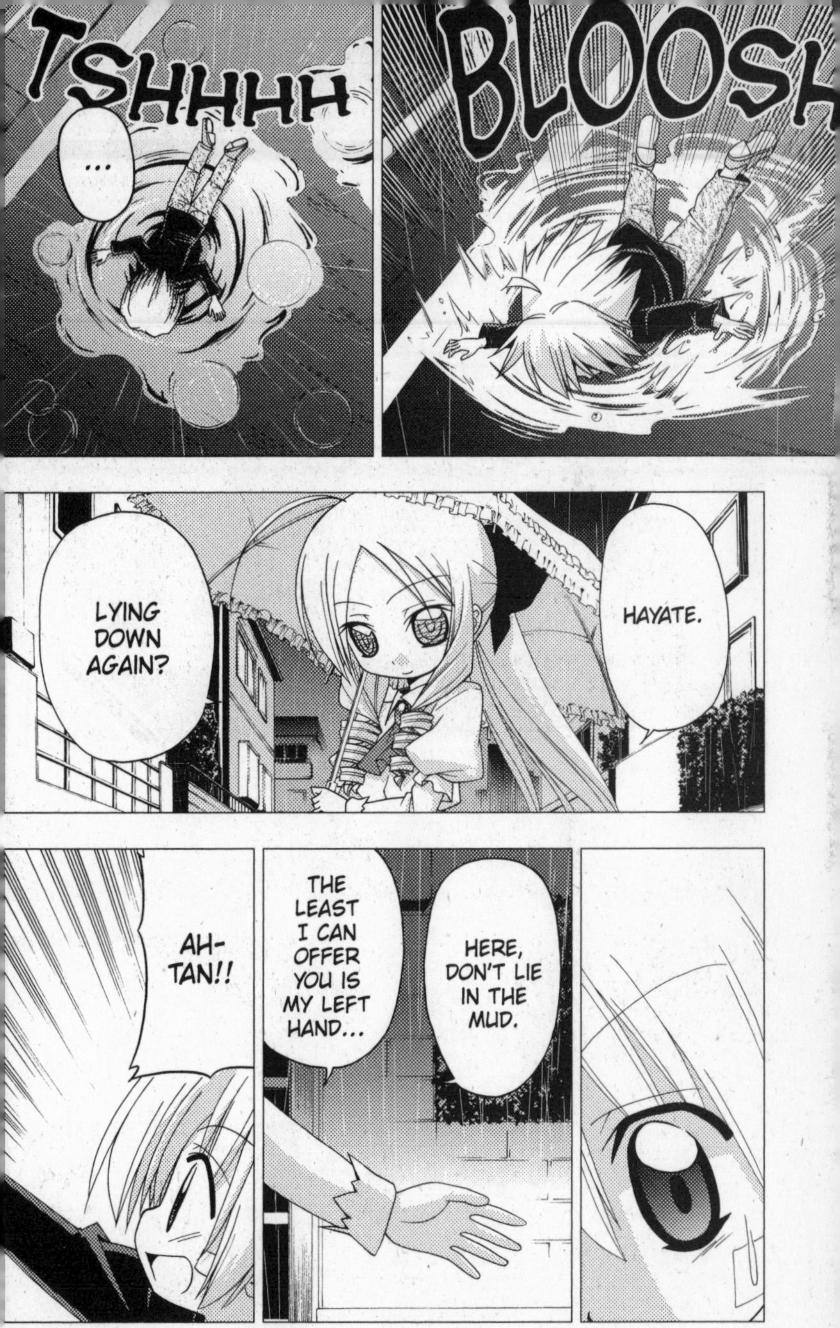
BLOOSH
TSHHHH
...
HAYATE.
LYING DOWN AGAIN?
HERE, DON'T LIE IN THE MUD.
THE LEAST I CAN OFFER YOU IS MY LEFT HAND...
AH-TAN!!

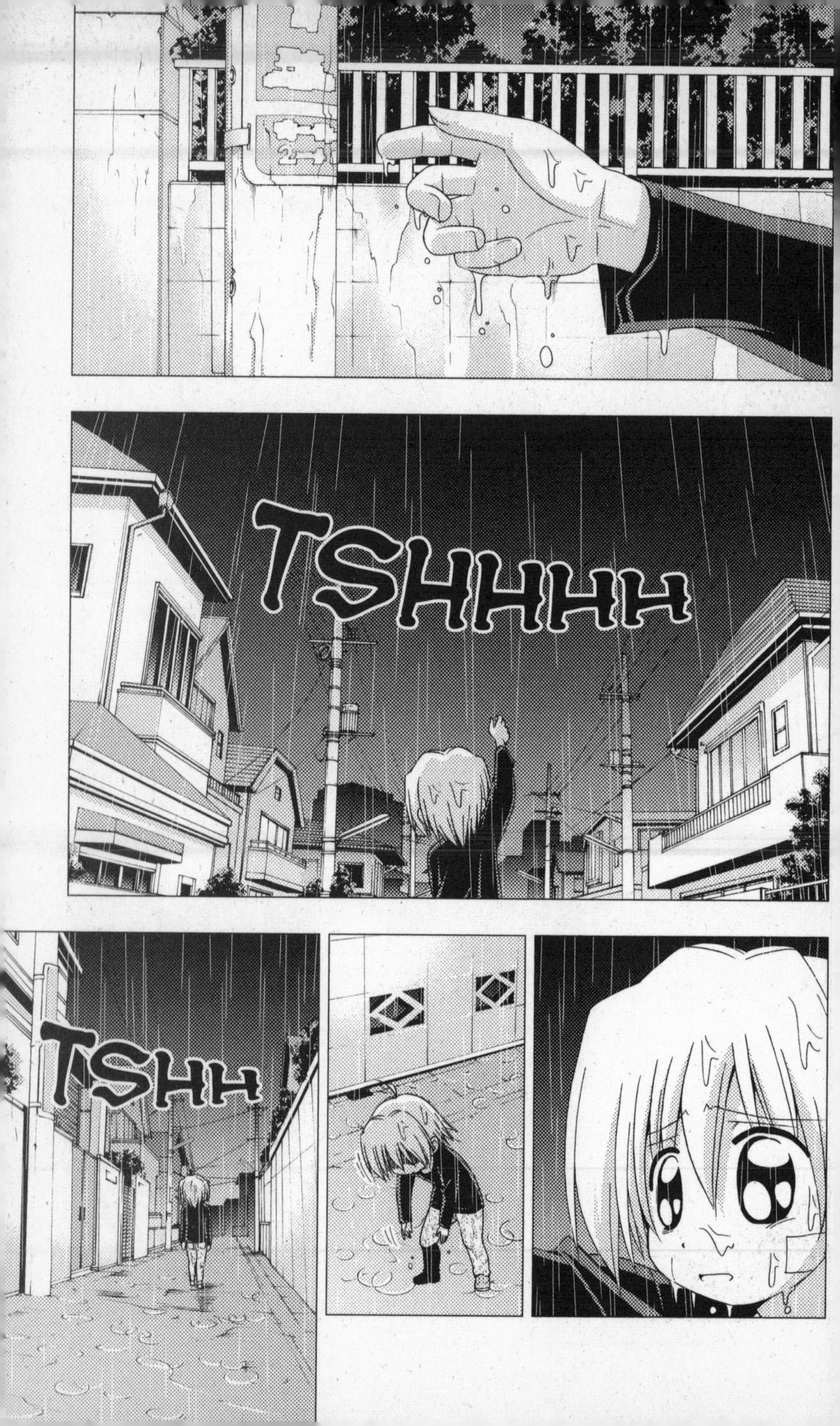
TSHHHH
TSHH

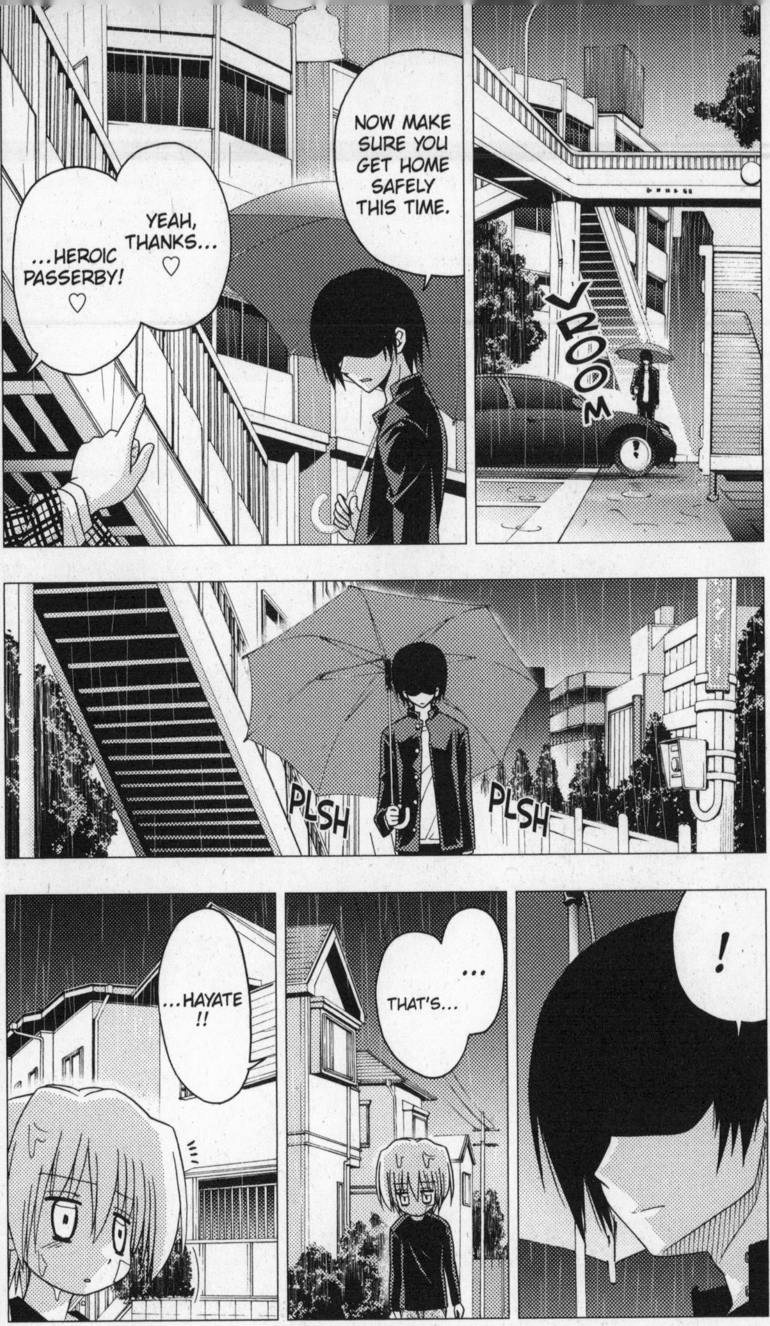
VROOM
NOW MAKE SURE YOU GET HOME SAFELY THIS TIME.
YEAH, THANKS... ♡
...HEROIC PASSERBY! ♡
PLSH
PLSH
!
... THAT'S...
...HAYATE !!

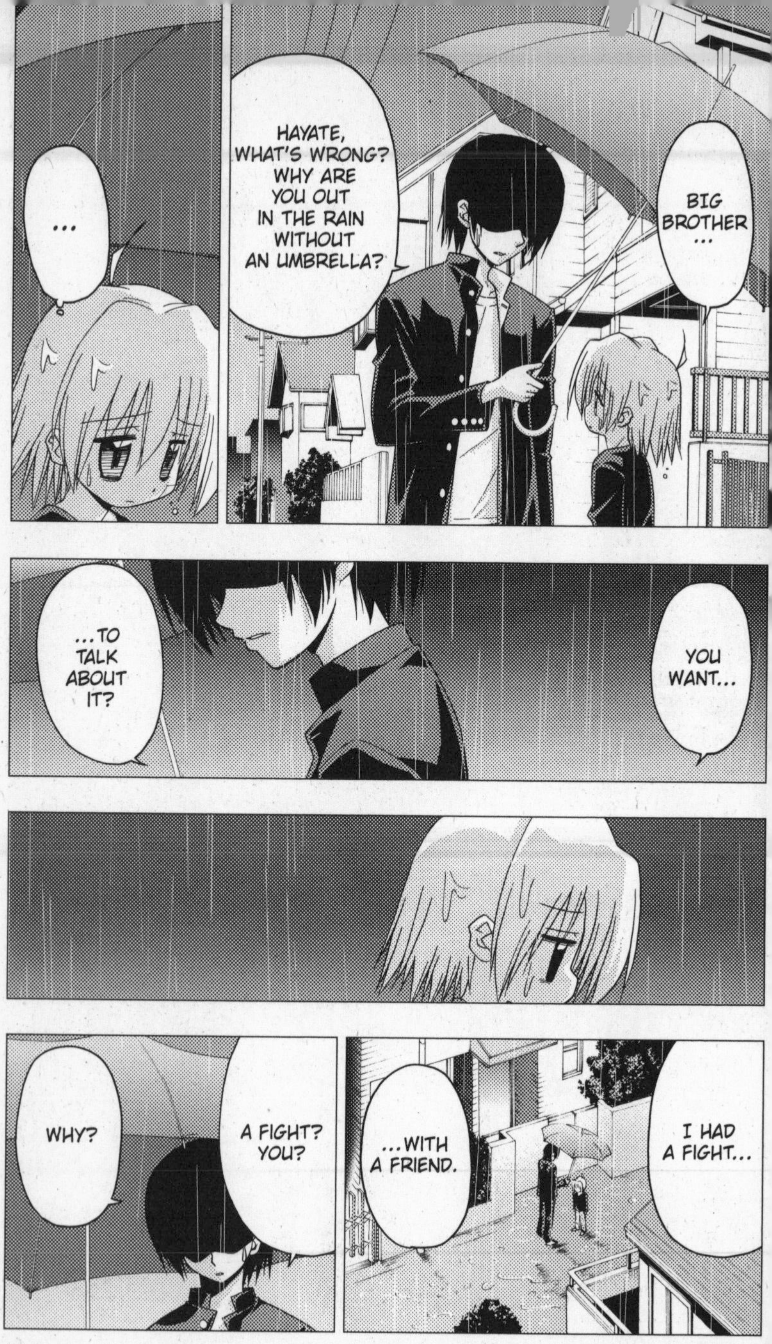
BIG BROTHER...
HAYATE, WHAT'S WRONG? WHY ARE YOU OUT IN THE RAIN WITHOUT AN UMBRELLA?
...
YOU WANT...
...TO TALK ABOUT IT?
I HAD A FIGHT...
...WITH A FRIEND.
A FIGHT? YOU?
WHY?

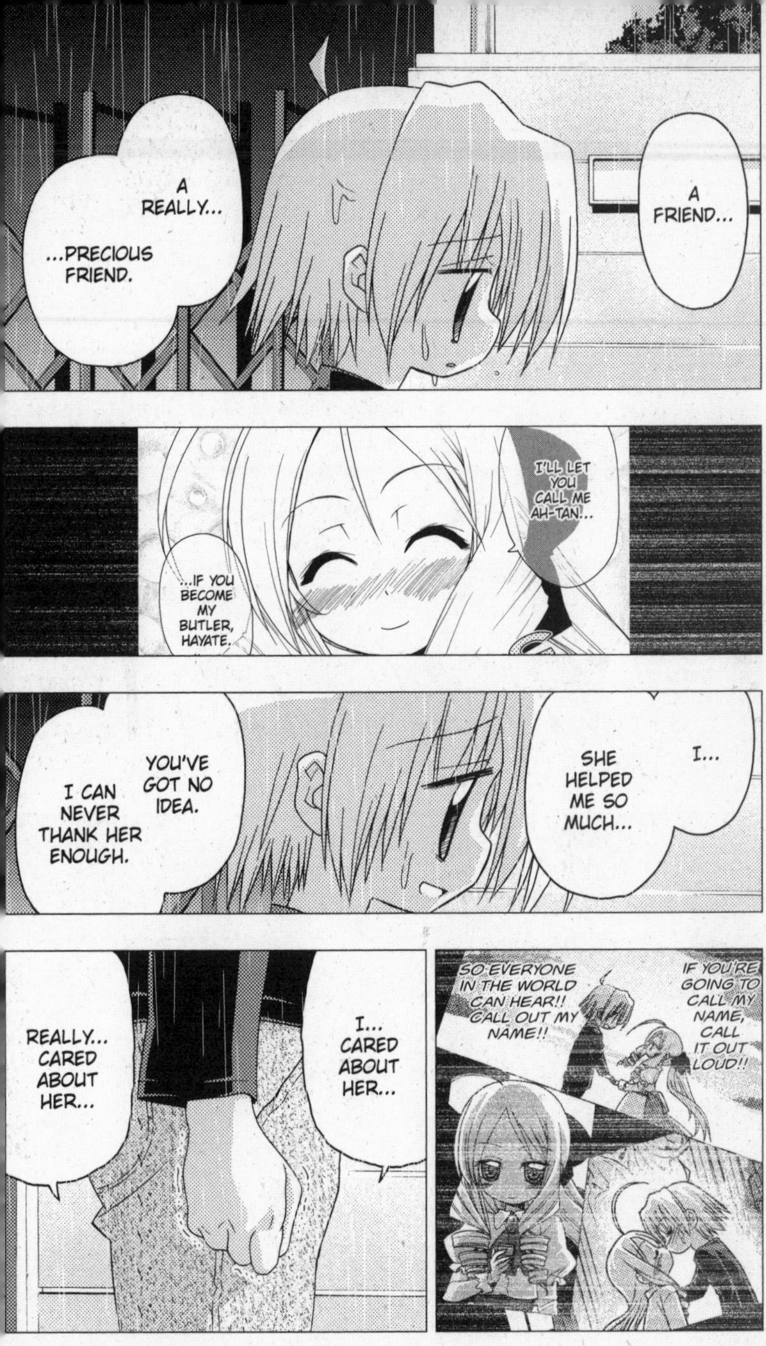
A FRIEND...
A REALLY... ...PRECIOUS FRIEND.
I'LL LET YOU CALL ME AH-TAN...
...IF YOU BECOME MY BUTLER, HAYATE.
I...
SHE HELPED ME SO MUCH...
YOU'VE GOT NO IDEA.
I CAN NEVER THANK HER ENOUGH.
IF YOU'RE GOING TO CALL MY NAME, CALL IT OUT LOUD!!
SO EVERYONE IN THE WORLD CAN HEAR!! CALL OUT MY NAME!!
I... CARED ABOUT HER...
REALLY... CARED ABOUT HER...

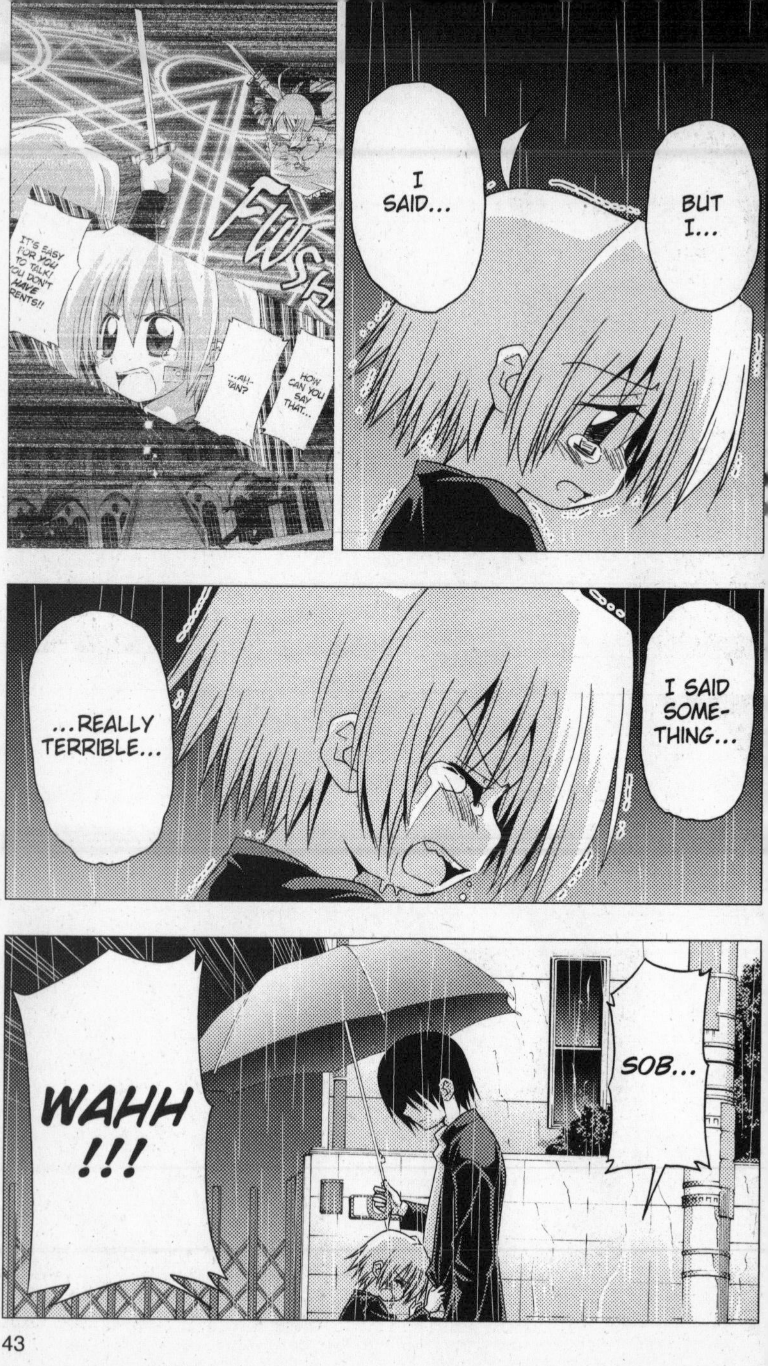
BUT I...
I SAID...
FWSH
HOW CAN YOU SAY THAT...
...AH-TAN?
IT'S EASY FOR YOU TO TALK! YOU DON'T HAVE RENTS!!
I SAID SOME-THING...
...REALLY TERRIBLE...
SOB...
WAHH!!!

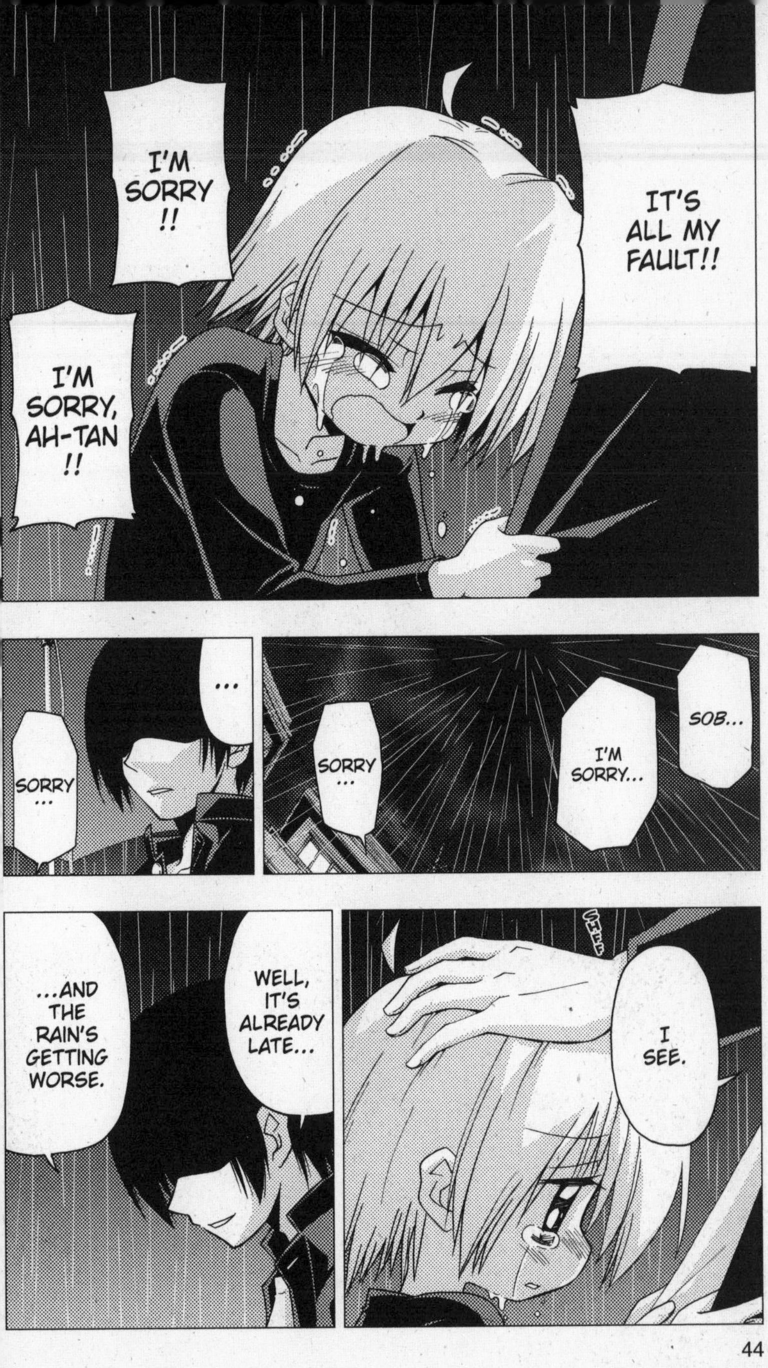
IT'S ALL MY FAULT!!
I'M SORRY!!
I'M SORRY, AH-TAN!!
SOB...
I'M SORRY...
SORRY...
...
SORRY...
SHFF
I SEE.
WELL, IT'S ALREADY LATE...
...AND THE RAIN'S GETTING WORSE.

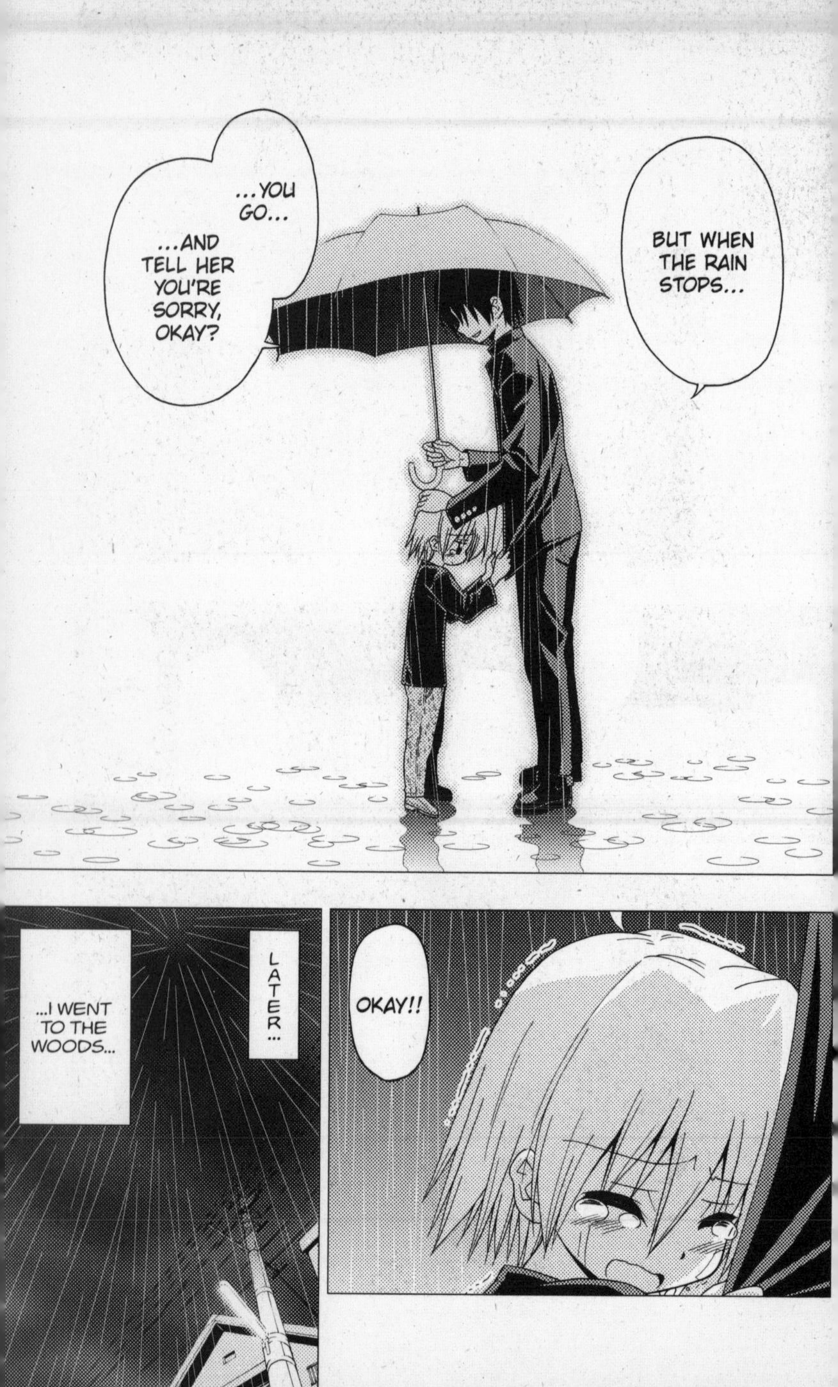
BUT WHEN THE RAIN STOPS...
...YOU GO...
...AND TELL HER YOU'RE SORRY, OKAY?
OKAY!!
LATER...
...I WENT TO THE WOODS...

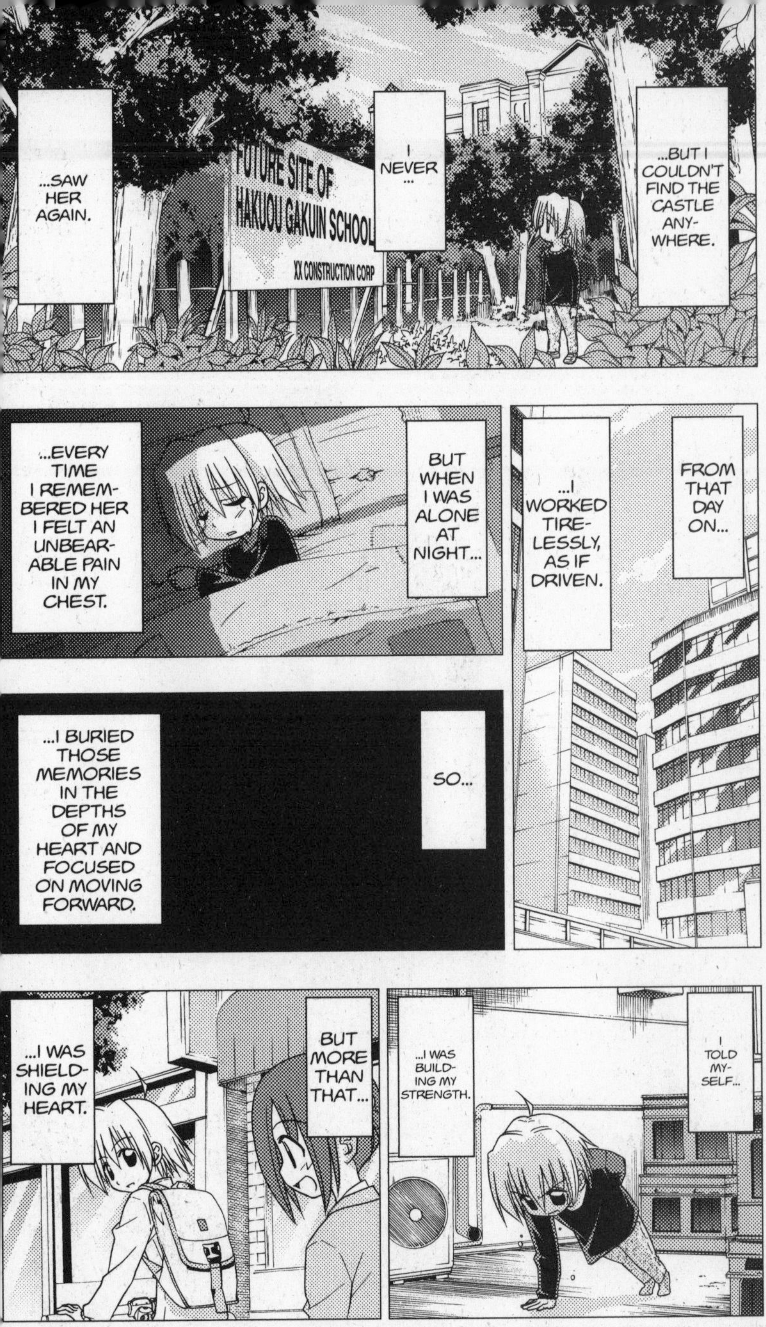
...BUT I COULDN'T FIND THE CASTLE ANYWHERE.
I NEVER...
FUTURE SITE OF HAKUOU GAKUIN SCHOOL
XX CONSTRUCTION CORP
...SAW HER AGAIN.
FROM THAT DAY ON...
...I WORKED TIRELESSLY, AS IF DRIVEN.
BUT WHEN I WAS ALONE AT NIGHT...
...EVERY TIME I REMEMBERED HER I FELT AN UNBEARABLE PAIN IN MY CHEST.
SO...
...I BURIED THOSE MEMORIES IN THE DEPTHS OF MY HEART AND FOCUSED ON MOVING FORWARD.
I TOLD MYSELF...
...I WAS BUILDING MY STRENGTH.
BUT MORE THAN THAT...
...I WAS SHIELDING MY HEART.

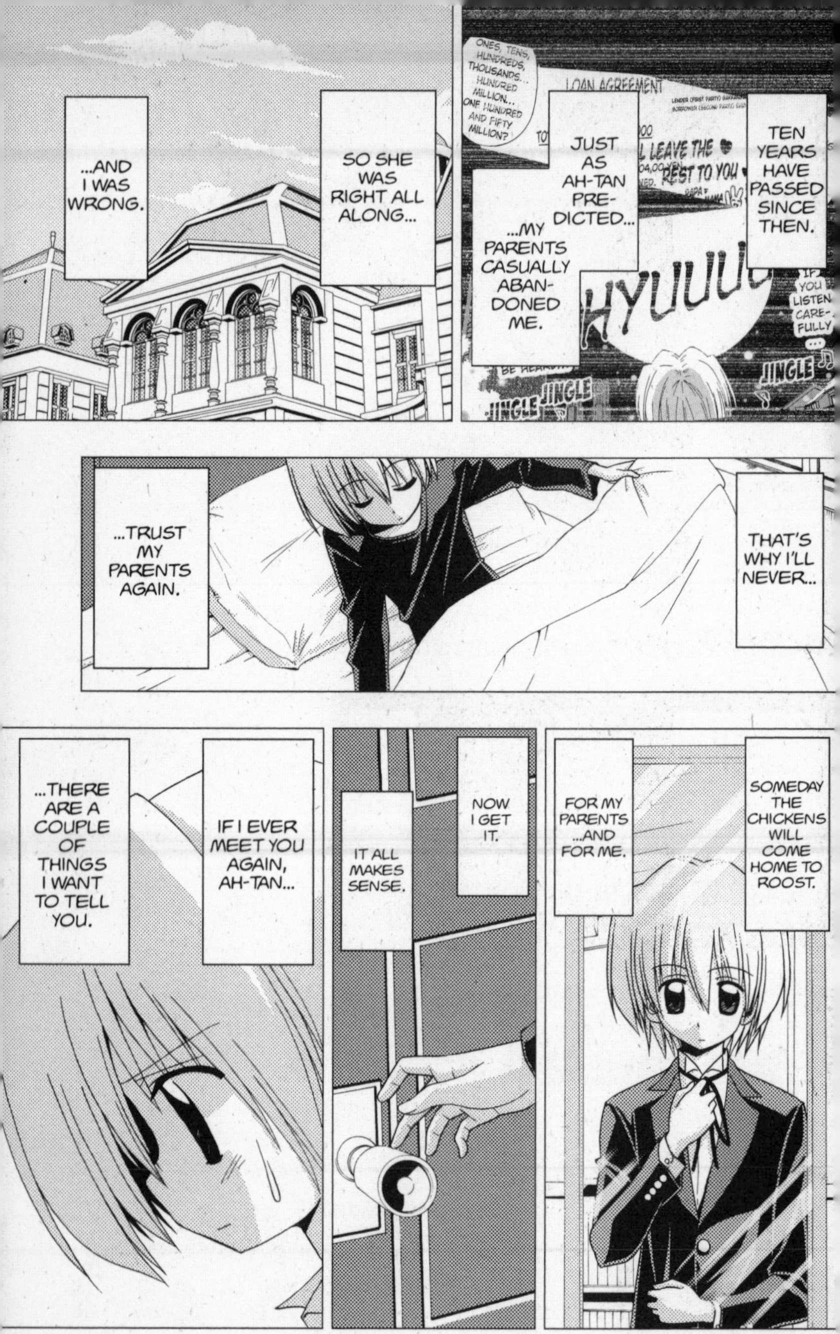
TEN YEARS HAVE PASSED SINCE THEN.
LOAN AGREEMENT
REST TO YOU
JUST AS AH-TAN PREDICTED...
ONES, TENS, HUNDREDS, THOUSANDS... HUNDRED MILLION... ONE HUNDRED AND FIFTY MILLION?
...MY PARENTS CASUALLY ABANDONED ME.
HYUUUU
IF YOU LISTEN CAREFULLY...
JINGLE
JINGLE JINGLE
SO SHE WAS RIGHT ALL ALONG...
...AND I WAS WRONG.
THAT'S WHY I'LL NEVER...
...TRUST MY PARENTS AGAIN.
SOMEDAY THE CHICKENS WILL COME HOME TO ROOST.
FOR MY PARENTS ...AND FOR ME.
NOW I GET IT.
IT ALL MAKES SENSE.
IF I EVER MEET YOU AGAIN, AH-TAN...
...THERE ARE A COUPLE OF THINGS I WANT TO TELL YOU.

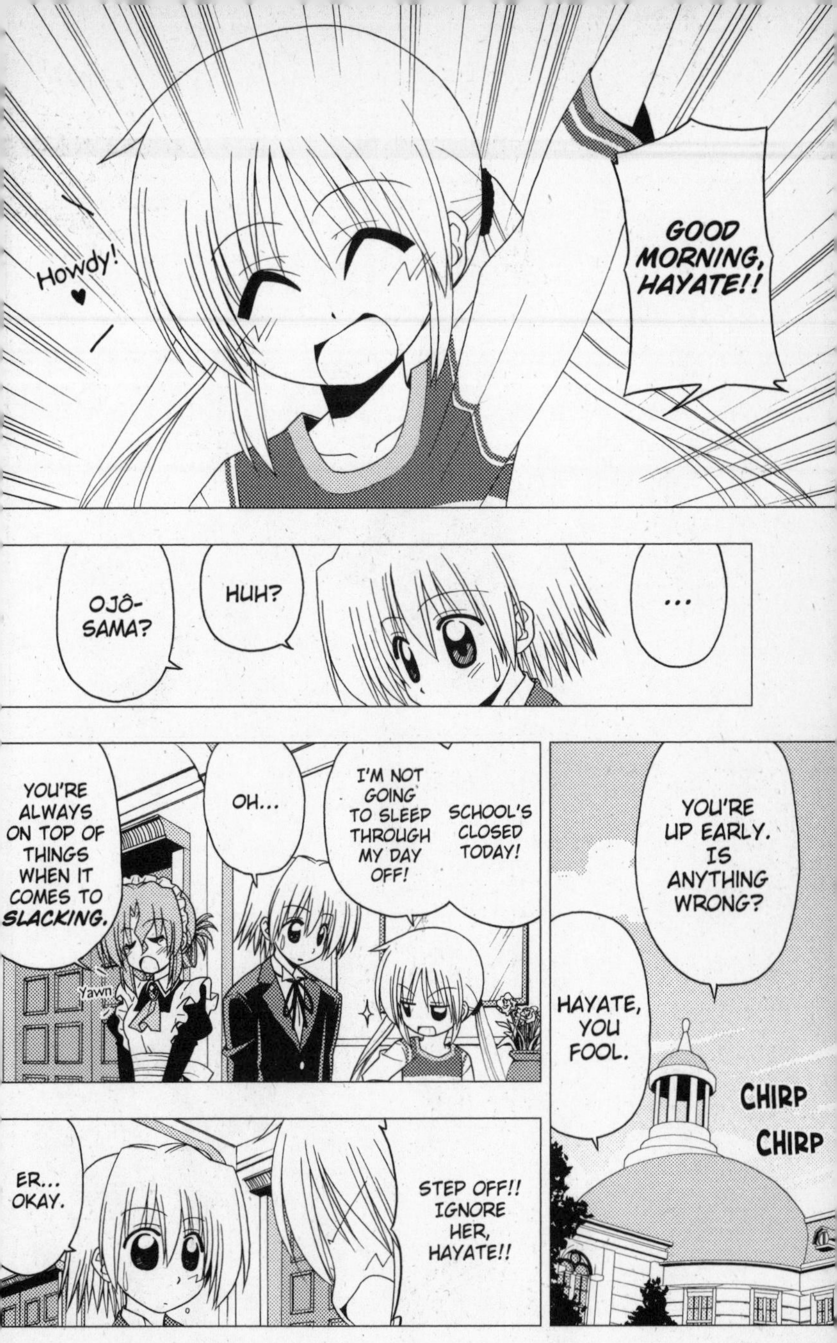
GOOD MORNING, HAYATE!!
Howdy! ♥
...
HUH?
OJÔ-SAMA?
YOU'RE UP EARLY. IS ANYTHING WRONG?
HAYATE, YOU FOOL.
CHIRP
CHIRP
SCHOOL'S CLOSED TODAY!
I'M NOT GOING TO SLEEP THROUGH MY DAY OFF!
OH...
YOU'RE ALWAYS ON TOP OF THINGS WHEN IT COMES TO *SLACKING.*
Yawn
STEP OFF!! IGNORE HER, HAYATE!!
ER... OKAY.

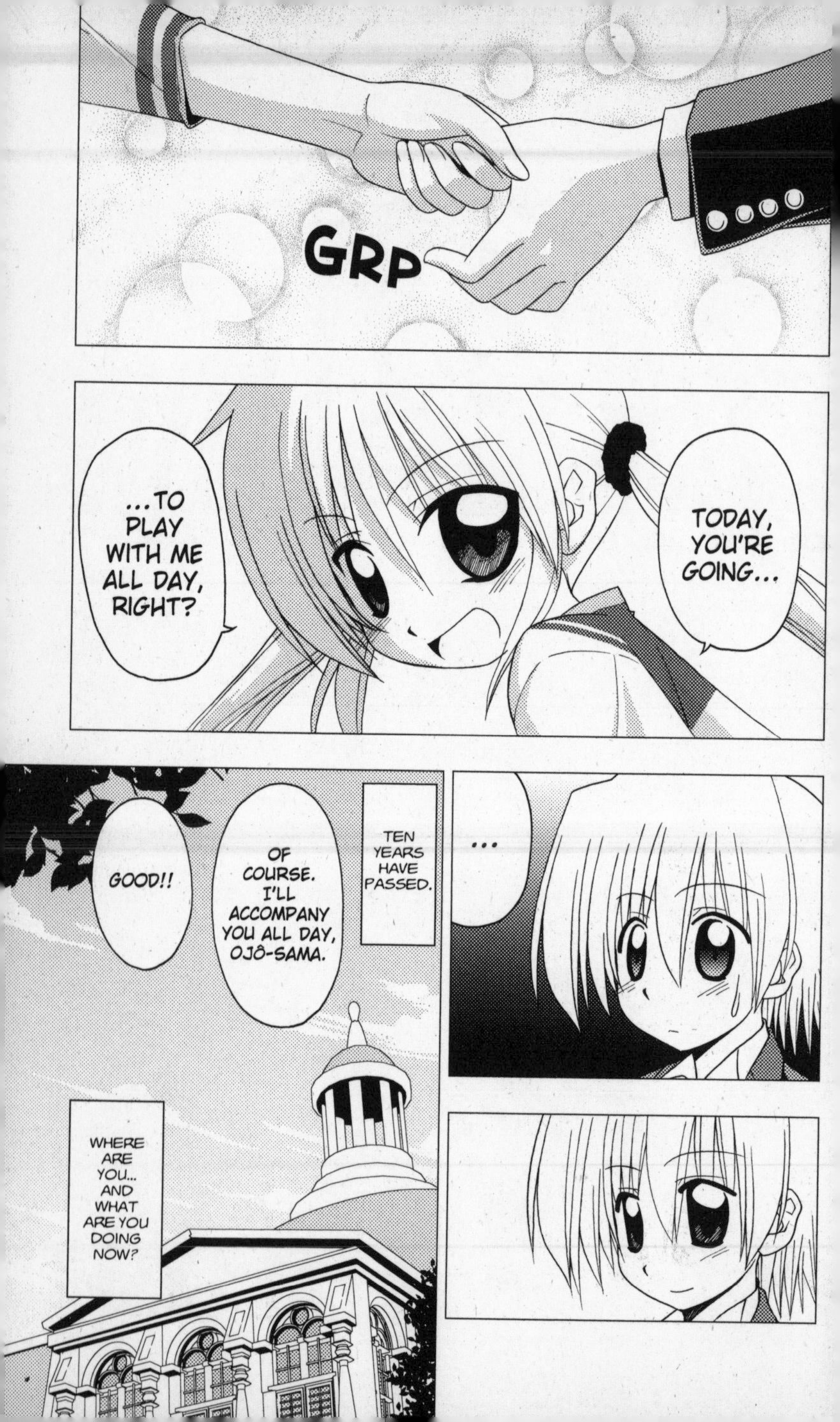
GRP
TODAY, YOU'RE GOING...
...TO PLAY WITH ME ALL DAY, RIGHT?
...
TEN YEARS HAVE PASSED.
OF COURSE. I'LL ACCOMPANY YOU ALL DAY, OJÔ-SAMA.
GOOD!!
WHERE ARE YOU... AND WHAT ARE YOU DOING NOW?

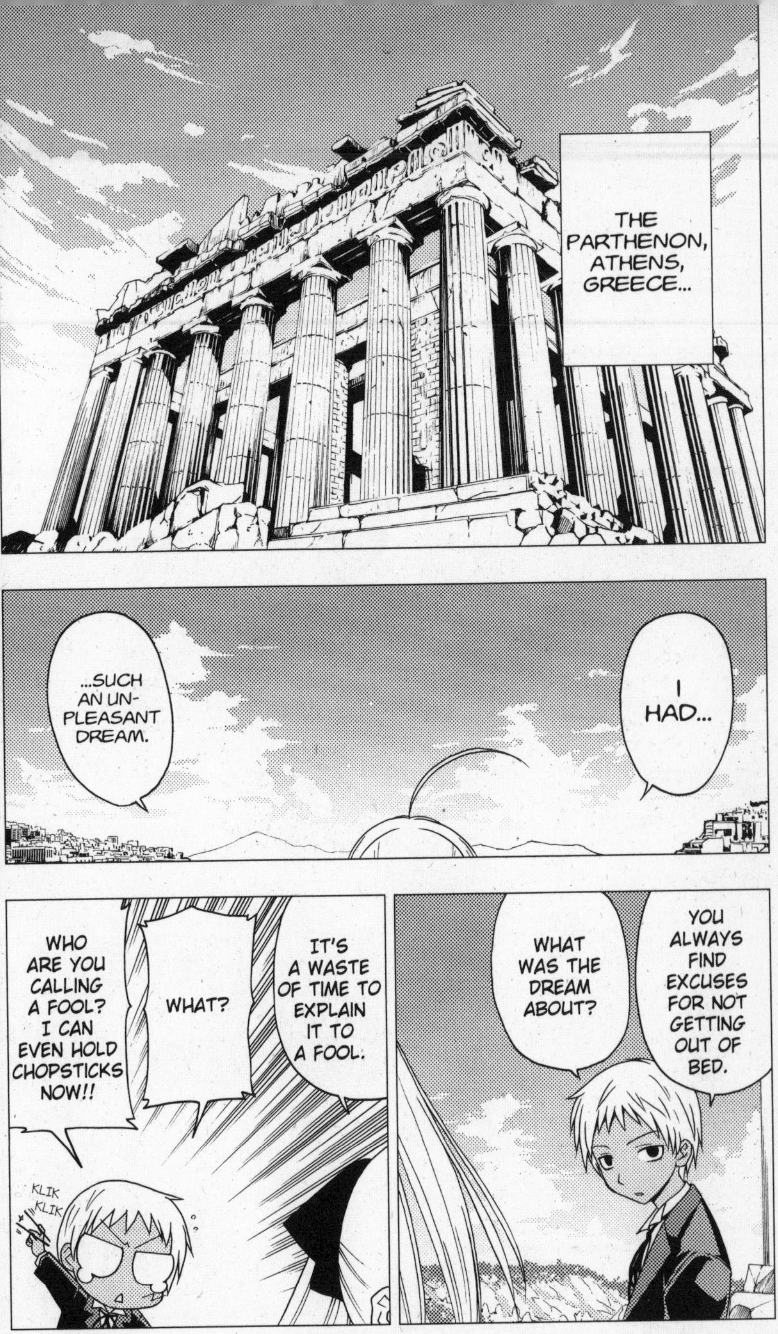
THE PARTHENON, ATHENS, GREECE...
I HAD...
...SUCH AN UNPLEASANT DREAM.
YOU ALWAYS FIND EXCUSES FOR NOT GETTING OUT OF BED.
WHAT WAS THE DREAM ABOUT?
IT'S A WASTE OF TIME TO EXPLAIN IT TO A FOOL.
WHAT?
WHO ARE YOU CALLING A FOOL? I CAN EVEN HOLD CHOPSTICKS NOW!!
KLIK KLIK

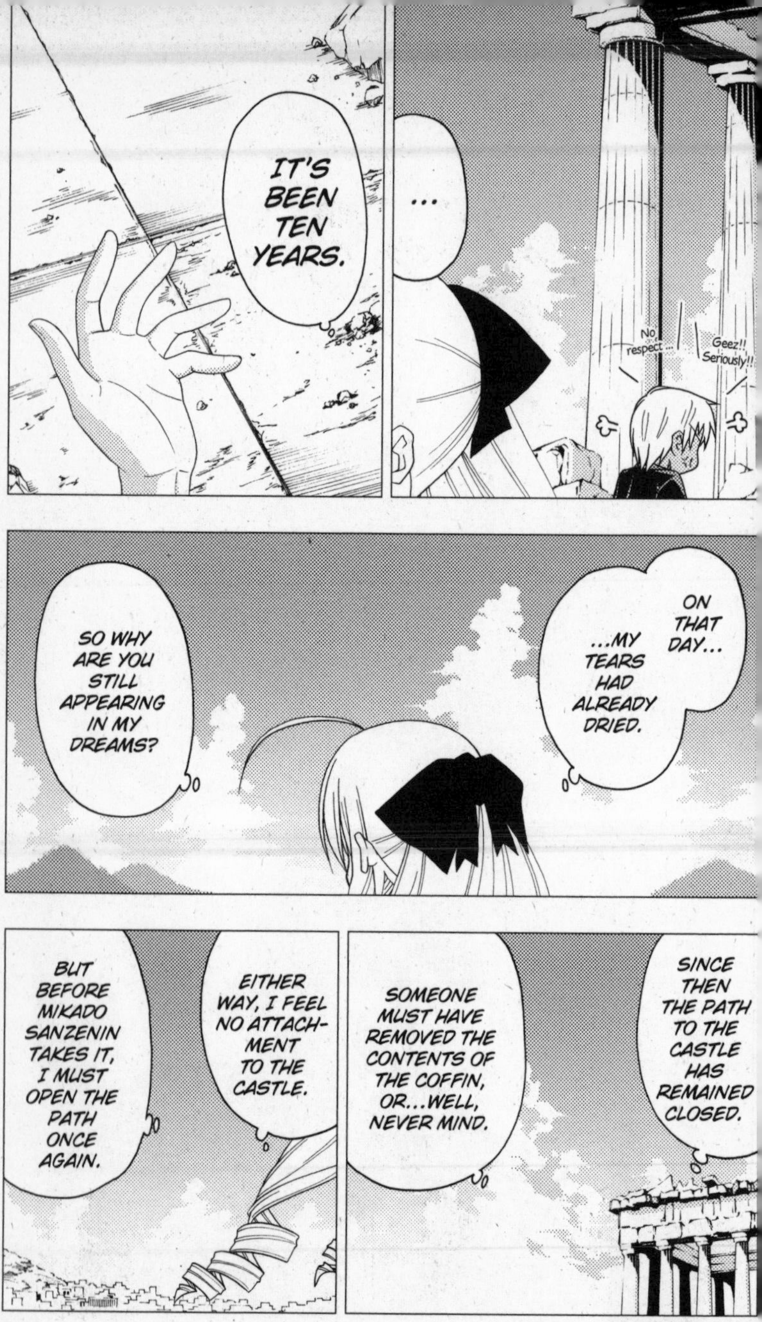
...
Geez!! Seriously!!
No respect...
IT'S BEEN TEN YEARS.
ON THAT DAY...
...MY TEARS HAD ALREADY DRIED.
SO WHY ARE YOU STILL APPEARING IN MY DREAMS?
SINCE THEN THE PATH TO THE CASTLE HAS REMAINED CLOSED.
SOMEONE MUST HAVE REMOVED THE CONTENTS OF THE COFFIN, OR...WELL, NEVER MIND.
EITHER WAY, I FEEL NO ATTACH-MENT TO THE CASTLE.
BUT BEFORE MIKADO SANZENIN TAKES IT, I MUST OPEN THE PATH ONCE AGAIN.

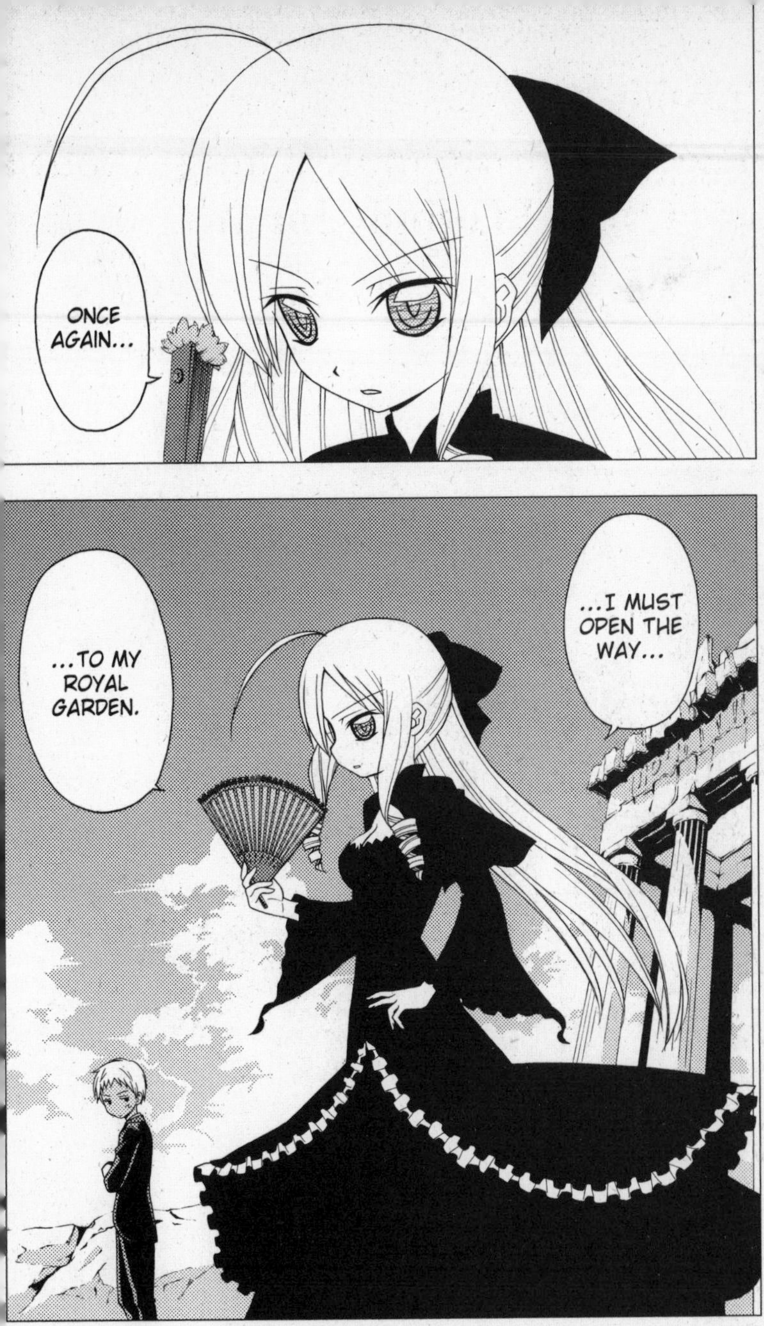
ONCE AGAIN...
...I MUST OPEN THE WAY...
...TO MY ROYAL GARDEN.

Episode 4:
"The Most Enjoyable Thing About
Day Off Is Planning for It"

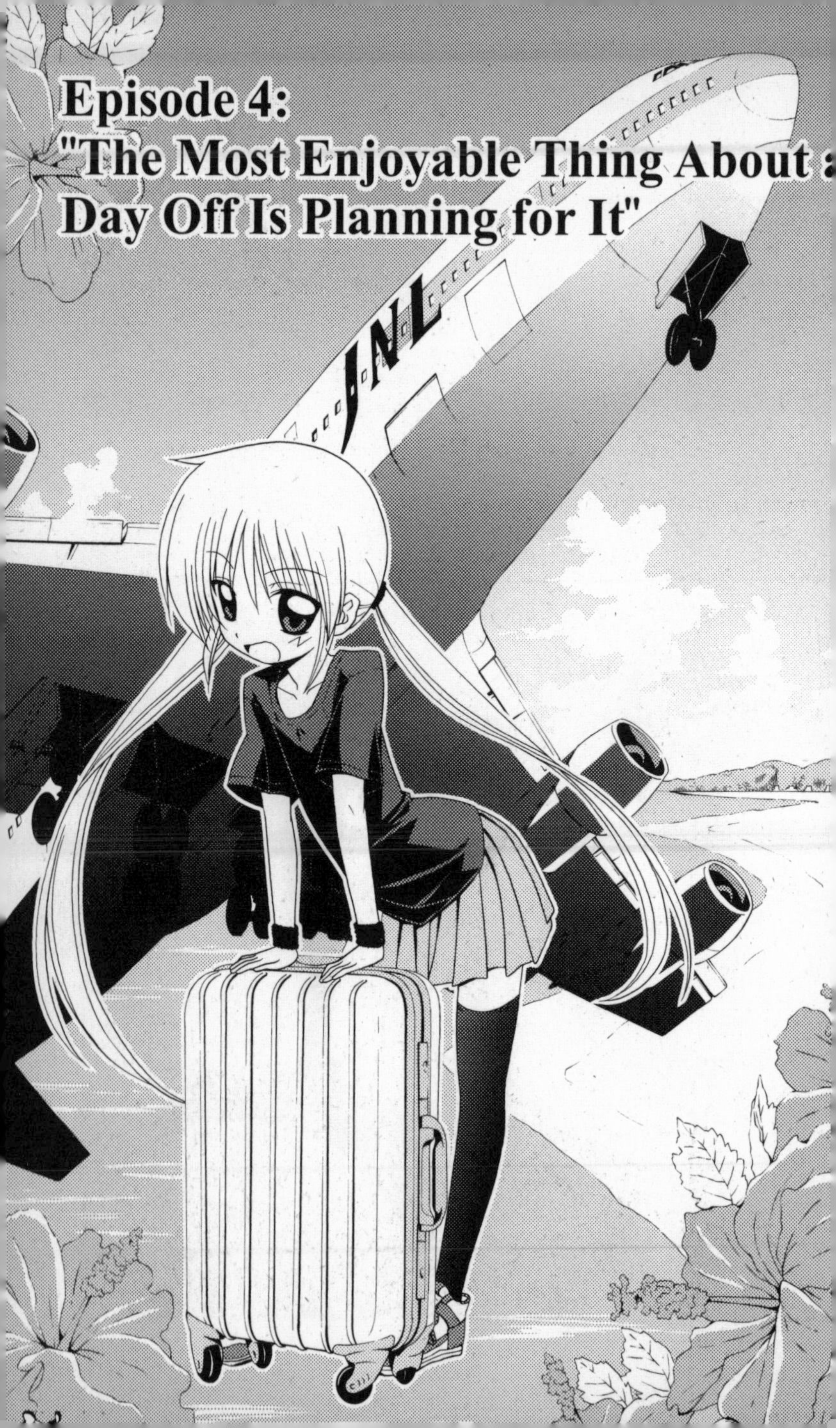
JNL

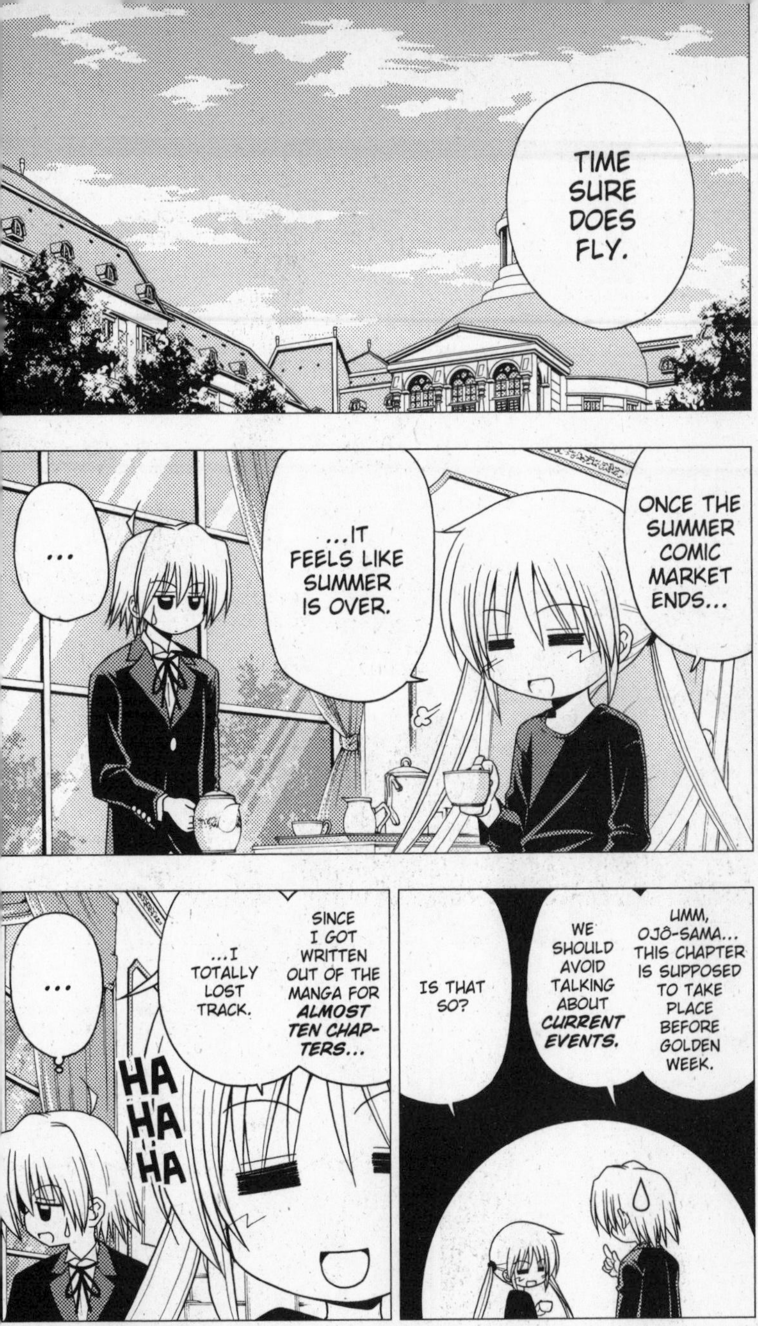
TIME SURE DOES FLY.
ONCE THE SUMMER COMIC MARKET ENDS...
...IT FEELS LIKE SUMMER IS OVER.
...
UMM, OJÔ-SAMA... THIS CHAPTER IS SUPPOSED TO TAKE PLACE BEFORE GOLDEN WEEK.
WE SHOULD AVOID TALKING ABOUT *CURRENT EVENTS.*
IS THAT SO?
SINCE I GOT WRITTEN OUT OF THE MANGA FOR *ALMOST TEN CHAPTERS...*
...I TOTALLY LOST TRACK.
...
HA HA HA HA

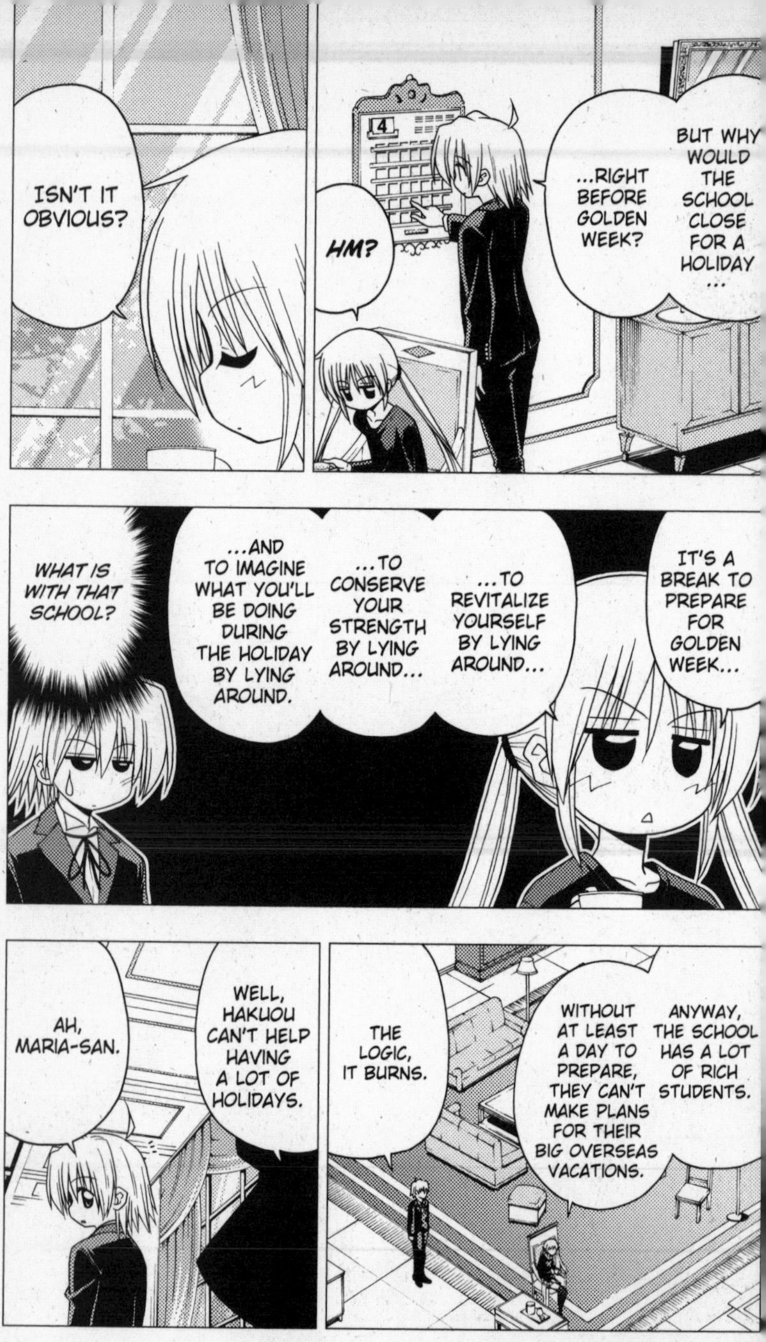
BUT WHY WOULD THE SCHOOL CLOSE FOR A HOLIDAY...
...RIGHT BEFORE GOLDEN WEEK?
HM?
ISN'T IT OBVIOUS?
IT'S A BREAK TO PREPARE FOR GOLDEN WEEK...
...TO REVITALIZE YOURSELF BY LYING AROUND...
...TO CONSERVE YOUR STRENGTH BY LYING AROUND...
...AND TO IMAGINE WHAT YOU'LL BE DOING DURING THE HOLIDAY BY LYING AROUND.
WHAT IS WITH THAT SCHOOL?
ANYWAY, THE SCHOOL HAS A LOT OF RICH STUDENTS.
WITHOUT AT LEAST A DAY TO PREPARE, THEY CAN'T MAKE PLANS FOR THEIR BIG OVERSEAS VACATIONS.
THE LOGIC, IT BURNS.
WELL, HAKUOU CAN'T HELP HAVING A LOT OF HOLIDAYS.
AH, MARIA-SAN.

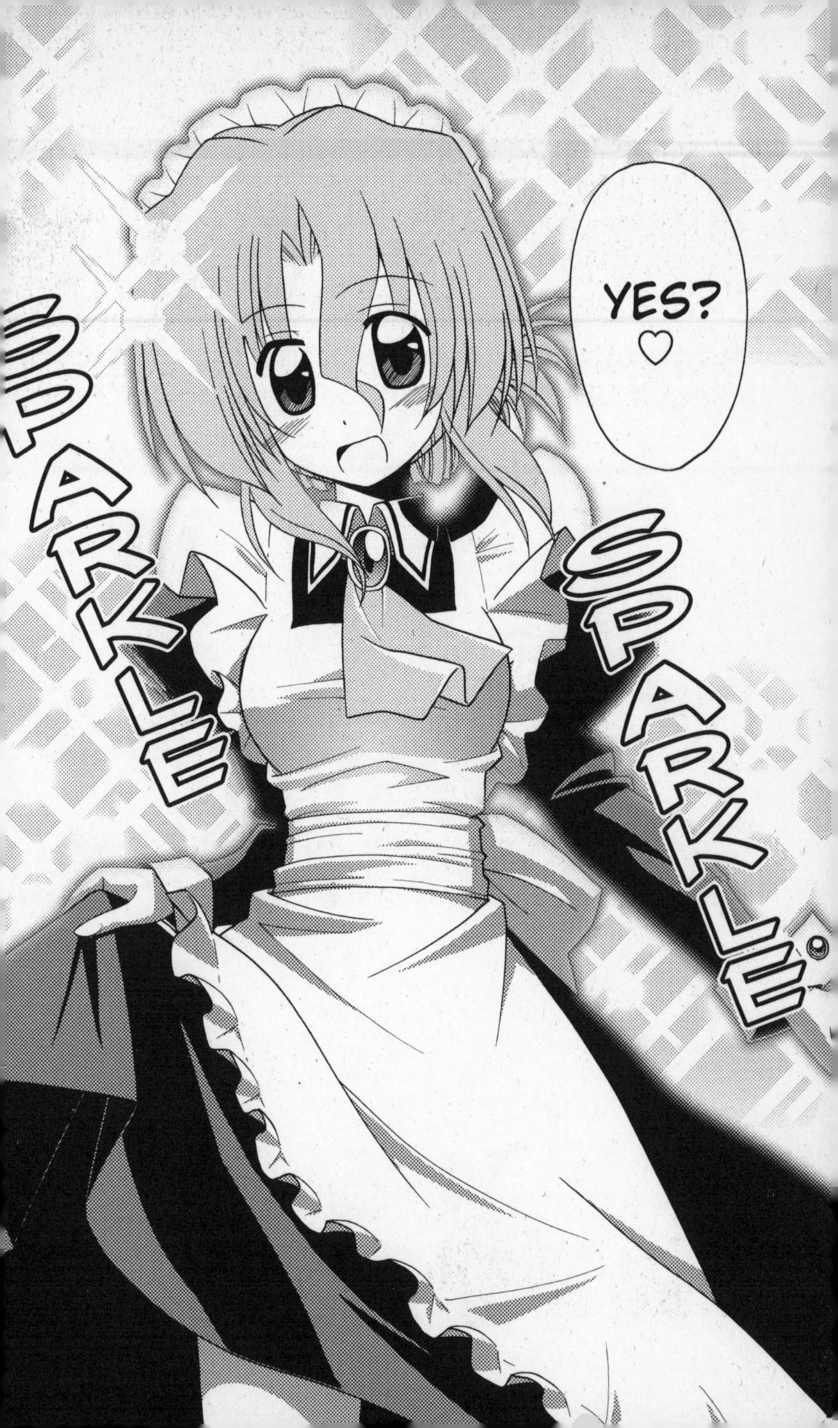
YES? ♡
SPARKLE
SPARKLE

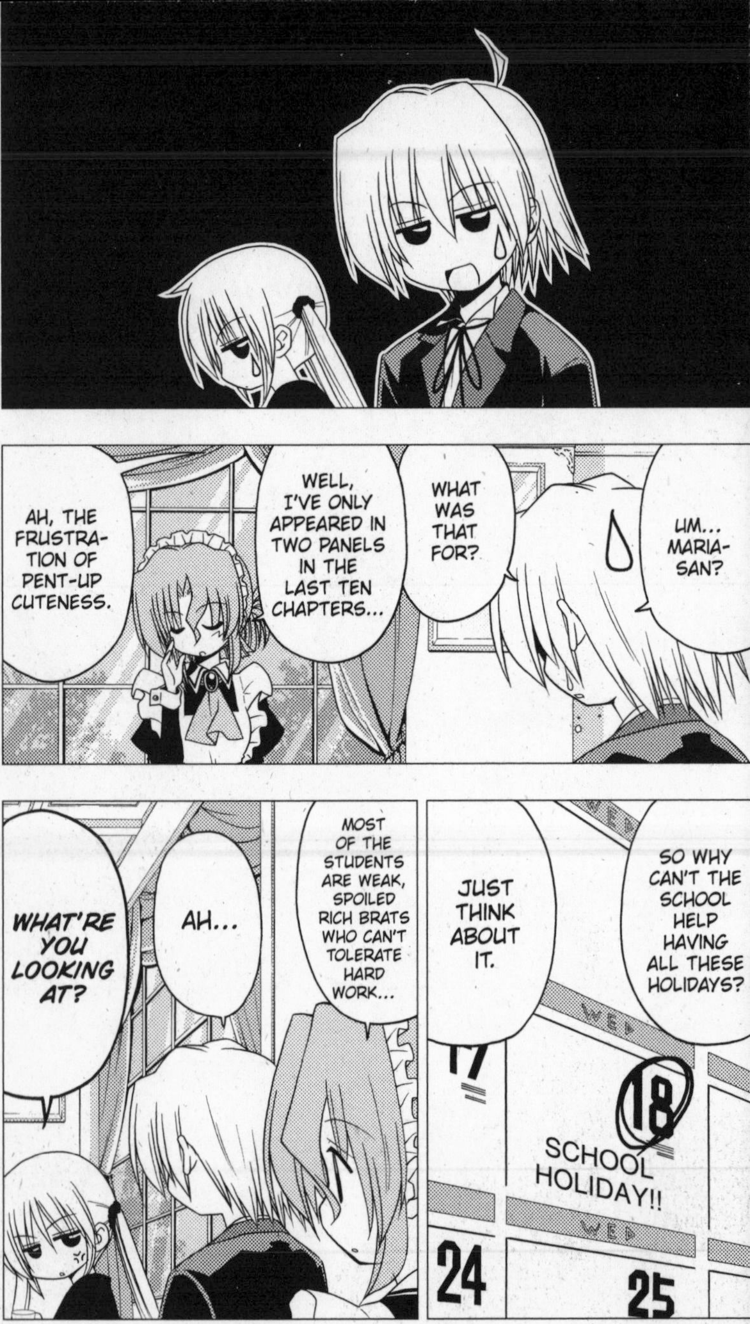
UM... MARIA-SAN?
WHAT WAS THAT FOR?
WELL, I'VE ONLY APPEARED IN TWO PANELS IN THE LAST TEN CHAPTERS...
AH, THE FRUSTRATION OF PENT-UP CUTENESS.
SO WHY CAN'T THE SCHOOL HELP HAVING ALL THESE HOLIDAYS?
JUST THINK ABOUT IT.
17
18
SCHOOL HOLIDAY!!
24
25
MOST OF THE STUDENTS ARE WEAK, SPOILED RICH BRATS WHO CAN'T TOLERATE HARD WORK...
AH...
WHAT'RE YOU LOOKING AT?

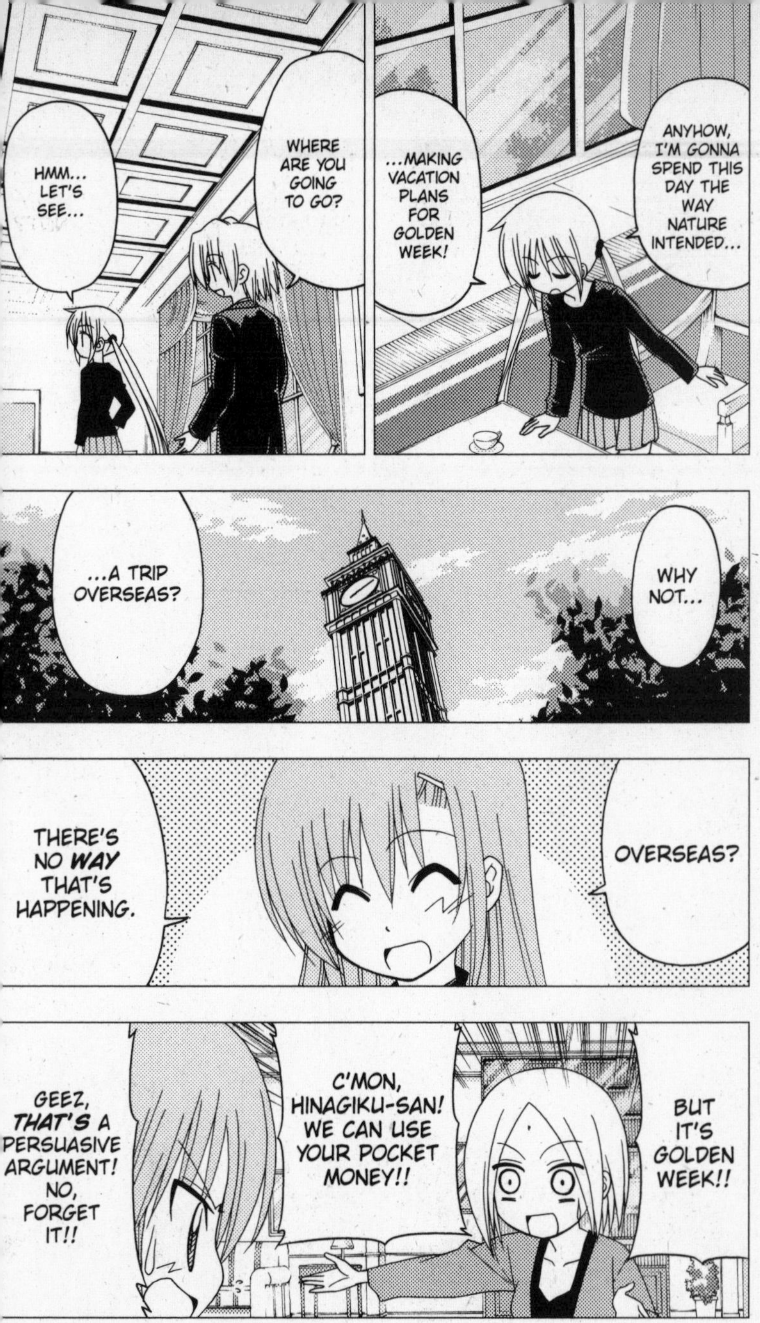
ANYHOW, I'M GONNA SPEND THIS DAY THE WAY NATURE INTENDED...
...MAKING VACATION PLANS FOR GOLDEN WEEK!
WHERE ARE YOU GOING TO GO?
HMM... LET'S SEE...
WHY NOT...
...A TRIP OVERSEAS?
OVERSEAS?
THERE'S NO WAY THAT'S HAPPENING.
BUT IT'S GOLDEN WEEK!!
C'MON, HINAGIKU-SAN! WE CAN USE YOUR POCKET MONEY!!
GEEZ, THAT'S A PERSUASIVE ARGUMENT! NO, FORGET IT!!

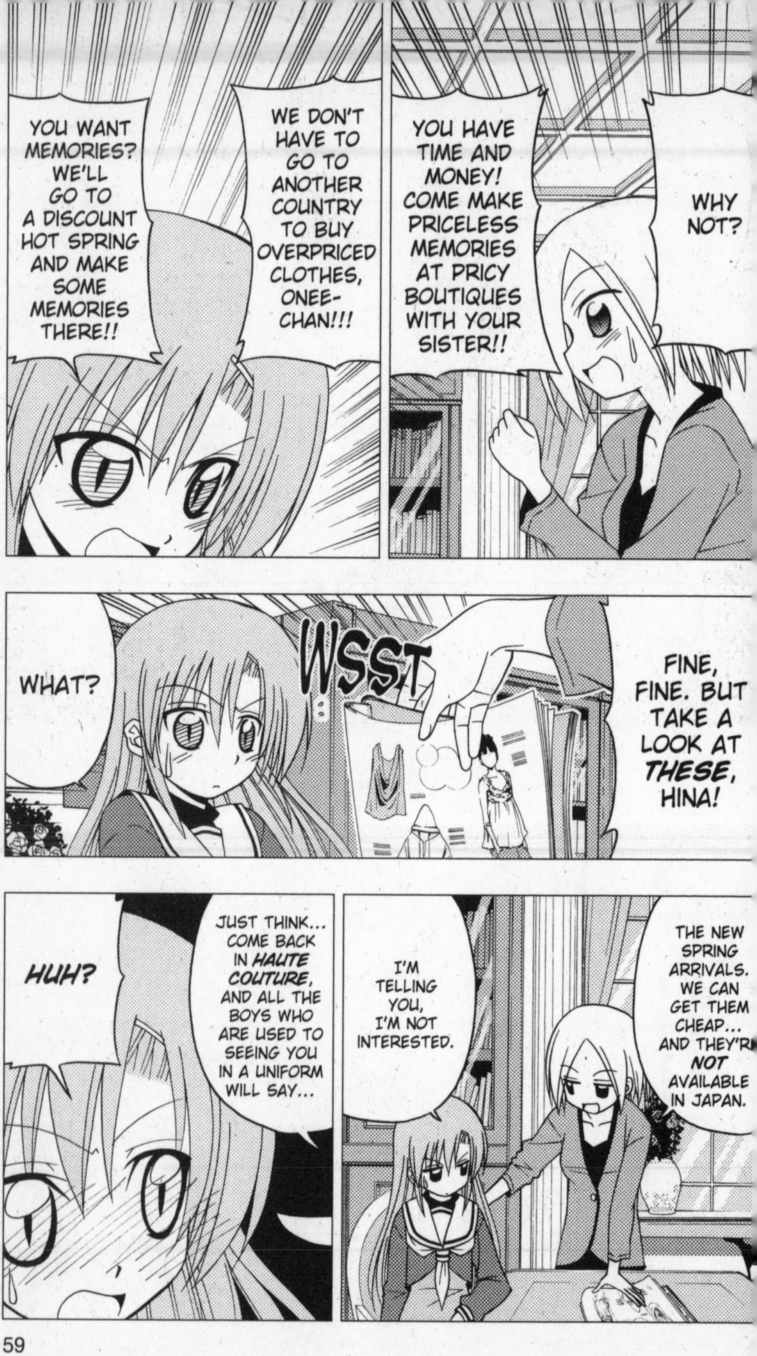

WHY NOT?
YOU HAVE TIME AND MONEY! COME MAKE PRICELESS MEMORIES AT PRICY BOUTIQUES WITH YOUR SISTER!!
WE DON'T HAVE TO GO TO ANOTHER COUNTRY TO BUY OVERPRICED CLOTHES, ONEE-CHAN!!!
YOU WANT MEMORIES? WE'LL GO TO A DISCOUNT HOT SPRING AND MAKE SOME MEMORIES THERE!!
FINE, FINE. BUT TAKE A LOOK AT *THESE*, HINA!
WSST
WHAT?
THE NEW SPRING ARRIVALS. WE CAN GET THEM CHEAP... AND THEY'R *NOT* AVAILABLE IN JAPAN.
I'M TELLING YOU, I'M NOT INTERESTED.
JUST THINK... COME BACK IN *HAUTE COUTURE*, AND ALL THE BOYS WHO ARE USED TO SEEING YOU IN A UNIFORM WILL SAY...
HUH?

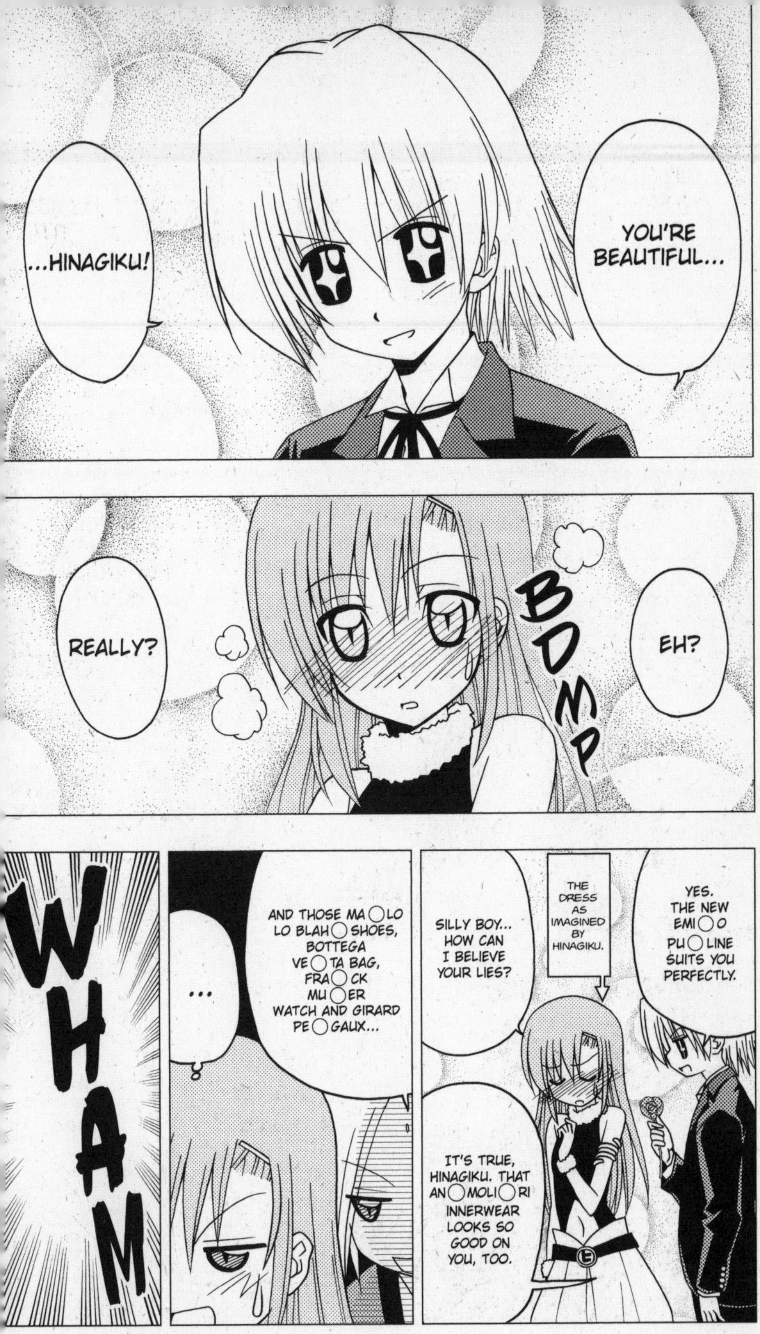
YOU'RE BEAUTIFUL...
...HINAGIKU!
EH?
BDMP
REALLY?
YES. THE NEW EMI◯O PU◯LINE SUITS YOU PERFECTLY.
THE DRESS AS IMAGINED BY HINAGIKU.
SILLY BOY... HOW CAN I BELIEVE YOUR LIES?
IT'S TRUE, HINAGIKU. THAT AN◯MOLI◯RI INNERWEAR LOOKS SO GOOD ON YOU, TOO.
AND THOSE MA◯LO LO BLAH◯ SHOES, BOTTEGA VE◯TA BAG, FRA◯CK MU◯ER WATCH AND GIRARD PE◯GAUX...
...
WHAM

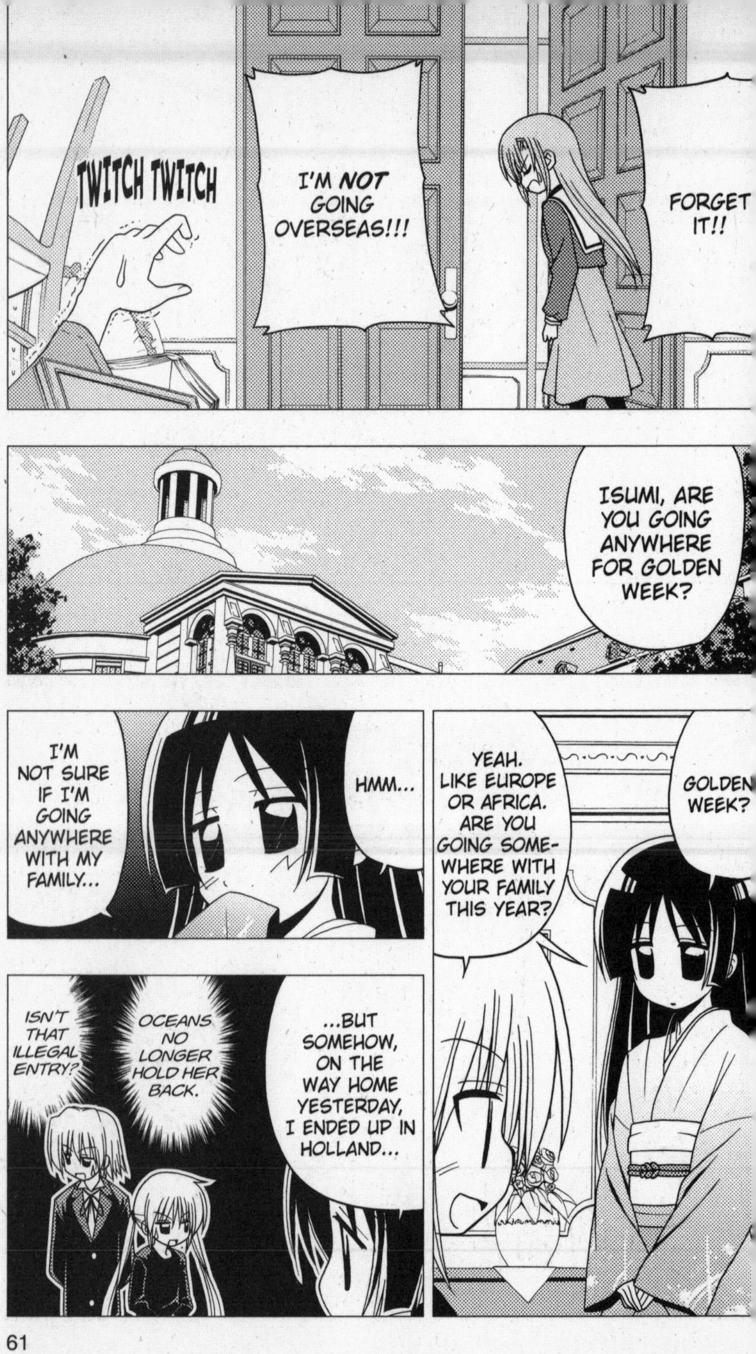
FORGET IT!!
I'M *NOT* GOING OVERSEAS!!!
TWITCH TWITCH
ISUMI, ARE YOU GOING ANYWHERE FOR GOLDEN WEEK?
GOLDEN WEEK?
YEAH. LIKE EUROPE OR AFRICA. ARE YOU GOING SOME-WHERE WITH YOUR FAMILY THIS YEAR?
HMM...
I'M NOT SURE IF I'M GOING ANYWHERE WITH MY FAMILY...
...BUT SOMEHOW, ON THE WAY HOME YESTERDAY, I ENDED UP IN HOLLAND...
OCEANS NO LONGER HOLD HER BACK.
ISN'T THAT ILLEGAL ENTRY?

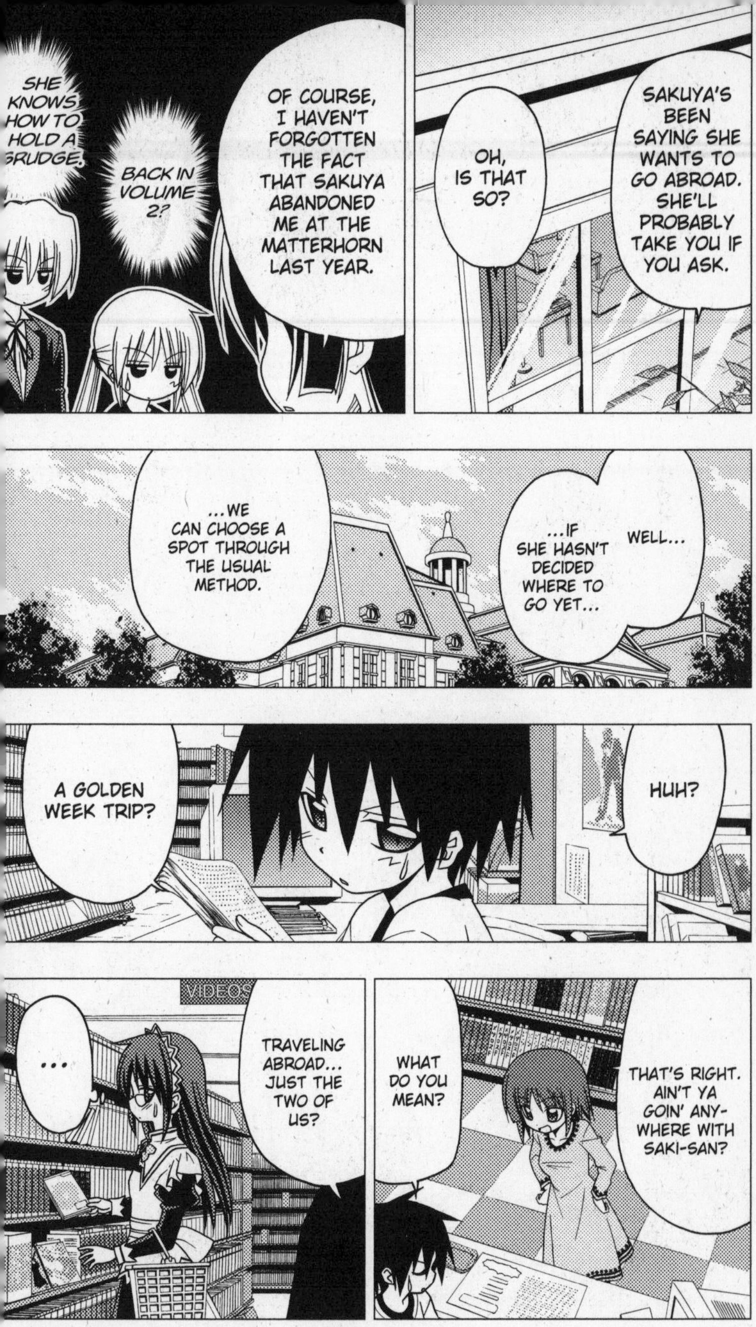
SAKUYA'S BEEN SAYING SHE WANTS TO GO ABROAD. SHE'LL PROBABLY TAKE YOU IF YOU ASK.
OH, IS THAT SO?
OF COURSE, I HAVEN'T FORGOTTEN THE FACT THAT SAKUYA ABANDONED ME AT THE MATTERHORN LAST YEAR.
BACK IN VOLUME 2?
SHE KNOWS HOW TO HOLD A GRUDGE.
WELL...
...IF SHE HASN'T DECIDED WHERE TO GO YET...
...WE CAN CHOOSE A SPOT THROUGH THE USUAL METHOD.
HUH?
A GOLDEN WEEK TRIP?
THAT'S RIGHT. AIN'T YA GOIN' ANY-WHERE WITH SAKI-SAN?
WHAT DO YOU MEAN?
TRAVELING ABROAD... JUST THE TWO OF US?
...
VIDEOS

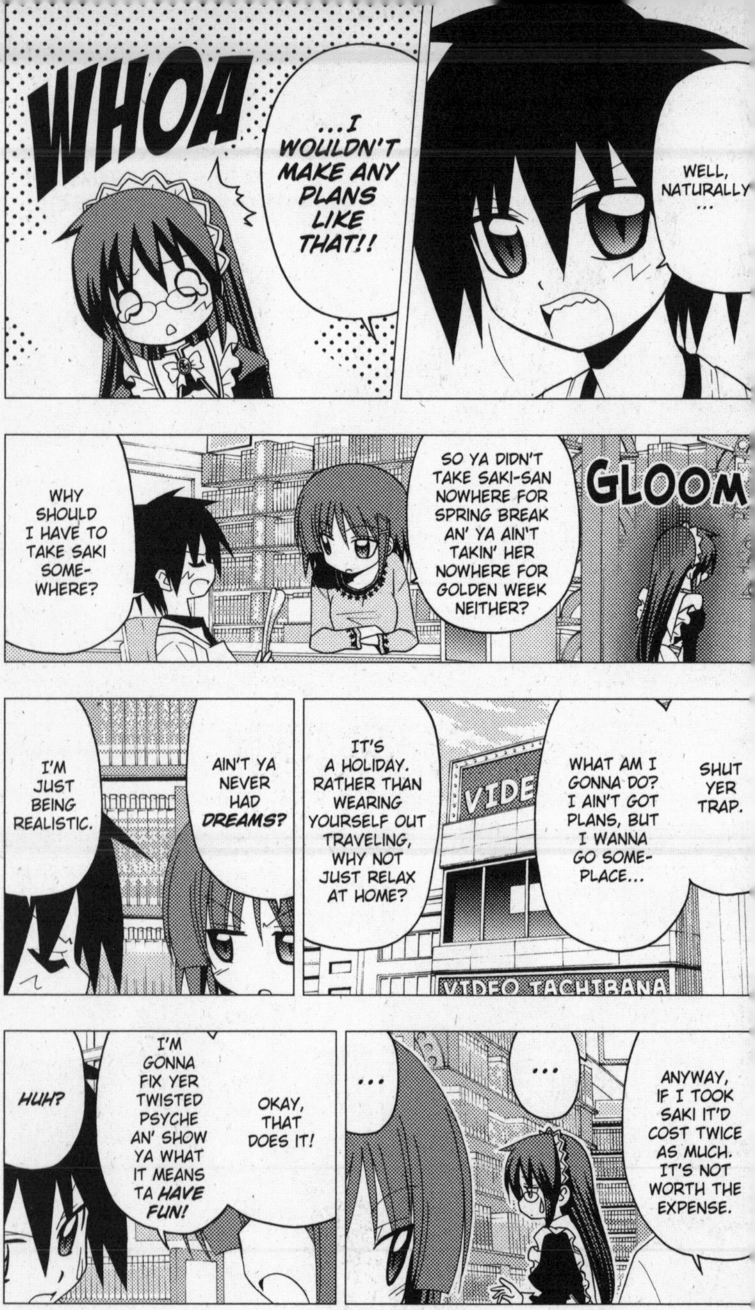
WELL, NATURALLY...
...I WOULDN'T MAKE ANY PLANS LIKE THAT!!
WHOA
GLOOM
SO YA DIDN'T TAKE SAKI-SAN NOWHERE FOR SPRING BREAK AN' YA AIN'T TAKIN' HER NOWHERE FOR GOLDEN WEEK NEITHER?
WHY SHOULD I HAVE TO TAKE SAKI SOME-WHERE?
SHUT YER TRAP.
WHAT AM I GONNA DO? I AIN'T GOT PLANS, BUT I WANNA GO SOME-PLACE...
VIDE
VIDEO TACHIBANA
IT'S A HOLIDAY. RATHER THAN WEARING YOURSELF OUT TRAVELING, WHY NOT JUST RELAX AT HOME?
AIN'T YA NEVER HAD *DREAMS?*
I'M JUST BEING REALISTIC.
ANYWAY, IF I TOOK SAKI IT'D COST TWICE AS MUCH. IT'S NOT WORTH THE EXPENSE.
...
...
OKAY, THAT DOES IT!
I'M GONNA FIX YER TWISTED PSYCHE AN' SHOW YA WHAT IT MEANS TA *HAVE FUN!*
HUH?

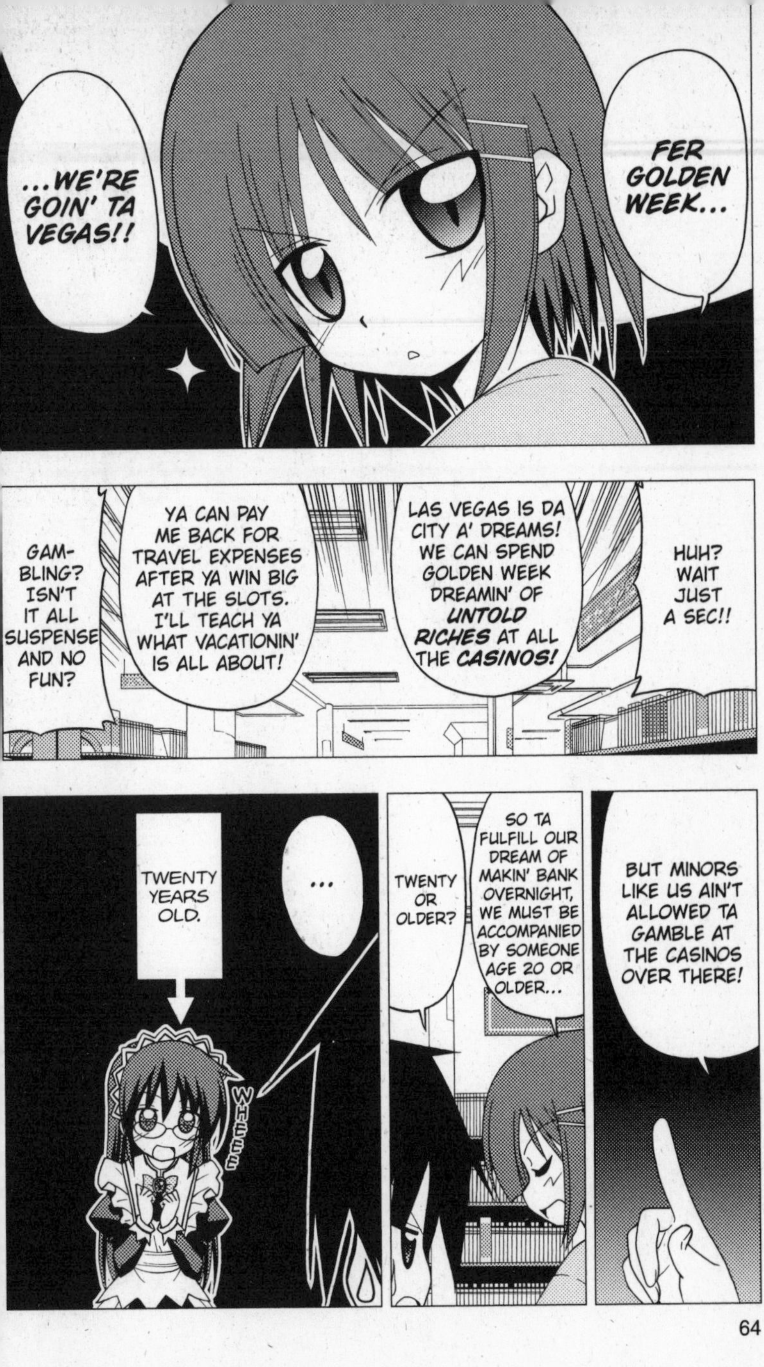
FER GOLDEN WEEK...
...WE'RE GOIN' TA VEGAS!!
HUH? WAIT JUST A SEC!!
LAS VEGAS IS DA CITY A' DREAMS! WE CAN SPEND GOLDEN WEEK DREAMIN' OF UNTOLD RICHES AT ALL THE CASINOS!
YA CAN PAY ME BACK FOR TRAVEL EXPENSES AFTER YA WIN BIG AT THE SLOTS. I'LL TEACH YA WHAT VACATIONIN' IS ALL ABOUT!
GAM-BLING? ISN'T IT ALL SUSPENSE AND NO FUN?
BUT MINORS LIKE US AIN'T ALLOWED TA GAMBLE AT THE CASINOS OVER THERE!
SO TA FULFILL OUR DREAM OF MAKIN' BANK OVERNIGHT, WE MUST BE ACCOMPANIED BY SOMEONE AGE 20 OR OLDER...
TWENTY OR OLDER?
...
TWENTY YEARS OLD.
WHEEEE

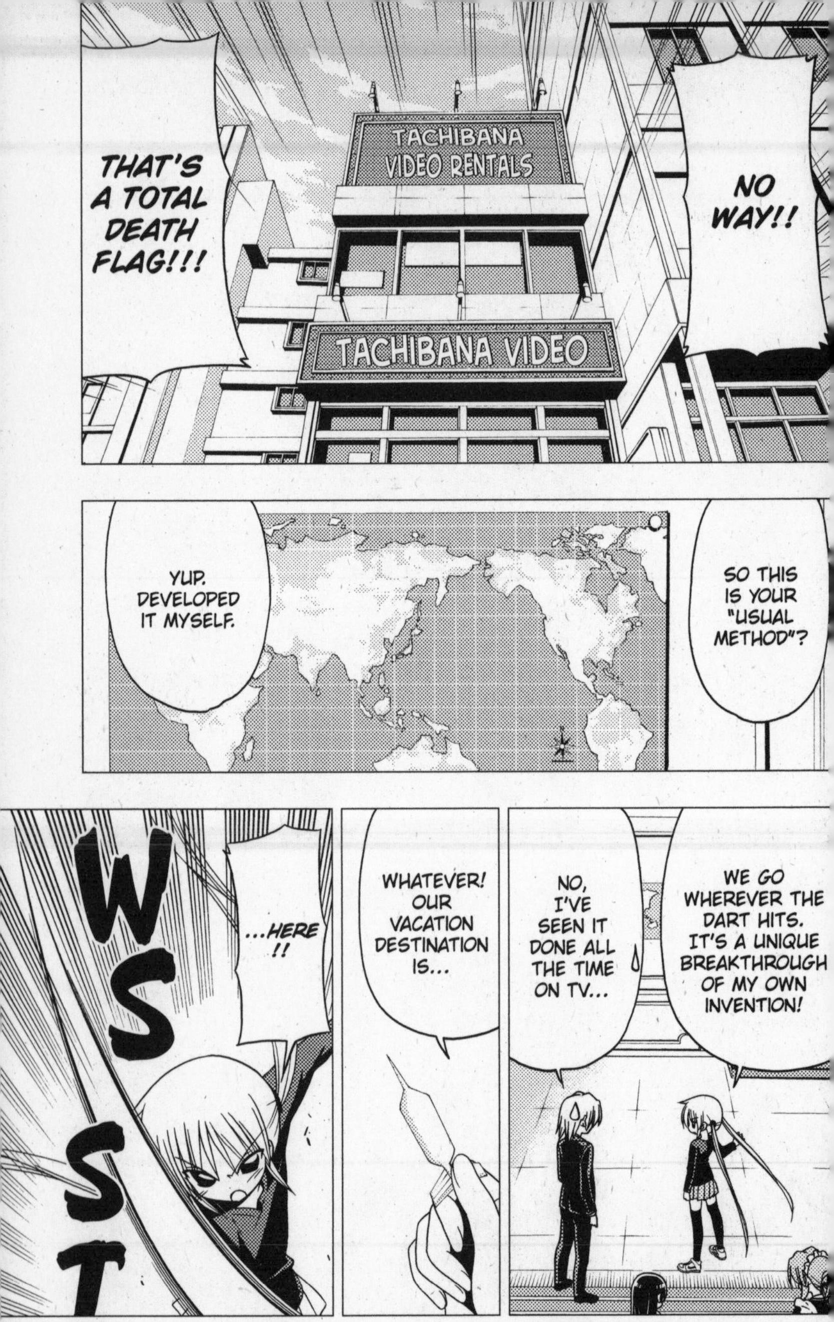
TACHIBANA VIDEO RENTALS
TACHIBANA VIDEO
NO WAY!!
THAT'S A TOTAL DEATH FLAG!!!
SO THIS IS YOUR "USUAL METHOD"?
YUP. DEVELOPED IT MYSELF.
WE GO WHEREVER THE DART HITS. IT'S A UNIQUE BREAKTHROUGH OF MY OWN INVENTION!
NO, I'VE SEEN IT DONE ALL THE TIME ON TV...
WHATEVER! OUR VACATION DESTINATION IS...
...HERE!!
WSST

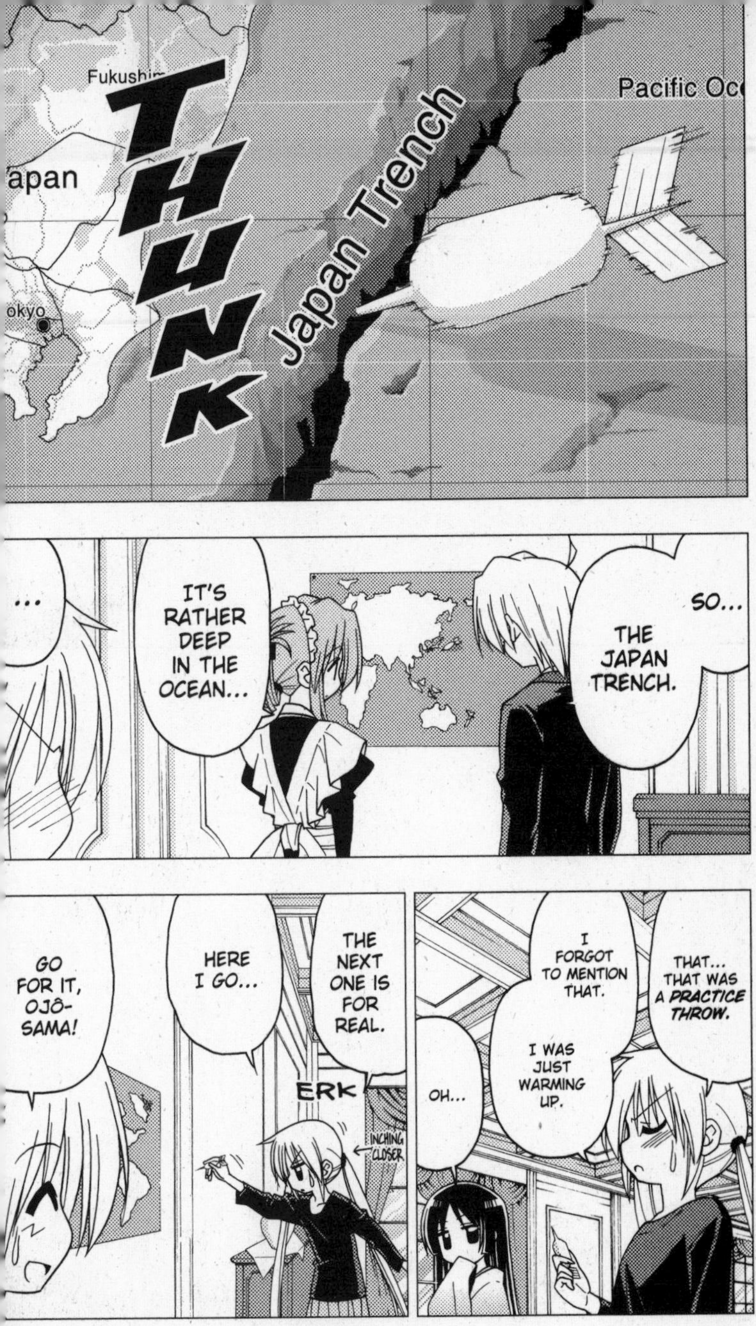
Fukushim
apan
okyo
THUNK
Japan Trench
Pacific Oc
SO... THE JAPAN TRENCH.
IT'S RATHER DEEP IN THE OCEAN...
...
THAT... THAT WAS A *PRACTICE THROW.*
I FORGOT TO MENTION THAT.
I WAS JUST WARMING UP.
OH...
THE NEXT ONE IS FOR REAL.
HERE I GO...
ERK
INCHING CLOSER
GO FOR IT, OJÔ-SAMA!

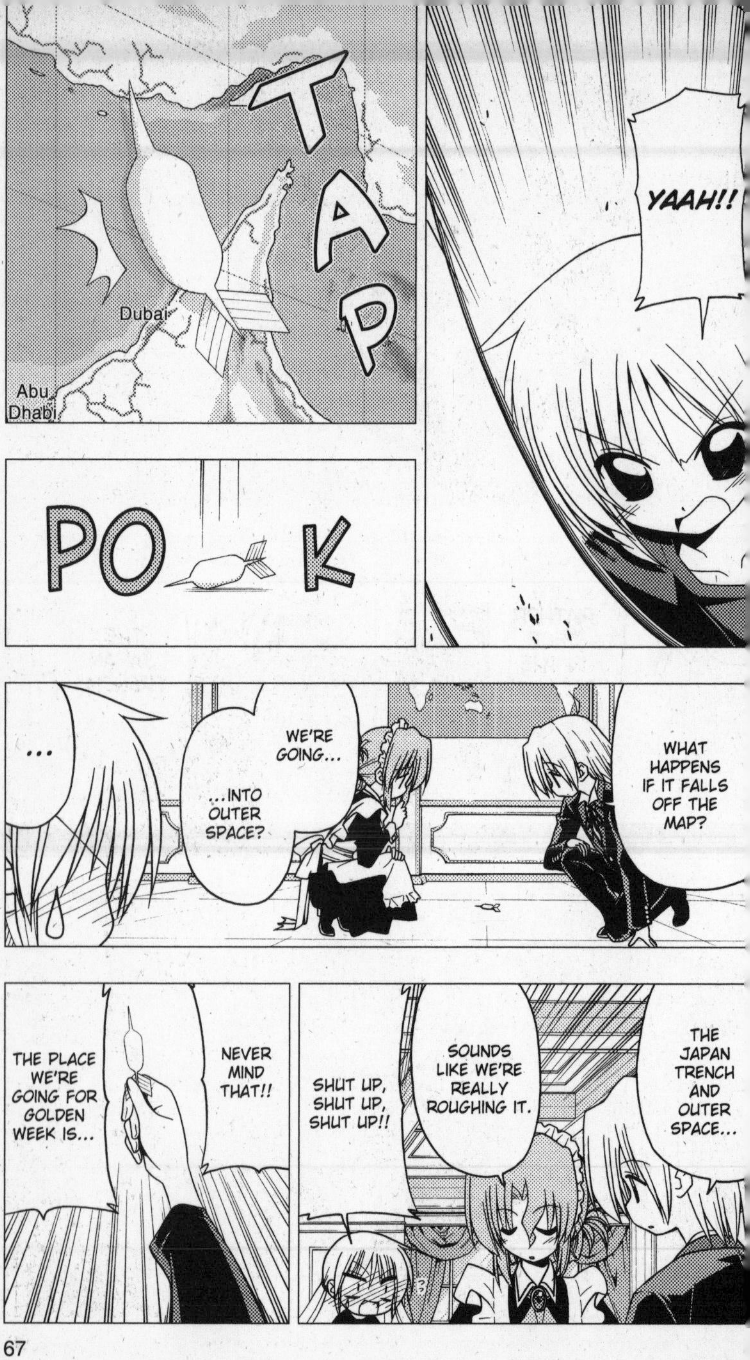
YAAH!!
TAP
Dubai
Abu Dhabi
PO K
WHAT HAPPENS IF IT FALLS OFF THE MAP?
WE'RE GOING...
...INTO OUTER SPACE?
...
THE JAPAN TRENCH AND OUTER SPACE...
SOUNDS LIKE WE'RE REALLY ROUGHING IT.
SHUT UP, SHUT UP, SHUT UP!!
NEVER MIND THAT!!
THE PLACE WE'RE GOING FOR GOLDEN WEEK IS...

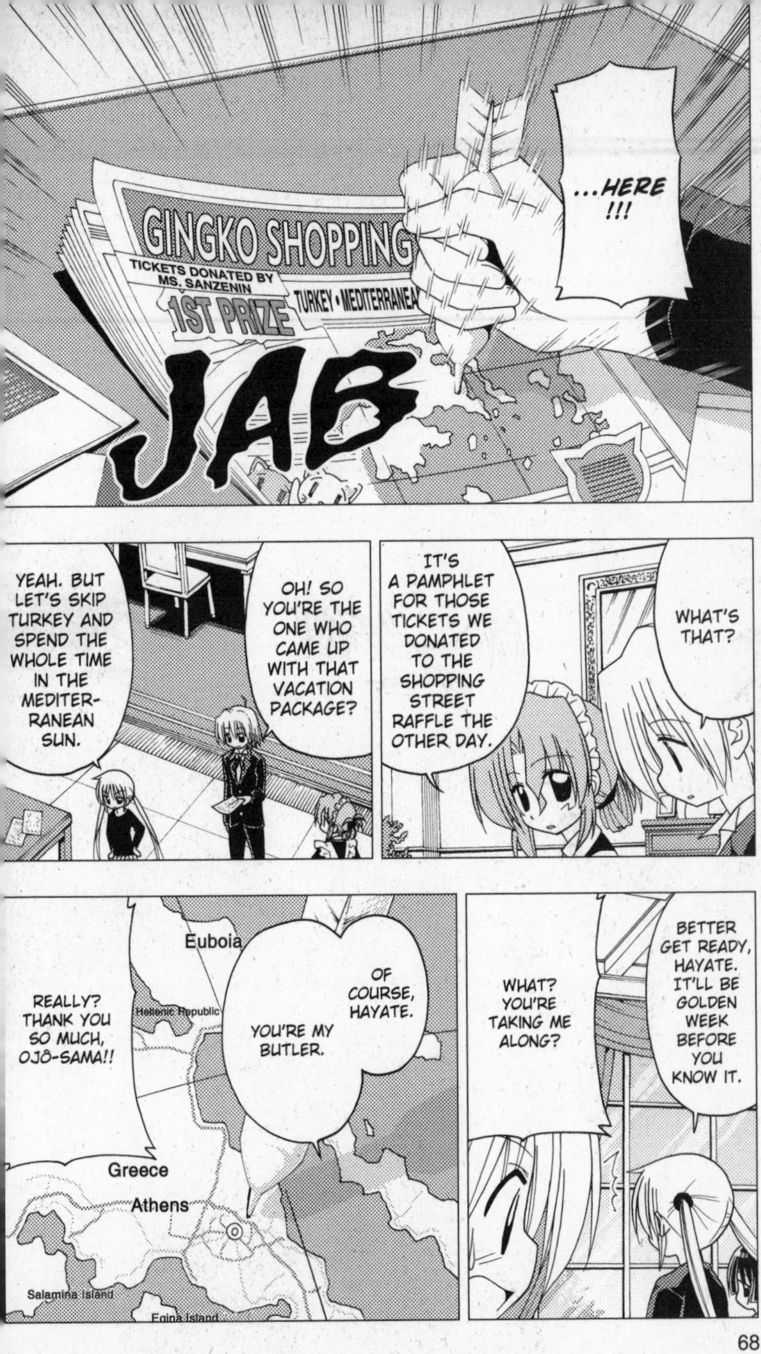
...HERE !!!
GINGKO SHOPPING
TICKETS DONATED BY MS. SANZENIN
1ST PRIZE
TURKEY • MEDITERRANEA
JAB
WHAT'S THAT?
IT'S A PAMPHLET FOR THOSE TICKETS WE DONATED TO THE SHOPPING STREET RAFFLE THE OTHER DAY.
OH! SO YOU'RE THE ONE WHO CAME UP WITH THAT VACATION PACKAGE?
YEAH. BUT LET'S SKIP TURKEY AND SPEND THE WHOLE TIME IN THE MEDITER-RANEAN SUN.
BETTER GET READY, HAYATE. IT'LL BE GOLDEN WEEK BEFORE YOU KNOW IT.
WHAT? YOU'RE TAKING ME ALONG?
OF COURSE, HAYATE.
YOU'RE MY BUTLER.
REALLY? THANK YOU SO MUCH, OJÔ-SAMA!!
Euboia
Hellenic Republic
Greece
Athens
Salamina Island
Egina Island

Episode 5: "Even the Holy Emperor Said Human Beings Suffer Because of Love"

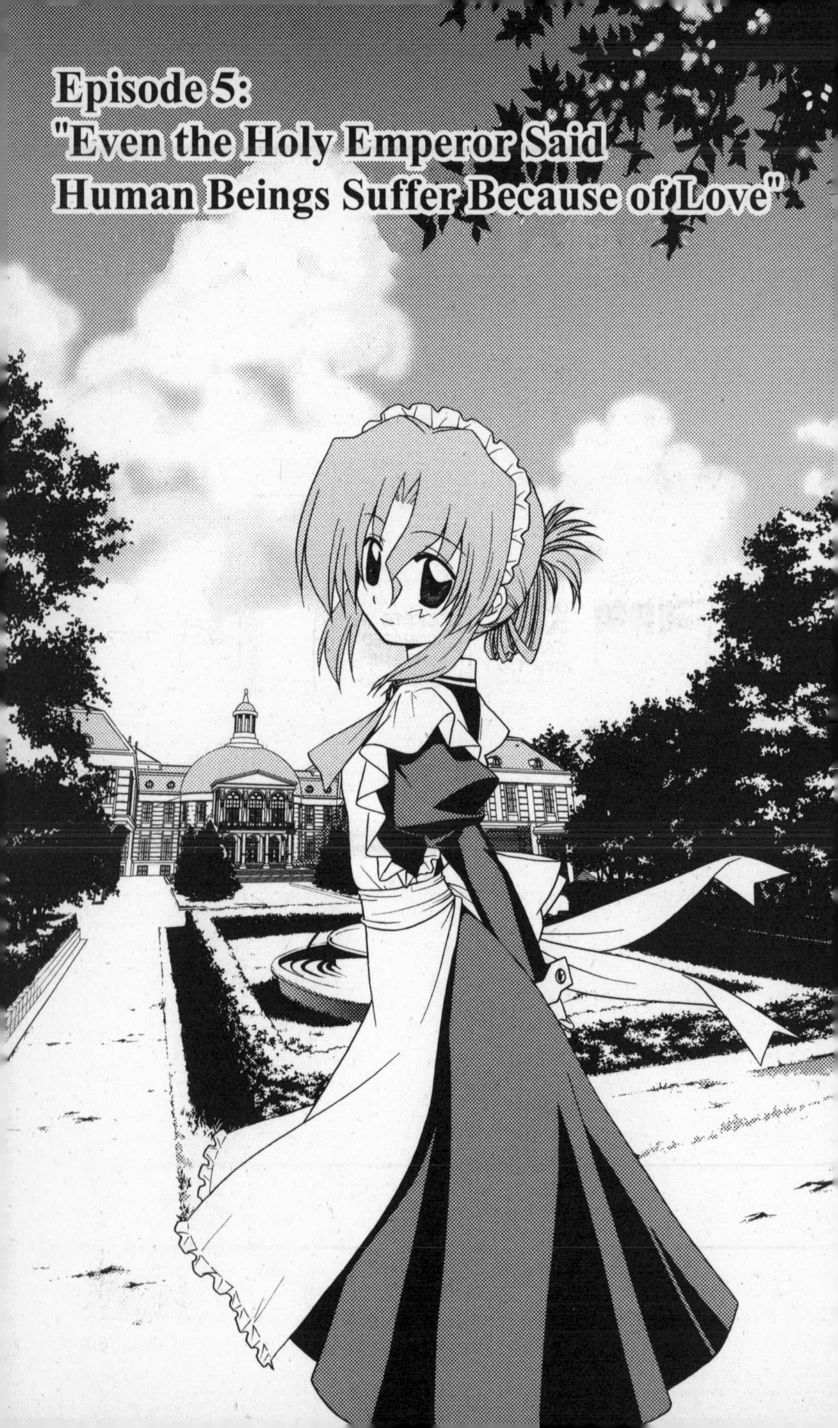

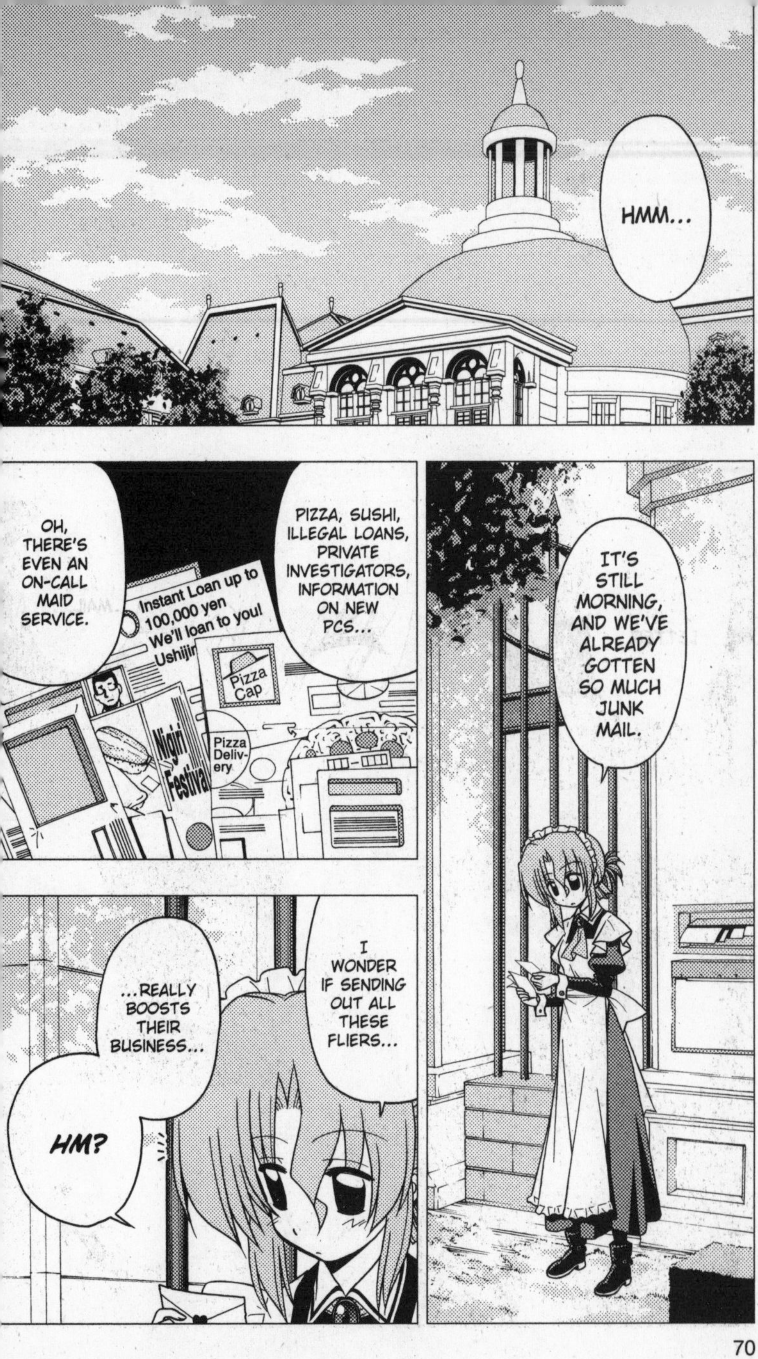
HMM...
IT'S STILL MORNING, AND WE'VE ALREADY GOTTEN SO MUCH JUNK MAIL.
PIZZA, SUSHI, ILLEGAL LOANS, PRIVATE INVESTIGATORS, INFORMATION ON NEW PCS...
OH, THERE'S EVEN AN ON-CALL MAID SERVICE.
Instant Loan up to 100,000 yen We'll loan to you!
Pizza Cap
Pizza Delivery
Nigiri Festival
I WONDER IF SENDING OUT ALL THESE FLIERS...
...REALLY BOOSTS THEIR BUSINESS...
HM?

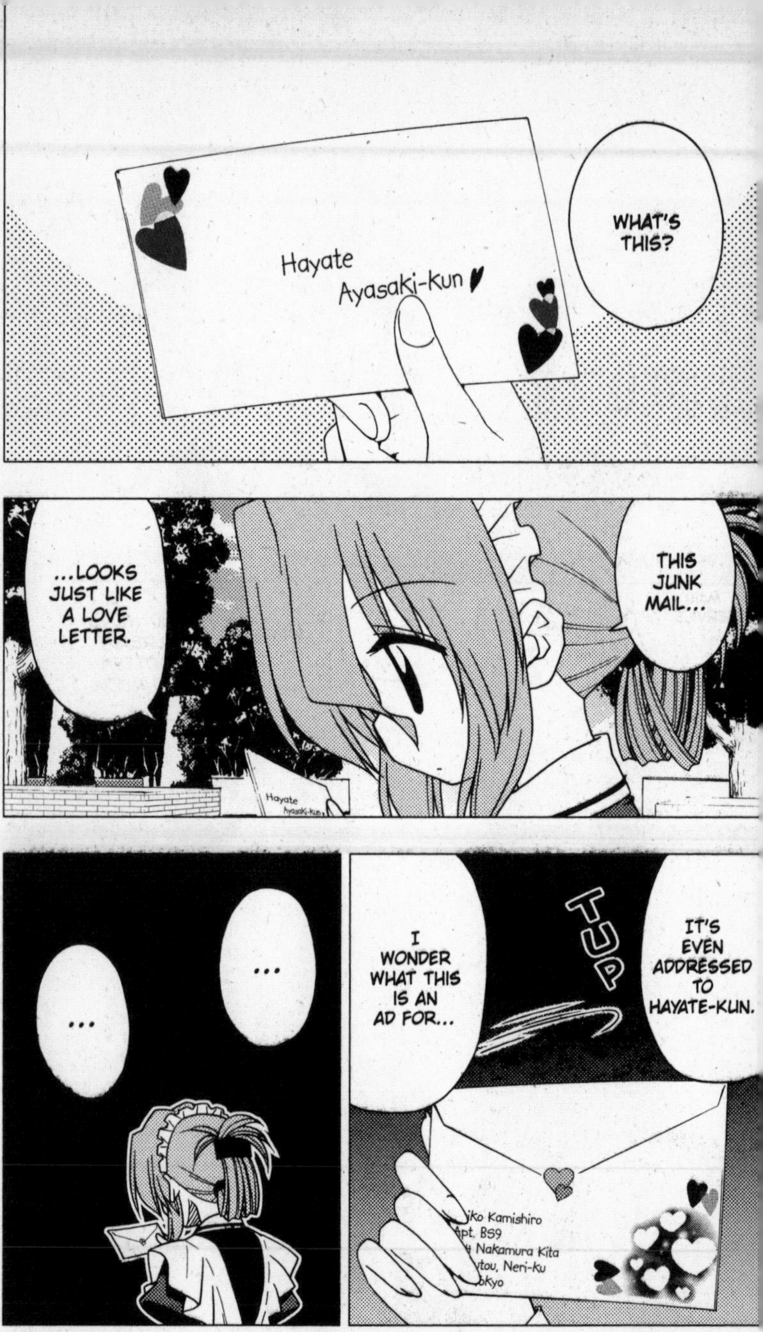
Hayate Ayasaki-Kun
WHAT'S THIS?
THIS JUNK MAIL...
...LOOKS JUST LIKE A LOVE LETTER.
Hayate Ayasaki-Kun
IT'S EVEN ADDRESSED TO HAYATE-KUN.
TUP
I WONDER WHAT THIS IS AN AD FOR...
Kamishiro
Apt. BS9
Nakamura Kita
Neri-Ku
...
...

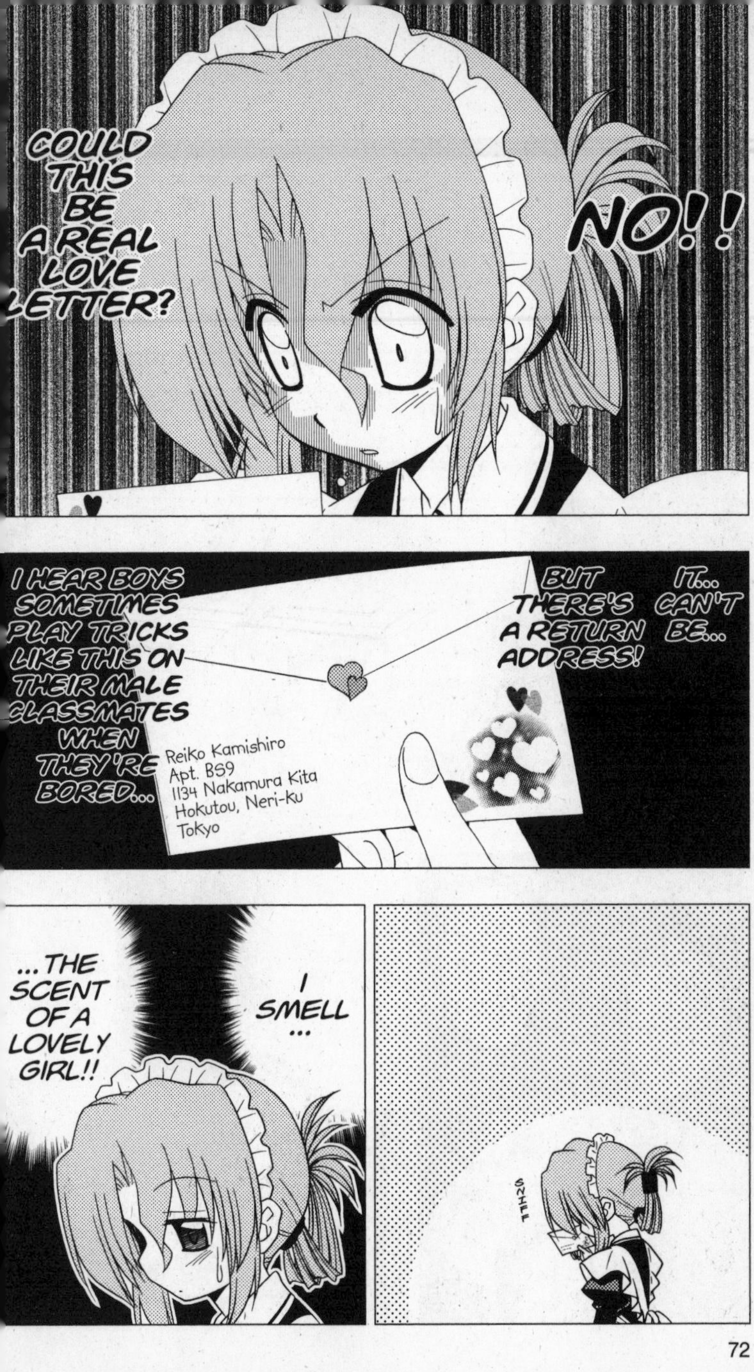
NO!!
COULD THIS BE A REAL LOVE LETTER?
IT... CAN'T BE...
BUT THERE'S A RETURN ADDRESS!
Reiko Kamishiro
Apt. BS9
1134 Nakamura Kita
Hokutou, Neri-Ku
Tokyo
I HEAR BOYS SOMETIMES PLAY TRICKS LIKE THIS ON THEIR MALE CLASSMATES WHEN THEY'RE BORED...
SNIFF
I SMELL...
...THE SCENT OF A LOVELY GIRL!!

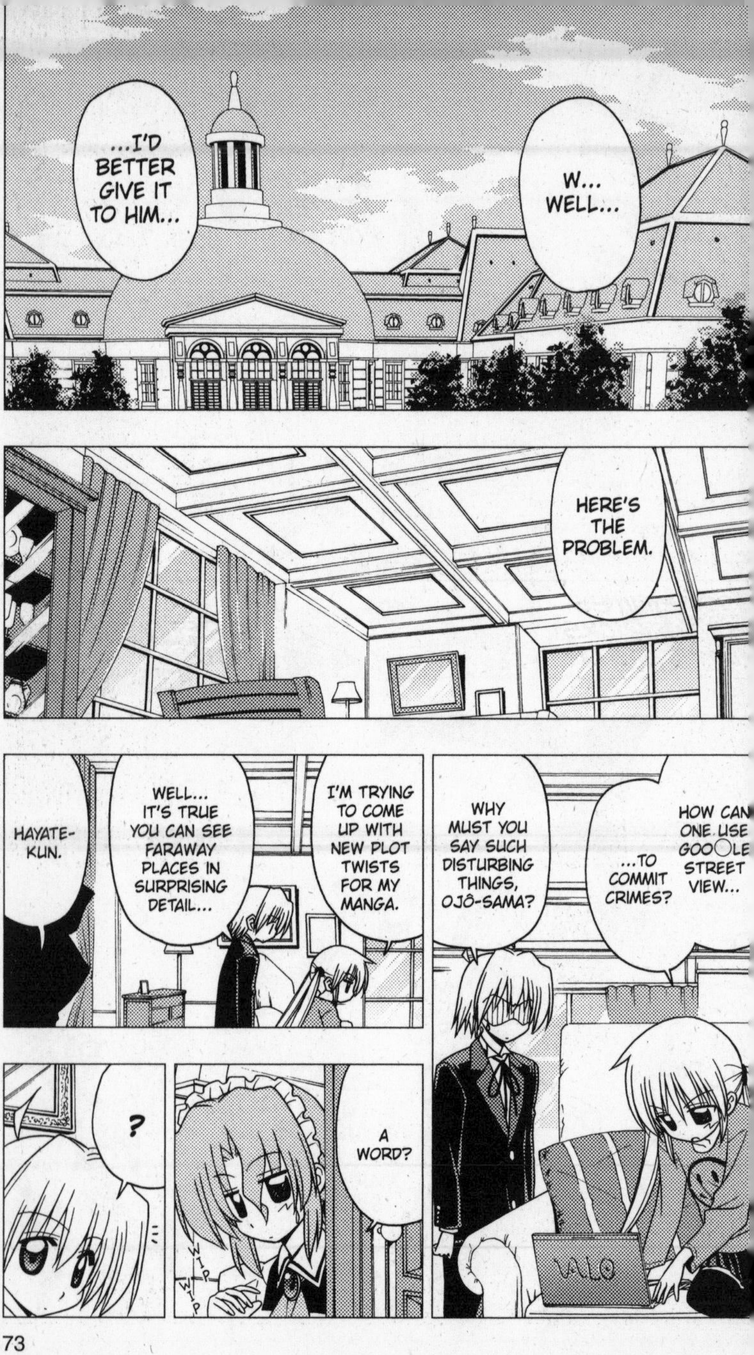
W... WELL...
...I'D BETTER GIVE IT TO HIM...
HERE'S THE PROBLEM.
HOW CAN ONE USE GOO◯LE STREET VIEW...
...TO COMMIT CRIMES?
WHY MUST YOU SAY SUCH DISTURBING THINGS, OJÔ-SAMA?
I'M TRYING TO COME UP WITH NEW PLOT TWISTS FOR MY MANGA.
WELL... IT'S TRUE YOU CAN SEE FARAWAY PLACES IN SURPRISING DETAIL...
HAYATE-KUN.
A WORD?
WIP WIP
?

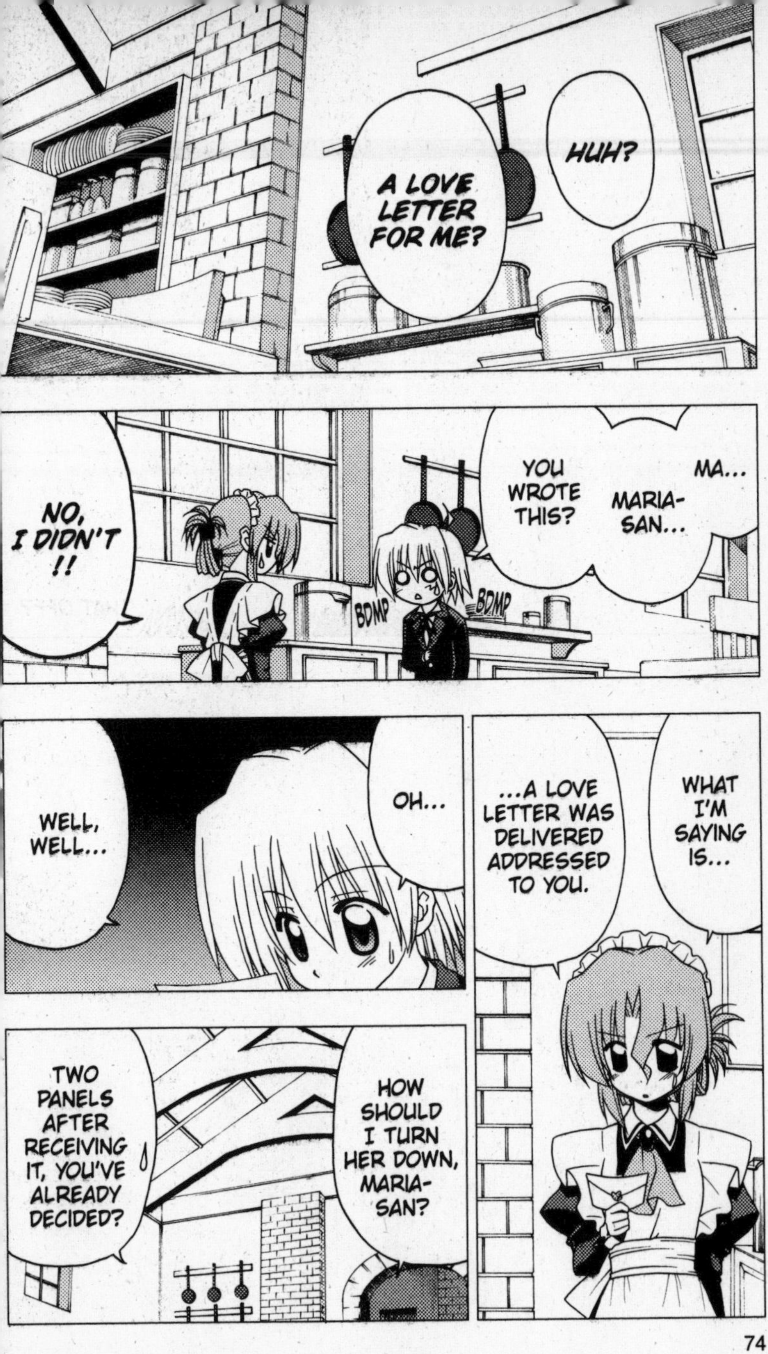
HUH?
A LOVE LETTER FOR ME?
MA... MARIA-SAN...
YOU WROTE THIS?
BDMP
BDMP
NO, I DIDN'T !!
WHAT I'M SAYING IS...
...A LOVE LETTER WAS DELIVERED ADDRESSED TO YOU.
OH...
WELL, WELL...
HOW SHOULD I TURN HER DOWN, MARIA-SAN?
TWO PANELS AFTER RECEIVING IT, YOU'VE ALREADY DECIDED?

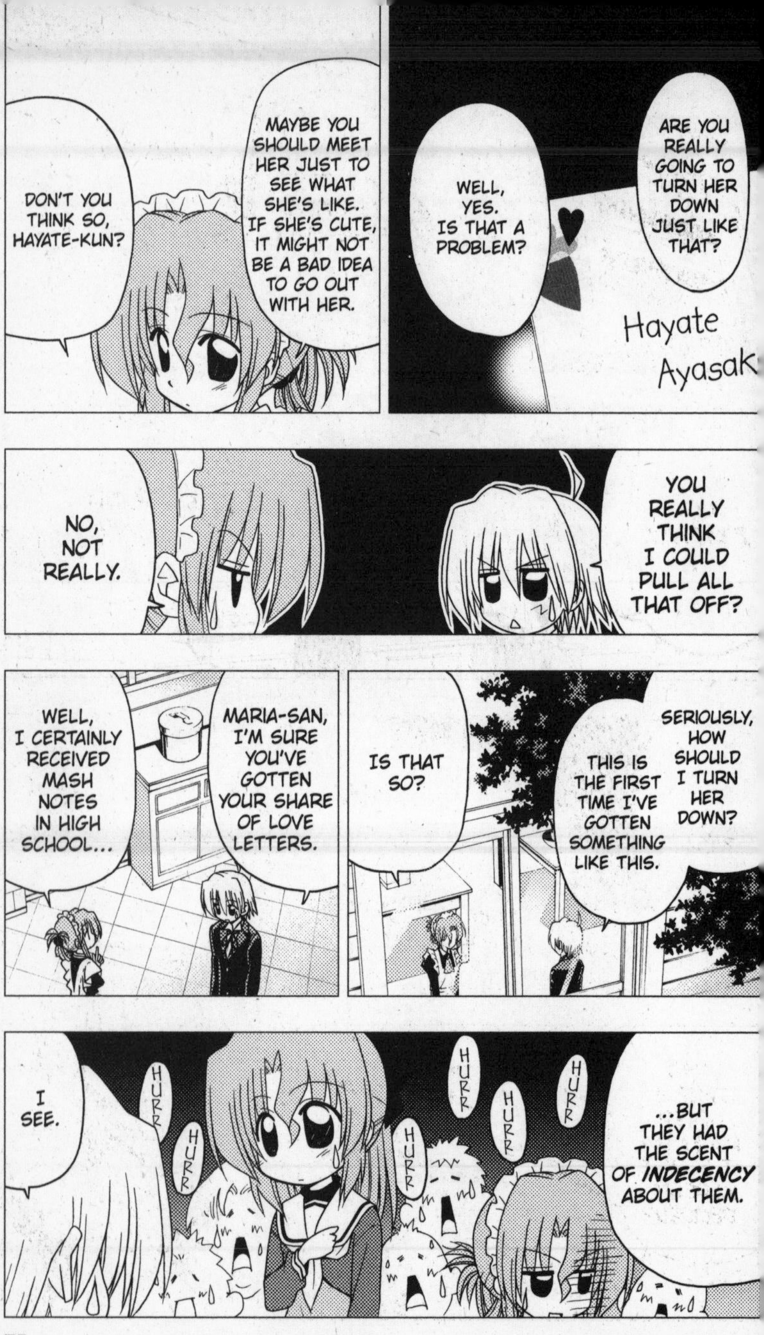
ARE YOU REALLY GOING TO TURN HER DOWN JUST LIKE THAT?
WELL, YES. IS THAT A PROBLEM?
Hayate Ayasak
MAYBE YOU SHOULD MEET HER JUST TO SEE WHAT SHE'S LIKE. IF SHE'S CUTE, IT MIGHT NOT BE A BAD IDEA TO GO OUT WITH HER.
DON'T YOU THINK SO, HAYATE-KUN?
YOU REALLY THINK I COULD PULL ALL THAT OFF?
NO, NOT REALLY.
SERIOUSLY, HOW SHOULD I TURN HER DOWN?
THIS IS THE FIRST TIME I'VE GOTTEN SOMETHING LIKE THIS.
IS THAT SO?
MARIA-SAN, I'M SURE YOU'VE GOTTEN YOUR SHARE OF LOVE LETTERS.
WELL, I CERTAINLY RECEIVED MASH NOTES IN HIGH SCHOOL...
...BUT THEY HAD THE SCENT OF ***INDECENCY*** ABOUT THEM.
HURR
HURR
HURR
HURR
HURR
HURR
I SEE.

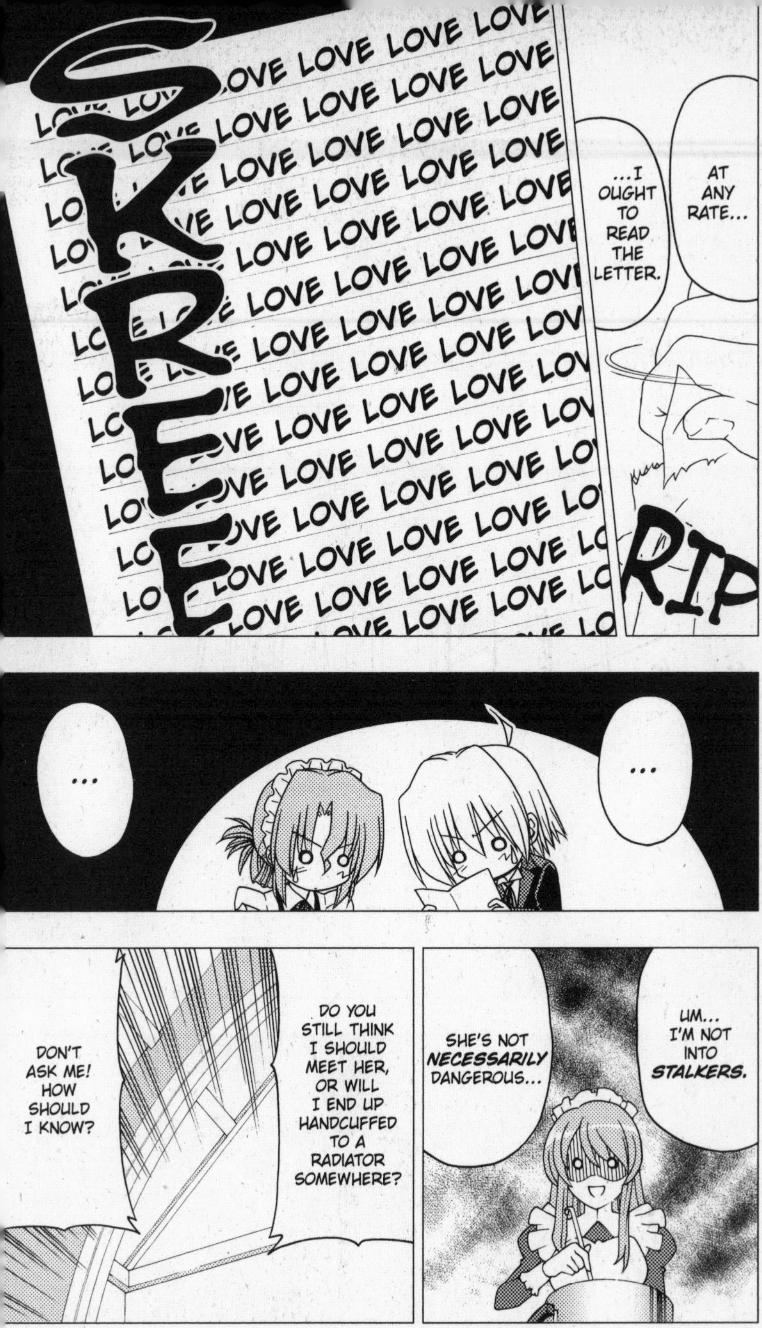
AT ANY RATE...
...I OUGHT TO READ THE LETTER.
RIP
LOVE LOVE LOVE LOVE
SKREE
...
...
UM... I'M NOT INTO **STALKERS.**
SHE'S NOT **NECESSARILY** DANGEROUS...
DO YOU STILL THINK I SHOULD MEET HER, OR WILL I END UP HANDCUFFED TO A RADIATOR SOMEWHERE?
DON'T ASK ME! HOW SHOULD I KNOW?

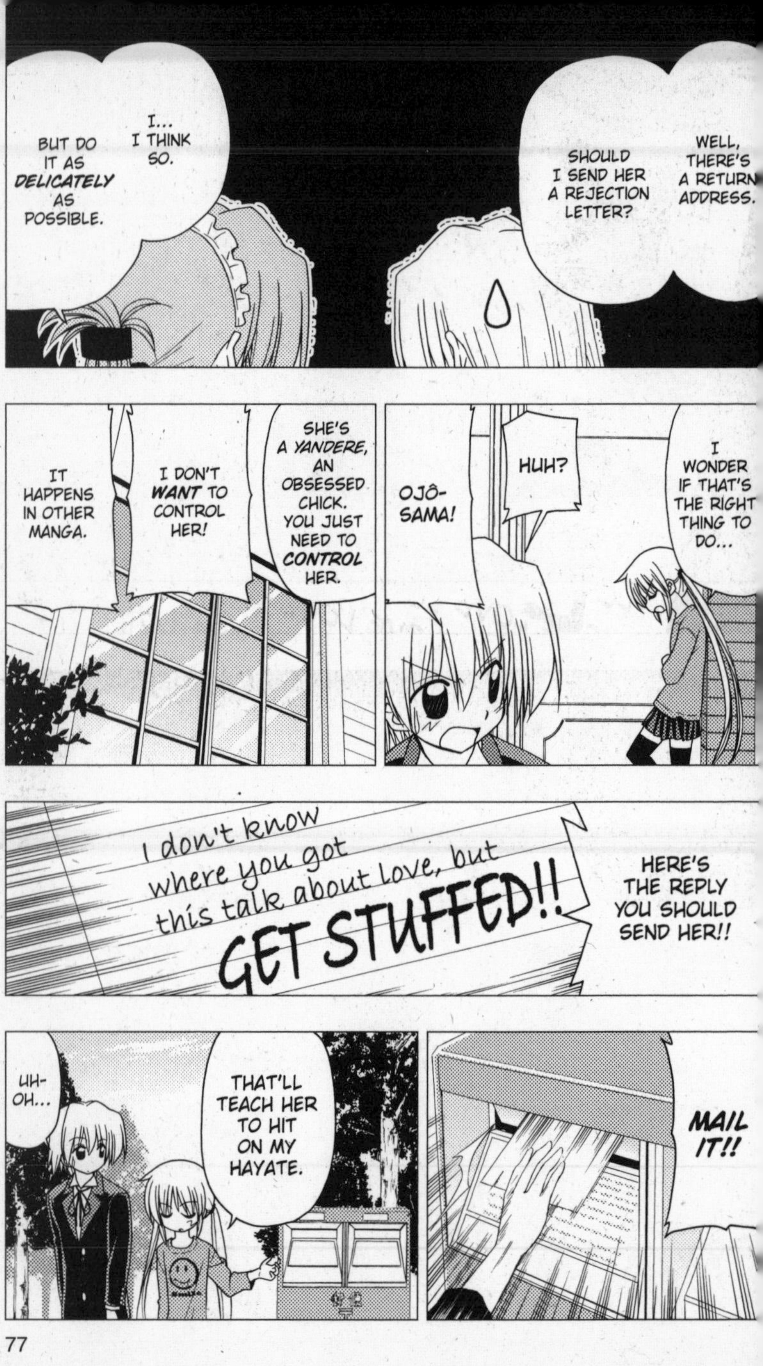
WELL, THERE'S A RETURN ADDRESS.
SHOULD I SEND HER A REJECTION LETTER?
I... I THINK SO.
BUT DO IT AS *DELICATELY* AS POSSIBLE.
I WONDER IF THAT'S THE RIGHT THING TO DO...
HUH?
OJÔ-SAMA!
SHE'S A *YANDERE*, AN OBSESSED CHICK. YOU JUST NEED TO *CONTROL* HER.
I DON'T *WANT* TO CONTROL HER!
IT HAPPENS IN OTHER MANGA.
HERE'S THE REPLY YOU SHOULD SEND HER!!
I don't know where you got this talk about love, but GET STUFFED!!
MAIL IT!!
THAT'LL TEACH HER TO HIT ON MY HAYATE.
UH-OH...

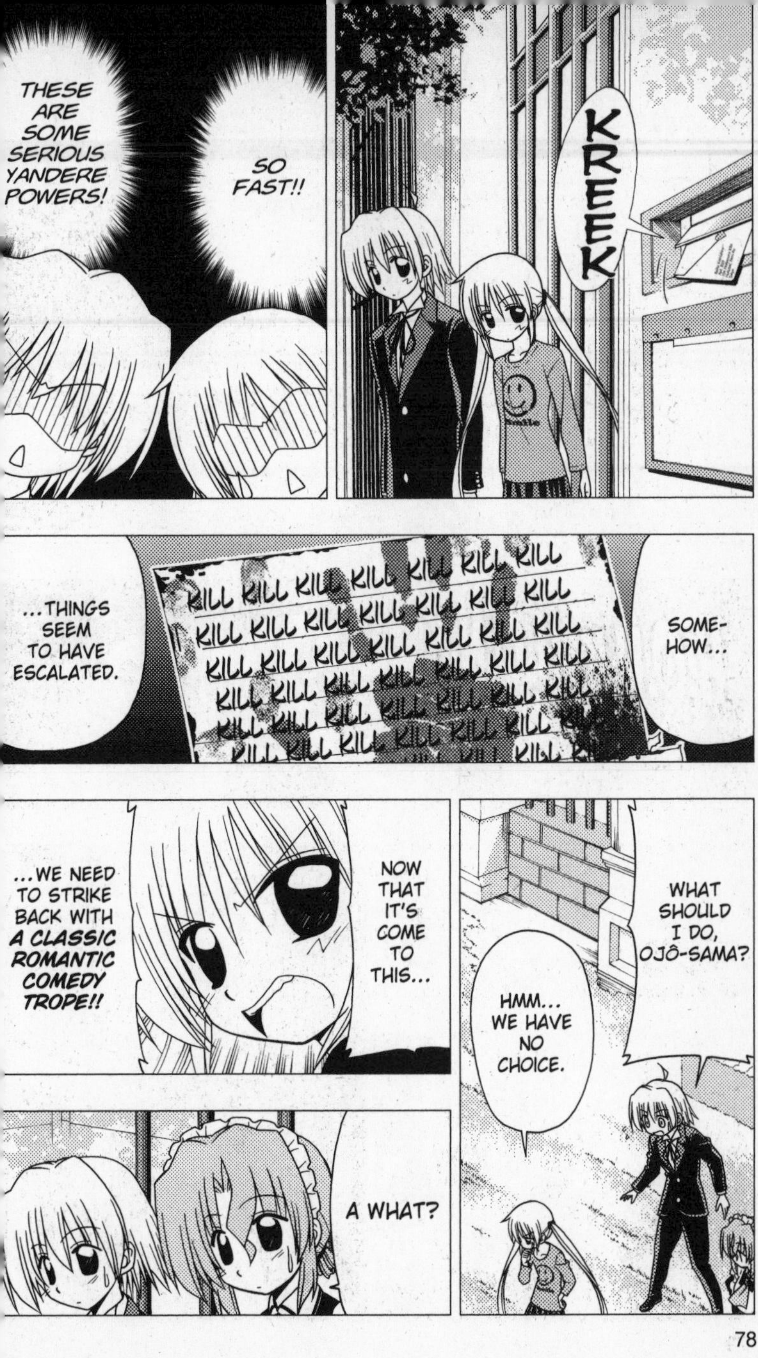
KREEK
SO FAST!!
THESE ARE SOME SERIOUS YANDERE POWERS!
SOME-HOW...
...THINGS SEEM TO HAVE ESCALATED.
KILL KILL KILL KILL
KILL KILL KILL KILL KILL KILL KILL
KILL KILL KILL KILL KILL KILL KILL
KILL KILL KILL KILL KILL KILL KILL
KILL KILL KILL KILL KILL KILL KILL
KILL KILL KILL KILL KILL KILL KILL
KILL KILL KILL KILL KILL KILL KILL
WHAT SHOULD I DO, OJÔ-SAMA?
HMM... WE HAVE NO CHOICE.
NOW THAT IT'S COME TO THIS...
...WE NEED TO STRIKE BACK WITH A CLASSIC ROMANTIC COMEDY TROPE!!
A WHAT?

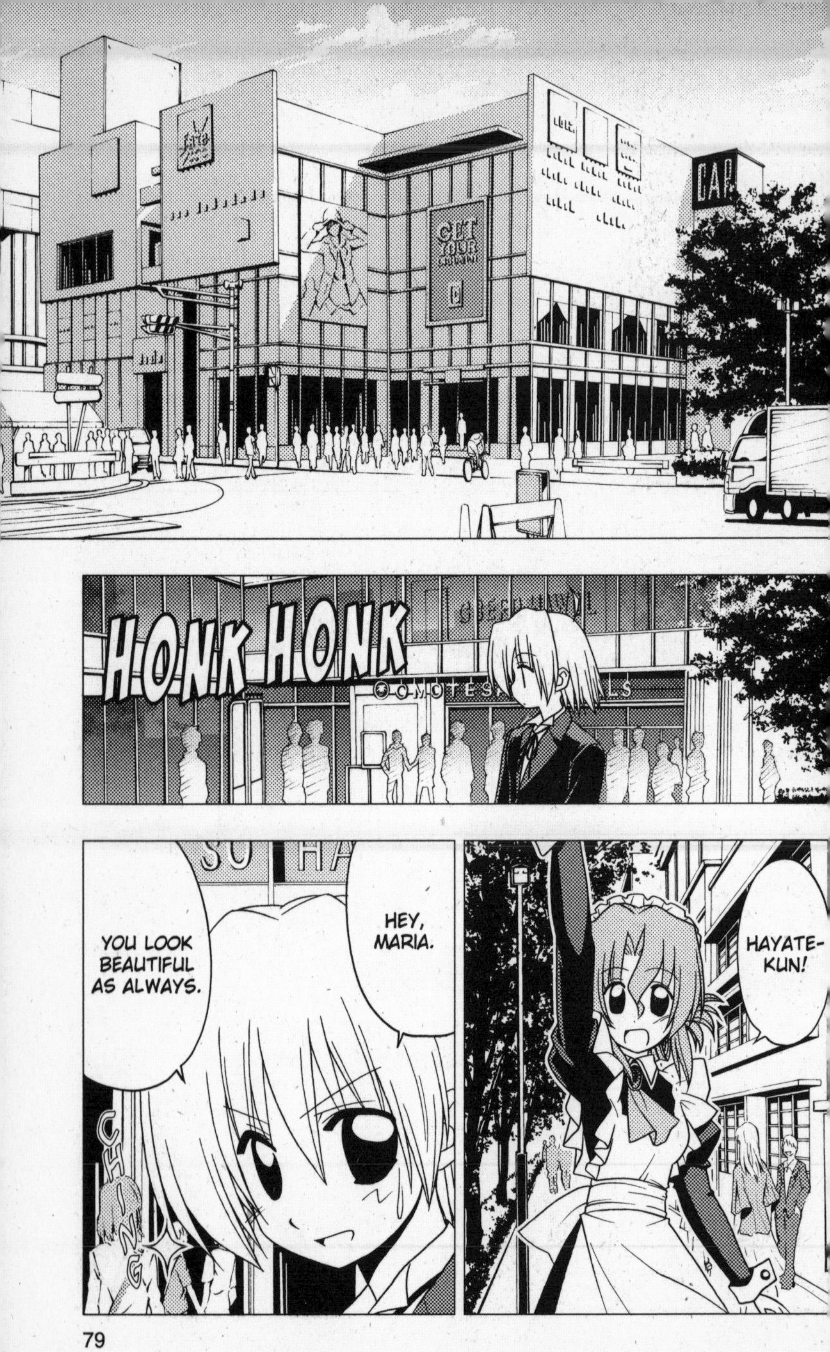
HONK HONK
HAYATE-KUN!
HEY, MARIA.
YOU LOOK BEAUTIFUL AS ALWAYS.
CHING

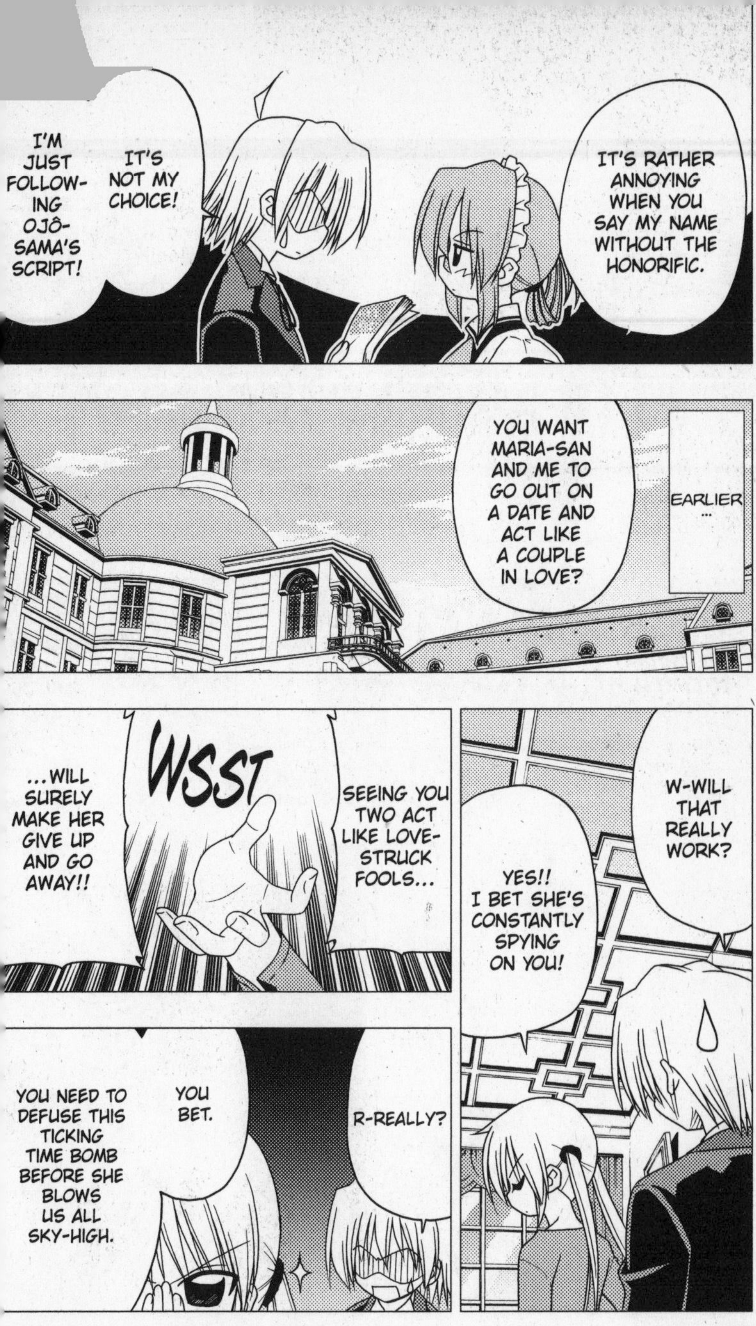
IT'S RATHER ANNOYING WHEN YOU SAY MY NAME WITHOUT THE HONORIFIC.
IT'S NOT MY CHOICE!
I'M JUST FOLLOWING OJÔ-SAMA'S SCRIPT!
EARLIER...
YOU WANT MARIA-SAN AND ME TO GO OUT ON A DATE AND ACT LIKE A COUPLE IN LOVE?
W-WILL THAT REALLY WORK?
YES!! I BET SHE'S CONSTANTLY SPYING ON YOU!
SEEING YOU TWO ACT LIKE LOVE-STRUCK FOOLS...
WSST
...WILL SURELY MAKE HER GIVE UP AND GO AWAY!!
R-REALLY?
YOU BET.
YOU NEED TO DEFUSE THIS TICKING TIME BOMB BEFORE SHE BLOWS US ALL SKY-HIGH.

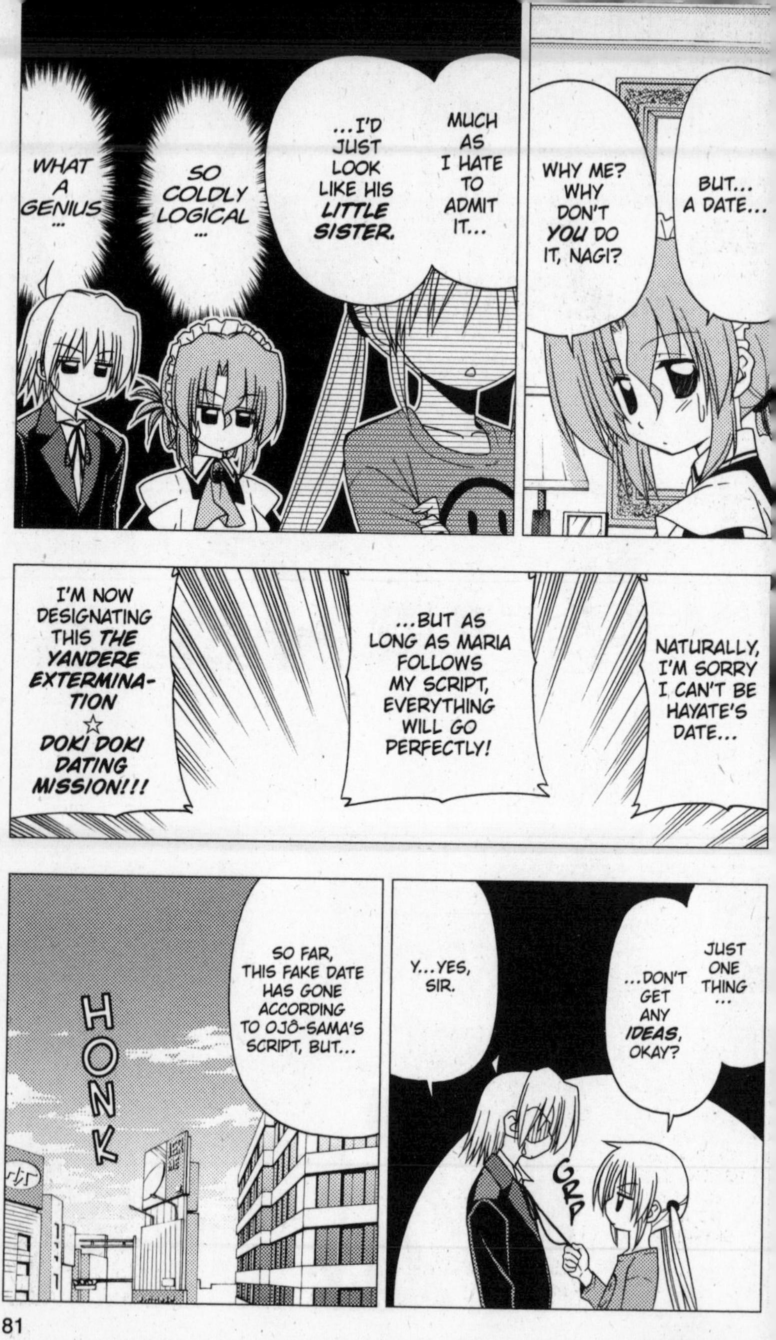
BUT... A DATE...
WHY ME? WHY DON'T YOU DO IT, NAGI?
MUCH AS I HATE TO ADMIT IT...
...I'D JUST LOOK LIKE HIS LITTLE SISTER.
SO COLDLY LOGICAL...
WHAT A GENIUS...
NATURALLY, I'M SORRY I CAN'T BE HAYATE'S DATE...
...BUT AS LONG AS MARIA FOLLOWS MY SCRIPT, EVERYTHING WILL GO PERFECTLY!
I'M NOW DESIGNATING THIS THE YANDERE EXTERMINATION ☆ DOKI DOKI DATING MISSION!!!
JUST ONE THING...
...DON'T GET ANY IDEAS, OKAY?
GRP
Y...YES, SIR.
SO FAR, THIS FAKE DATE HAS GONE ACCORDING TO OJÔ-SAMA'S SCRIPT, BUT...
HONK

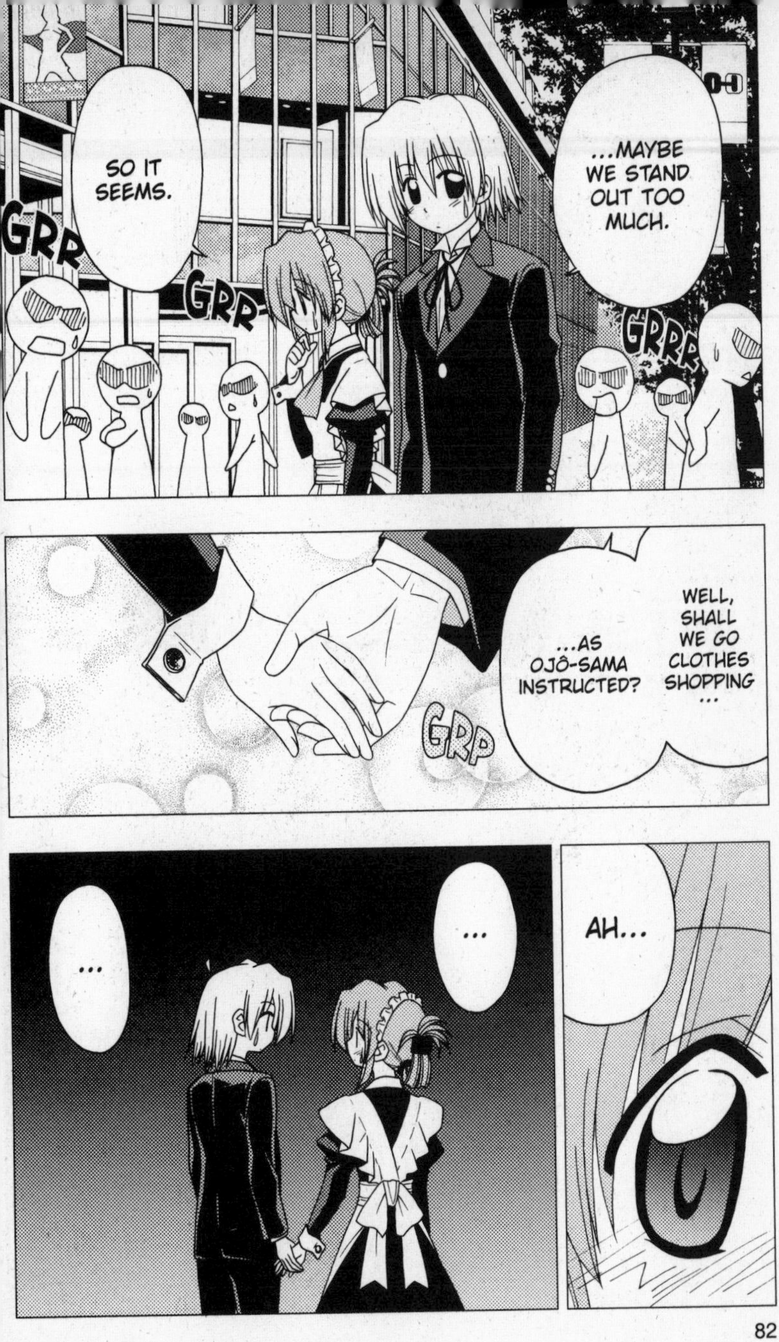
...MAYBE WE STAND OUT TOO MUCH.
GRRRR
SO IT SEEMS.
GRR
GRR
WELL, SHALL WE GO CLOTHES SHOPPING ...
...AS OJÔ-SAMA INSTRUCTED?
GRP
AH...
...
...

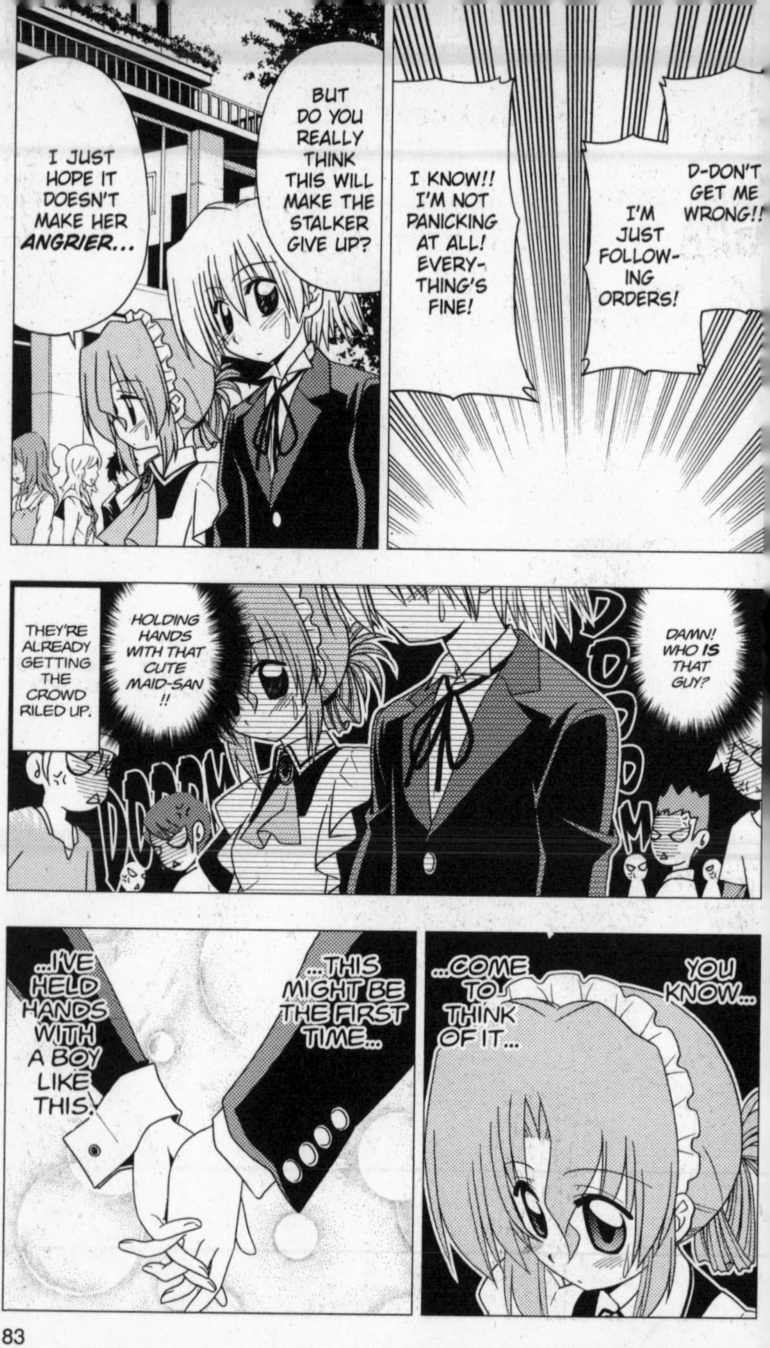
D-DON'T GET ME WRONG!!
I'M JUST FOLLOWING ORDERS!
I KNOW!! I'M NOT PANICKING AT ALL! EVERYTHING'S FINE!
BUT DO YOU REALLY THINK THIS WILL MAKE THE STALKER GIVE UP?
I JUST HOPE IT DOESN'T MAKE HER *ANGRIER*...
DAMN! WHO **IS** THAT GUY?
DDDDDM
HOLDING HANDS WITH THAT CUTE MAID-SAN !!
DDDDM
THEY'RE ALREADY GETTING THE CROWD RILED UP.
YOU KNOW...
...COME TO THINK OF IT...
...THIS MIGHT BE THE FIRST TIME...
...I'VE HELD HANDS WITH A BOY LIKE THIS.

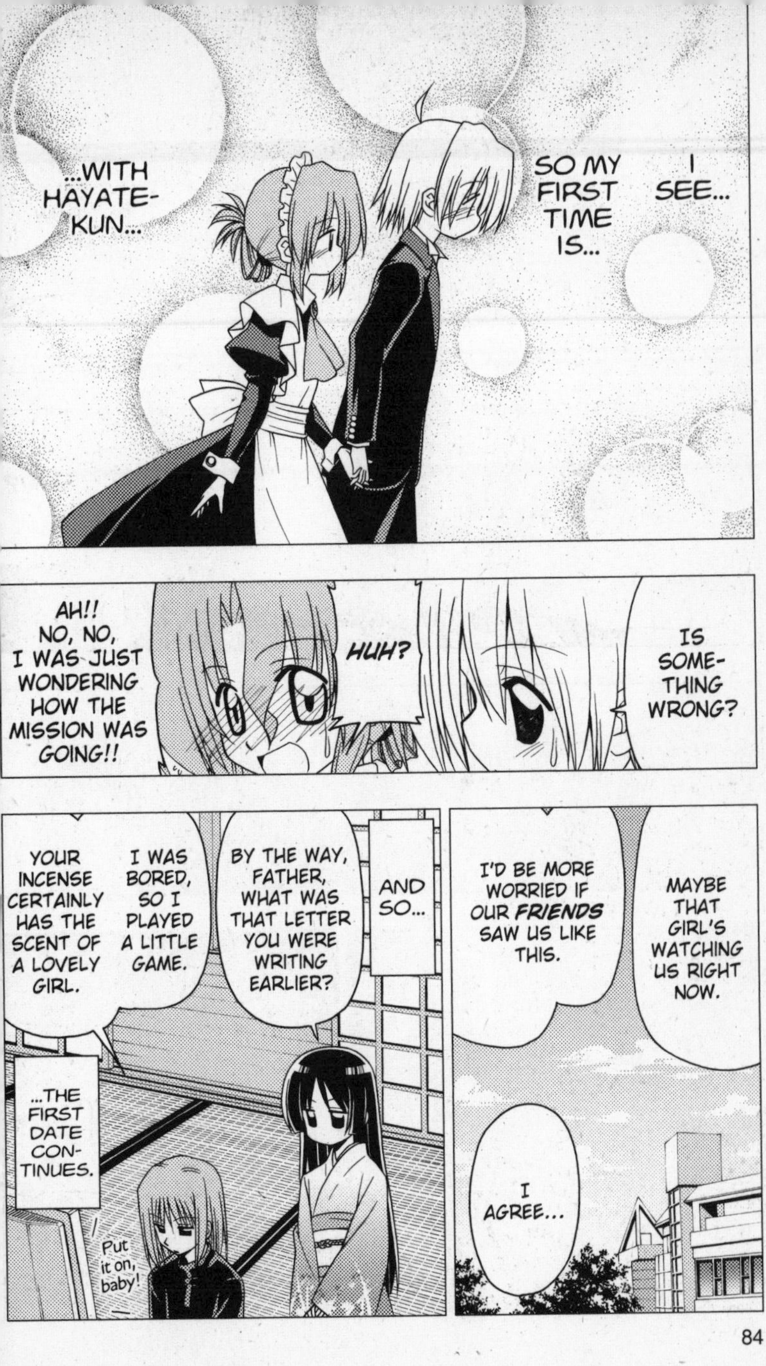
I SEE...
SO MY FIRST TIME IS...
...WITH HAYATE-KUN...
IS SOMETHING WRONG?
HUH?
AH!! NO, NO, I WAS JUST WONDERING HOW THE MISSION WAS GOING!!
MAYBE THAT GIRL'S WATCHING US RIGHT NOW.
I'D BE MORE WORRIED IF OUR FRIENDS SAW US LIKE THIS.
I AGREE...
AND SO...
BY THE WAY, FATHER, WHAT WAS THAT LETTER YOU WERE WRITING EARLIER?
I WAS BORED, SO I PLAYED A LITTLE GAME.
YOUR INCENSE CERTAINLY HAS THE SCENT OF A LOVELY GIRL.
...THE FIRST DATE CONTINUES.
Put it on, baby!

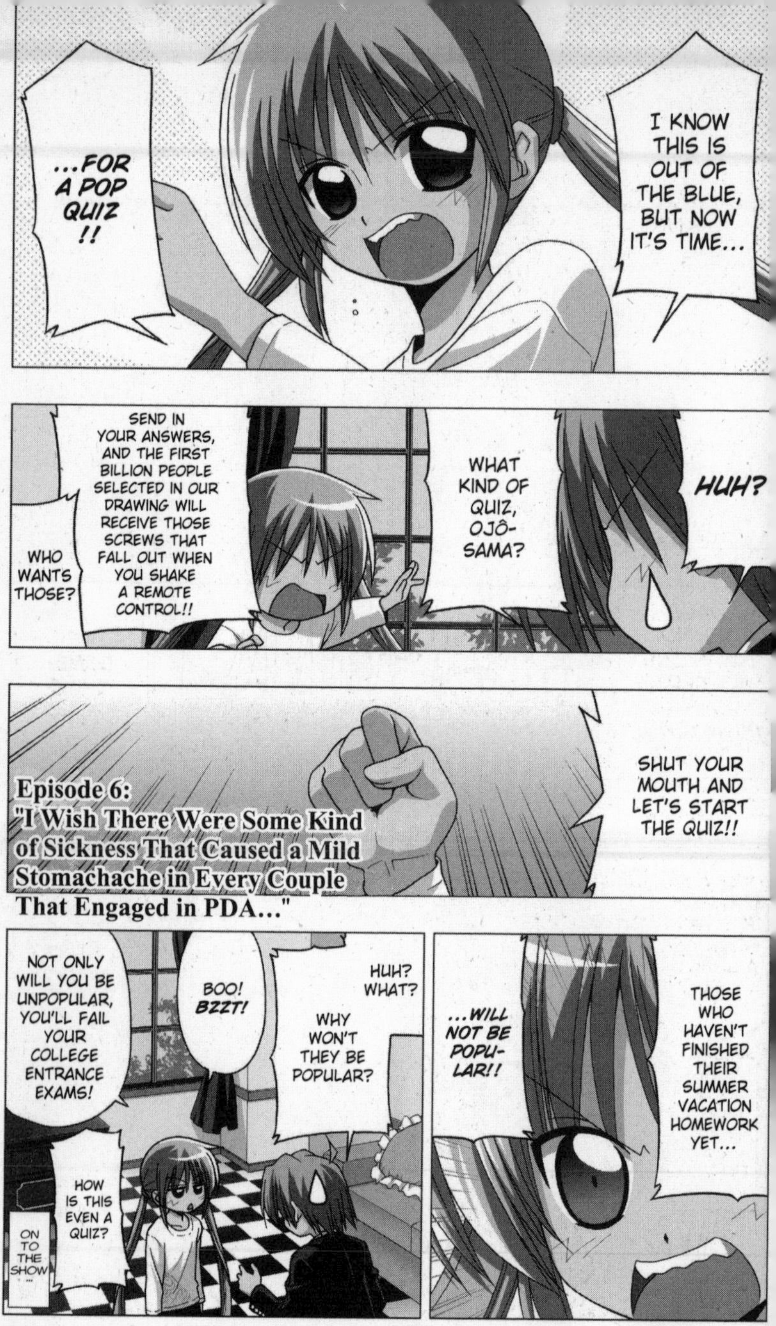
I KNOW THIS IS OUT OF THE BLUE, BUT NOW IT'S TIME...
...FOR A POP QUIZ!!
HUH?
WHAT KIND OF QUIZ, OJÔ-SAMA?
SEND IN YOUR ANSWERS, AND THE FIRST BILLION PEOPLE SELECTED IN OUR DRAWING WILL RECEIVE THOSE SCREWS THAT FALL OUT WHEN YOU SHAKE A REMOTE CONTROL!!
WHO WANTS THOSE?
SHUT YOUR MOUTH AND LET'S START THE QUIZ!!
Episode 6: "I Wish There Were Some Kind of Sickness That Caused a Mild Stomachache in Every Couple That Engaged in PDA..."
THOSE WHO HAVEN'T FINISHED THEIR SUMMER VACATION HOMEWORK YET...
...WILL NOT BE POPULAR!!
HUH? WHAT?
WHY WON'T THEY BE POPULAR?
BOO! BZZT!
NOT ONLY WILL YOU BE UNPOPULAR, YOU'LL FAIL YOUR COLLEGE ENTRANCE EXAMS!
HOW IS THIS EVEN A QUIZ?
ON TO THE SHOW...

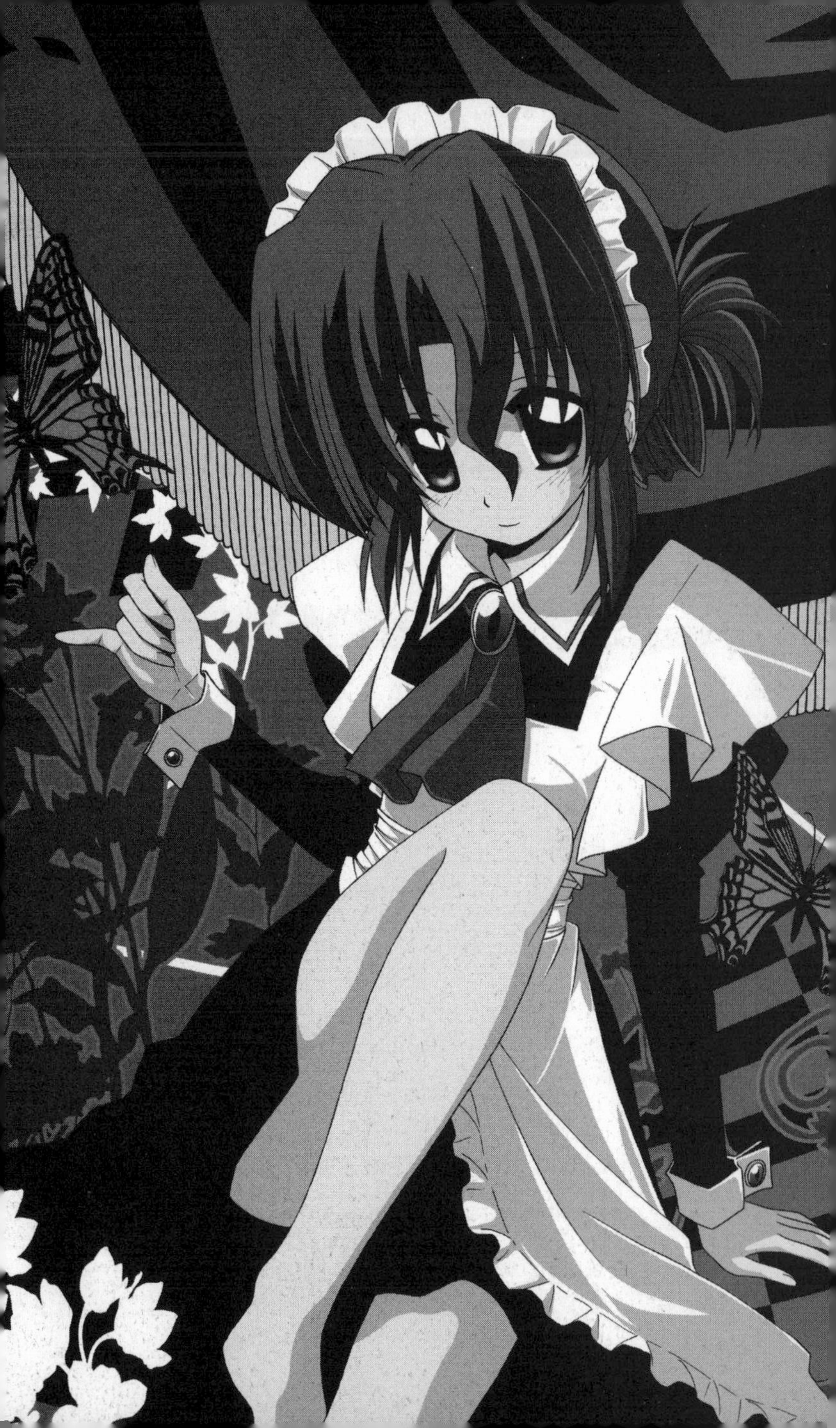

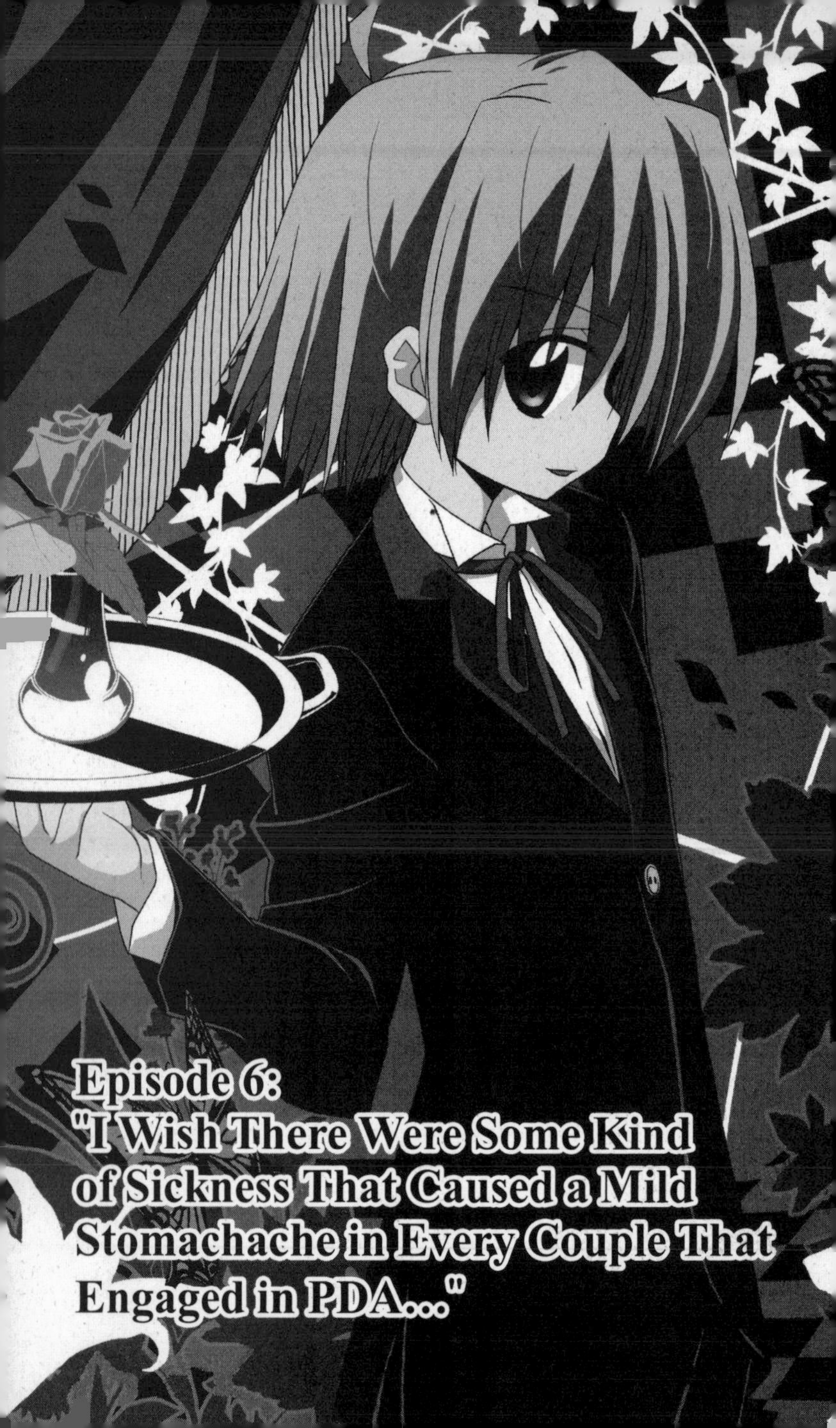
Episode 6:
"I Wish There Were Some Kind of Sickness That Caused a Mild Stomachache in Every Couple That Engaged in PDA..."

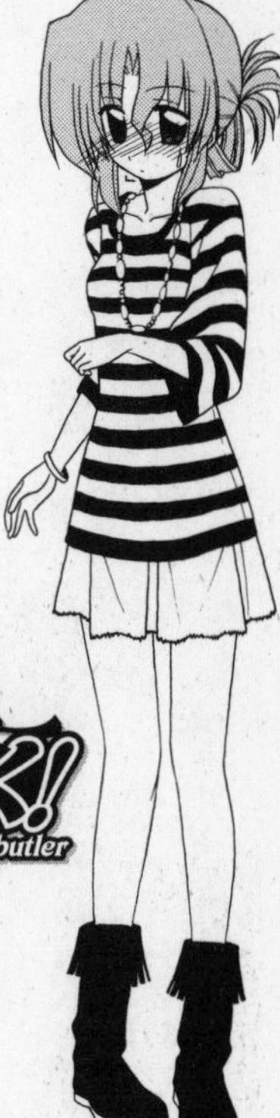

ハヤテのごとく!
Hayate the combat butler

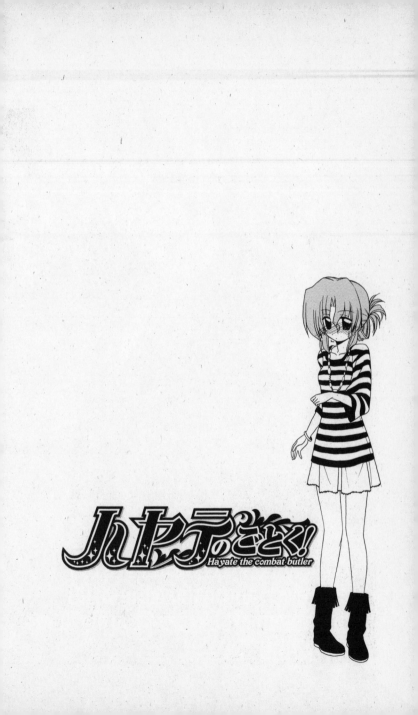

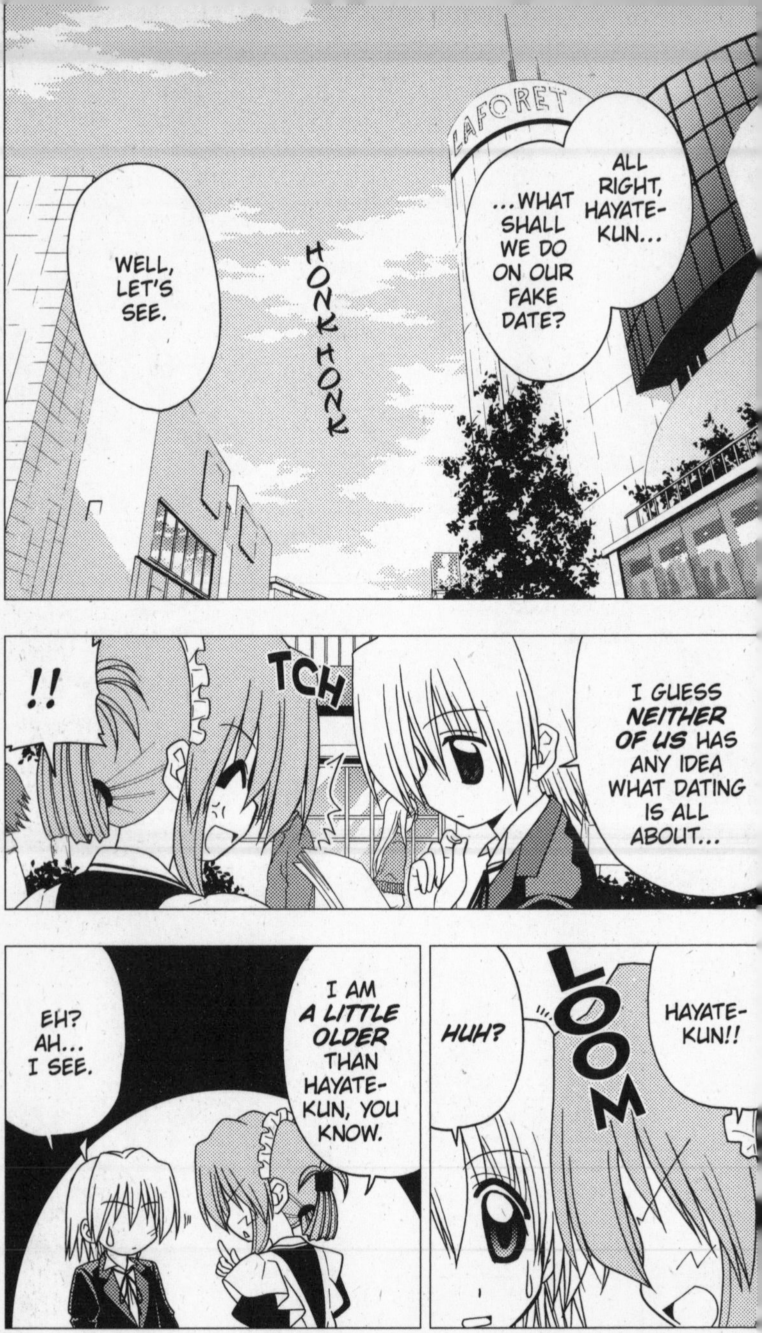
ALL RIGHT, HAYATE-KUN...
...WHAT SHALL WE DO ON OUR FAKE DATE?
HONK HONK
WELL, LET'S SEE.
LAFORET
I GUESS *NEITHER OF US* HAS ANY IDEA WHAT DATING IS ALL ABOUT...
TCH
!!
HAYATE-KUN!!
LOOM
HUH?
I AM *A LITTLE OLDER* THAN HAYATE-KUN, YOU KNOW.
EH? AH... I SEE.

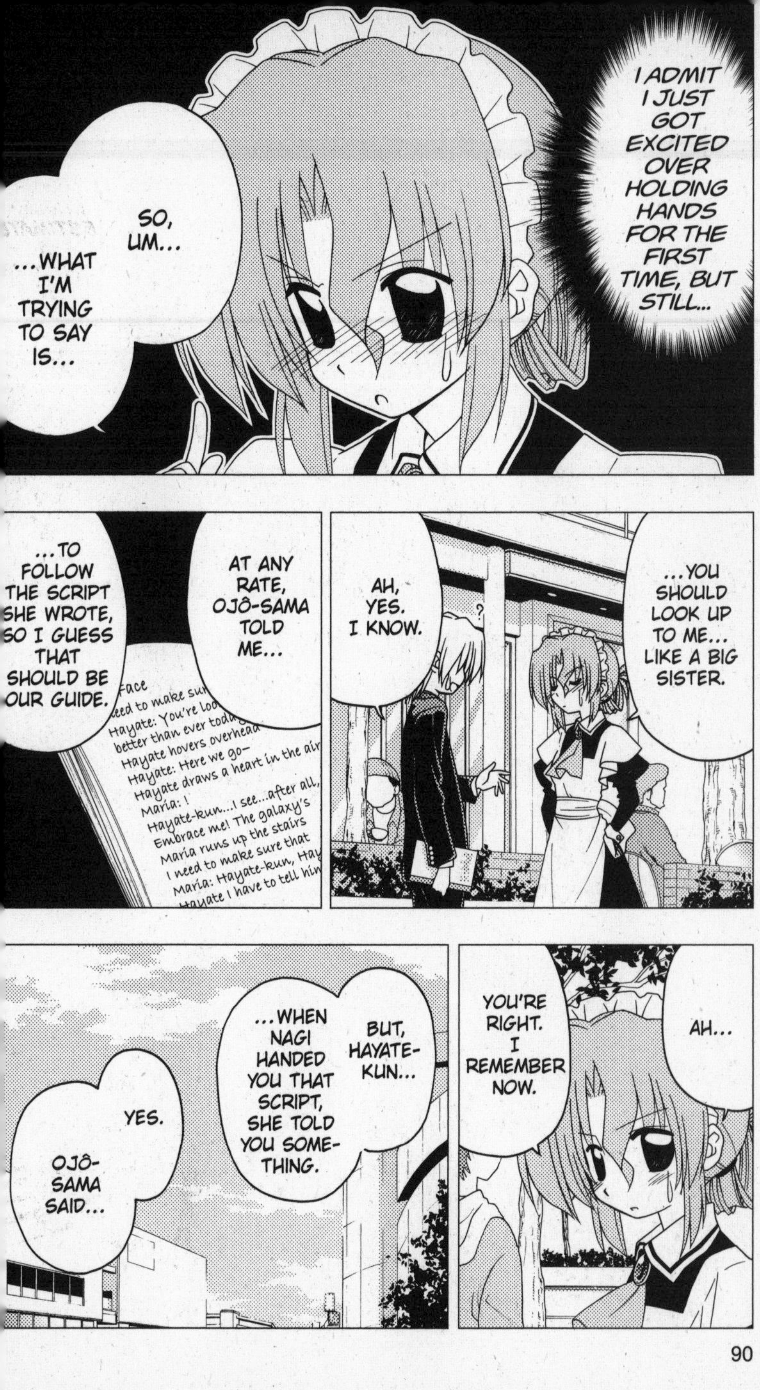
I ADMIT I JUST GOT EXCITED OVER HOLDING HANDS FOR THE FIRST TIME, BUT STILL...
SO, UM...
...WHAT I'M TRYING TO SAY IS...
...YOU SHOULD LOOK UP TO ME... LIKE A BIG SISTER.
AH, YES. I KNOW.
?
AT ANY RATE, OJÔ-SAMA TOLD ME...
...TO FOLLOW THE SCRIPT SHE WROTE, SO I GUESS THAT SHOULD BE OUR GUIDE.
Hayate hovers overhead
Hayate: Here we go—
Hayate draws a heart in the air
Maria: !
Maria runs up the stairs
AH...
YOU'RE RIGHT. I REMEMBER NOW.
BUT, HAYATE-KUN...
...WHEN NAGI HANDED YOU THAT SCRIPT, SHE TOLD YOU SOMETHING.
YES.
OJÔ-SAMA SAID...

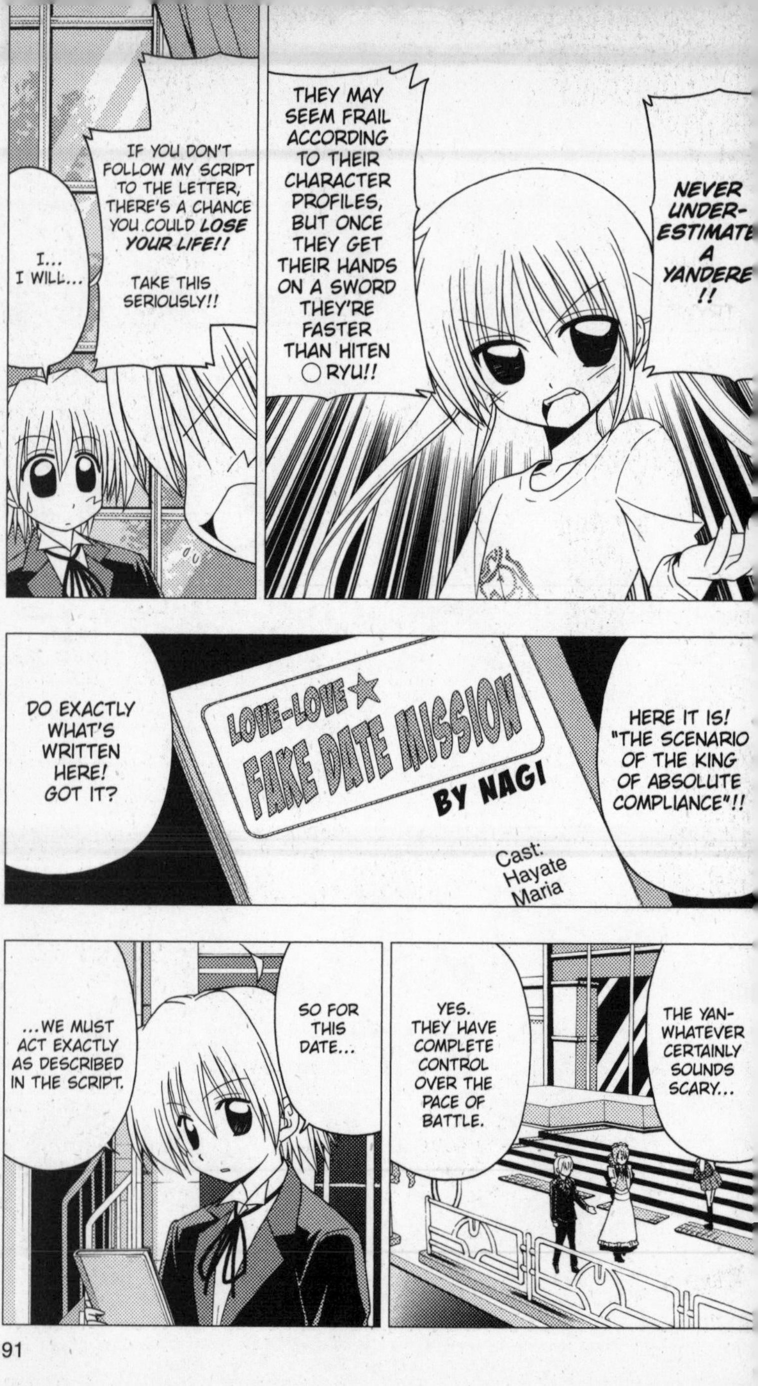
NEVER UNDER-ESTIMATE A YANDERE!!
THEY MAY SEEM FRAIL ACCORDING TO THEIR CHARACTER PROFILES, BUT ONCE THEY GET THEIR HANDS ON A SWORD THEY'RE FASTER THAN HITEN ○ RYU!!
IF YOU DON'T FOLLOW MY SCRIPT TO THE LETTER, THERE'S A CHANCE YOU COULD LOSE YOUR LIFE!!
TAKE THIS SERIOUSLY!!
I... I WILL...
HERE IT IS! "THE SCENARIO OF THE KING OF ABSOLUTE COMPLIANCE"!!
LOVE-LOVE★ FAKE DATE MISSION
BY NAGI
Cast: Hayate Maria
DO EXACTLY WHAT'S WRITTEN HERE! GOT IT?
THE YAN-WHATEVER CERTAINLY SOUNDS SCARY...
YES. THEY HAVE COMPLETE CONTROL OVER THE PACE OF BATTLE.
SO FOR THIS DATE...
...WE MUST ACT EXACTLY AS DESCRIBED IN THE SCRIPT.

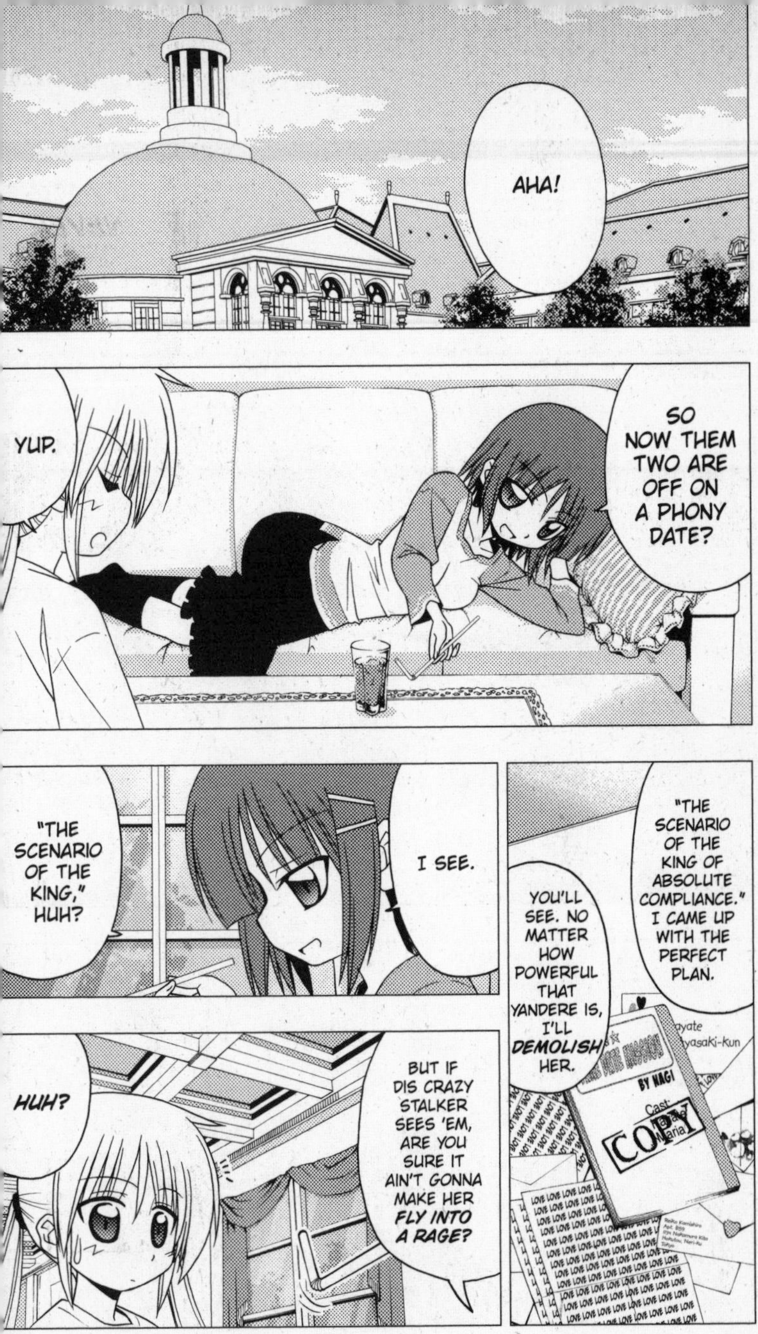
AHA!
SO NOW THEM TWO ARE OFF ON A PHONY DATE?
YUP.
"THE SCENARIO OF THE KING OF ABSOLUTE COMPLIANCE." I CAME UP WITH THE PERFECT PLAN.
YOU'LL SEE. NO MATTER HOW POWERFUL THAT YANDERE IS, I'LL ***DEMOLISH*** HER.
BY NAGI
Cast:
COPY
I SEE.
"THE SCENARIO OF THE KING," HUH?
BUT IF DIS CRAZY STALKER SEES 'EM, ARE YOU SURE IT AIN'T GONNA MAKE HER ***FLY INTO A RAGE?***
HUH?

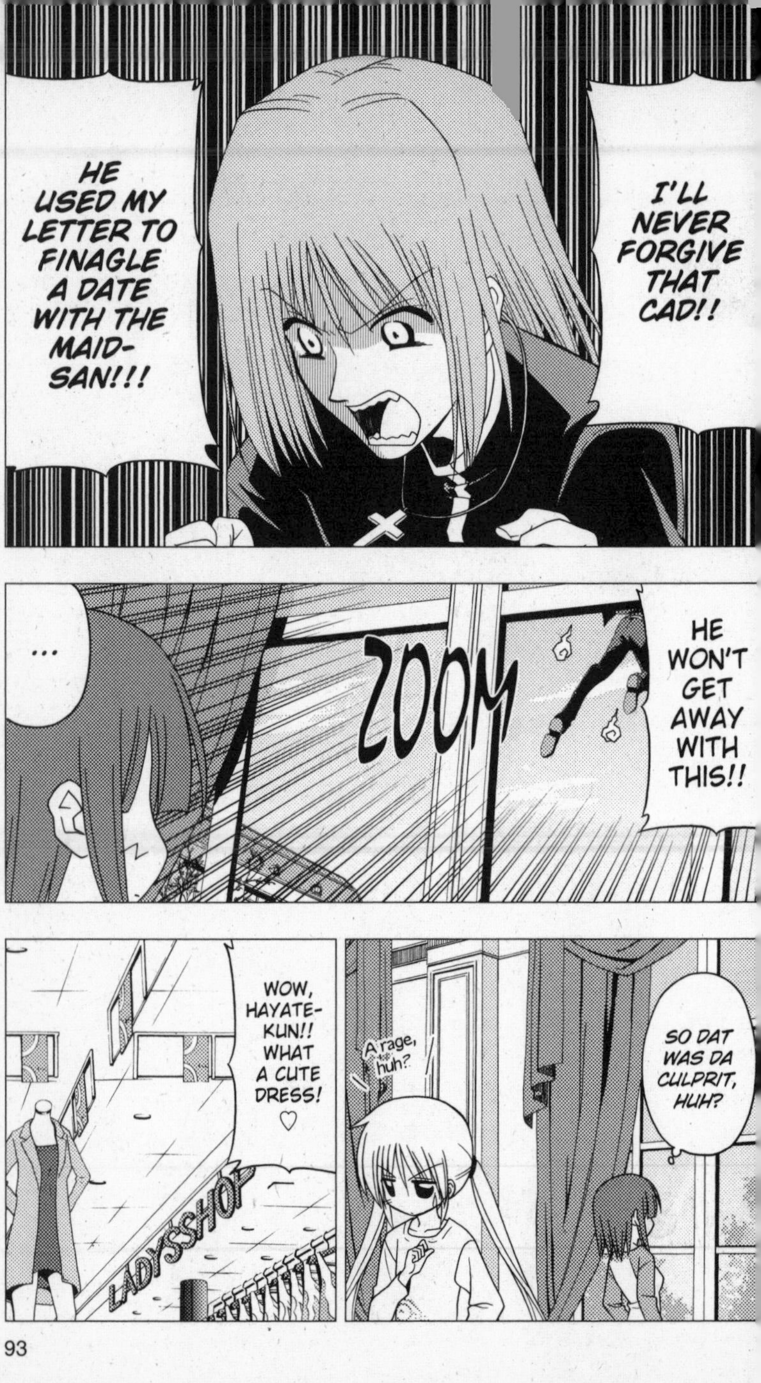
I'LL NEVER FORGIVE THAT CAD!!
HE USED MY LETTER TO FINAGLE A DATE WITH THE MAID-SAN!!!
HE WON'T GET AWAY WITH THIS!!
ZOOM
...
SO DAT WAS DA CULPRIT, HUH?
A rage, huh?
WOW, HAYATE-KUN!! WHAT A CUTE DRESS! ♡
LADYSSHOP

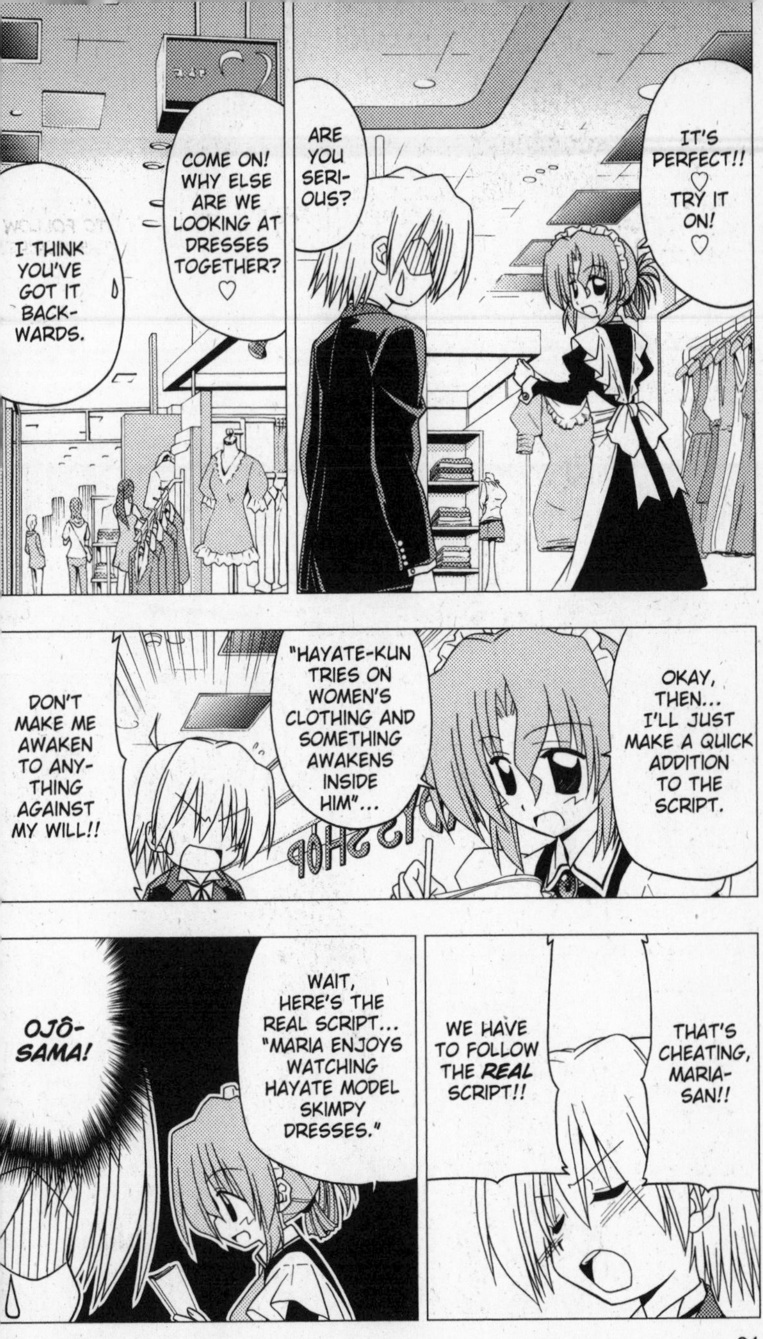
IT'S PERFECT!! ♡ TRY IT ON! ♡
ARE YOU SERI-OUS?
COME ON! WHY ELSE ARE WE LOOKING AT DRESSES TOGETHER? ♡
I THINK YOU'VE GOT IT BACK-WARDS.
OKAY, THEN... I'LL JUST MAKE A QUICK ADDITION TO THE SCRIPT.
"HAYATE-KUN TRIES ON WOMEN'S CLOTHING AND SOMETHING AWAKENS INSIDE HIM"...
DON'T MAKE ME AWAKEN TO ANY-THING AGAINST MY WILL!!
THAT'S CHEATING, MARIA-SAN!!
WE HAVE TO FOLLOW THE ***REAL*** SCRIPT!!
WAIT, HERE'S THE REAL SCRIPT... "MARIA ENJOYS WATCHING HAYATE MODEL SKIMPY DRESSES."
OJÔ-SAMA!

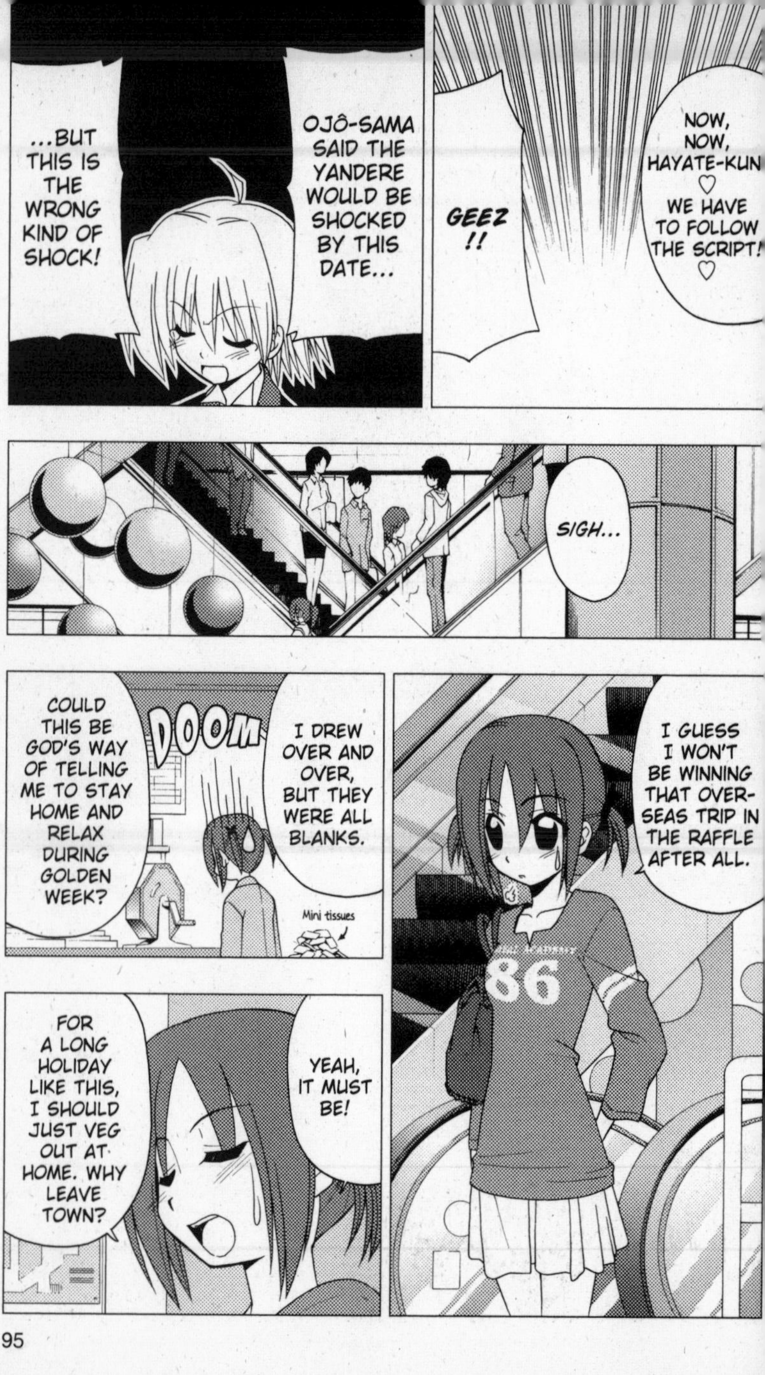
NOW, NOW, HAYATE-KUN ♡ WE HAVE TO FOLLOW THE SCRIPT! ♡
GEEZ!!
OJÔ-SAMA SAID THE YANDERE WOULD BE SHOCKED BY THIS DATE...
...BUT THIS IS THE WRONG KIND OF SHOCK!
SIGH...
I GUESS I WON'T BE WINNING THAT OVER-SEAS TRIP IN THE RAFFLE AFTER ALL.
I DREW OVER AND OVER, BUT THEY WERE ALL BLANKS.
DOOM
COULD THIS BE GOD'S WAY OF TELLING ME TO STAY HOME AND RELAX DURING GOLDEN WEEK?
Mini tissues
86
YEAH, IT MUST BE!
FOR A LONG HOLIDAY LIKE THIS, I SHOULD JUST VEG OUT AT HOME. WHY LEAVE TOWN?

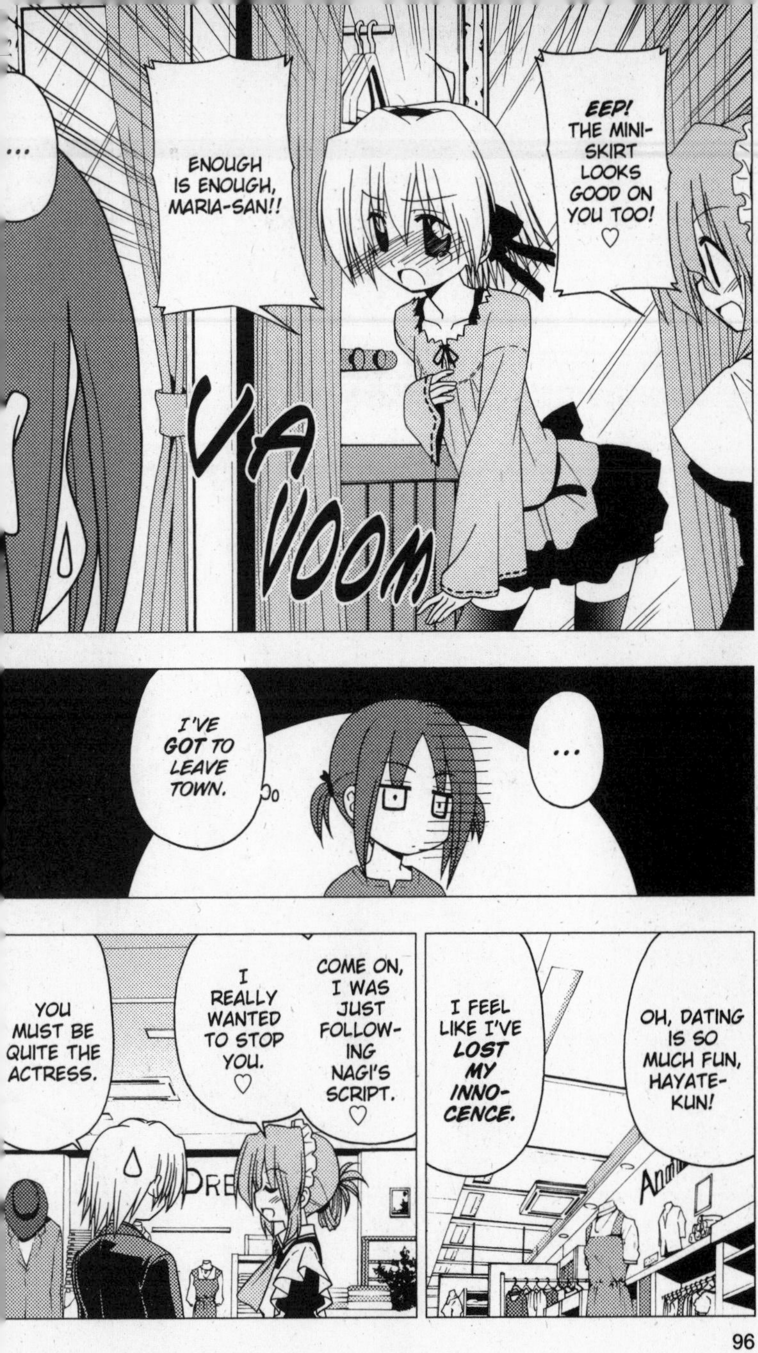
EEP! THE MINI-SKIRT LOOKS GOOD ON YOU TOO! ♡
ENOUGH IS ENOUGH, MARIA-SAN!!
...
VA VOOM
...
I'VE GOT TO LEAVE TOWN.
OH, DATING IS SO MUCH FUN, HAYATE-KUN!
I FEEL LIKE I'VE LOST MY INNOCENCE.
COME ON, I WAS JUST FOLLOWING NAGI'S SCRIPT. ♡
I REALLY WANTED TO STOP YOU. ♡
YOU MUST BE QUITE THE ACTRESS.

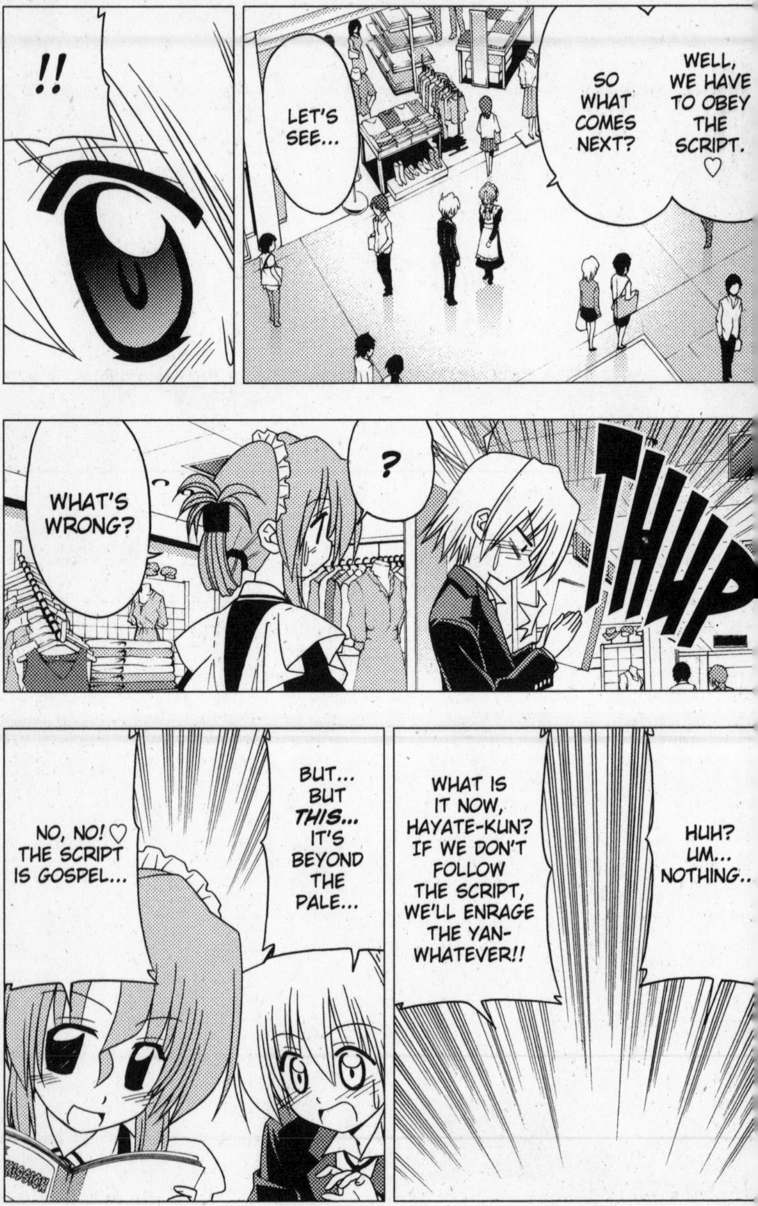
WELL, WE HAVE TO OBEY THE SCRIPT. ♡
SO WHAT COMES NEXT?
LET'S SEE...
!!
THUP
?
WHAT'S WRONG?
HUH? UM... NOTHING..
WHAT IS IT NOW, HAYATE-KUN? IF WE DON'T FOLLOW THE SCRIPT, WE'LL ENRAGE THE YAN-WHATEVER!!
BUT... BUT *THIS*... IT'S BEYOND THE PALE...
NO, NO! ♡ THE SCRIPT IS GOSPEL...

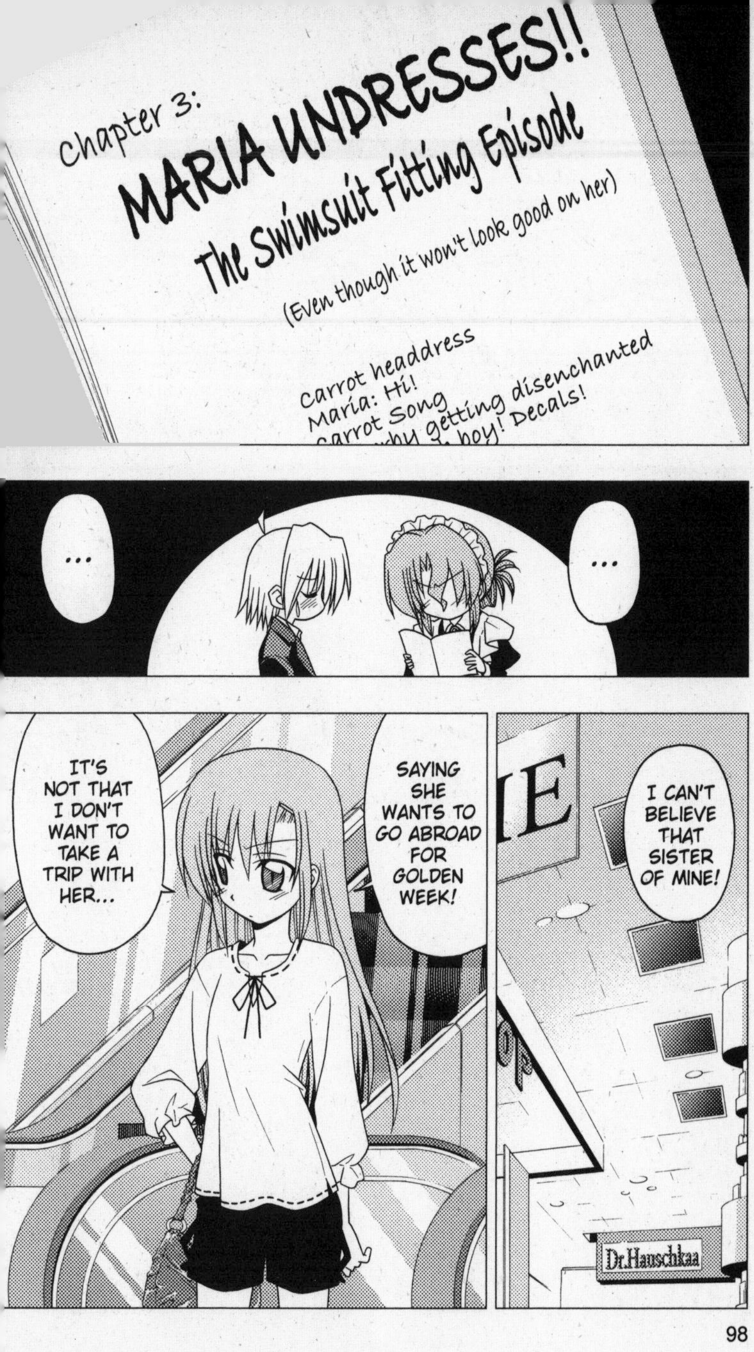
Chapter 3:
MARIA UNDRESSES!!
The Swimsuit Fitting Episode
(Even though it won't look good on her)
Carrot headdress
Maria: Hi!
Carrot Song
...
...
I CAN'T BELIEVE THAT SISTER OF MINE!
Dr.Hauschkaa
SAYING SHE WANTS TO GO ABROAD FOR GOLDEN WEEK!
IT'S NOT THAT I DON'T WANT TO TAKE A TRIP WITH HER...

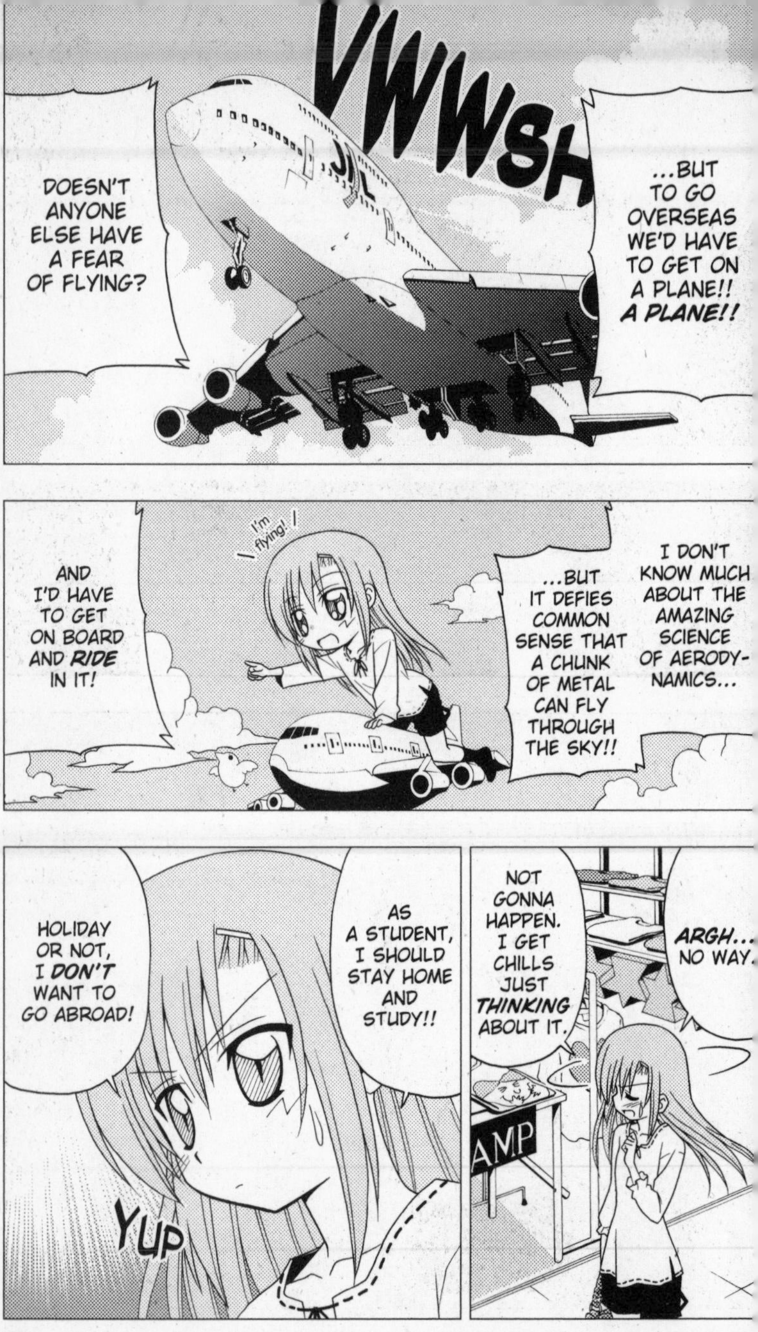
...BUT TO GO OVERSEAS WE'D HAVE TO GET ON A PLANE!! *A PLANE!!*
VWWSH
DOESN'T ANYONE ELSE HAVE A FEAR OF FLYING?
I DON'T KNOW MUCH ABOUT THE AMAZING SCIENCE OF AERODY-NAMICS...
...BUT IT DEFIES COMMON SENSE THAT A CHUNK OF METAL CAN FLY THROUGH THE SKY!!
I'm flying!
AND I'D HAVE TO GET ON BOARD AND ***RIDE*** IN IT!
ARGH... NO WAY.
NOT GONNA HAPPEN. I GET CHILLS JUST ***THINKING*** ABOUT IT.
AMP
AS A STUDENT, I SHOULD STAY HOME AND STUDY!!
HOLIDAY OR NOT, I ***DON'T*** WANT TO GO ABROAD!
YUP

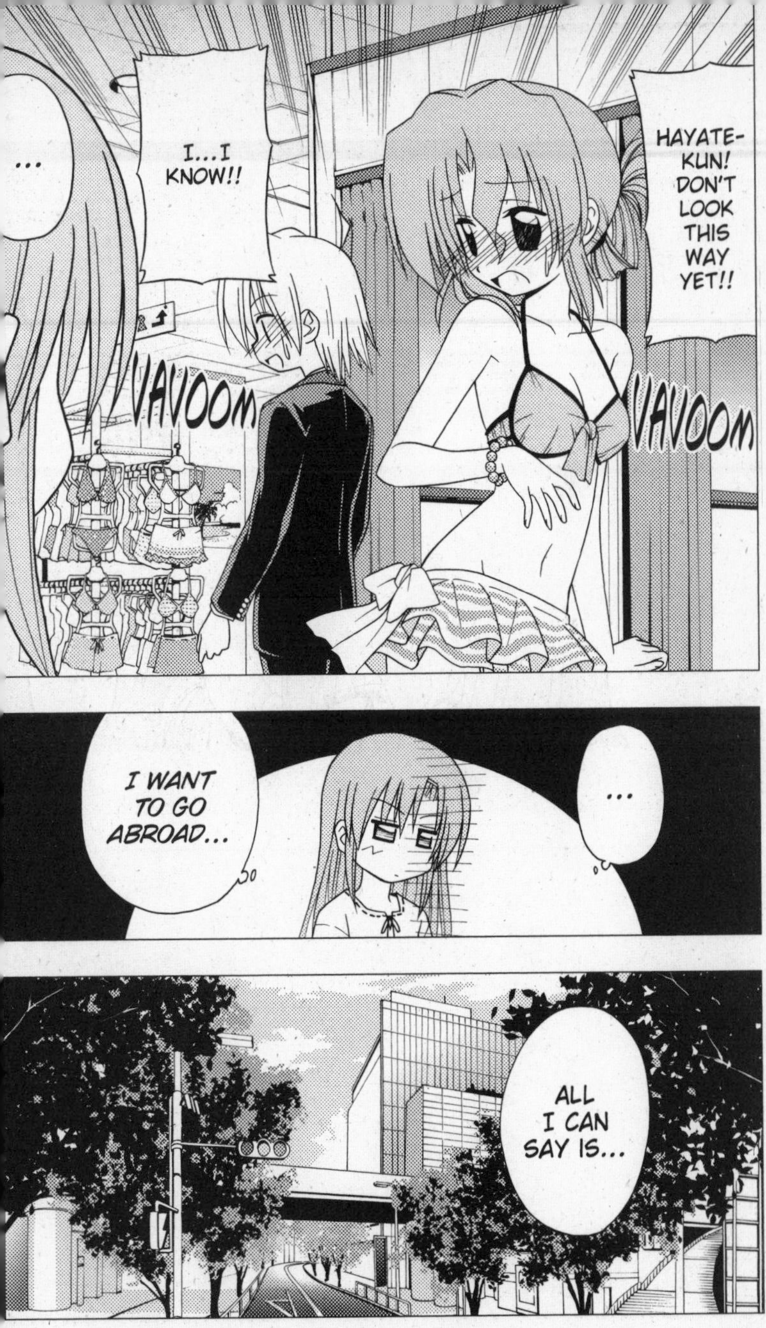
HAYATE-KUN! DON'T LOOK THIS WAY YET!!
VAVOOM
I...I KNOW!!
VAVOOM
...
...
I WANT TO GO ABROAD...
ALL I CAN SAY IS...

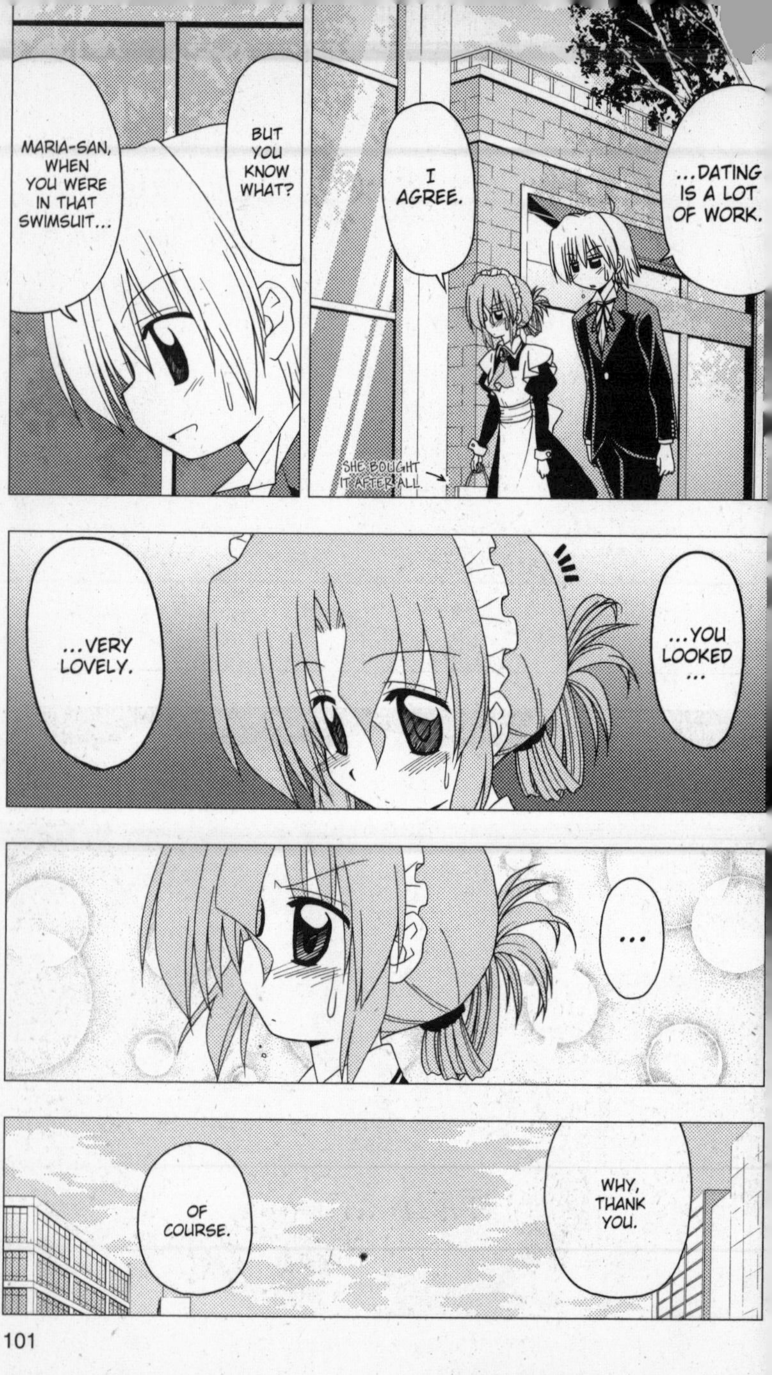
...DATING IS A LOT OF WORK.
I AGREE.
SHE BOUGHT IT AFTER ALL.
BUT YOU KNOW WHAT?
MARIA-SAN, WHEN YOU WERE IN THAT SWIMSUIT...
...YOU LOOKED...
...VERY LOVELY.
...
WHY, THANK YOU.
OF COURSE.

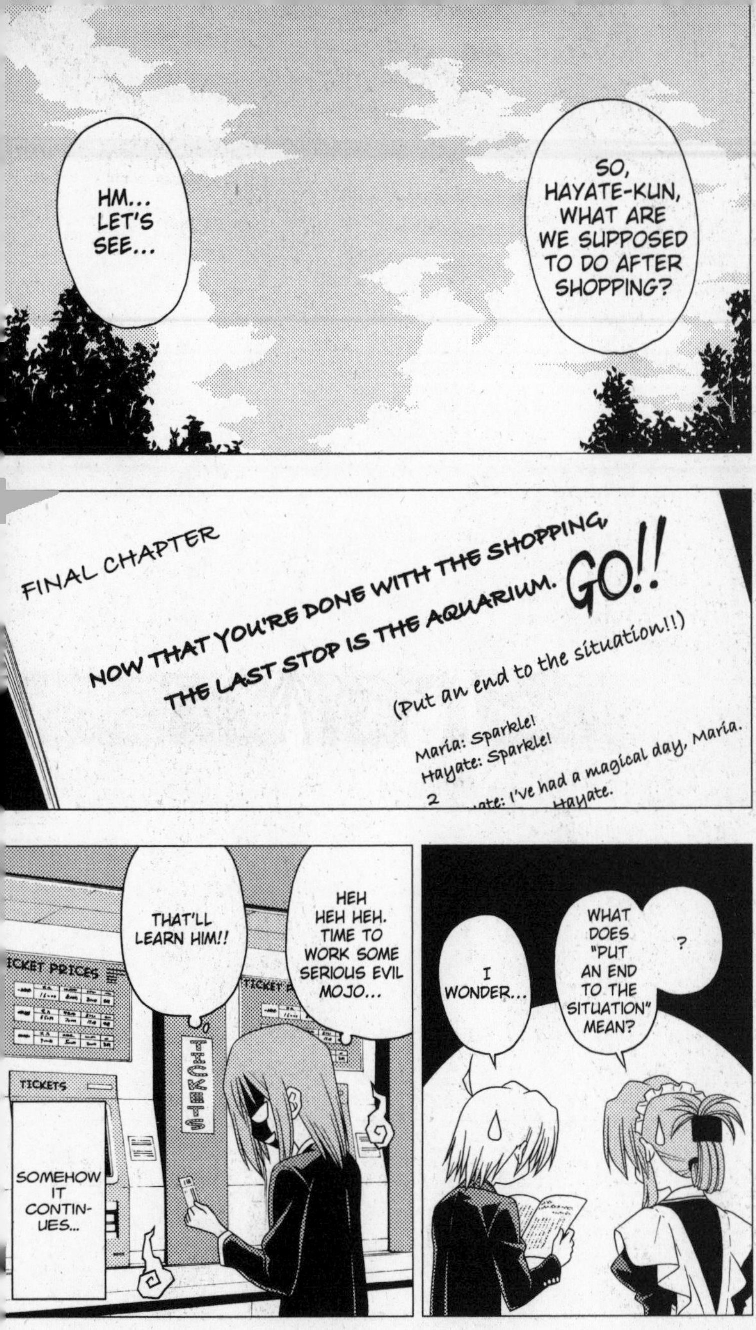
SO, HAYATE-KUN, WHAT ARE WE SUPPOSED TO DO AFTER SHOPPING?
HM... LET'S SEE...
FINAL CHAPTER
NOW THAT YOU'RE DONE WITH THE SHOPPING
THE LAST STOP IS THE AQUARIUM. GO!!
(Put an end to the situation!!)
Maria: Sparkle!
Hayate: Sparkle!
?
WHAT DOES "PUT AN END TO THE SITUATION" MEAN?
I WONDER...
HEH HEH HEH. TIME TO WORK SOME SERIOUS EVIL MOJO...
THAT'LL LEARN HIM!!
TICKET PRICES
TICKETS
TICKETS
SOMEHOW IT CONTIN-UES...

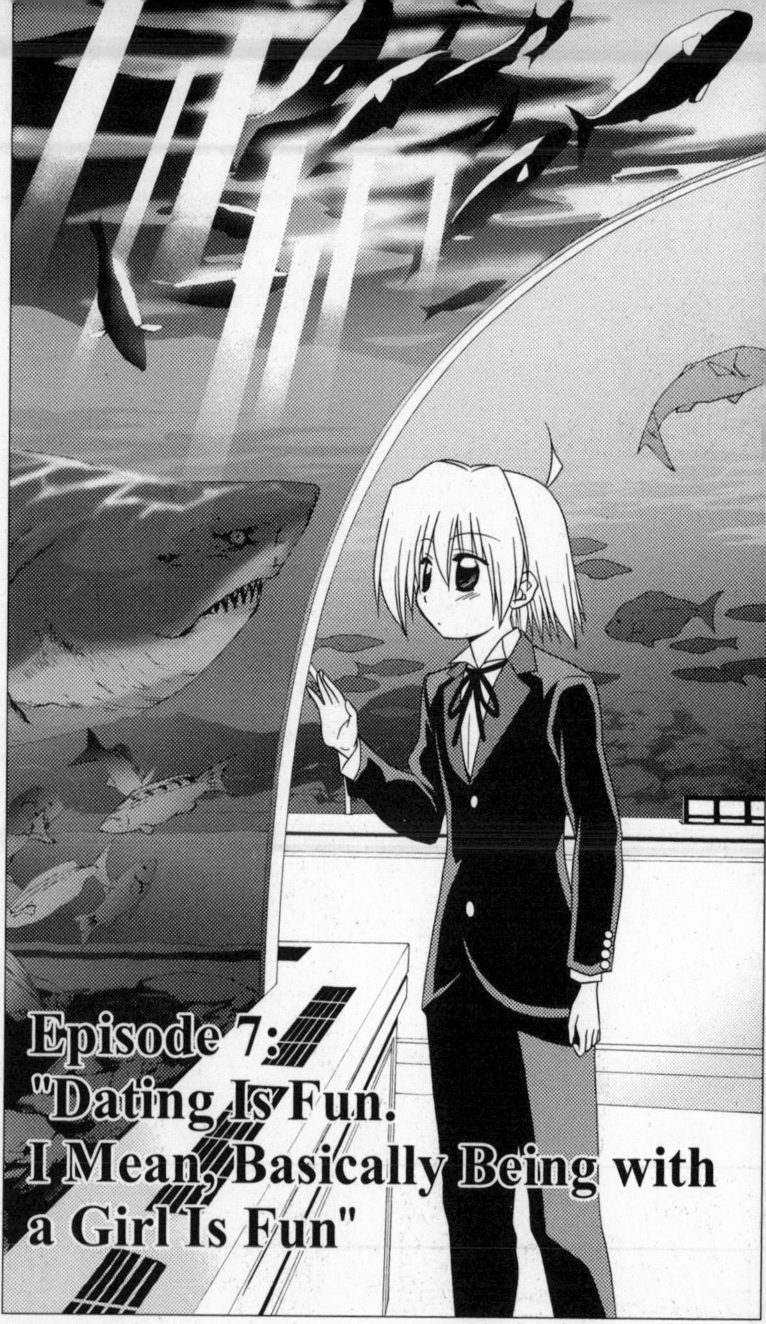
Episode 7:
"Dating Is Fun.
I Mean, Basically Being with a Girl Is Fun"

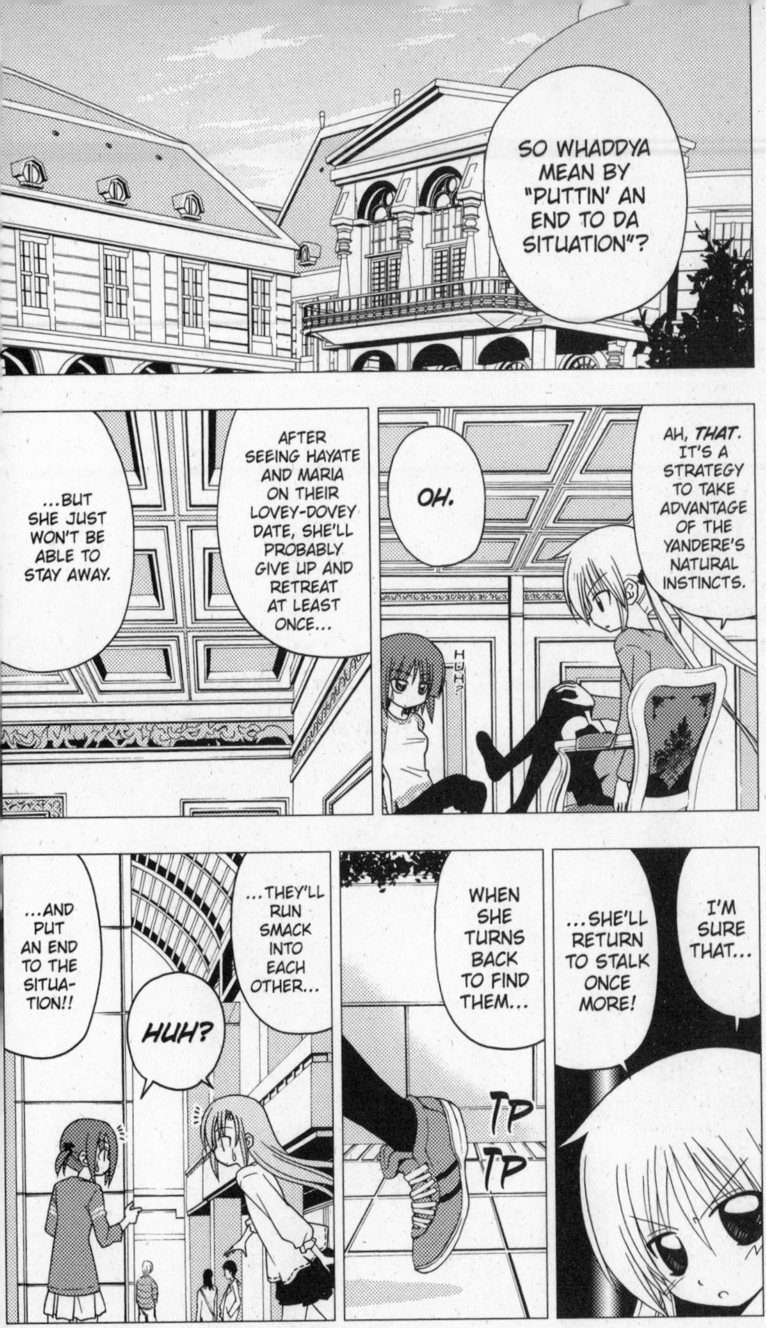

SO WHADDYA MEAN BY "PUTTIN' AN END TO DA SITUATION"?
AH, *THAT*. IT'S A STRATEGY TO TAKE ADVANTAGE OF THE YANDERE'S NATURAL INSTINCTS.
OH.
HUH?
AFTER SEEING HAYATE AND MARIA ON THEIR LOVEY-DOVEY DATE, SHE'LL PROBABLY GIVE UP AND RETREAT AT LEAST ONCE...
...BUT SHE JUST WON'T BE ABLE TO STAY AWAY.
I'M SURE THAT...
...SHE'LL RETURN TO STALK ONCE MORE!
WHEN SHE TURNS BACK TO FIND THEM...
TP
TP
...THEY'LL RUN SMACK INTO EACH OTHER...
...AND PUT AN END TO THE SITUATION!!
HUH?

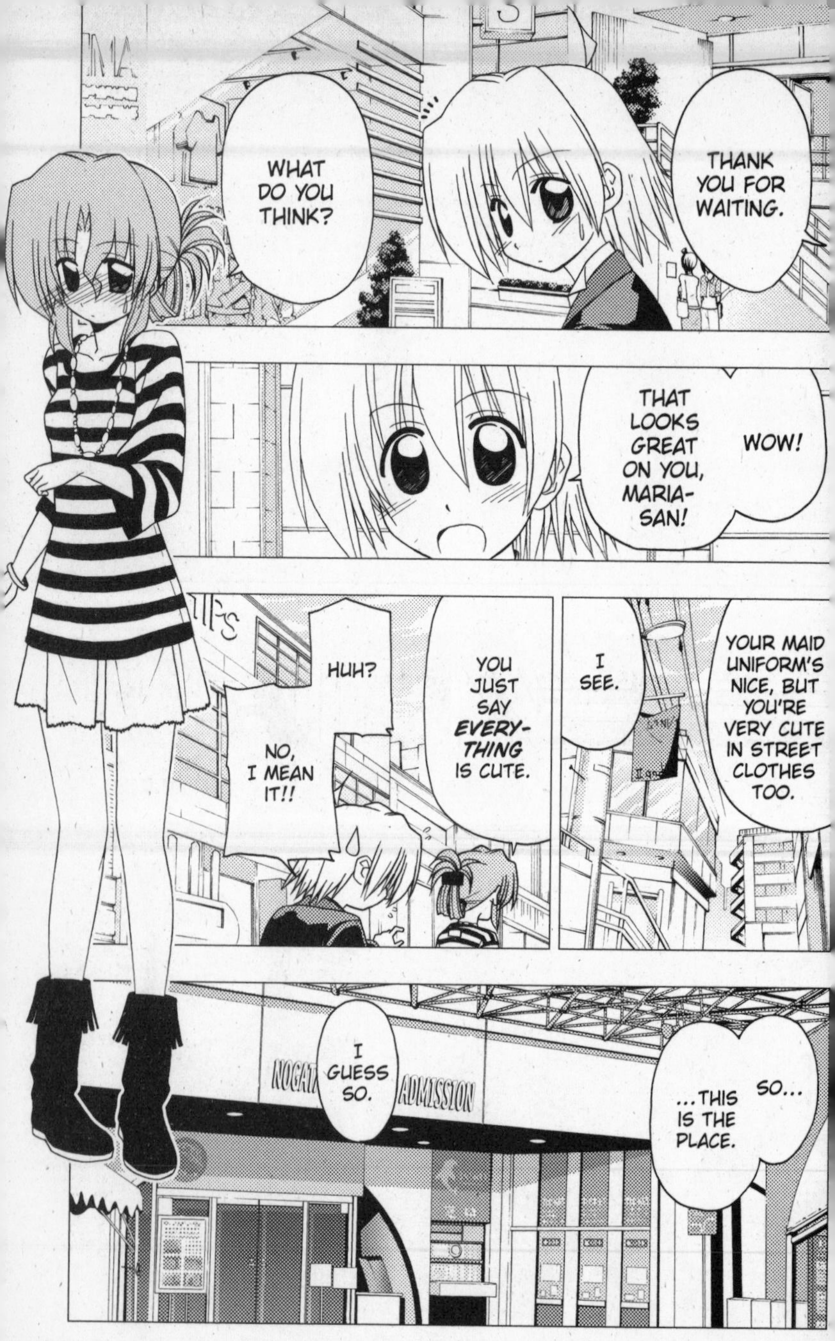
THANK YOU FOR WAITING.
WHAT DO YOU THINK?
WOW!
THAT LOOKS GREAT ON YOU, MARIA-SAN!
YOUR MAID UNIFORM'S NICE, BUT YOU'RE VERY CUTE IN STREET CLOTHES TOO.
I SEE.
YOU JUST SAY *EVERYTHING* IS CUTE.
HUH?
NO, I MEAN IT!!
SO...
...THIS IS THE PLACE.
ADMISSION
I GUESS SO.
NOGATA

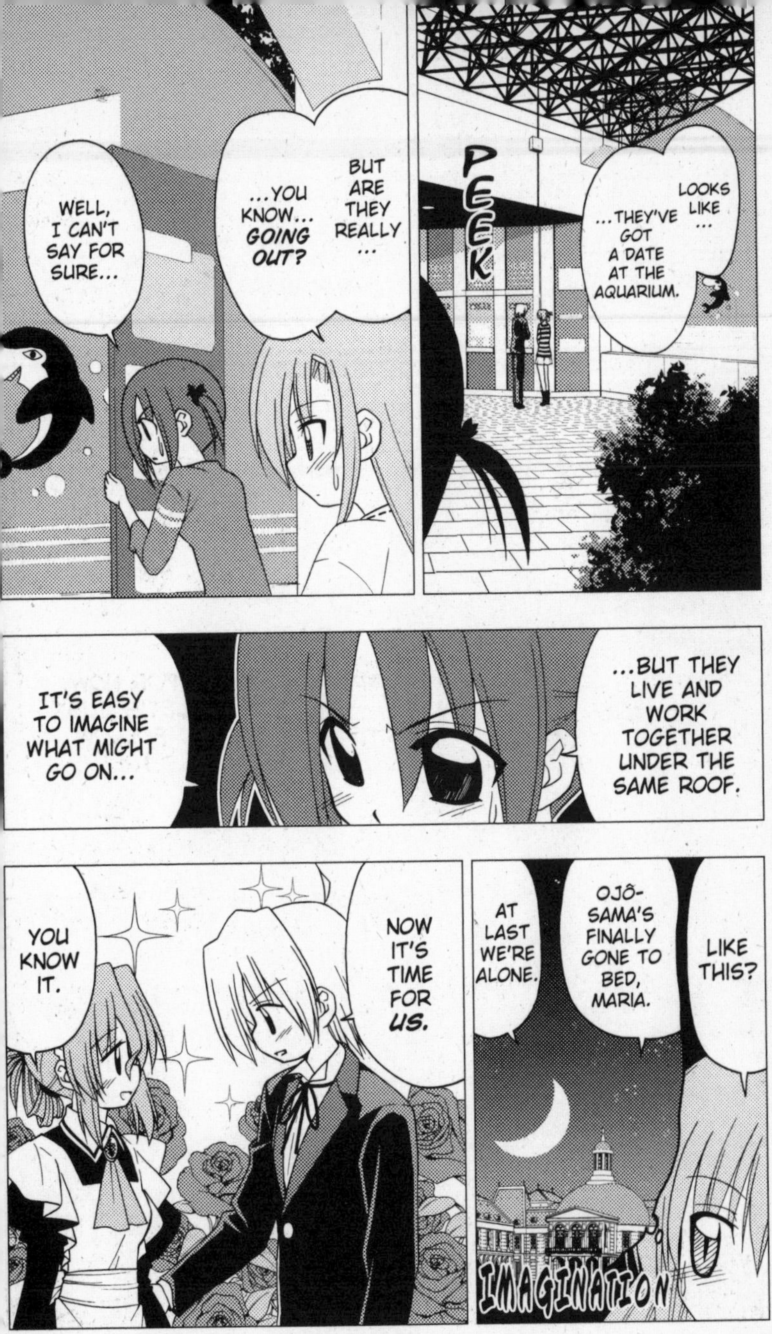
LOOKS LIKE...
...THEY'VE GOT A DATE AT THE AQUARIUM.
PEEK
BUT ARE THEY REALLY...
...YOU KNOW... GOING OUT?
WELL, I CAN'T SAY FOR SURE...
...BUT THEY LIVE AND WORK TOGETHER UNDER THE SAME ROOF.
IT'S EASY TO IMAGINE WHAT MIGHT GO ON...
LIKE THIS?
OJÔ-SAMA'S FINALLY GONE TO BED, MARIA.
AT LAST WE'RE ALONE.
IMAGINATION
NOW IT'S TIME FOR US.
YOU KNOW IT.

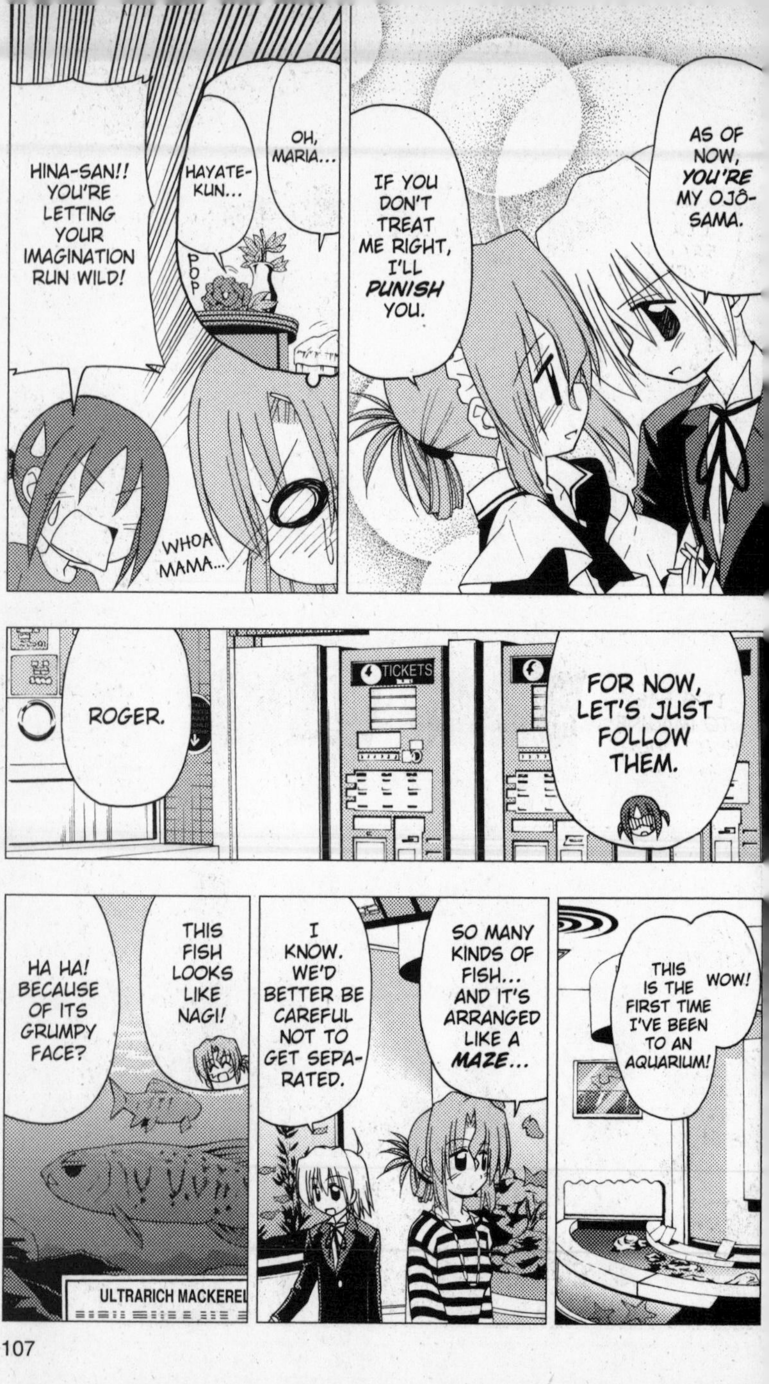
AS OF NOW, *YOU'RE* MY OJÔ-SAMA.
IF YOU DON'T TREAT ME RIGHT, I'LL *PUNISH* YOU.
OH, MARIA...
HAYATE-KUN...
POP
HINA-SAN!! YOU'RE LETTING YOUR IMAGINATION RUN WILD!
WHOA MAMA...
FOR NOW, LET'S JUST FOLLOW THEM.
TICKETS
ROGER.
WOW!
THIS IS THE FIRST TIME I'VE BEEN TO AN AQUARIUM!
SO MANY KINDS OF FISH... AND IT'S ARRANGED LIKE A *MAZE*...
I KNOW. WE'D BETTER BE CAREFUL NOT TO GET SEPA-RATED.
THIS FISH LOOKS LIKE NAGI!
HA HA! BECAUSE OF ITS GRUMPY FACE?
ULTRARICH MACKEREL

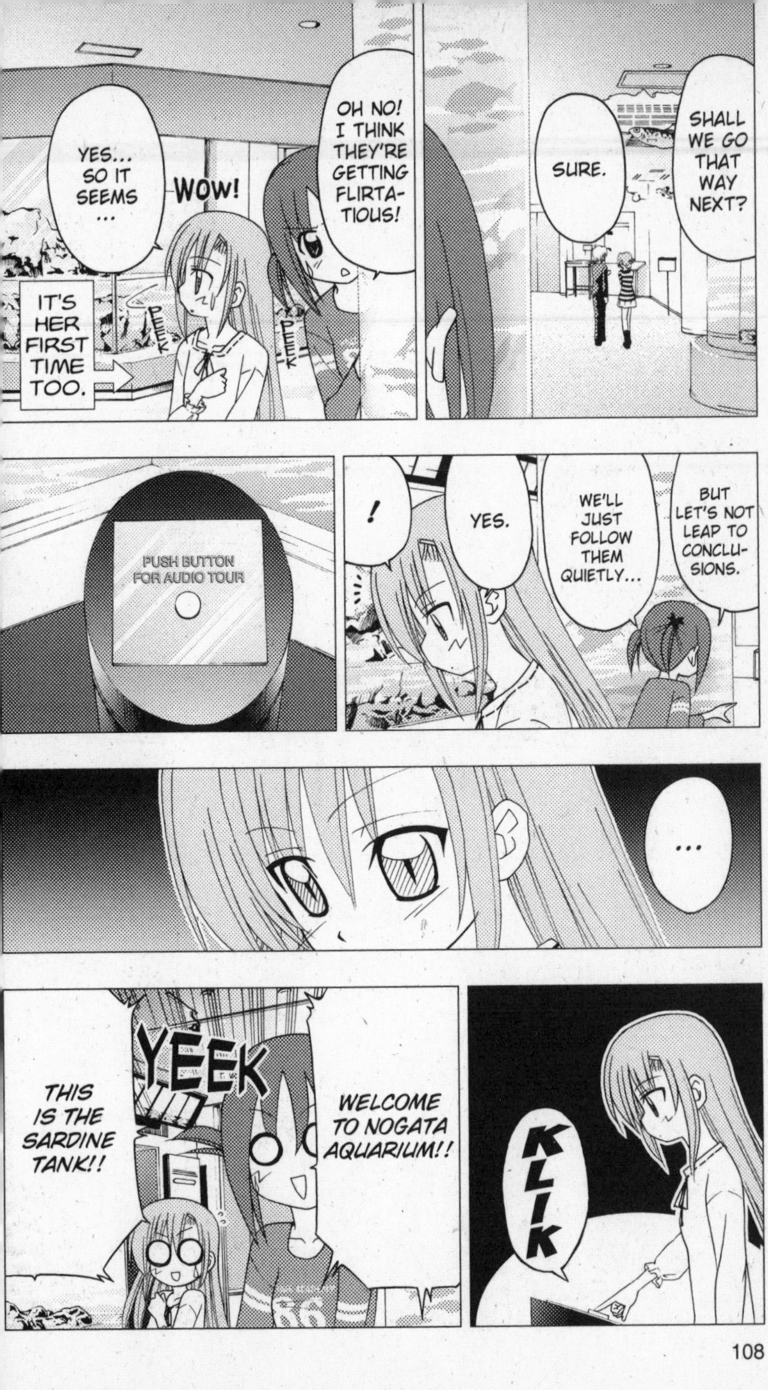
SHALL WE GO THAT WAY NEXT?
SURE.
OH NO! I THINK THEY'RE GETTING FLIRTA-TIOUS!
WOW!
YES... SO IT SEEMS...
PEEK
PEEK
IT'S HER FIRST TIME TOO.
BUT LET'S NOT LEAP TO CONCLU-SIONS.
WE'LL JUST FOLLOW THEM QUIETLY...
YES.
!
PUSH BUTTON FOR AUDIO TOUR
...
KLIK
WELCOME TO NOGATA AQUARIUM!!
YEEK
THIS IS THE SARDINE TANK!!

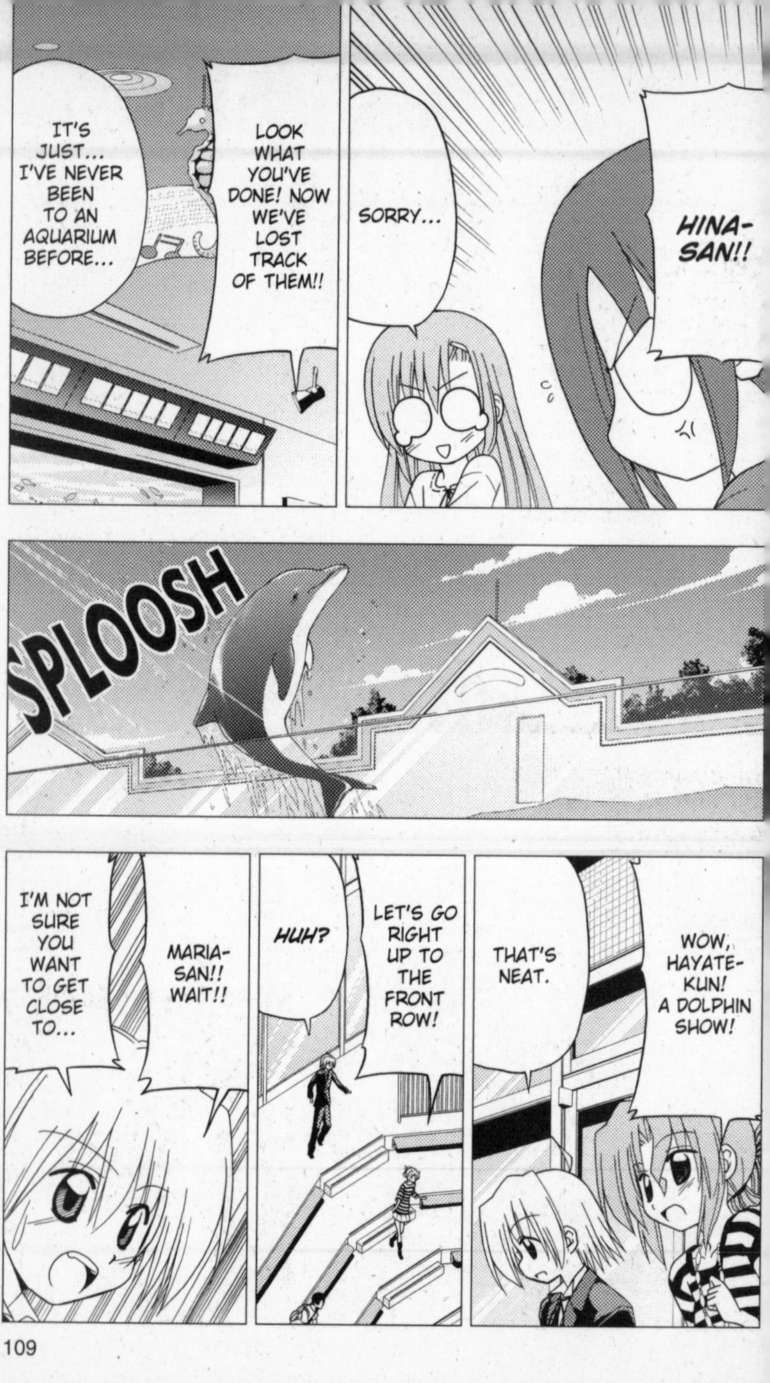
HINA-SAN!!
SORRY...
LOOK WHAT YOU'VE DONE! NOW WE'VE LOST TRACK OF THEM!!
IT'S JUST... I'VE NEVER BEEN TO AN AQUARIUM BEFORE...
SPLOOSH
WOW, HAYATE-KUN! A DOLPHIN SHOW!
THAT'S NEAT.
LET'S GO RIGHT UP TO THE FRONT ROW!
HUH?
MARIA-SAN!! WAIT!!
I'M NOT SURE YOU WANT TO GET CLOSE TO...

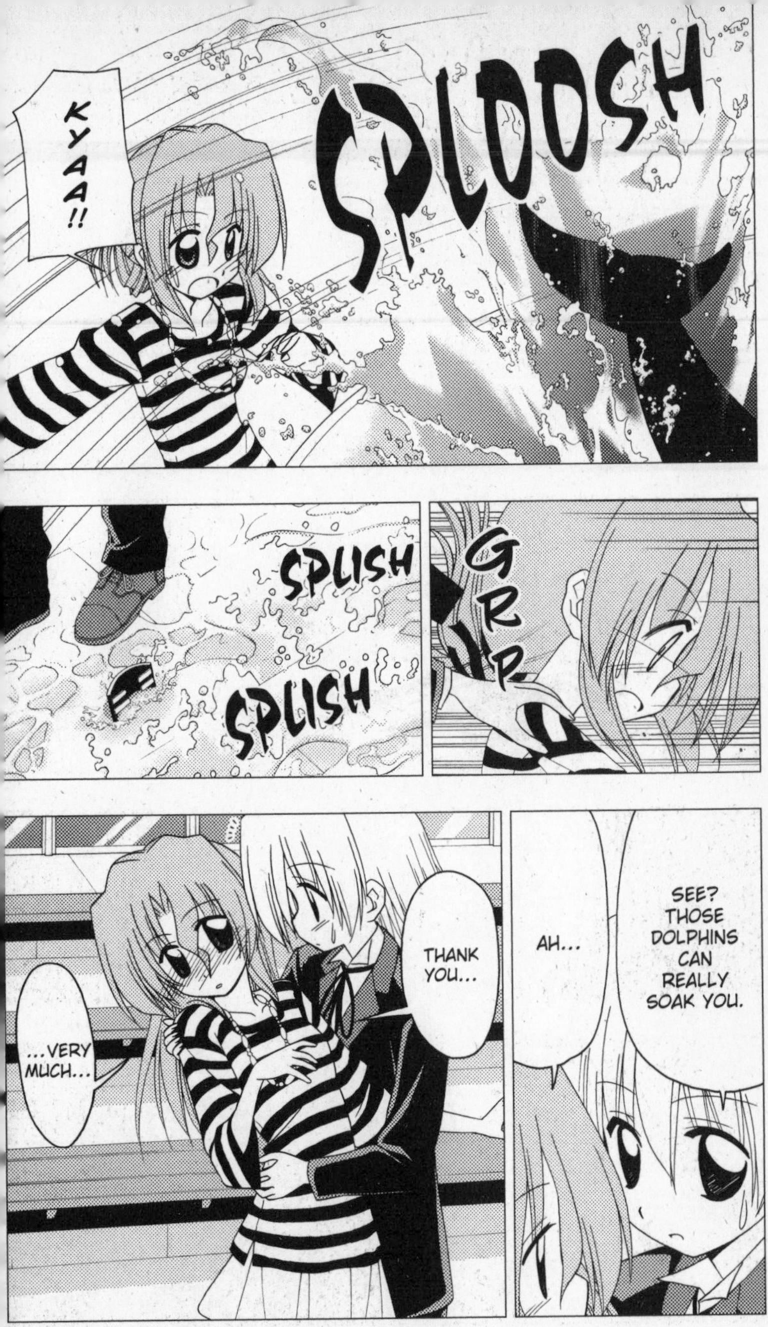
SPLOOSH
KYAA!!
GRP
SPLISH
SPLISH
SEE? THOSE DOLPHINS CAN REALLY SOAK YOU.
AH...
THANK YOU...
...VERY MUCH...

...
...
BLUSSSSH
ERK!! UM... SORRY!!
ER, NO... IT'S MY FAULT... ER...
UM... DOLPHINS ARE PRETTY CUTE, HUH?
THEY CERTAINLY ARE.
HOW CARELESS OF ME!
PANICKING OVER SOMETHING LIKE THAT!
I'M SUPPOSED TO BE THE "BIG SISTER"!
IN A DELICATE SITUATION LIKE THIS, I NEED TO APPEAR ABOVE IT ALL!
HAYATE-KUN!!
YES?

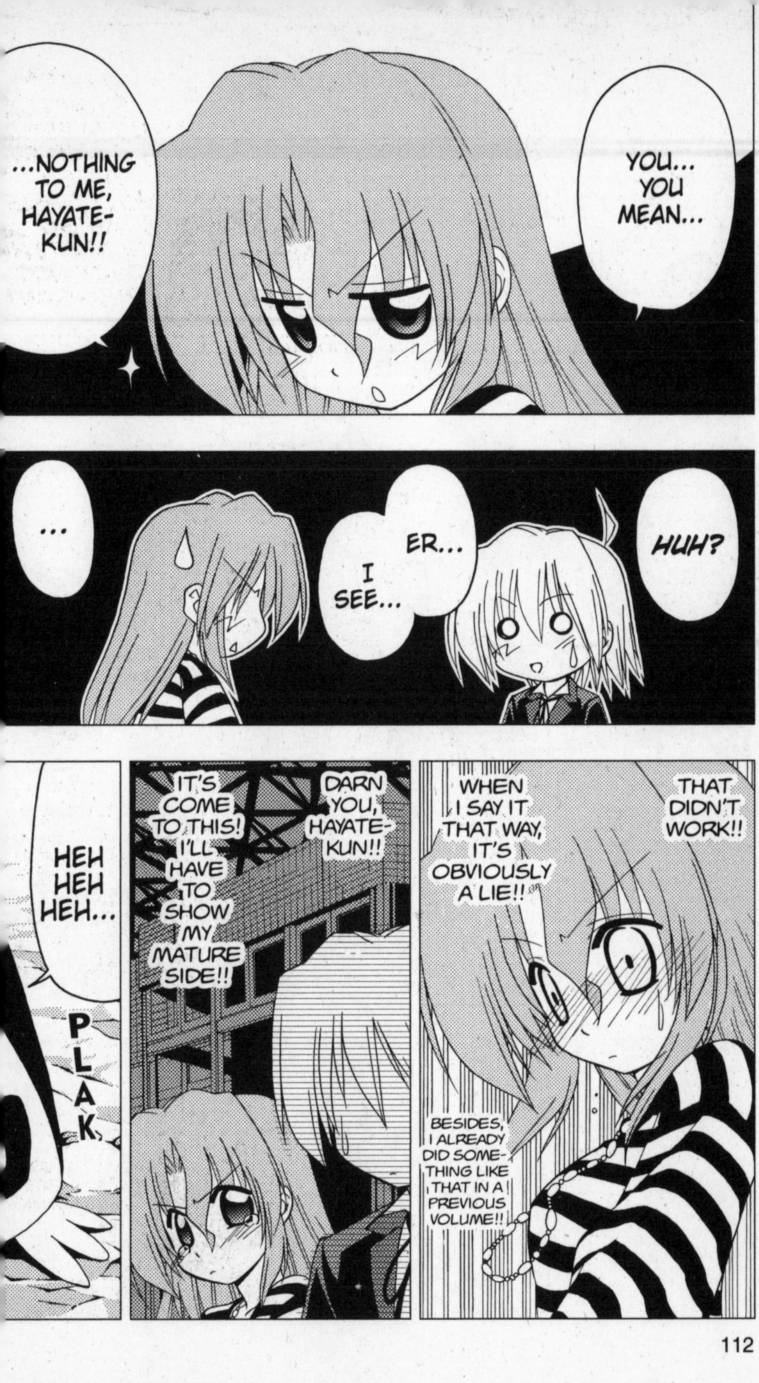
YOU... YOU MEAN...
...NOTHING TO ME, HAYATE-KUN!!
HUH?
ER...
I SEE...
...
THAT DIDN'T WORK!!
WHEN I SAY IT THAT WAY, IT'S OBVIOUSLY A LIE!!
BESIDES, I ALREADY DID SOME-THING LIKE THAT IN A PREVIOUS VOLUME!!
DARN YOU, HAYATE-KUN!!
IT'S COME TO THIS! I'LL HAVE TO SHOW MY MATURE SIDE!!
HEH HEH HEH...
PLAK

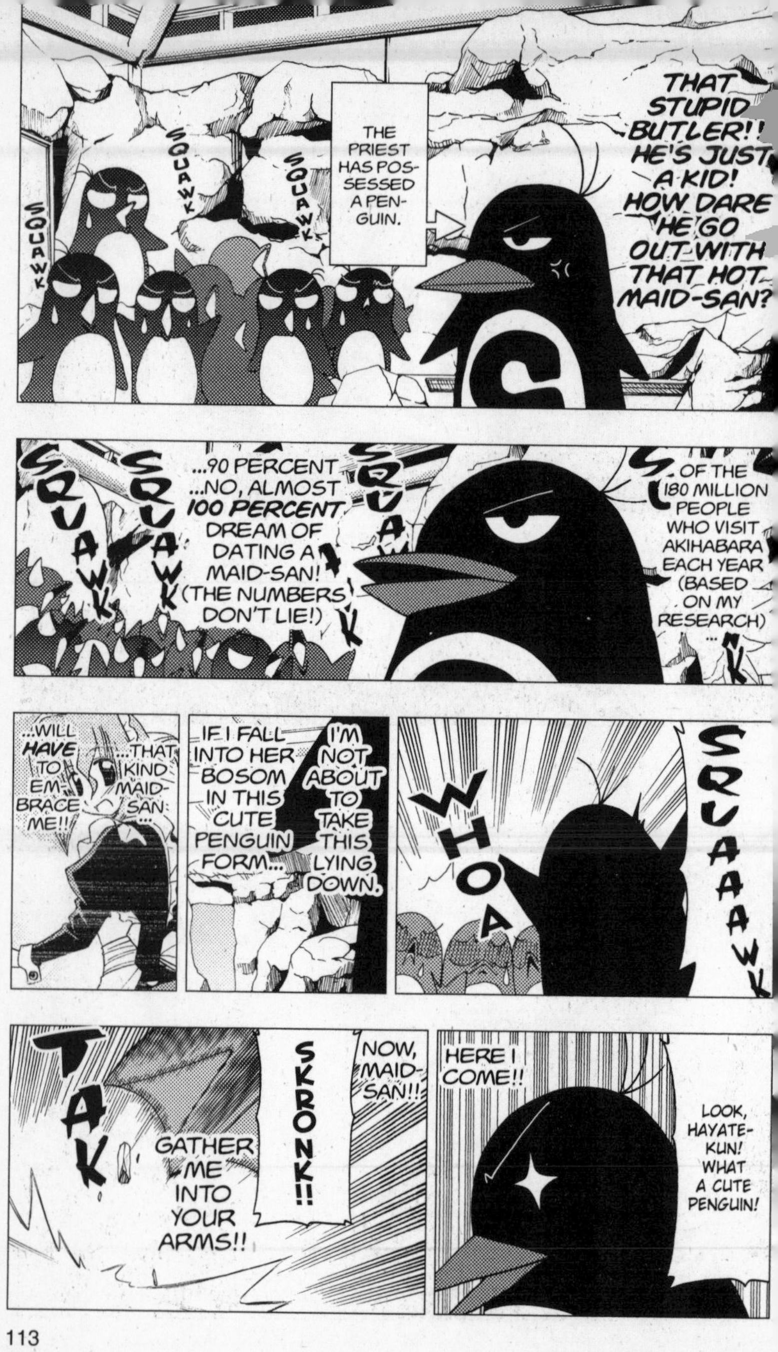
THAT STUPID BUTLER!! HE'S JUST A KID! HOW DARE HE GO OUT WITH THAT HOT MAID-SAN?
THE PRIEST HAS POSSESSED A PENGUIN.
SQUAWK
SQUAWK
SQUAWK
...OF THE 180 MILLION PEOPLE WHO VISIT AKIHABARA EACH YEAR (BASED ON MY RESEARCH)...
...90 PERCENT ...NO, ALMOST **100 PERCENT** DREAM OF DATING A MAID-SAN! (THE NUMBERS DON'T LIE!)
SQUAWK
SQUAWK
SQUAWK
SQUAAAAWK
WHOA
I'M NOT ABOUT TO TAKE THIS LYING DOWN.
IF I FALL INTO HER BOSOM IN THIS CUTE PENGUIN FORM...
...THAT KIND MAID-SAN...
...WILL **HAVE** TO EMBRACE ME!!
LOOK, HAYATE-KUN! WHAT A CUTE PENGUIN!
HERE I COME!!
NOW, MAID-SAN!!
SKRONK!!
GATHER ME INTO YOUR ARMS!!
TAK

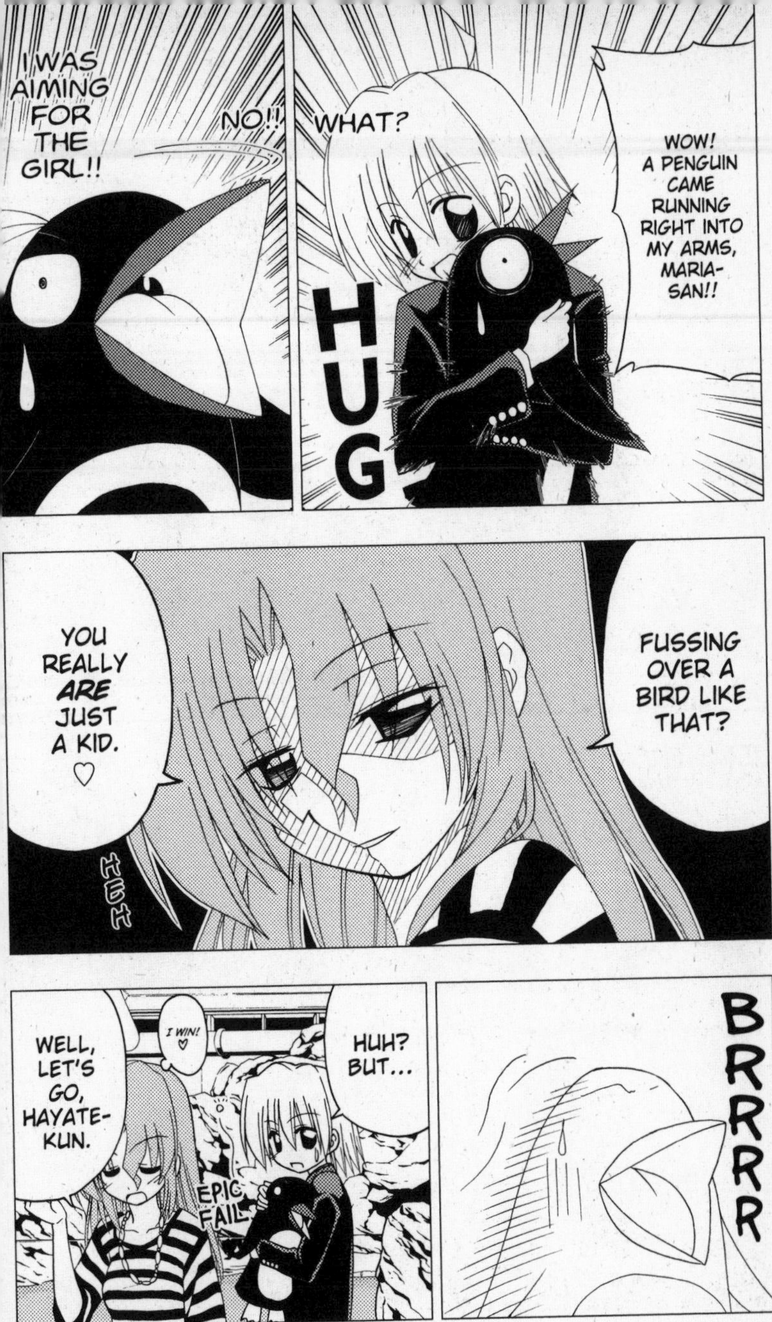

WOW! A PENGUIN CAME RUNNING RIGHT INTO MY ARMS, MARIA-SAN!!
WHAT?
HUG
NO!!
I WAS AIMING FOR THE GIRL!!
FUSSING OVER A BIRD LIKE THAT?
YOU REALLY *ARE* JUST A KID. ♡
HEH
BRRRR
HUH? BUT...
I WIN! ♡
WELL, LET'S GO, HAYATE-KUN.
EPIC FAIL

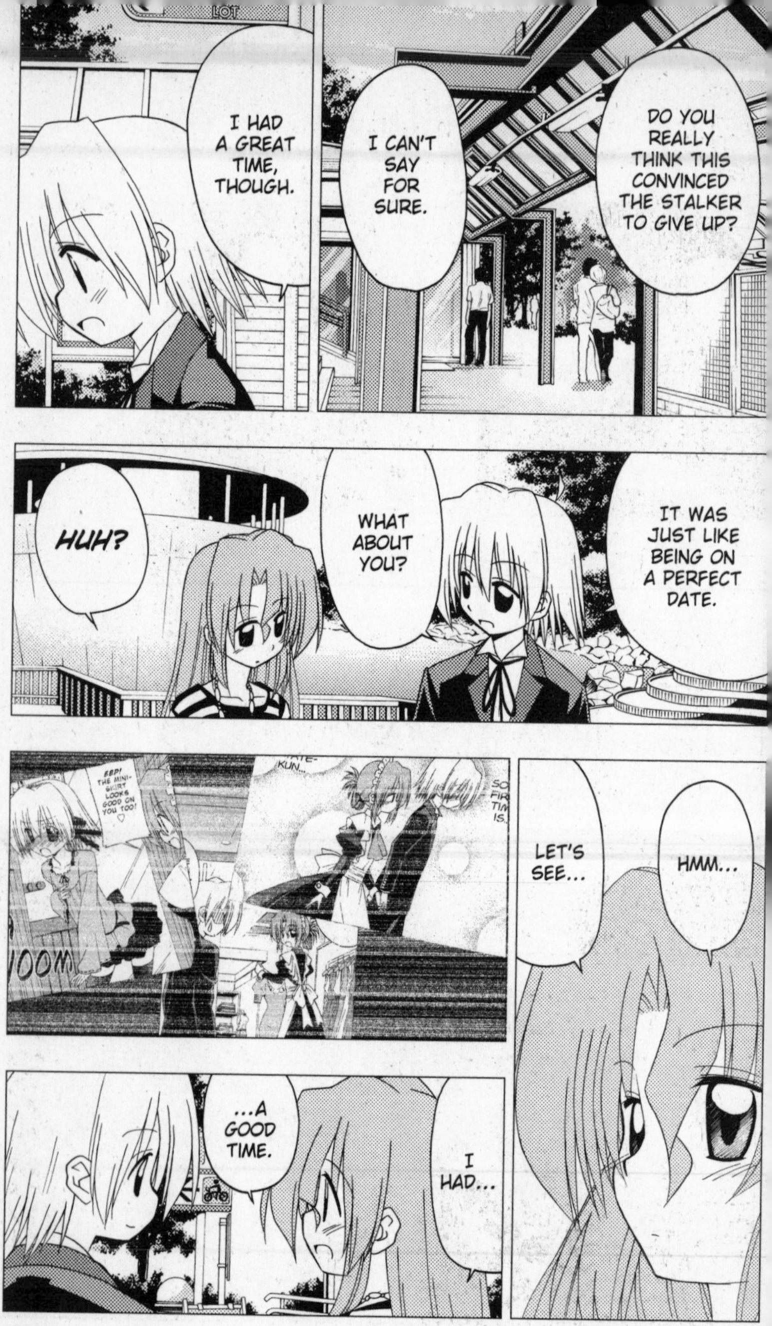
DO YOU REALLY THINK THIS CONVINCED THE STALKER TO GIVE UP?
I CAN'T SAY FOR SURE.
I HAD A GREAT TIME, THOUGH.
IT WAS JUST LIKE BEING ON A PERFECT DATE.
WHAT ABOUT YOU?
HUH?
HMM...
LET'S SEE...
EEP! THE MINI-SKIRT LOOKS GOOD ON YOU TOO! ♡
I HAD...
...A GOOD TIME.

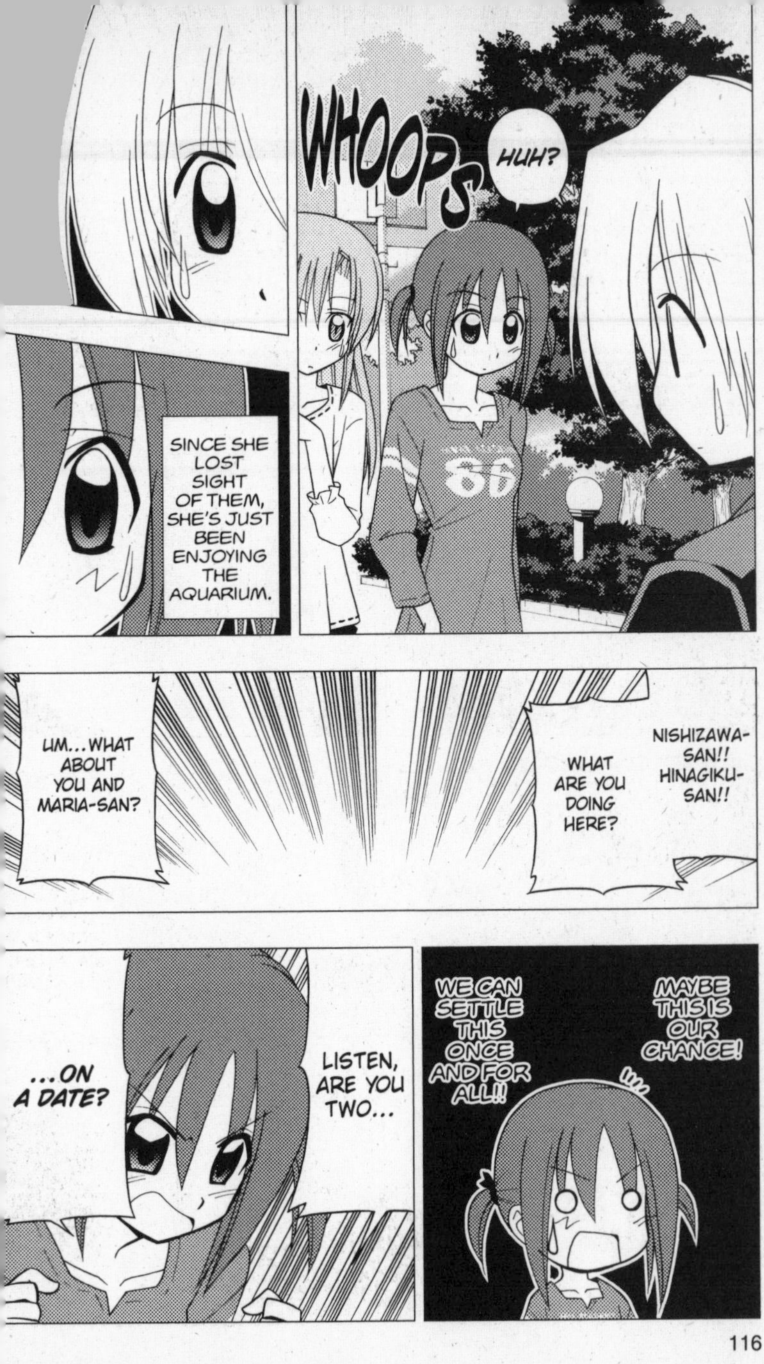
HUH?
WHOOPS
SINCE SHE LOST SIGHT OF THEM, SHE'S JUST BEEN ENJOYING THE AQUARIUM.
NISHIZAWA-SAN!! HINAGIKU-SAN!!
WHAT ARE YOU DOING HERE?
UM...WHAT ABOUT YOU AND MARIA-SAN?
MAYBE THIS IS OUR CHANCE!
WE CAN SETTLE THIS ONCE AND FOR ALL!!
LISTEN, ARE YOU TWO...
...ON A DATE?

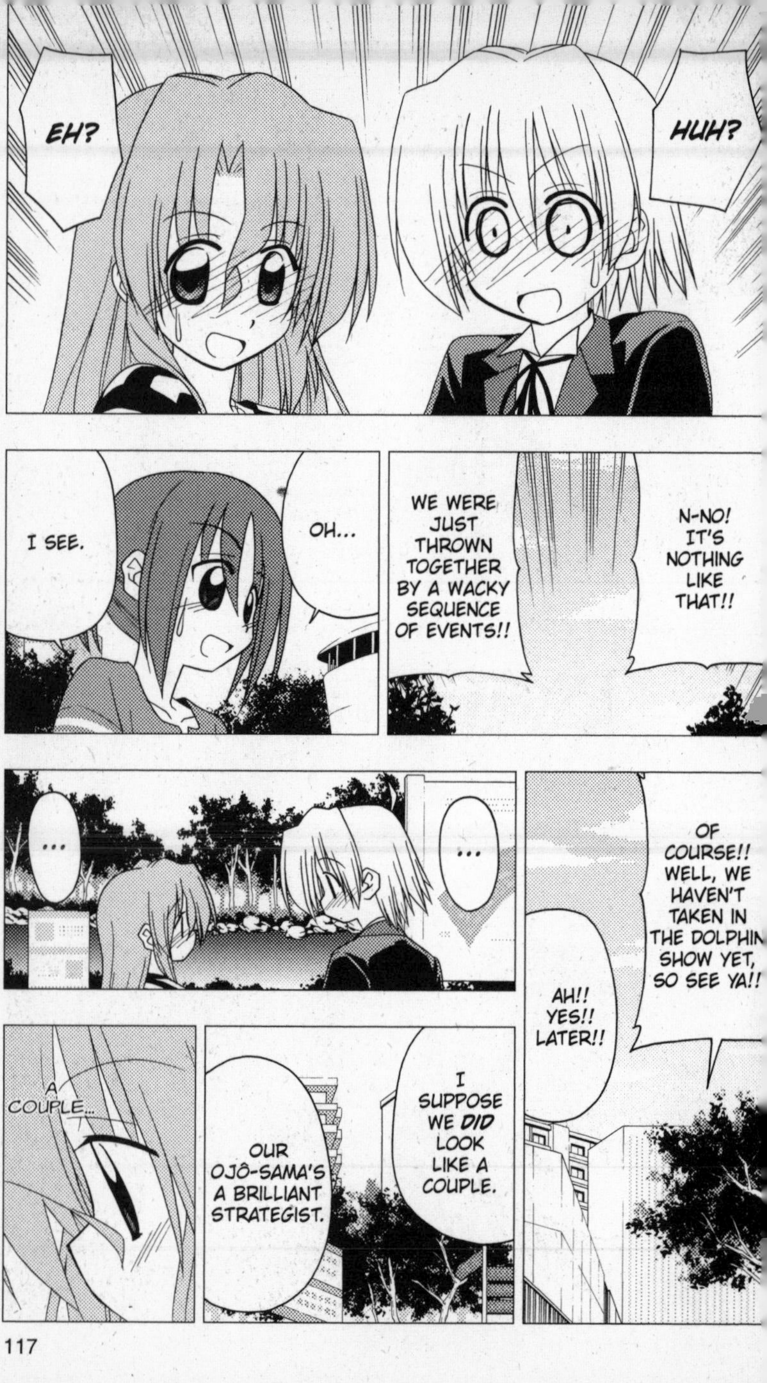
HUH?
EH?
N-NO! IT'S NOTHING LIKE THAT!!
WE WERE JUST THROWN TOGETHER BY A WACKY SEQUENCE OF EVENTS!!
OH...
I SEE.
OF COURSE!! WELL, WE HAVEN'T TAKEN IN THE DOLPHIN SHOW YET, SO SEE YA!!
AH!! YES!! LATER!!
...
...
I SUPPOSE WE *DID* LOOK LIKE A COUPLE.
OUR OJÔ-SAMA'S A BRILLIANT STRATEGIST.
A COUPLE...

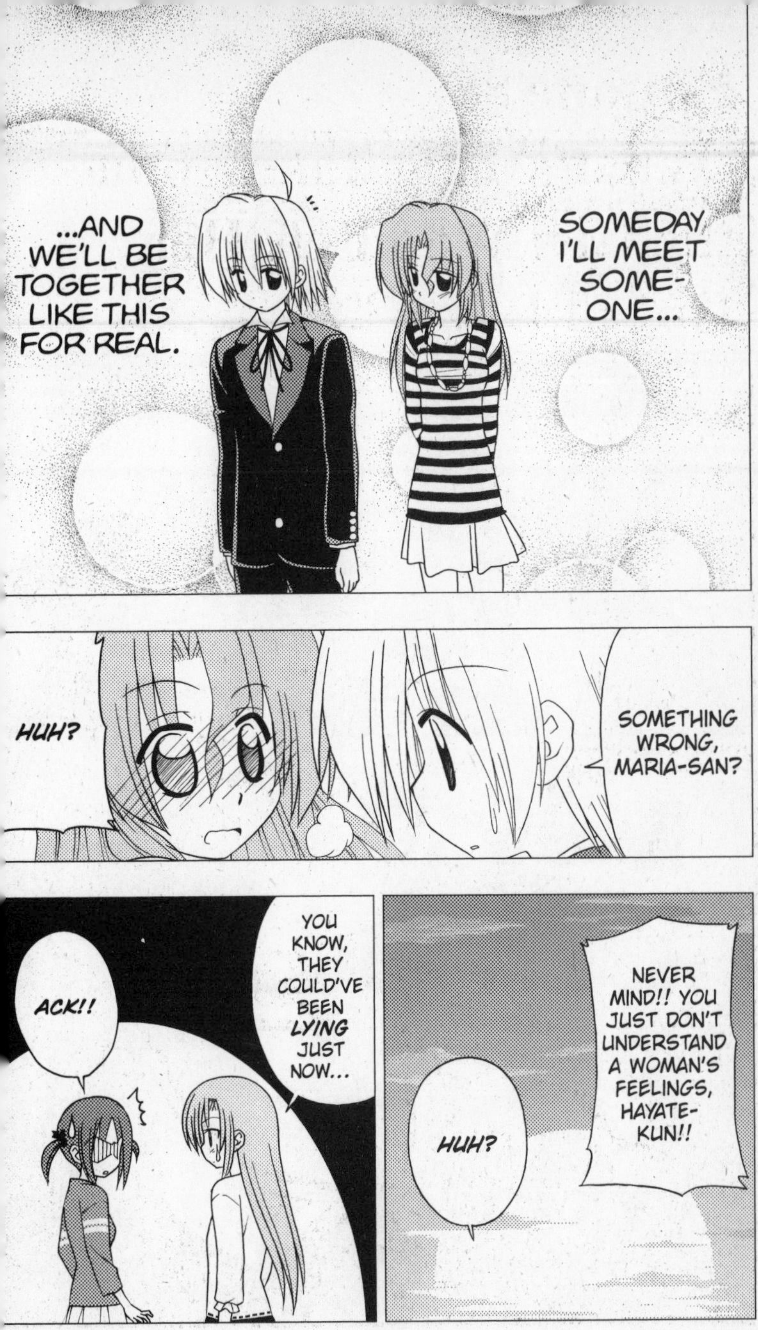
SOMEDAY I'LL MEET SOME-ONE...
...AND WE'LL BE TOGETHER LIKE THIS FOR REAL.
SOMETHING WRONG, MARIA-SAN?
HUH?
NEVER MIND!! YOU JUST DON'T UNDERSTAND A WOMAN'S FEELINGS, HAYATE-KUN!!
HUH?
YOU KNOW, THEY COULD'VE BEEN *LYING* JUST NOW...
ACK!!

Episode 8:

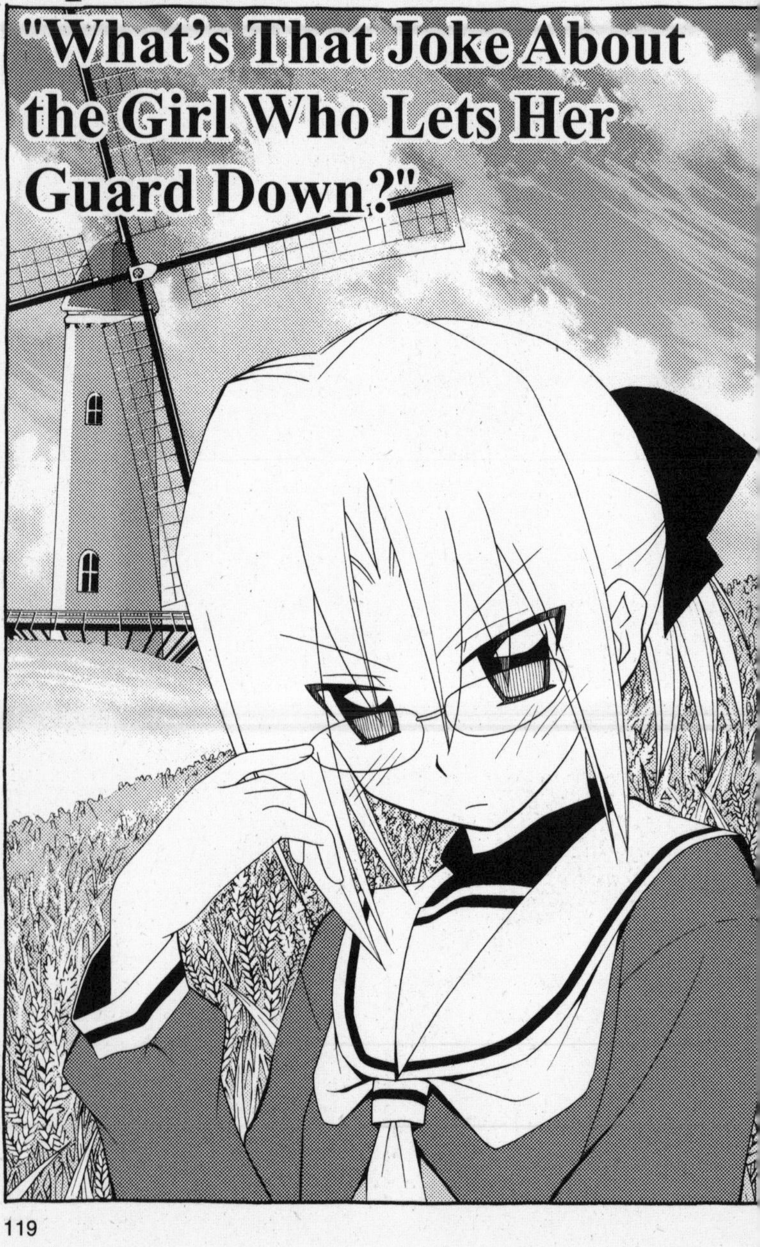
"What's That Joke About the Girl Who Lets Her Guard Down?"

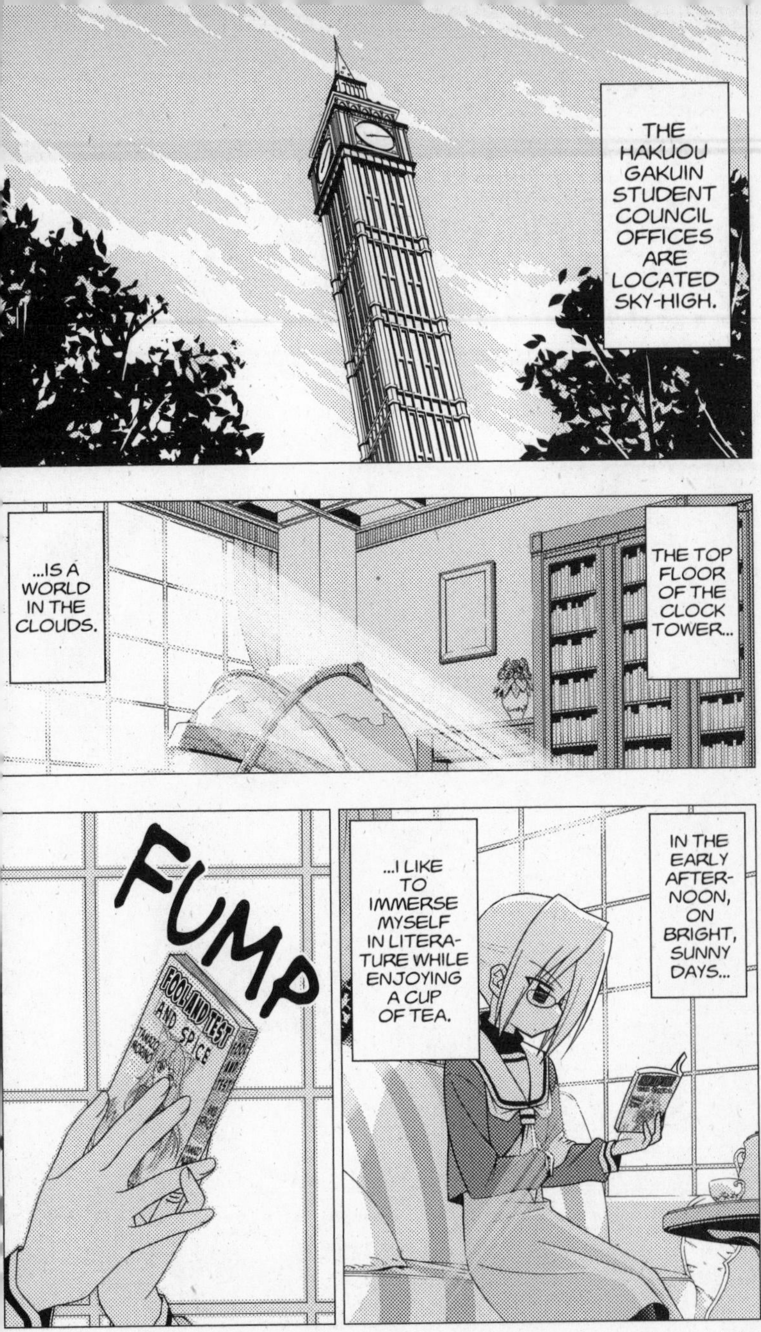
THE HAKUOU GAKUIN STUDENT COUNCIL OFFICES ARE LOCATED SKY-HIGH.
THE TOP FLOOR OF THE CLOCK TOWER...
...IS A WORLD IN THE CLOUDS.
IN THE EARLY AFTER-NOON, ON BRIGHT, SUNNY DAYS...
...I LIKE TO IMMERSE MYSELF IN LITERA-TURE WHILE ENJOYING A CUP OF TEA.
FUMP
FOOL AND TEST AND SPICE

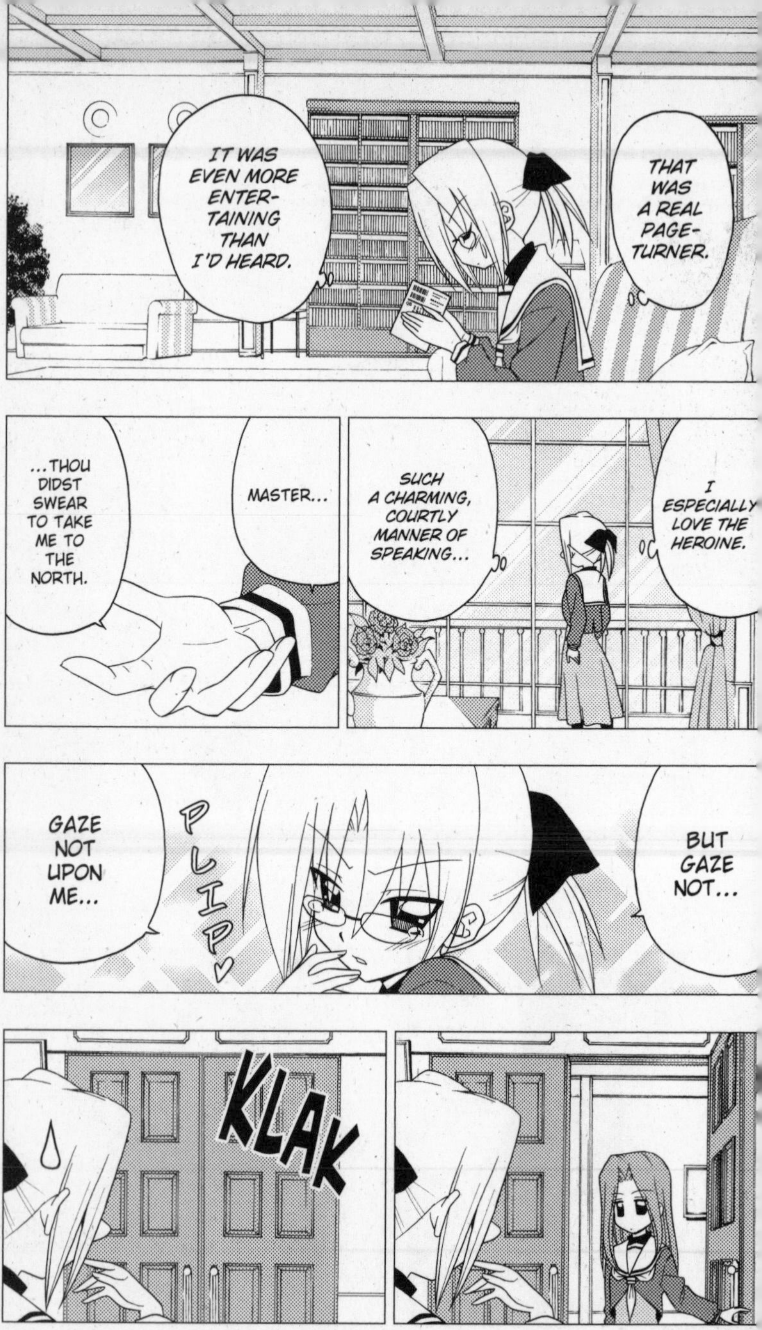
THAT WAS A REAL PAGE-TURNER.
IT WAS EVEN MORE ENTER-TAINING THAN I'D HEARD.
I ESPECIALLY LOVE THE HEROINE.
SUCH A CHARMING, COURTLY MANNER OF SPEAKING...
MASTER...
...THOU DIDST SWEAR TO TAKE ME TO THE NORTH.
BUT GAZE NOT...
PLIP♥
GAZE NOT UPON ME...
KLAK

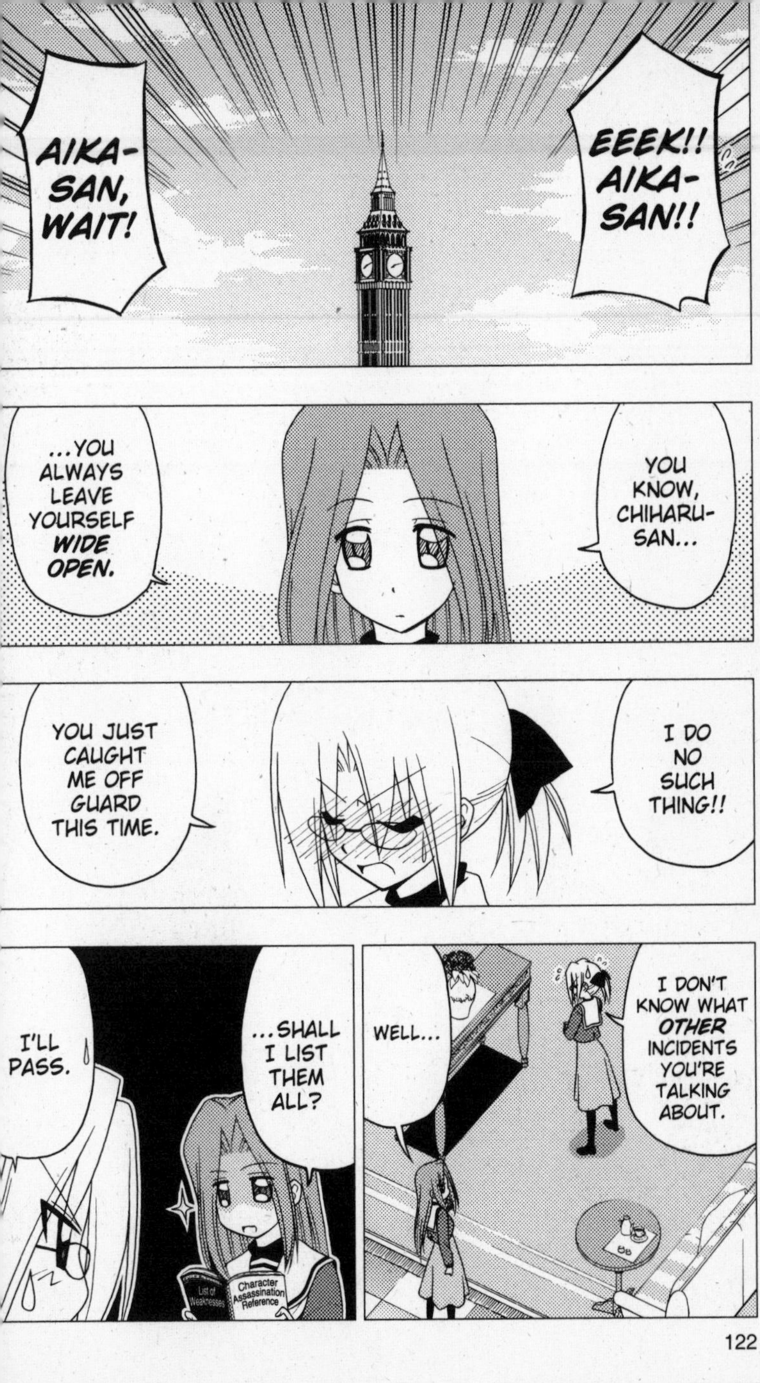
EEEK!! AIKA-SAN!!
AIKA-SAN, WAIT!
YOU KNOW, CHIHARU-SAN...
...YOU ALWAYS LEAVE YOURSELF WIDE OPEN.
I DO NO SUCH THING!!
YOU JUST CAUGHT ME OFF GUARD THIS TIME.
I DON'T KNOW WHAT OTHER INCIDENTS YOU'RE TALKING ABOUT.
WELL...
...SHALL I LIST THEM ALL?
Character Assassination Reference
List of Weaknesses
I'LL PASS.

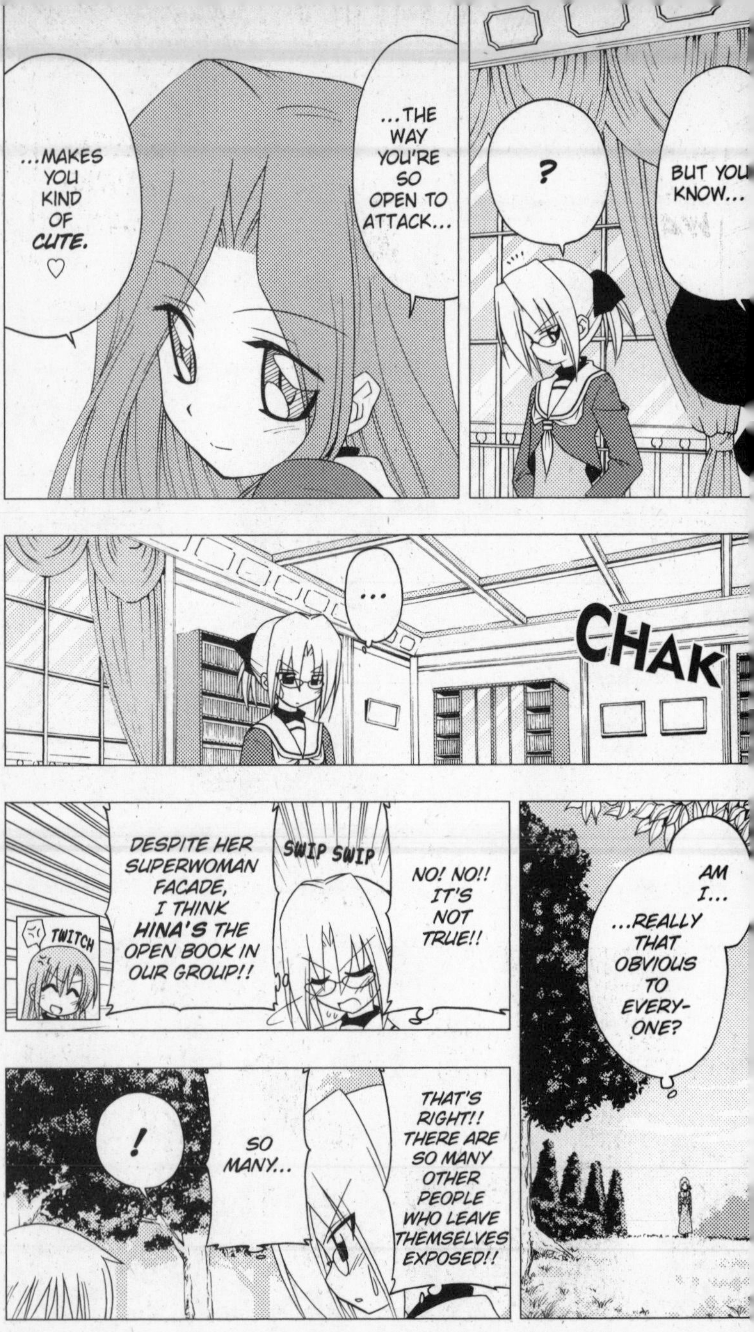
BUT YOU KNOW...
?
...THE WAY YOU'RE SO OPEN TO ATTACK...
...MAKES YOU KIND OF CUTE. ♡
CHAK
...
AM I... ...REALLY THAT OBVIOUS TO EVERYONE?
NO! NO!! IT'S NOT TRUE!!
SWIP SWIP
DESPITE HER SUPERWOMAN FACADE, I THINK HINA'S THE OPEN BOOK IN OUR GROUP!!
TWITCH
THAT'S RIGHT!! THERE ARE SO MANY OTHER PEOPLE WHO LEAVE THEMSELVES EXPOSED!!
SO MANY...
!

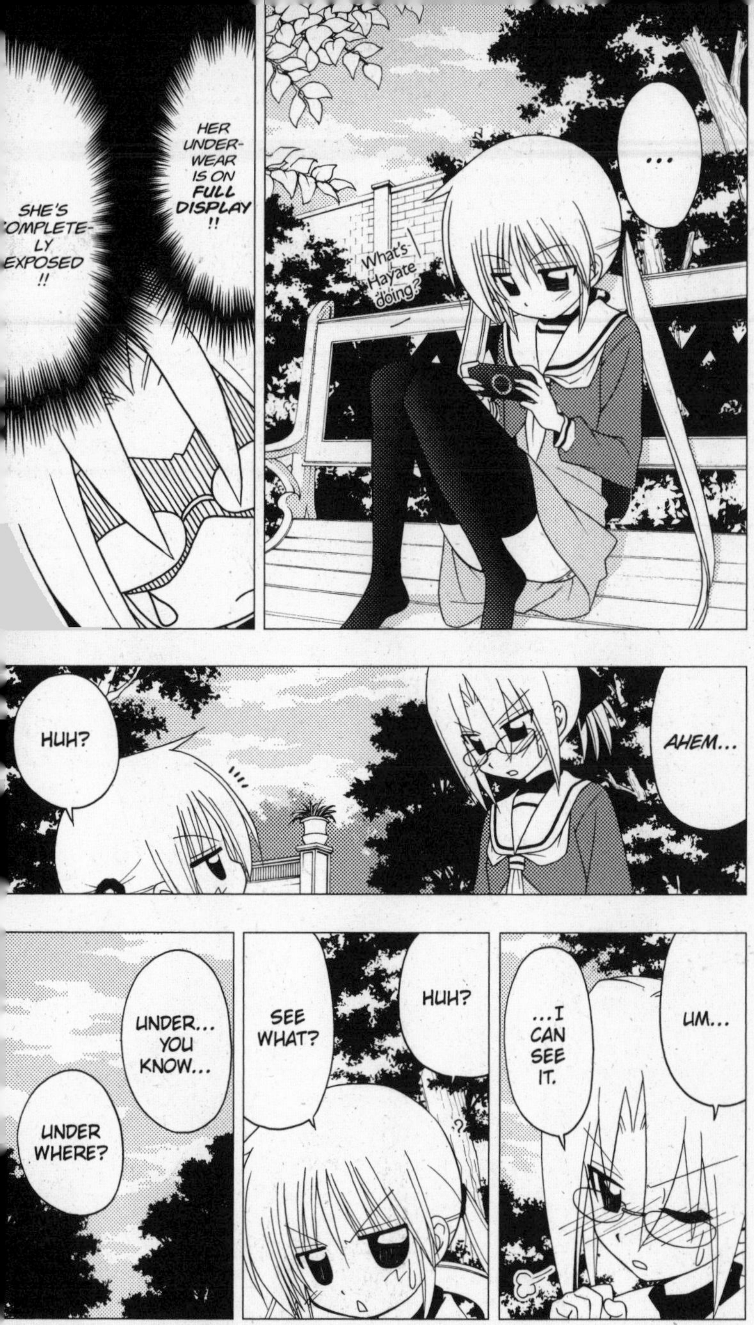
...
What's Hayate doing?
HER UNDERWEAR IS ON FULL DISPLAY!!
SHE'S OMPLETELY EXPOSED!!
AHEM...
HUH?
UM...
...I CAN SEE IT.
HUH?
SEE WHAT?
UNDER... YOU KNOW...
UNDER WHERE?

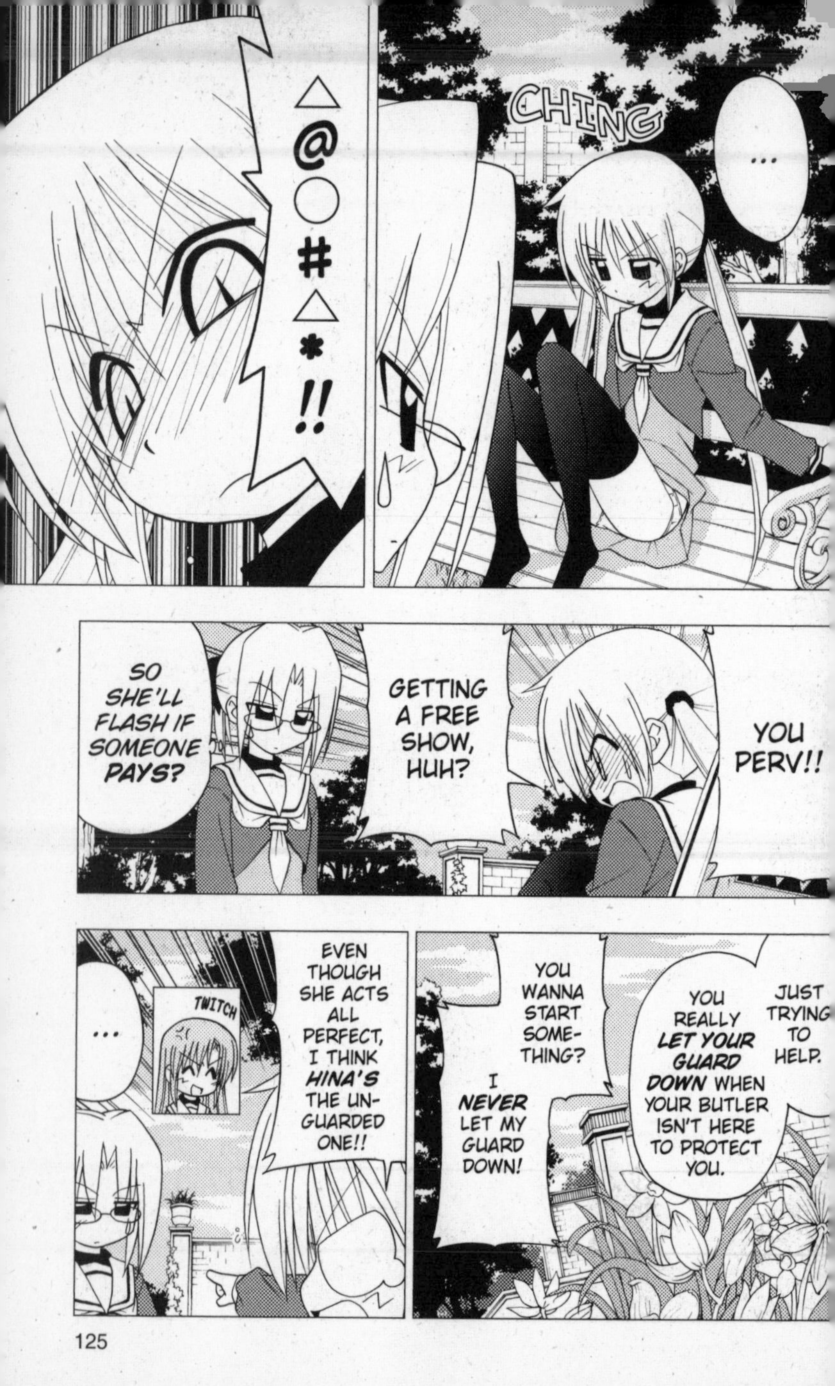

CHING
...
△@○#△*!!
YOU PERV!!
GETTING A FREE SHOW, HUH?
SO SHE'LL FLASH IF SOMEONE PAYS?
JUST TRYING TO HELP.
YOU REALLY LET YOUR GUARD DOWN WHEN YOUR BUTLER ISN'T HERE TO PROTECT YOU.
YOU WANNA START SOME-THING?
I NEVER LET MY GUARD DOWN!
EVEN THOUGH SHE ACTS ALL PERFECT, I THINK HINA'S THE UN-GUARDED ONE!!
TWITCH
...

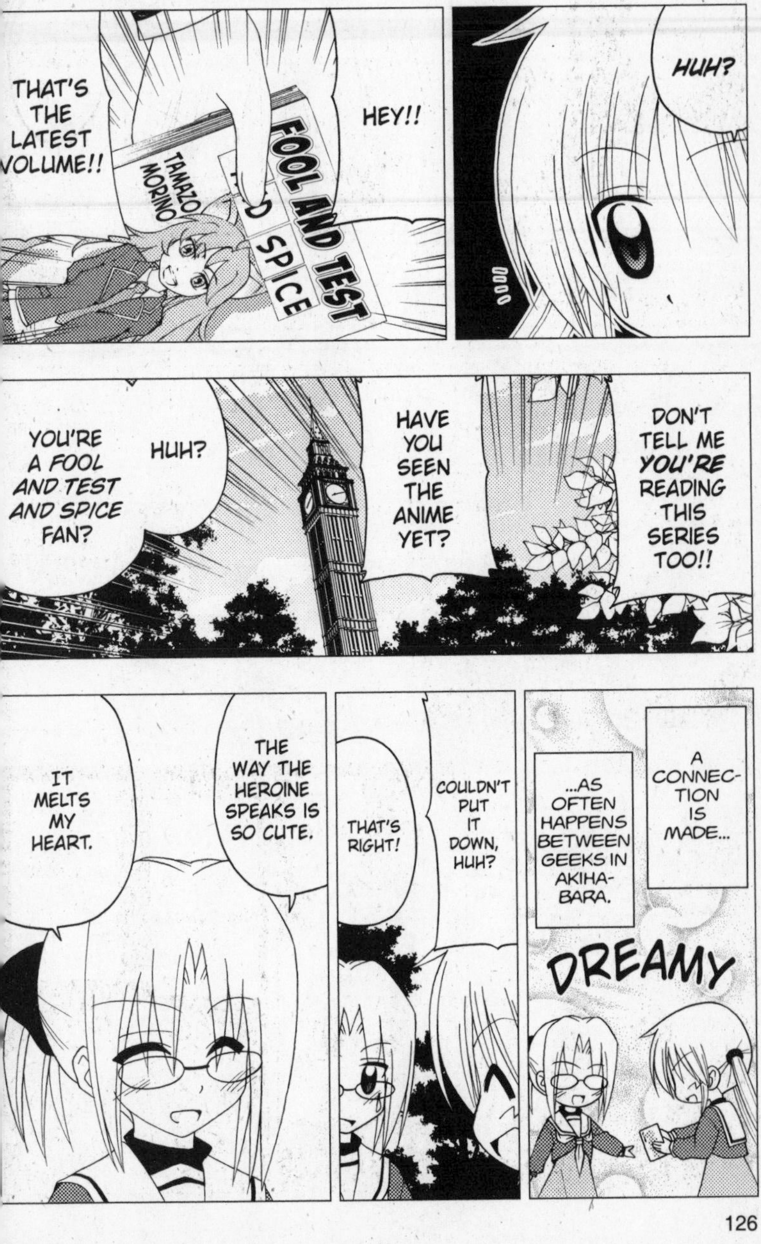
HUH?
HEY!!
FOOL AND TEST
D SPICE
TAMAZO MORINO
THAT'S THE LATEST VOLUME!!
DON'T TELL ME *YOU'RE* READING THIS SERIES TOO!!
HAVE YOU SEEN THE ANIME YET?
HUH?
YOU'RE A *FOOL AND TEST AND SPICE* FAN?
A CONNECTION IS MADE...
...AS OFTEN HAPPENS BETWEEN GEEKS IN AKIHABARA.
DREAMY
COULDN'T PUT IT DOWN, HUH?
THAT'S RIGHT!
THE WAY THE HEROINE SPEAKS IS SO CUTE.
IT MELTS MY HEART.

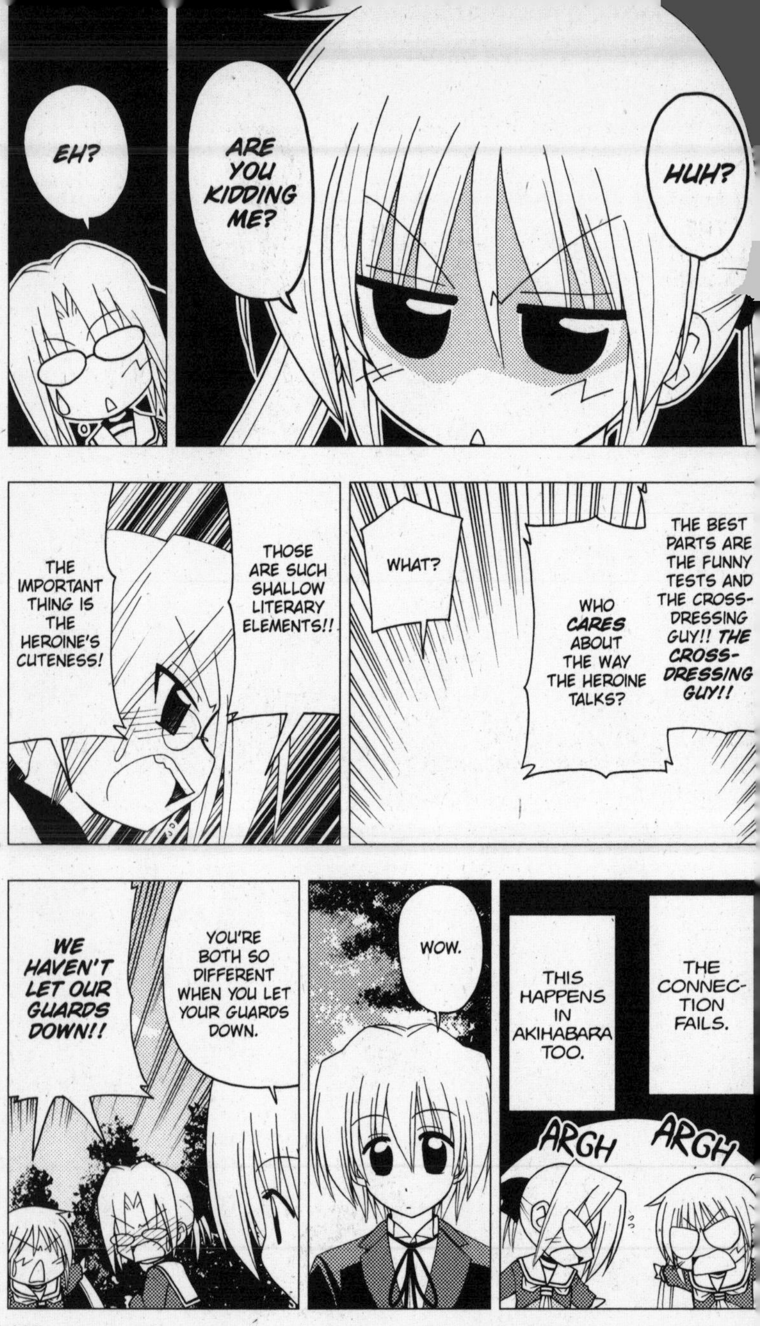
HUH?
ARE YOU KIDDING ME?
EH?
THE BEST PARTS ARE THE FUNNY TESTS AND THE CROSS-DRESSING GUY!! ***THE CROSS-DRESSING GUY!!***
WHO ***CARES*** ABOUT THE WAY THE HEROINE TALKS?
WHAT?
THOSE ARE SUCH SHALLOW LITERARY ELEMENTS!!
THE IMPORTANT THING IS THE HEROINE'S CUTENESS!
THE CONNECTION FAILS.
THIS HAPPENS IN AKIHABARA TOO.
ARGH
ARGH
WOW.
YOU'RE BOTH SO DIFFERENT WHEN YOU LET YOUR GUARDS DOWN.
WE HAVEN'T LET OUR GUARDS DOWN!!

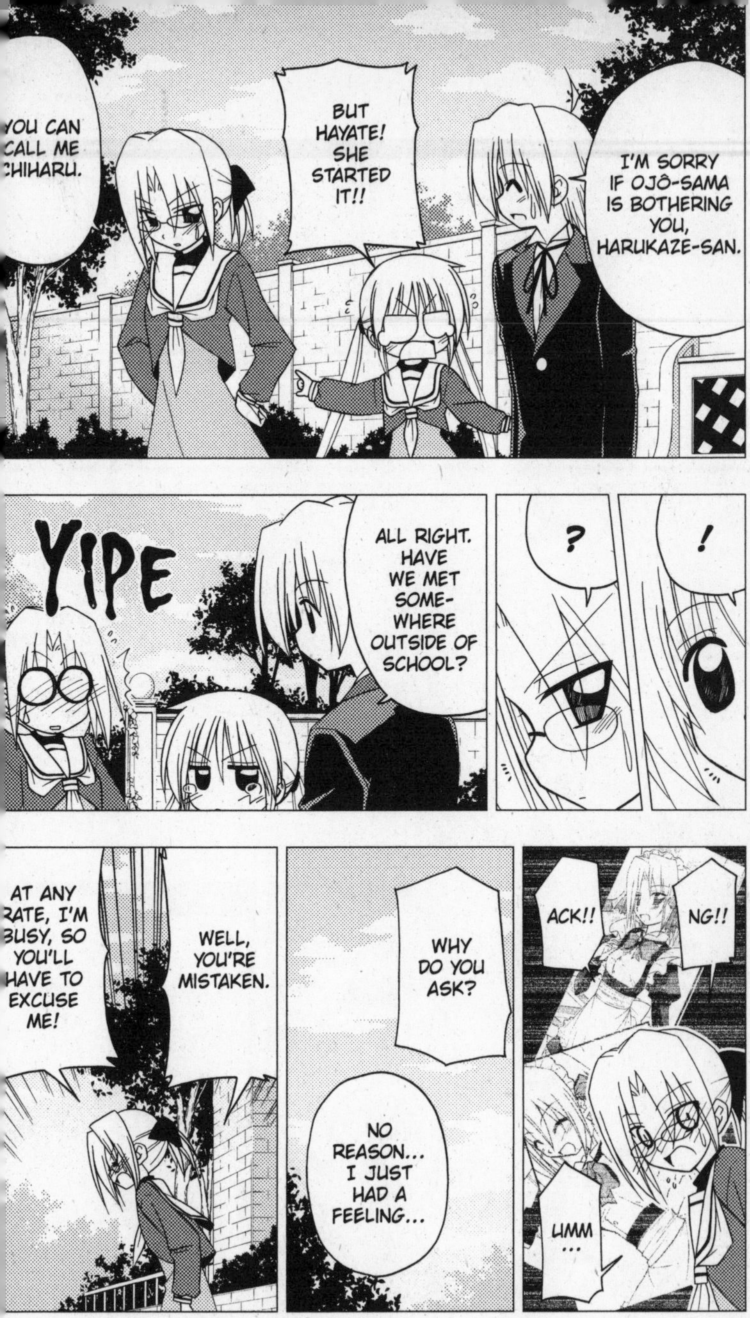
I'M SORRY IF OJÔ-SAMA IS BOTHERING YOU, HARUKAZE-SAN.
BUT HAYATE! SHE STARTED IT!!
YOU CAN CALL ME CHIHARU.
!
?
ALL RIGHT. HAVE WE MET SOME-WHERE OUTSIDE OF SCHOOL?
YIPE
NG!!
ACK!!
UMM...
WHY DO YOU ASK?
NO REASON... I JUST HAD A FEELING...
WELL, YOU'RE MISTAKEN.
AT ANY RATE, I'M BUSY, SO YOU'LL HAVE TO EXCUSE ME!

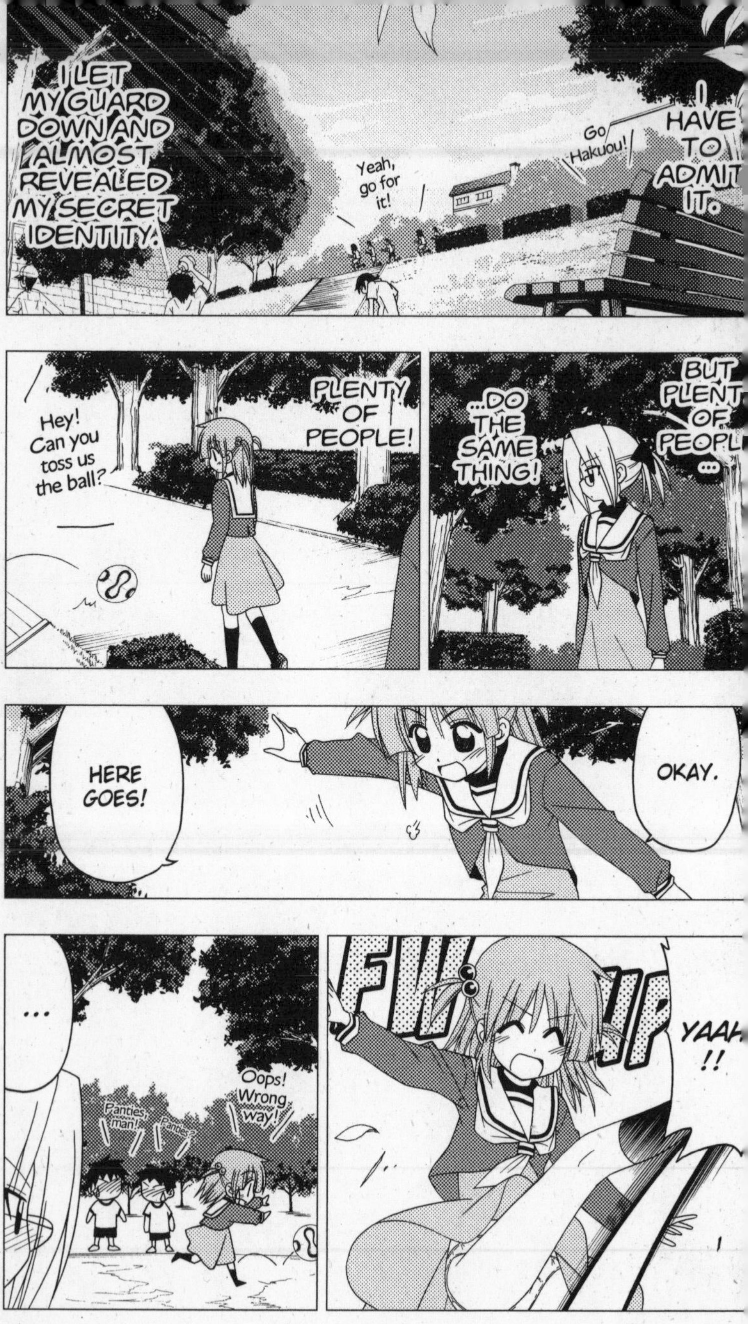
I HAVE TO ADMIT IT.
Go Hakuou!
Yeah, go for it!
I LET MY GUARD DOWN AND ALMOST REVEALED MY SECRET IDENTITY.
BUT PLENT OF PEOPL ...
...DO THE SAME THING!
PLENTY OF PEOPLE!
Hey! Can you toss us the ball?
OKAY.
HERE GOES!
YAAK !!
Oops! Wrong way!
Panties, man!
Panties
...

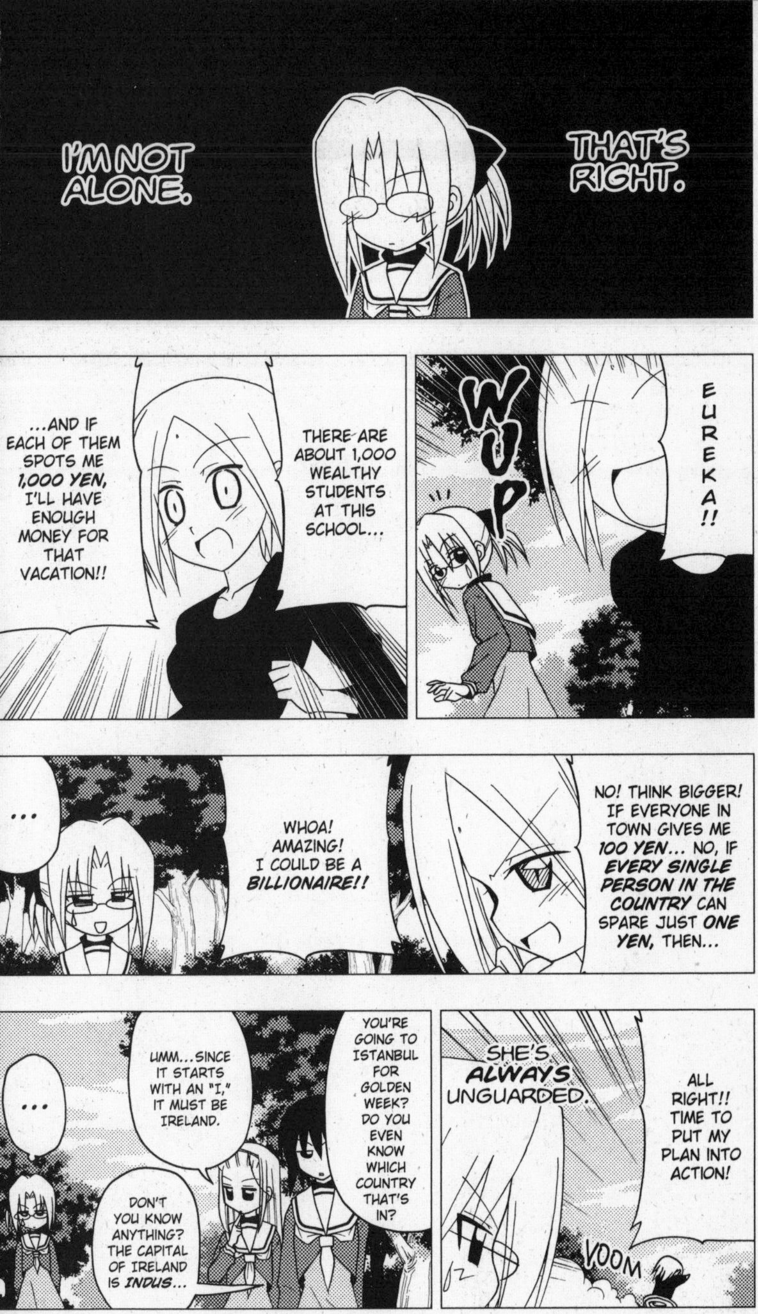
THAT'S RIGHT.
I'M NOT ALONE.
EUREKA!!
WUP
THERE ARE ABOUT 1,000 WEALTHY STUDENTS AT THIS SCHOOL...
...AND IF EACH OF THEM SPOTS ME 1,000 YEN, I'LL HAVE ENOUGH MONEY FOR THAT VACATION!!
NO! THINK BIGGER! IF EVERYONE IN TOWN GIVES ME 100 YEN... NO, IF EVERY SINGLE PERSON IN THE COUNTRY CAN SPARE JUST ONE YEN, THEN...
WHOA! AMAZING! I COULD BE A BILLIONAIRE!!
...
ALL RIGHT!! TIME TO PUT MY PLAN INTO ACTION!
SHE'S ALWAYS UNGUARDED.
VOOM
YOU'RE GOING TO ISTANBUL FOR GOLDEN WEEK? DO YOU EVEN KNOW WHICH COUNTRY THAT'S IN?
UMM...SINCE IT STARTS WITH AN "I," IT MUST BE IRELAND.
DON'T YOU KNOW ANYTHING? THE CAPITAL OF IRELAND IS INDUS...
...

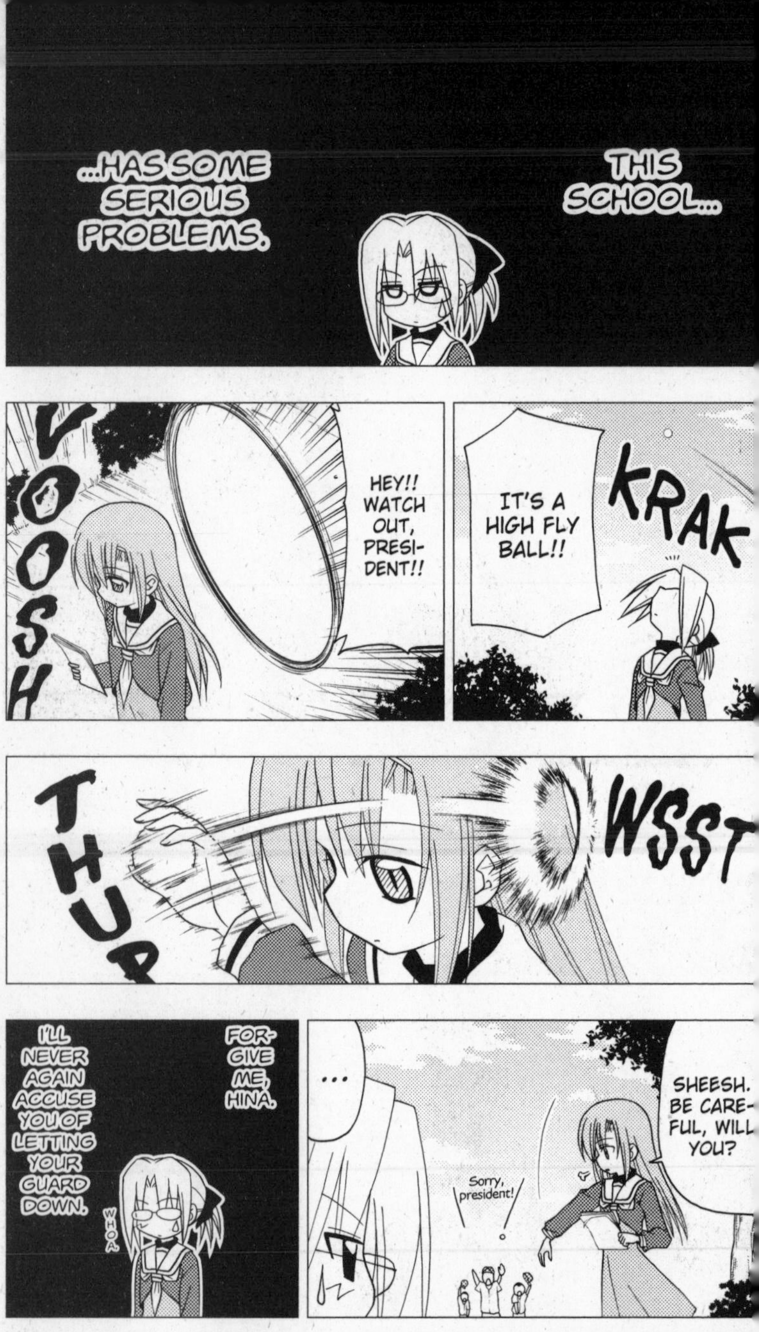
THIS SCHOOL...
...HAS SOME SERIOUS PROBLEMS.
KRAK
IT'S A HIGH FLY BALL!!
HEY!! WATCH OUT, PRESI-DENT!!
VOOSH
WSST
THUP
SHEESH. BE CARE-FUL, WILL YOU?
Sorry, president!
...
FOR-GIVE ME, HINA.
I'LL NEVER AGAIN ACCUSE YOU OF LETTING YOUR GUARD DOWN.
WHOA.

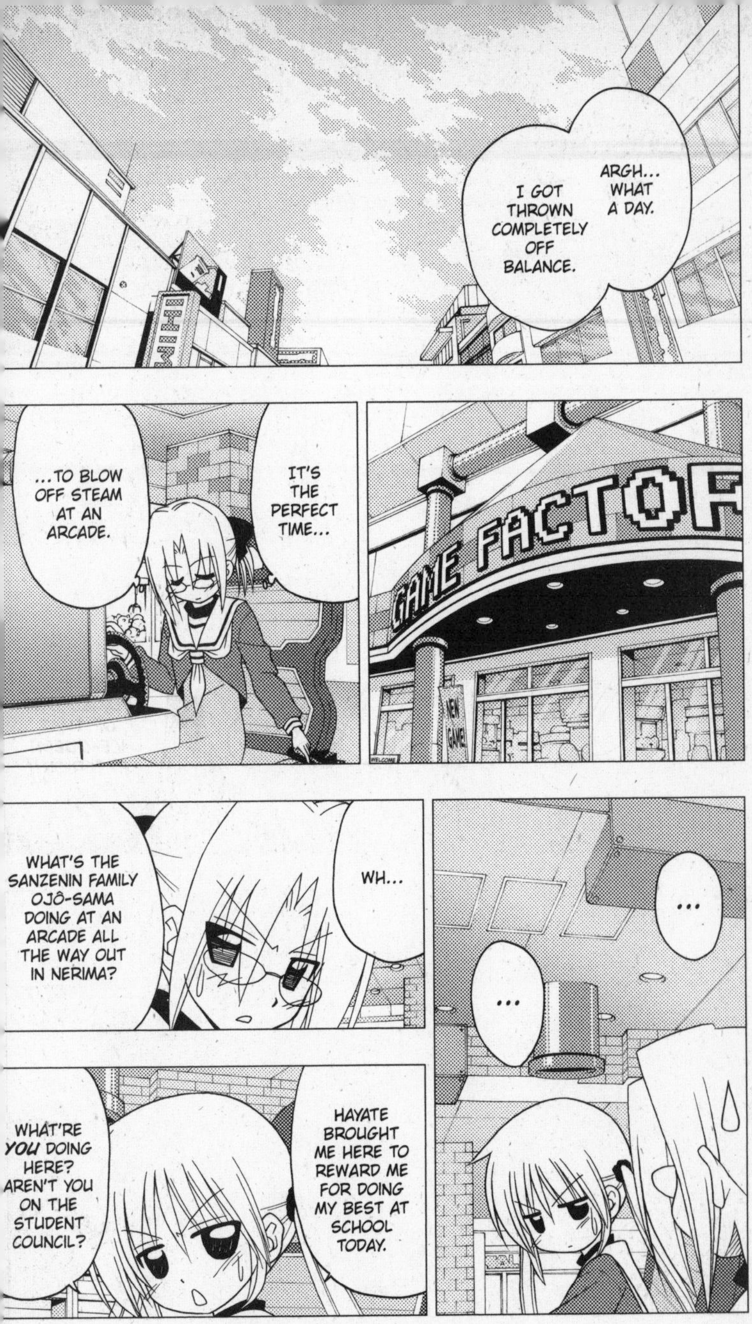
ARGH... WHAT A DAY.
I GOT THROWN COMPLETELY OFF BALANCE.
GAME FACTOR
NEW GAME!
WELCOME
IT'S THE PERFECT TIME...
...TO BLOW OFF STEAM AT AN ARCADE.
...
...
WH...
WHAT'S THE SANZENIN FAMILY OJÔ-SAMA DOING AT AN ARCADE ALL THE WAY OUT IN NERIMA?
HAYATE BROUGHT ME HERE TO REWARD ME FOR DOING MY BEST AT SCHOOL TODAY.
WHAT'RE *YOU* DOING HERE? AREN'T YOU ON THE STUDENT COUNCIL?

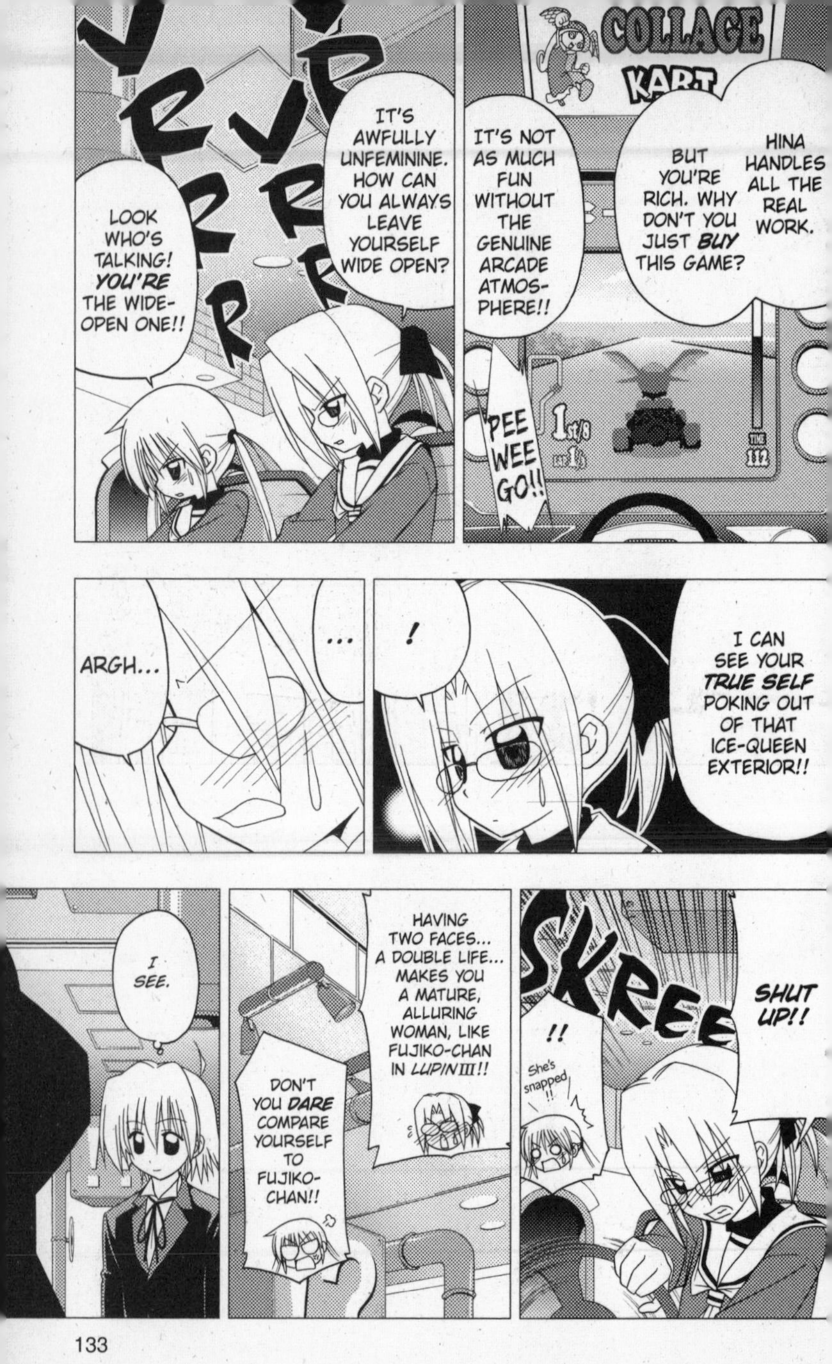
COLLAGE KART
HINA HANDLES ALL THE REAL WORK.
BUT YOU'RE RICH. WHY DON'T YOU JUST *BUY* THIS GAME?
IT'S NOT AS MUCH FUN WITHOUT THE GENUINE ARCADE ATMOSPHERE!!
PEE WEE GO!!
1st/8
TIME 112
IT'S AWFULLY UNFEMININE. HOW CAN YOU ALWAYS LEAVE YOURSELF WIDE OPEN?
LOOK WHO'S TALKING! *YOU'RE* THE WIDE-OPEN ONE!!
I CAN SEE YOUR *TRUE SELF* POKING OUT OF THAT ICE-QUEEN EXTERIOR!!
!
...
ARGH...
SKREE
SHUT UP!!
!!
She's snapped!!
HAVING TWO FACES... A DOUBLE LIFE... MAKES YOU A MATURE, ALLURING WOMAN, LIKE FUJIKO-CHAN IN *LUPIN III*!!
DON'T YOU *DARE* COMPARE YOURSELF TO FUJIKO-CHAN!!
I SEE.

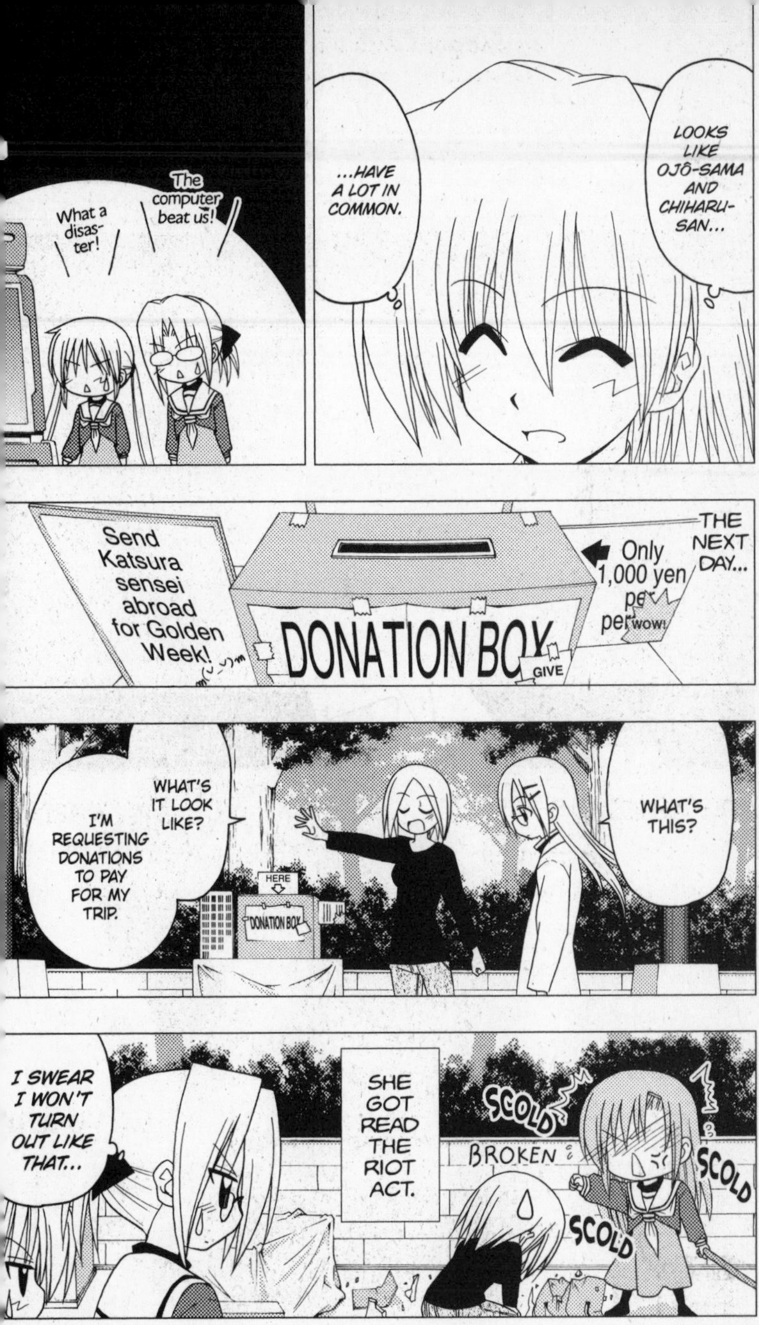
LOOKS LIKE OJÔ-SAMA AND CHIHARU-SAN...
...HAVE A LOT IN COMMON.
The computer beat us!
What a disaster!
THE NEXT DAY...
Only 1,000 yen pe per
WOW!
Send Katsura sensei abroad for Golden Week!
DONATION BOX
GIVE
WHAT'S THIS?
WHAT'S IT LOOK LIKE? I'M REQUESTING DONATIONS TO PAY FOR MY TRIP.
HERE
DONATION BOX
SCOLD
SCOLD
SCOLD
BROKEN
SHE GOT READ THE RIOT ACT.
I SWEAR I WON'T TURN OUT LIKE THAT...

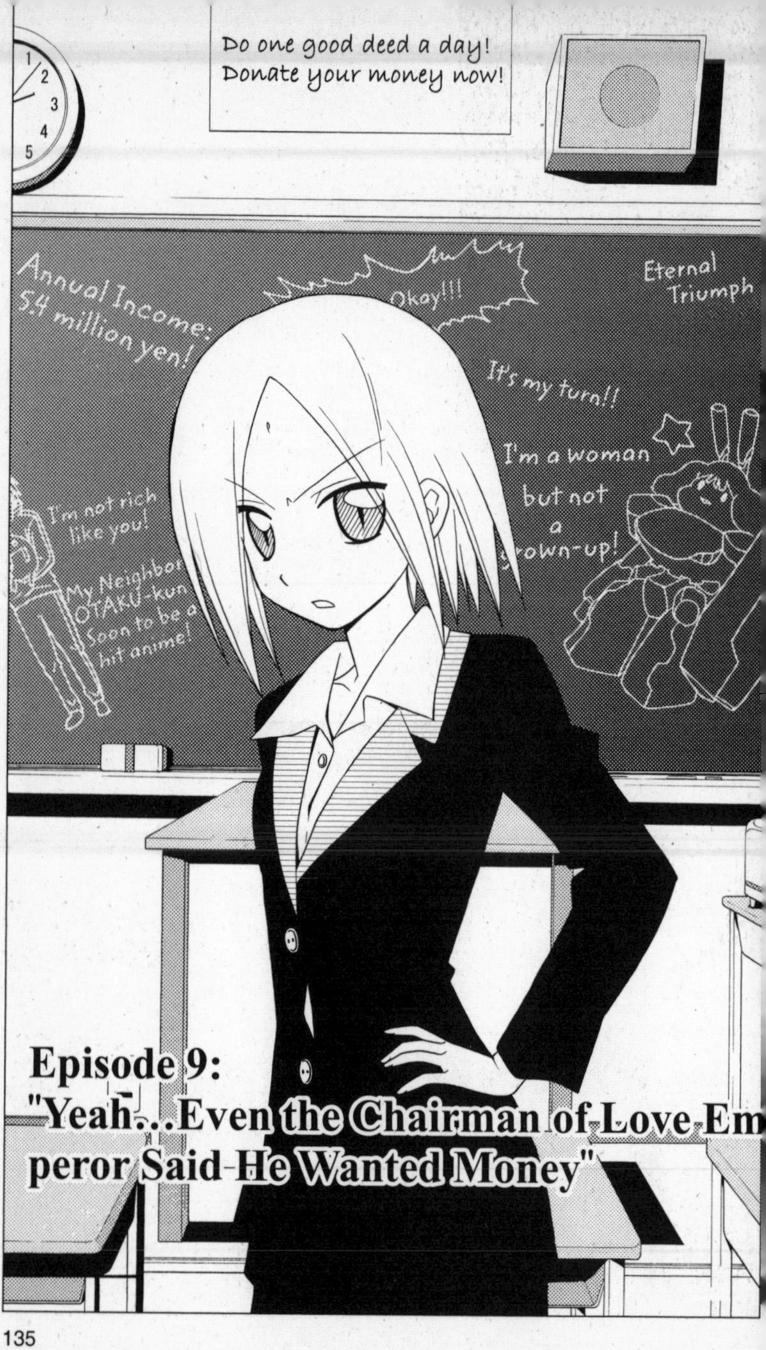
Do one good deed a day!
Donate your money now!
Eternal Triumph
Okay!!!
Annual Income: 5.4 million yen!
It's my turn!!
I'm a woman but not a grown-up!
I'm not rich like you!
My Neighbor OTAKU-kun Soon to be a hit anime!

Episode 9: "Yeah...Even the Chairman of Love Emperor Said He Wanted Money"

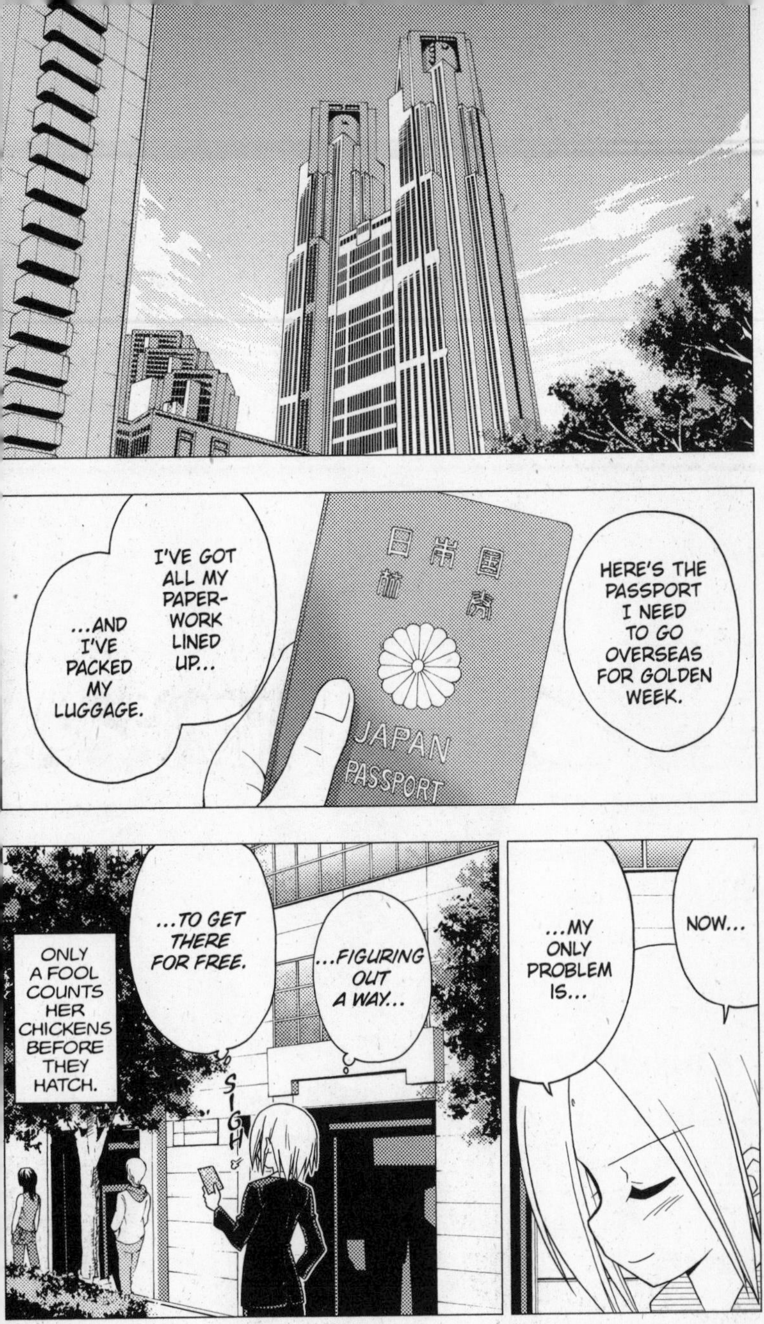
HERE'S THE PASSPORT I NEED TO GO OVERSEAS FOR GOLDEN WEEK.
JAPAN PASSPORT
I'VE GOT ALL MY PAPER-WORK LINED UP...
...AND I'VE PACKED MY LUGGAGE.
NOW...
...MY ONLY PROBLEM IS...
...FIGURING OUT A WAY...
...TO GET THERE FOR FREE.
SIGH
ONLY A FOOL COUNTS HER CHICKENS BEFORE THEY HATCH.

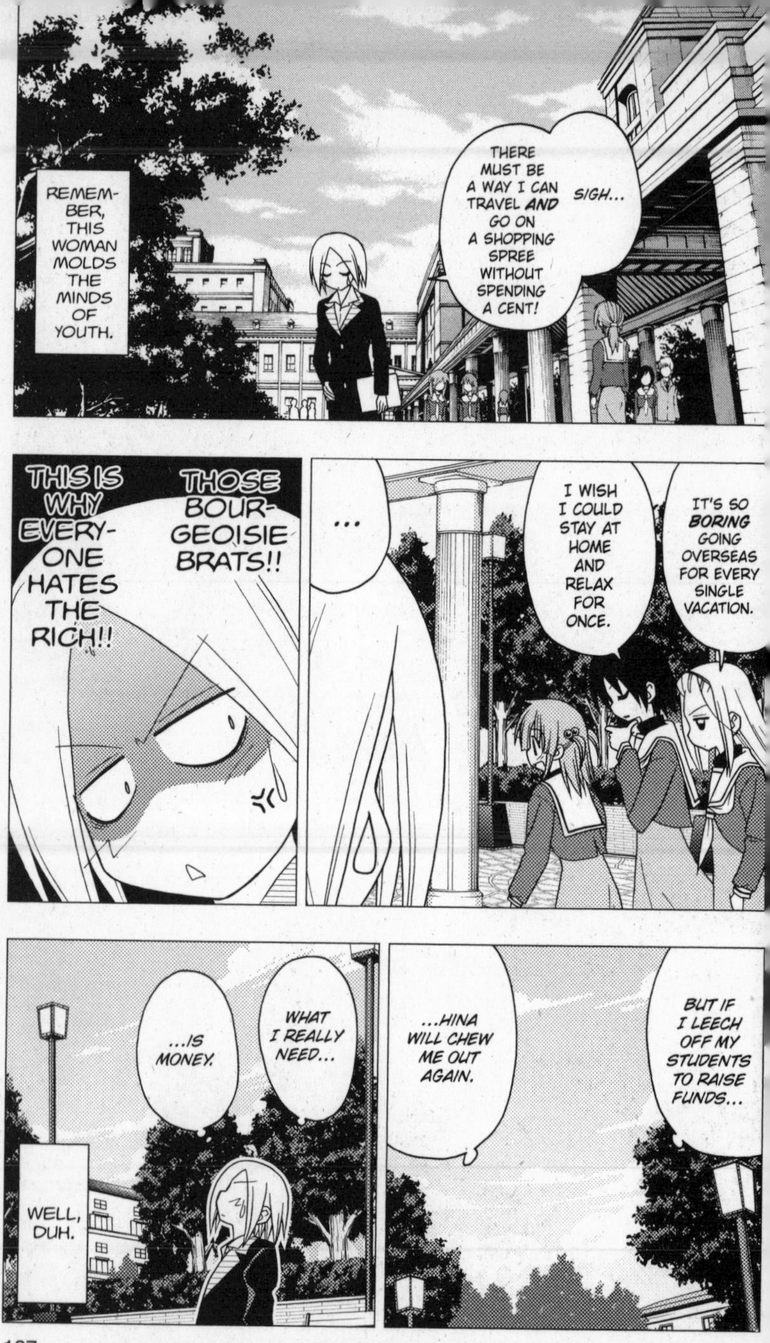
SIGH...
THERE MUST BE A WAY I CAN TRAVEL AND GO ON A SHOPPING SPREE WITHOUT SPENDING A CENT!
REMEMBER, THIS WOMAN MOLDS THE MINDS OF YOUTH.
IT'S SO BORING GOING OVERSEAS FOR EVERY SINGLE VACATION.
I WISH I COULD STAY AT HOME AND RELAX FOR ONCE.
...
THOSE BOURGEOISIE BRATS!!
THIS IS WHY EVERYONE HATES THE RICH!!
BUT IF I LEECH OFF MY STUDENTS TO RAISE FUNDS...
...HINA WILL CHEW ME OUT AGAIN.
WHAT I REALLY NEED...
...IS MONEY.
WELL, DUH.

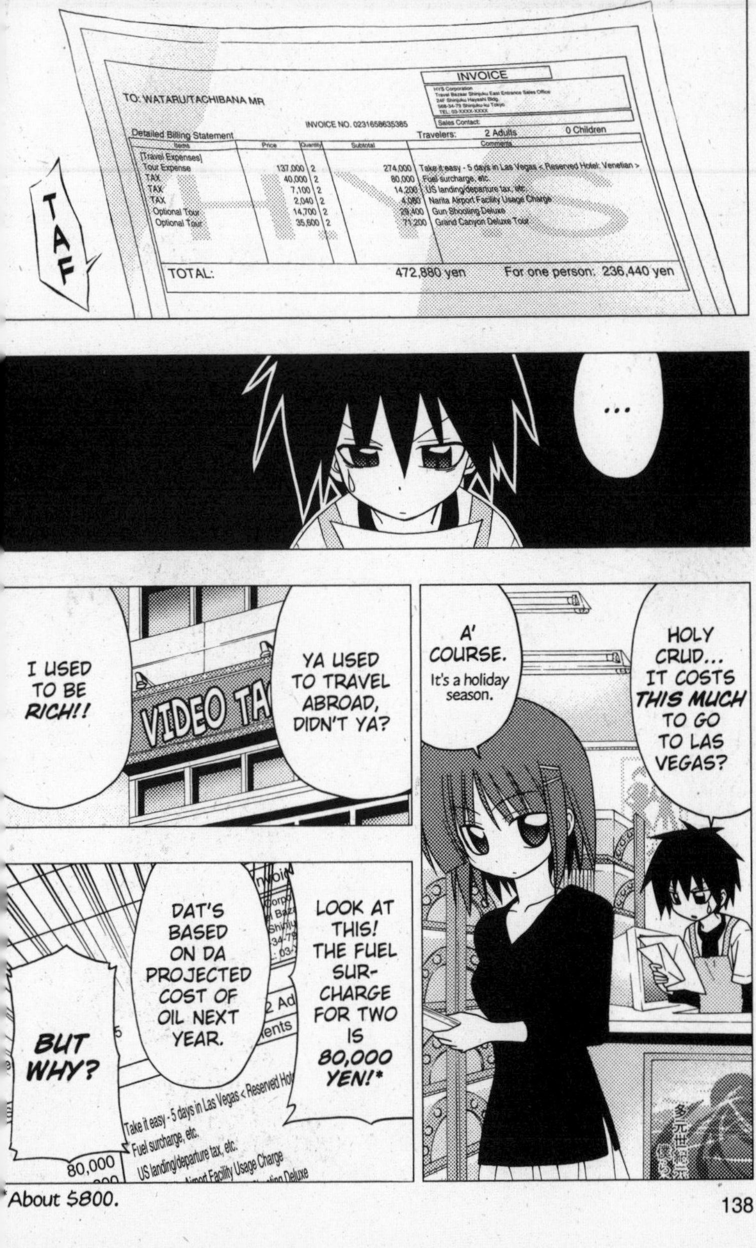
INVOICE
HYS Corporation
Travel Bazaar Shinjuku East Entrance Sales Office
24F Shinjuku Hayashi Bldg.
Shinjuku-ku Tokyo
Sales Contact:
TO: WATARU/TACHIBANA MR
INVOICE NO. 0231658635385
Detailed Billing Statement
Travelers: 2 Adults 0 Children
Items Price Quantity Subtotal Comments
[Travel Expenses]
Tour Expense 137,000 2 274,000 Take it easy - 5 days in Las Vegas < Reserved Hotel: Venetian >
TAX 40,000 2 80,000 Fuel surcharge, etc.
TAX 7,100 2 14,200 US landing/departure tax, etc.
TAX 2,040 2 4,080 Narita Airport Facility Usage Charge
Optional Tour 14,700 2 29,400 Gun Shooting Deluxe
Optional Tour 35,600 2 71,200 Grand Canyon Deluxe Tour
TOTAL: 472,880 yen For one person: 236,440 yen
TAF
...
HOLY CRUD... IT COSTS THIS MUCH TO GO TO LAS VEGAS?
A' COURSE. It's a holiday season.
YA USED TO TRAVEL ABROAD, DIDN'T YA?
I USED TO BE RICH!!
VIDEO TA
LOOK AT THIS! THE FUEL SUR-CHARGE FOR TWO IS 80,000 YEN!*
DAT'S BASED ON DA PROJECTED COST OF OIL NEXT YEAR.
BUT WHY?
Take it easy - 5 days in Las Vegas < Reserved Hot
Fuel surcharge, etc.
US landing/departure tax, etc.
80,000

*About $800.

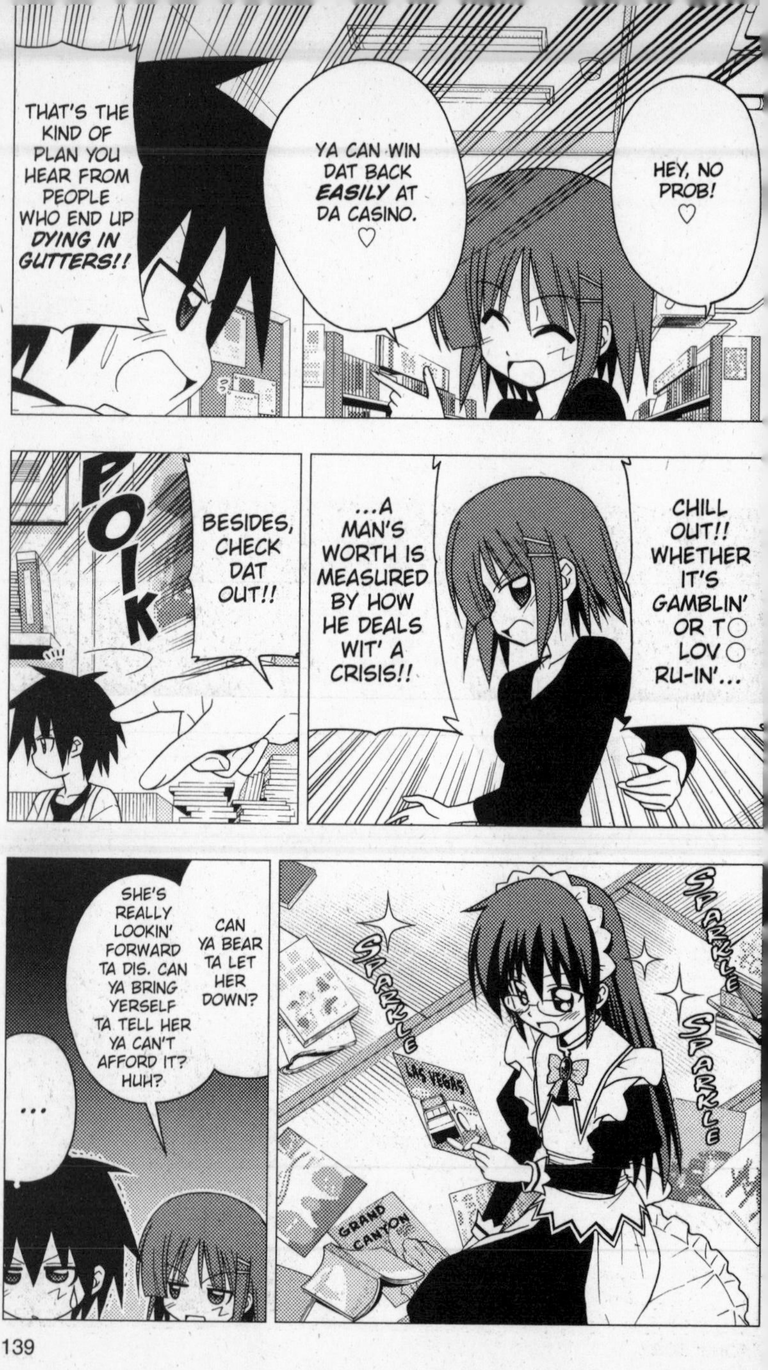
HEY, NO PROB! ♡
YA CAN WIN DAT BACK EASILY AT DA CASINO. ♡
THAT'S THE KIND OF PLAN YOU HEAR FROM PEOPLE WHO END UP DYING IN GUTTERS!!
CHILL OUT!! WHETHER IT'S GAMBLIN' OR T○ LOV○ RU-IN'...
...A MAN'S WORTH IS MEASURED BY HOW HE DEALS WIT' A CRISIS!!
BESIDES, CHECK DAT OUT!!
POIK
SPARKLE
SPARKLE
SPARKLE
LAS VEGAS
GRAND CANYON
CAN YA BEAR TA LET HER DOWN?
SHE'S REALLY LOOKIN' FORWARD TA DIS. CAN YA BRING YERSELF TA TELL HER YA CAN'T AFFORD IT? HUH?
...

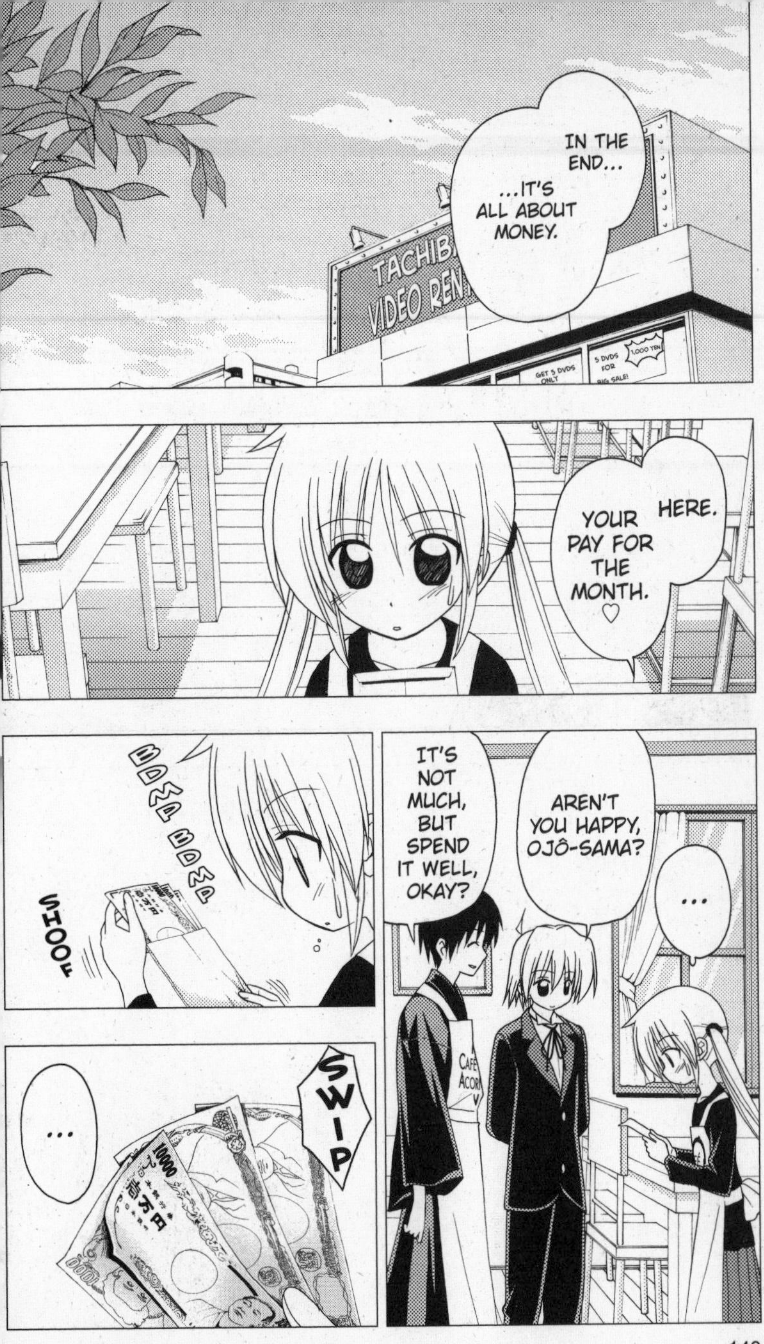
IN THE END...
...IT'S ALL ABOUT MONEY.
5 DVDS FOR
1,000 YEN
BIG SALE!
HERE.
YOUR PAY FOR THE MONTH. ♡
AREN'T YOU HAPPY, OJÔ-SAMA?
IT'S NOT MUCH, BUT SPEND IT WELL, OKAY?
...
BDMP BDMP
SHOOF
SWIP
...

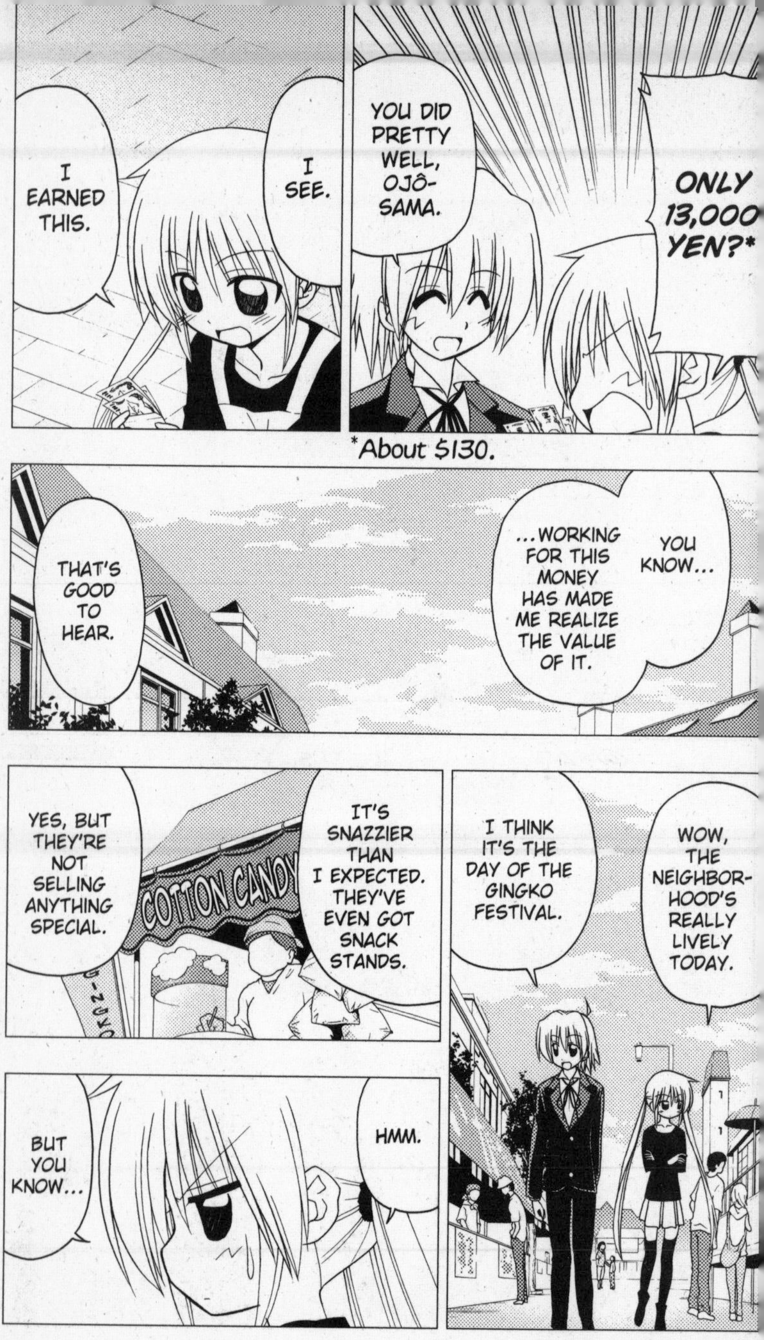
ONLY 13,000 YEN?*
YOU DID PRETTY WELL, OJÔ-SAMA.
I SEE.
I EARNED THIS.
YOU KNOW...
...WORKING FOR THIS MONEY HAS MADE ME REALIZE THE VALUE OF IT.
THAT'S GOOD TO HEAR.
WOW, THE NEIGHBOR-HOOD'S REALLY LIVELY TODAY.
I THINK IT'S THE DAY OF THE GINGKO FESTIVAL.
IT'S SNAZZIER THAN I EXPECTED. THEY'VE EVEN GOT SNACK STANDS.
COTTON CANDY
YES, BUT THEY'RE NOT SELLING ANYTHING SPECIAL.
HMM.
BUT YOU KNOW...

*About $130.

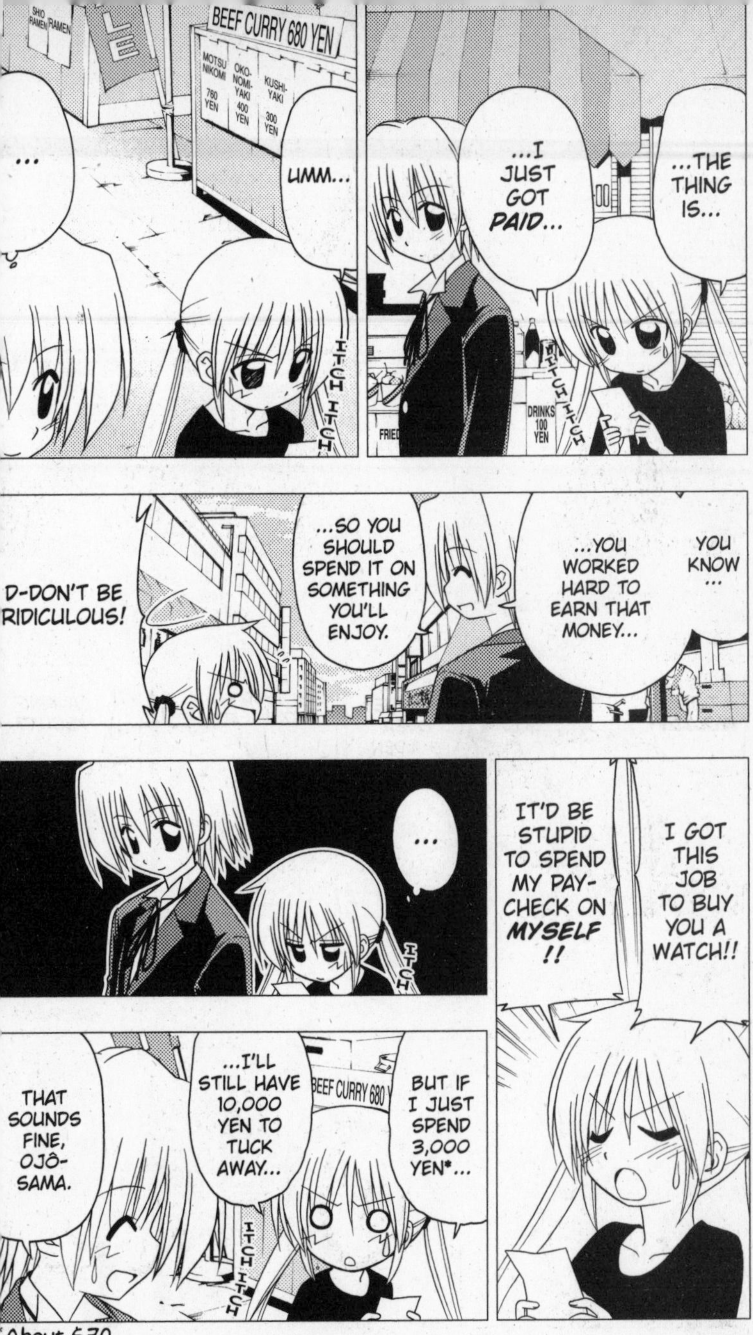
...THE THING IS...
...I JUST GOT PAID...
ITCH ITCH
DRINKS 100 YEN
FRIED
BEEF CURRY 680 YEN
MOTSU NIKOMI 760 YEN
OKO-NOMI-YAKI 400 YEN
KUSHI-YAKI 300 YEN
SHIO RAMEN
RAMEN
UMM...
ITCH ITCH
...
YOU KNOW...
...YOU WORKED HARD TO EARN THAT MONEY...
...SO YOU SHOULD SPEND IT ON SOMETHING YOU'LL ENJOY.
D-DON'T BE RIDICULOUS!
I GOT THIS JOB TO BUY YOU A WATCH!!
IT'D BE STUPID TO SPEND MY PAY-CHECK ON MYSELF!!
...
ITCH
BUT IF I JUST SPEND 3,000 YEN*...
...I'LL STILL HAVE 10,000 YEN TO TUCK AWAY...
BEEF CURRY 680
THAT SOUNDS FINE, OJÔ-SAMA.
ITCH ITCH

*About $30.

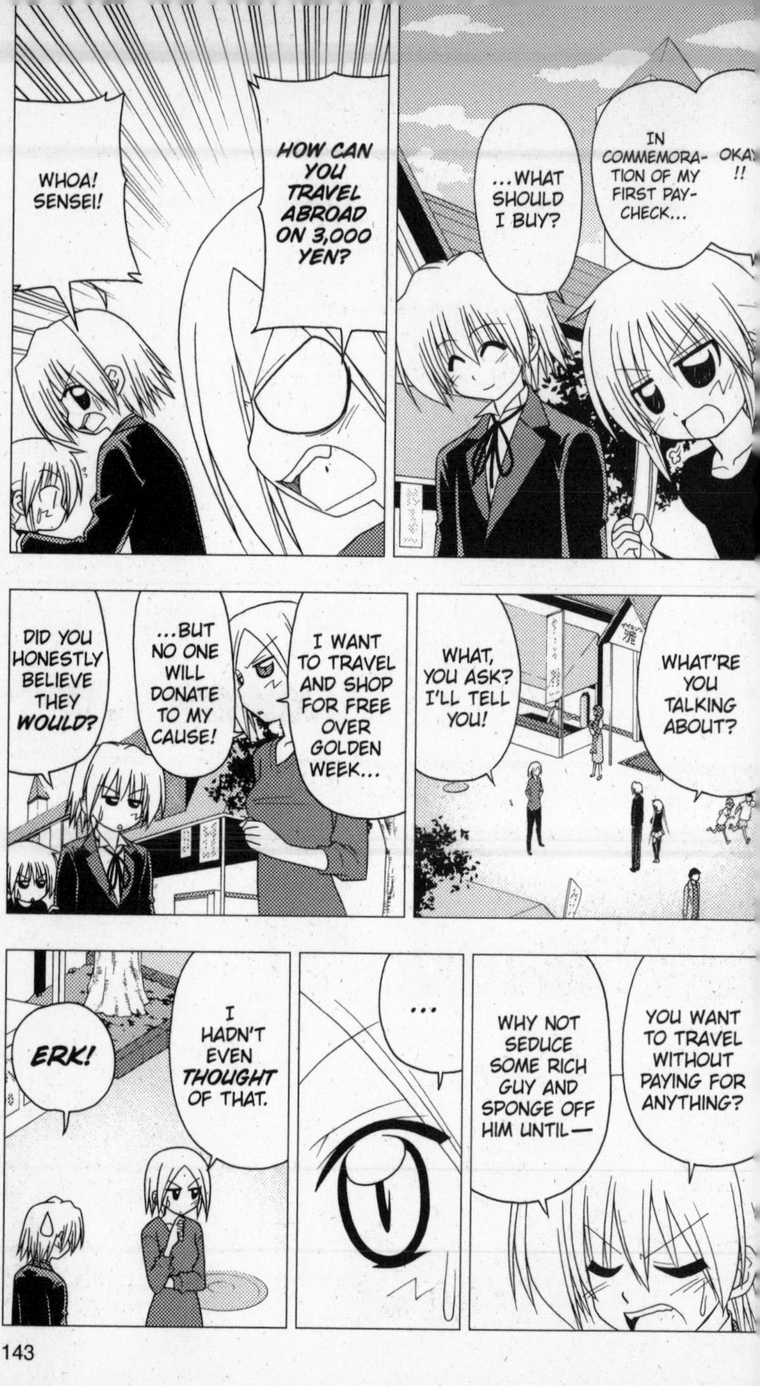
IN COMMEMORATION OF MY FIRST PAYCHECK... OKAY !!
...WHAT SHOULD I BUY?
HOW CAN YOU TRAVEL ABROAD ON 3,000 YEN?
WHOA! SENSEI!
WHAT'RE YOU TALKING ABOUT?
WHAT, YOU ASK? I'LL TELL YOU!
I WANT TO TRAVEL AND SHOP FOR FREE OVER GOLDEN WEEK...
...BUT NO ONE WILL DONATE TO MY CAUSE!
DID YOU HONESTLY BELIEVE THEY WOULD?
YOU WANT TO TRAVEL WITHOUT PAYING FOR ANYTHING?
WHY NOT SEDUCE SOME RICH GUY AND SPONGE OFF HIM UNTIL—
...
I HADN'T EVEN THOUGHT OF THAT.
ERK!

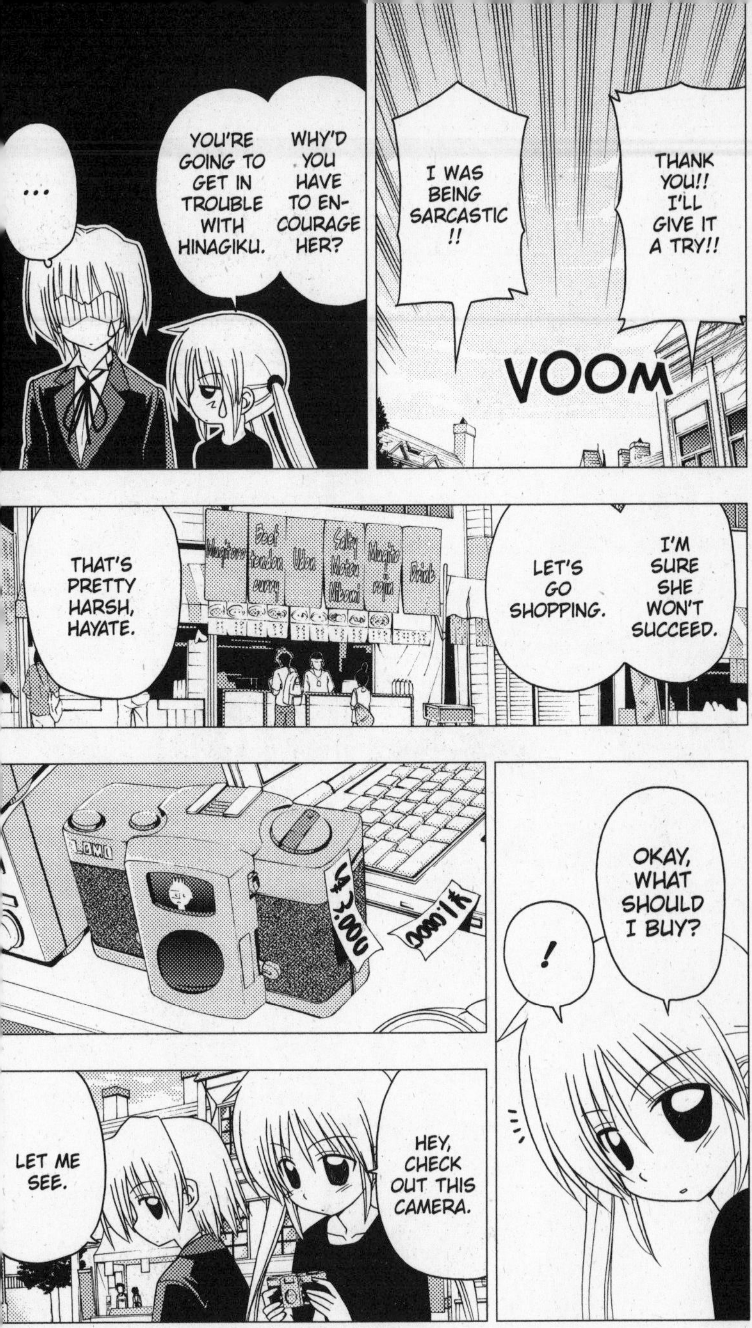
THANK YOU!! I'LL GIVE IT A TRY!!
I WAS BEING SARCASTIC!!
VOOM
WHY'D YOU HAVE TO EN-COURAGE HER?
YOU'RE GOING TO GET IN TROUBLE WITH HINAGIKU.
...
I'M SURE SHE WON'T SUCCEED.
LET'S GO SHOPPING.
Drink
Udon
Beef tendon curry
THAT'S PRETTY HARSH, HAYATE.
OKAY, WHAT SHOULD I BUY?
!
HEY, CHECK OUT THIS CAMERA.
LET ME SEE.

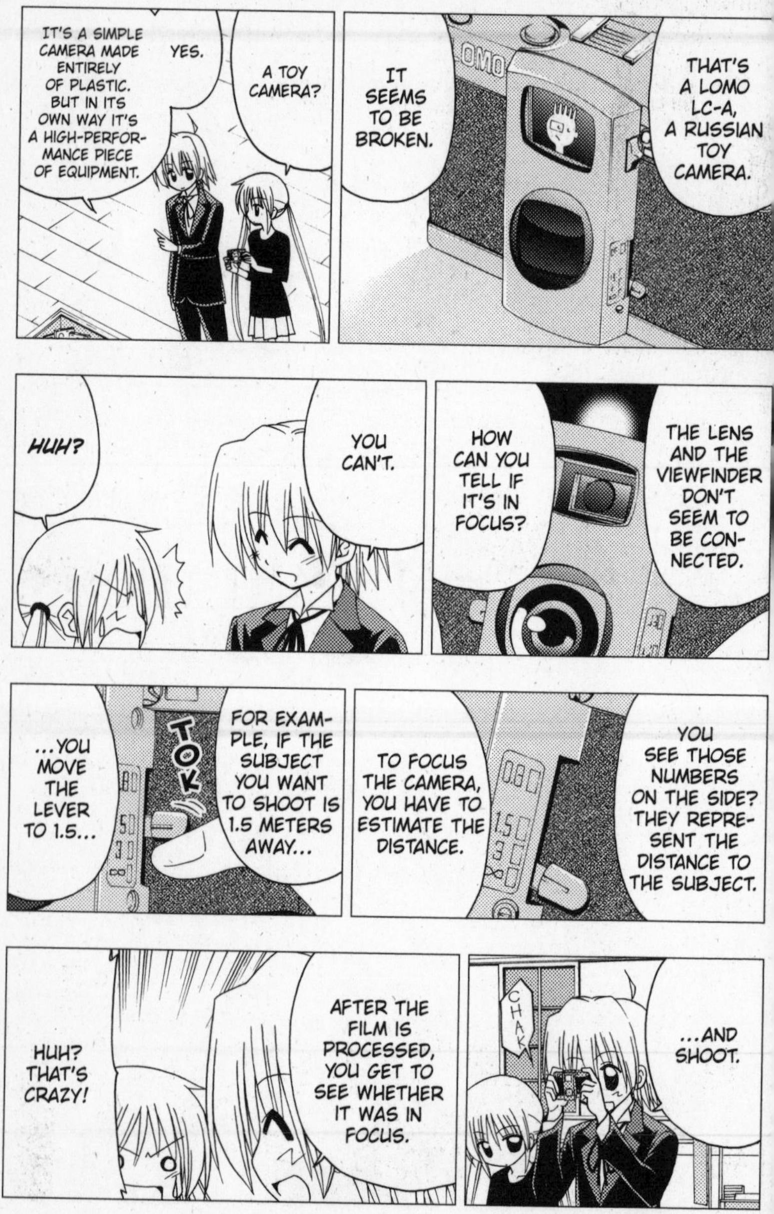
THAT'S A LOMO LC-A, A RUSSIAN TOY CAMERA.
IT SEEMS TO BE BROKEN.
A TOY CAMERA?
YES.
IT'S A SIMPLE CAMERA MADE ENTIRELY OF PLASTIC. BUT IN ITS OWN WAY IT'S A HIGH-PERFORMANCE PIECE OF EQUIPMENT.
THE LENS AND THE VIEWFINDER DON'T SEEM TO BE CONNECTED.
HOW CAN YOU TELL IF IT'S IN FOCUS?
YOU CAN'T.
HUH?
YOU SEE THOSE NUMBERS ON THE SIDE? THEY REPRESENT THE DISTANCE TO THE SUBJECT.
TO FOCUS THE CAMERA, YOU HAVE TO ESTIMATE THE DISTANCE.
FOR EXAMPLE, IF THE SUBJECT YOU WANT TO SHOOT IS 1.5 METERS AWAY...
TOK
...YOU MOVE THE LEVER TO 1.5...
...AND SHOOT.
CHAK
AFTER THE FILM IS PROCESSED, YOU GET TO SEE WHETHER IT WAS IN FOCUS.
HUH? THAT'S CRAZY!

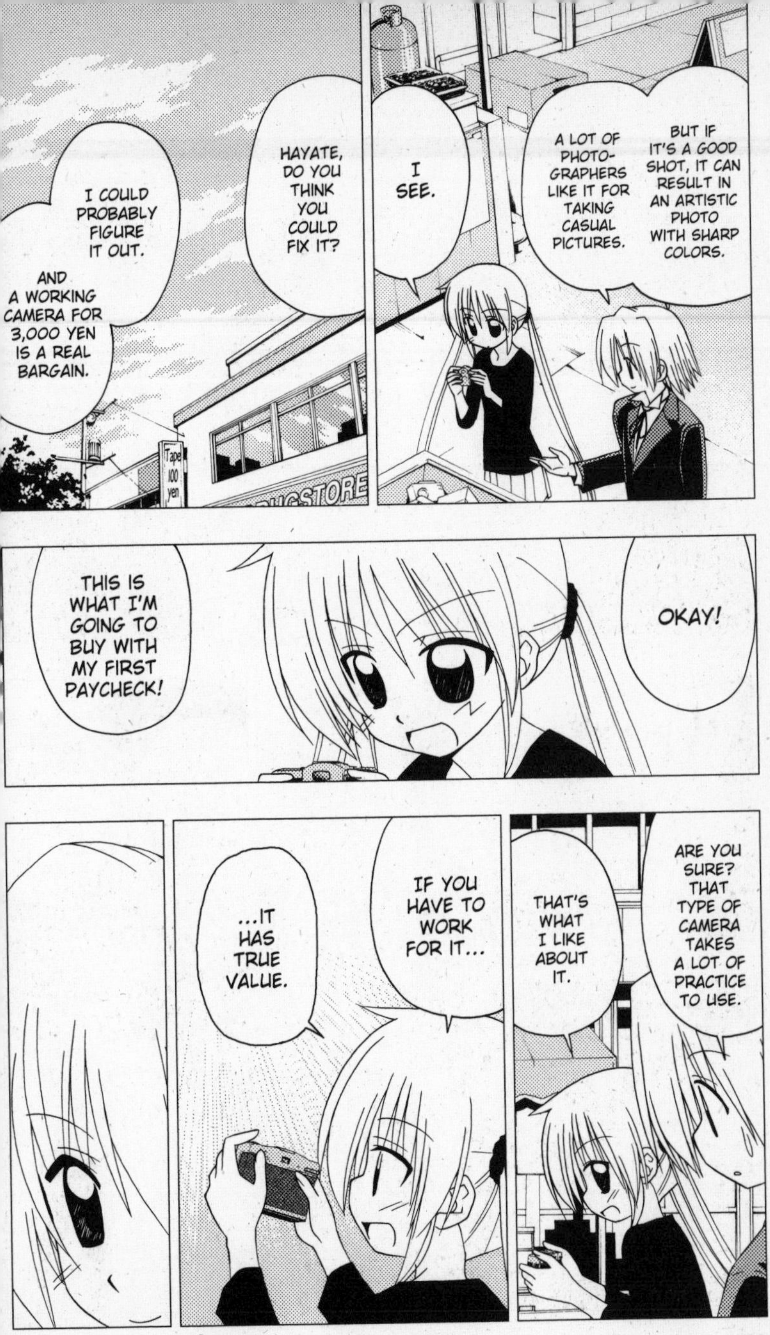

A LOT OF PHOTOGRAPHERS LIKE IT FOR TAKING CASUAL PICTURES.
BUT IF IT'S A GOOD SHOT, IT CAN RESULT IN AN ARTISTIC PHOTO WITH SHARP COLORS.
I SEE.
HAYATE, DO YOU THINK YOU COULD FIX IT?
I COULD PROBABLY FIGURE IT OUT.
AND A WORKING CAMERA FOR 3,000 YEN IS A REAL BARGAIN.
Tape 100 yen
OKAY!
THIS IS WHAT I'M GOING TO BUY WITH MY FIRST PAYCHECK!
ARE YOU SURE? THAT TYPE OF CAMERA TAKES A LOT OF PRACTICE TO USE.
THAT'S WHAT I LIKE ABOUT IT.
IF YOU HAVE TO WORK FOR IT...
...IT HAS TRUE VALUE.

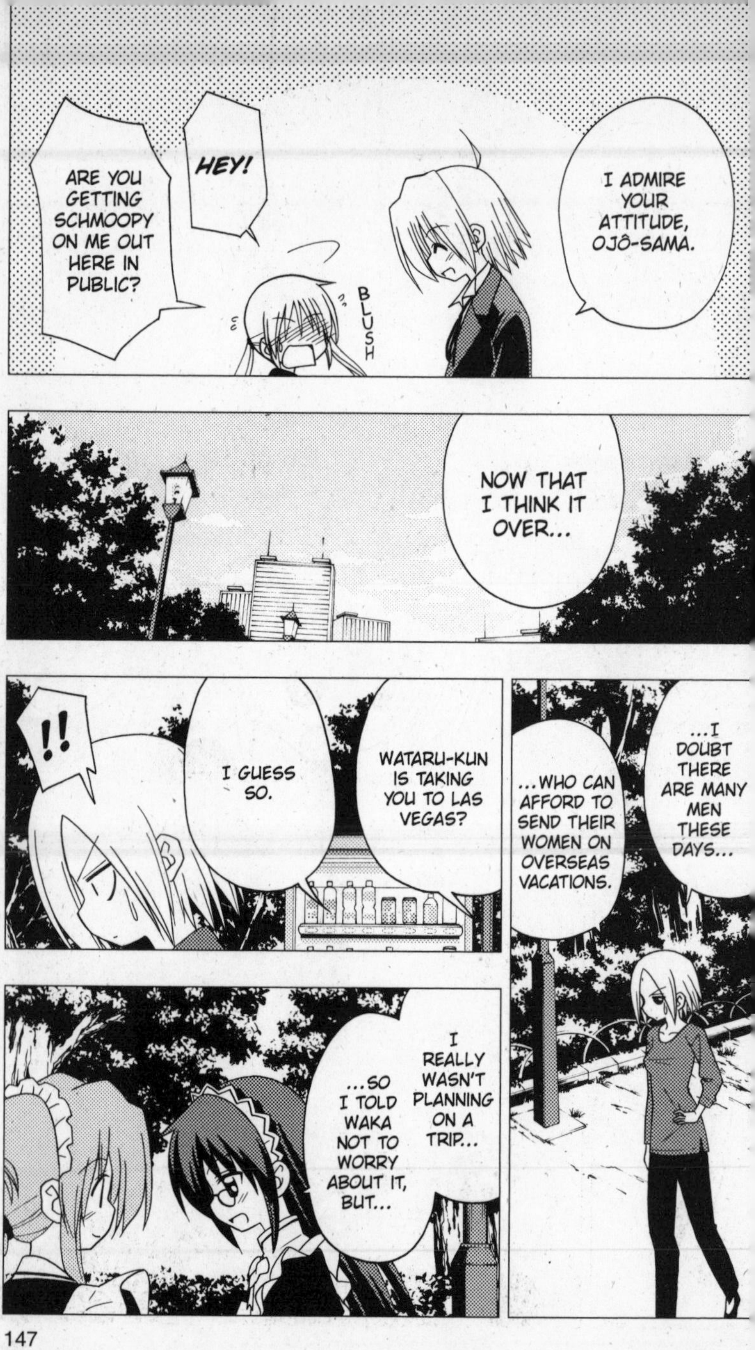
I ADMIRE YOUR ATTITUDE, OJÔ-SAMA.
HEY!
ARE YOU GETTING SCHMOOPY ON ME OUT HERE IN PUBLIC?
BLUSH
NOW THAT I THINK IT OVER...
...I DOUBT THERE ARE MANY MEN THESE DAYS...
...WHO CAN AFFORD TO SEND THEIR WOMEN ON OVERSEAS VACATIONS.
WATARU-KUN IS TAKING YOU TO LAS VEGAS?
I GUESS SO.
!!
I REALLY WASN'T PLANNING ON A TRIP...
...SO I TOLD WAKA NOT TO WORRY ABOUT IT, BUT...

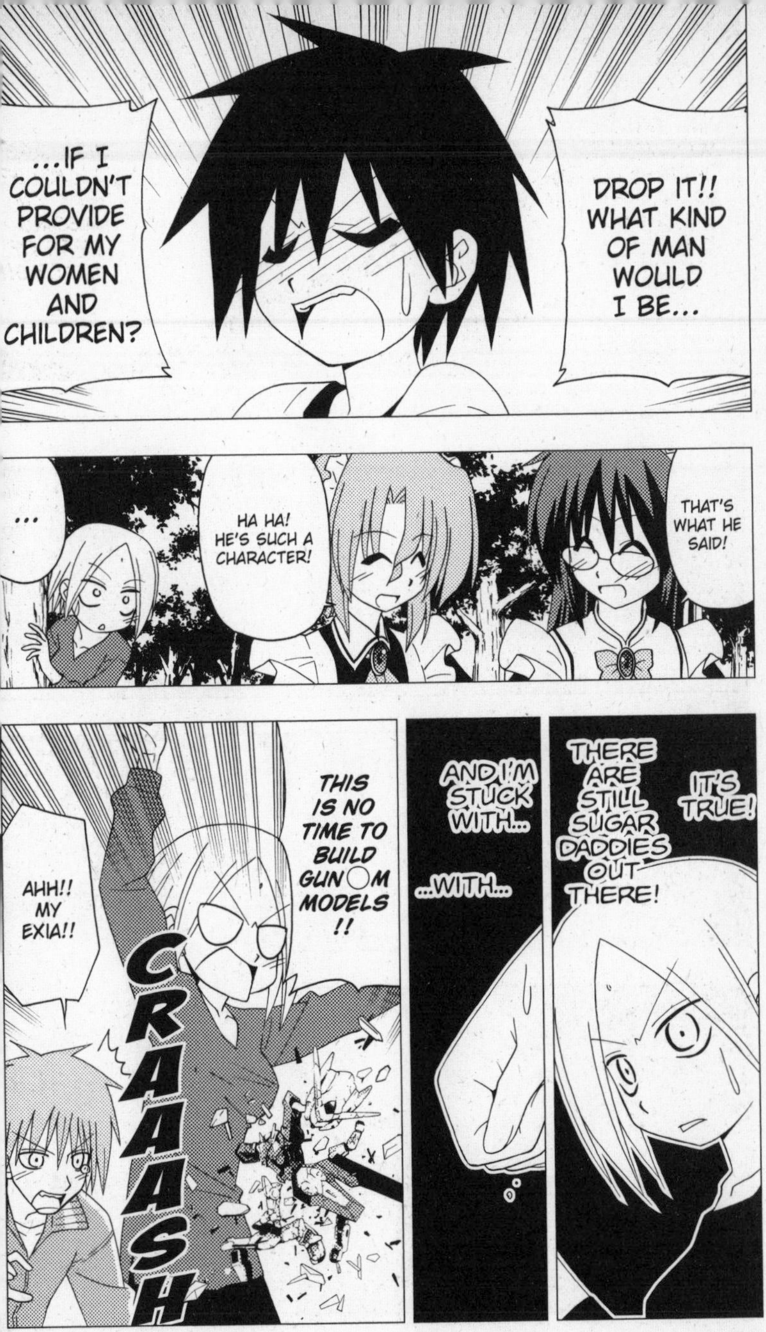
DROP IT!! WHAT KIND OF MAN WOULD I BE...
...IF I COULDN'T PROVIDE FOR MY WOMEN AND CHILDREN?
THAT'S WHAT HE SAID!
HA HA! HE'S SUCH A CHARACTER!
...
IT'S TRUE!
THERE ARE STILL SUGAR DADDIES OUT THERE!
AND I'M STUCK WITH...
...WITH...
THIS IS NO TIME TO BUILD GUN◯M MODELS!!
CRAAASH
AHH!! MY EXIA!!

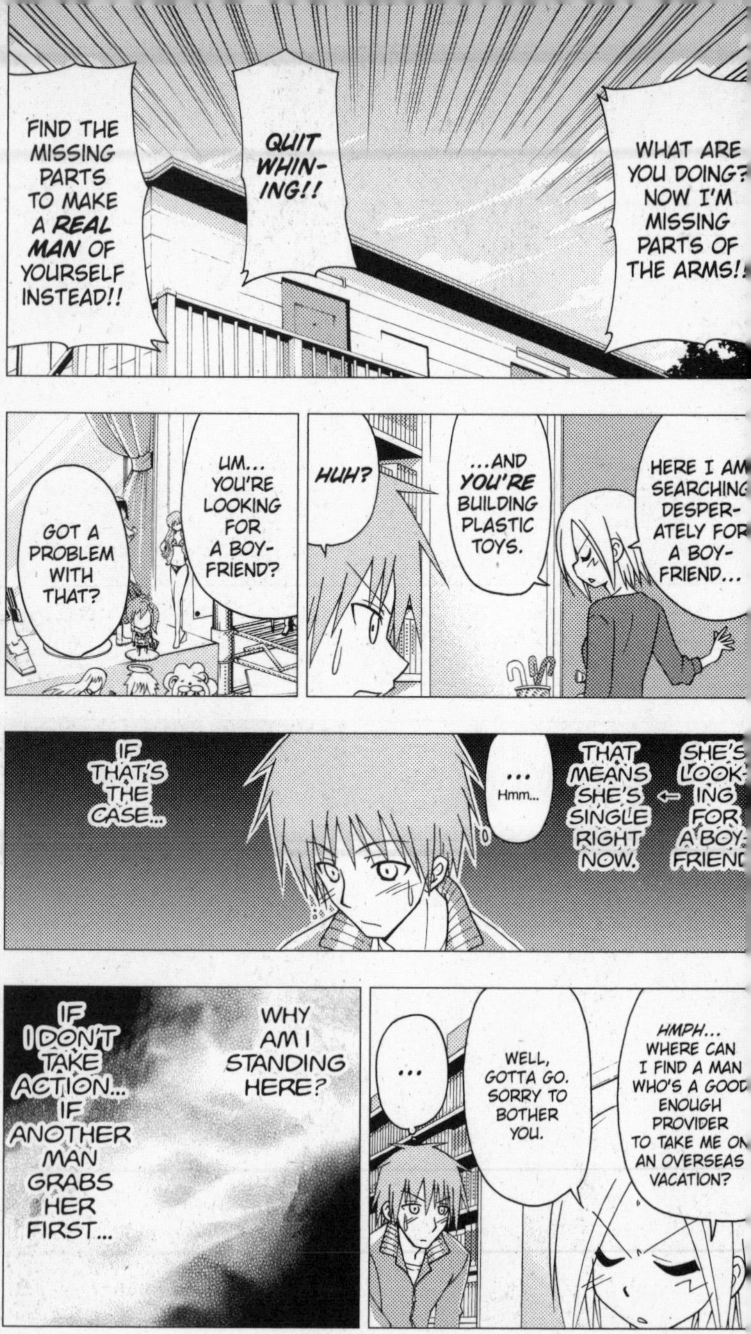
WHAT ARE YOU DOING? NOW I'M MISSING PARTS OF THE ARMS!!
QUIT WHINING!!
FIND THE MISSING PARTS TO MAKE A REAL MAN OF YOURSELF INSTEAD!!
HERE I AM SEARCHING DESPERATELY FOR A BOYFRIEND...
...AND YOU'RE BUILDING PLASTIC TOYS.
HUH?
UM... YOU'RE LOOKING FOR A BOYFRIEND?
GOT A PROBLEM WITH THAT?
SHE'S LOOKING FOR A BOYFRIEN
THAT MEANS SHE'S SINGLE RIGHT NOW.
... Hmm...
IF THAT'S THE CASE...
HMPH... WHERE CAN I FIND A MAN WHO'S A GOO ENOUGH PROVIDER TO TAKE ME O AN OVERSEAS VACATION?
WELL, GOTTA GO. SORRY TO BOTHER YOU.
...
WHY AM I STANDING HERE?
IF I DON'T TAKE ACTION... IF ANOTHER MAN GRABS HER FIRST...

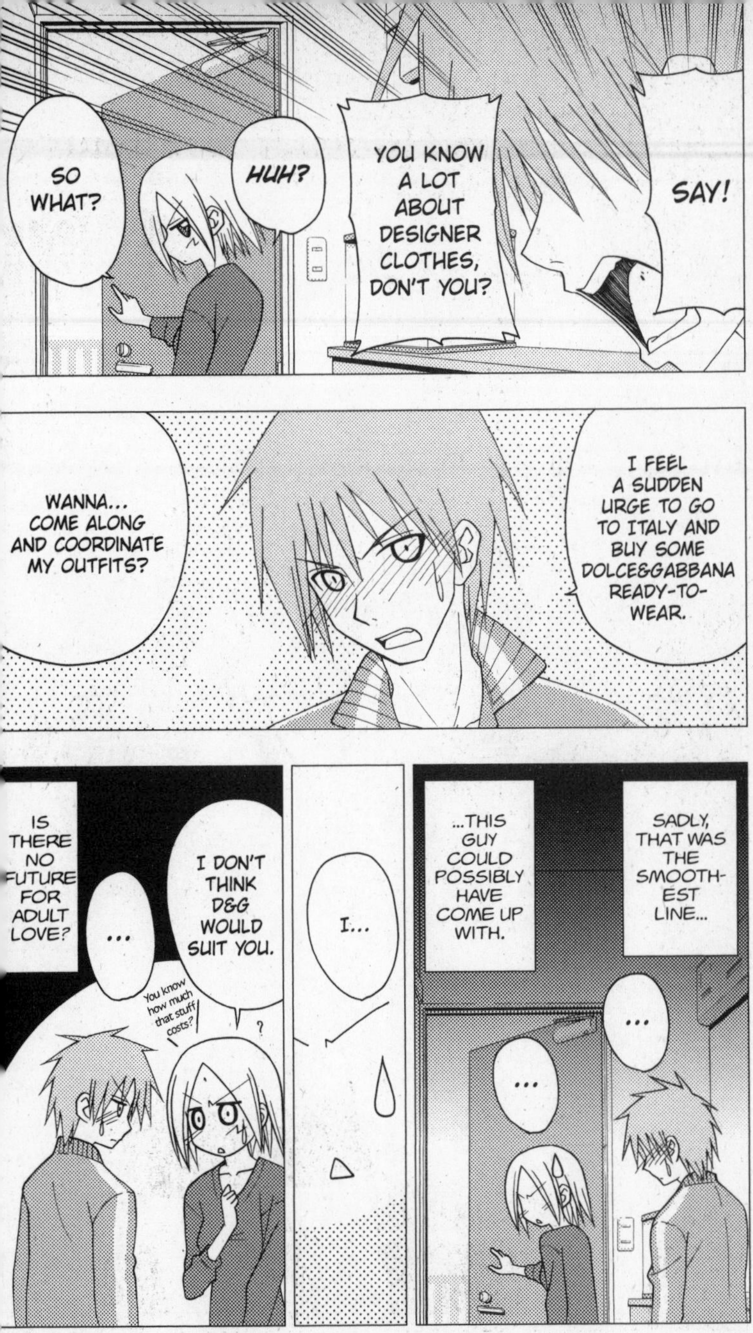
SAY!
YOU KNOW A LOT ABOUT DESIGNER CLOTHES, DON'T YOU?
HUH?
SO WHAT?
I FEEL A SUDDEN URGE TO GO TO ITALY AND BUY SOME DOLCE&GABBANA READY-TO-WEAR.
WANNA... COME ALONG AND COORDINATE MY OUTFITS?
SADLY, THAT WAS THE SMOOTH-EST LINE...
...THIS GUY COULD POSSIBLY HAVE COME UP WITH.
...
...
I...
I DON'T THINK D&G WOULD SUIT YOU.
...
IS THERE NO FUTURE FOR ADULT LOVE?
You know how much that stuff costs?
?

Episode 10: "Quiz Magic Hamster Academy"

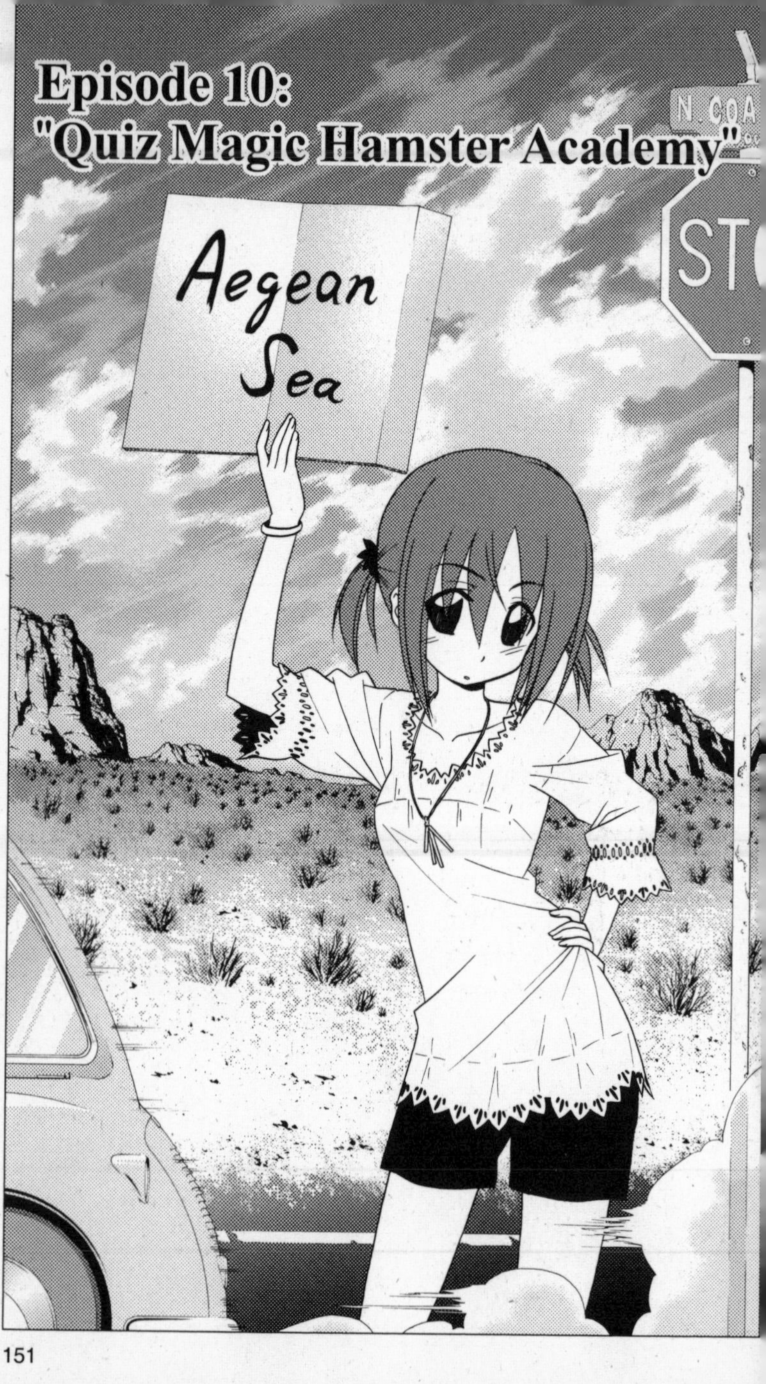
Aegean Sea

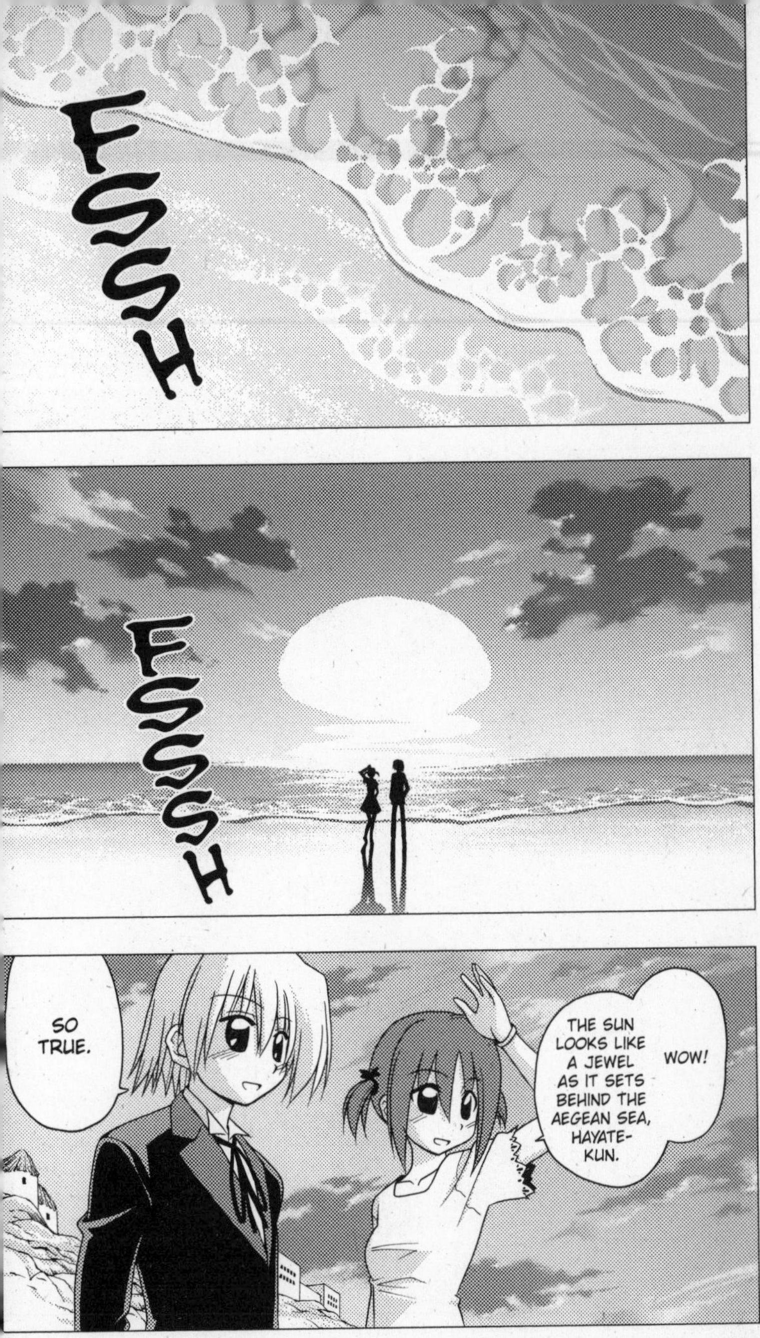
FSSH
FSSSH
WOW!
THE SUN LOOKS LIKE A JEWEL AS IT SETS BEHIND THE AEGEAN SEA, HAYATE-KUN.
SO TRUE.

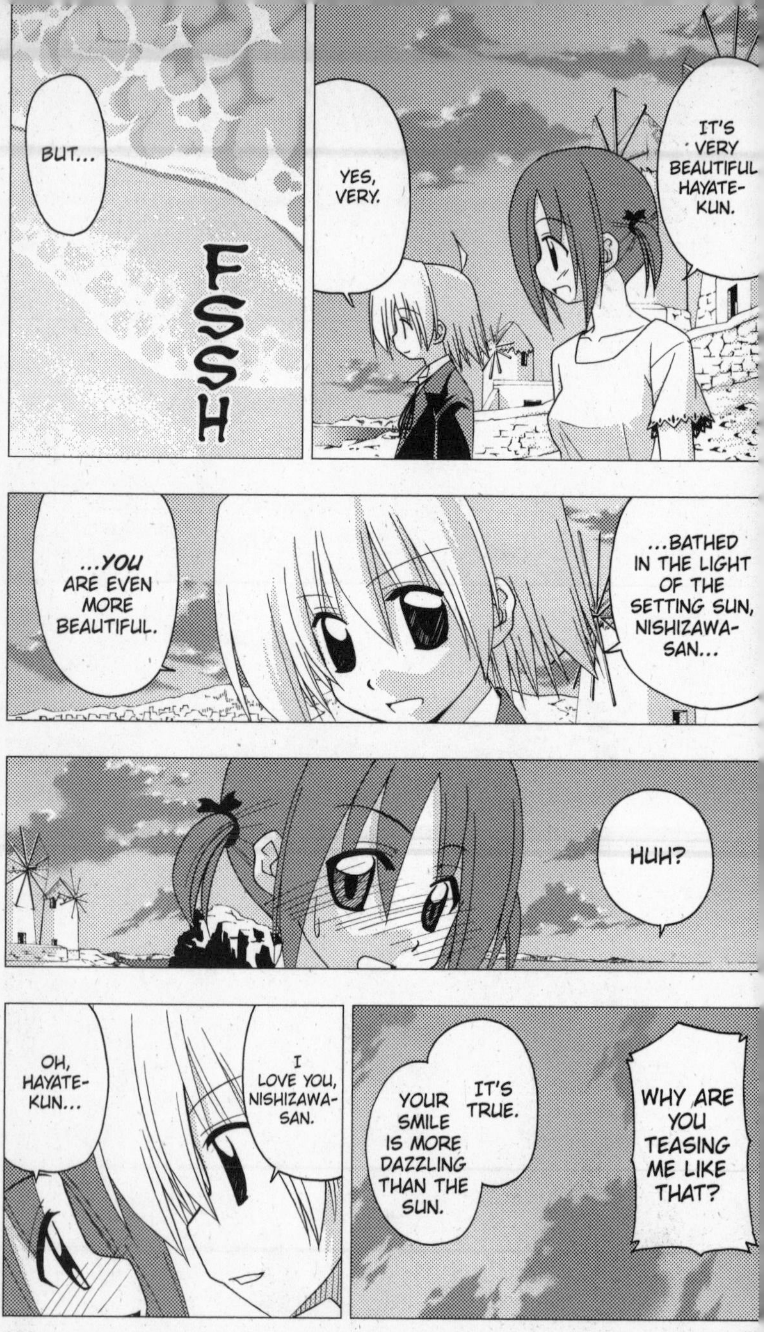
IT'S VERY BEAUTIFUL HAYATE-KUN.
YES, VERY.
BUT...
FSSH
...BATHED IN THE LIGHT OF THE SETTING SUN, NISHIZAWA-SAN...
...YOU ARE EVEN MORE BEAUTIFUL.
HUH?
WHY ARE YOU TEASING ME LIKE THAT?
IT'S TRUE.
YOUR SMILE IS MORE DAZZLING THAN THE SUN.
I LOVE YOU, NISHIZAWA-SAN.
OH, HAYATE-KUN...

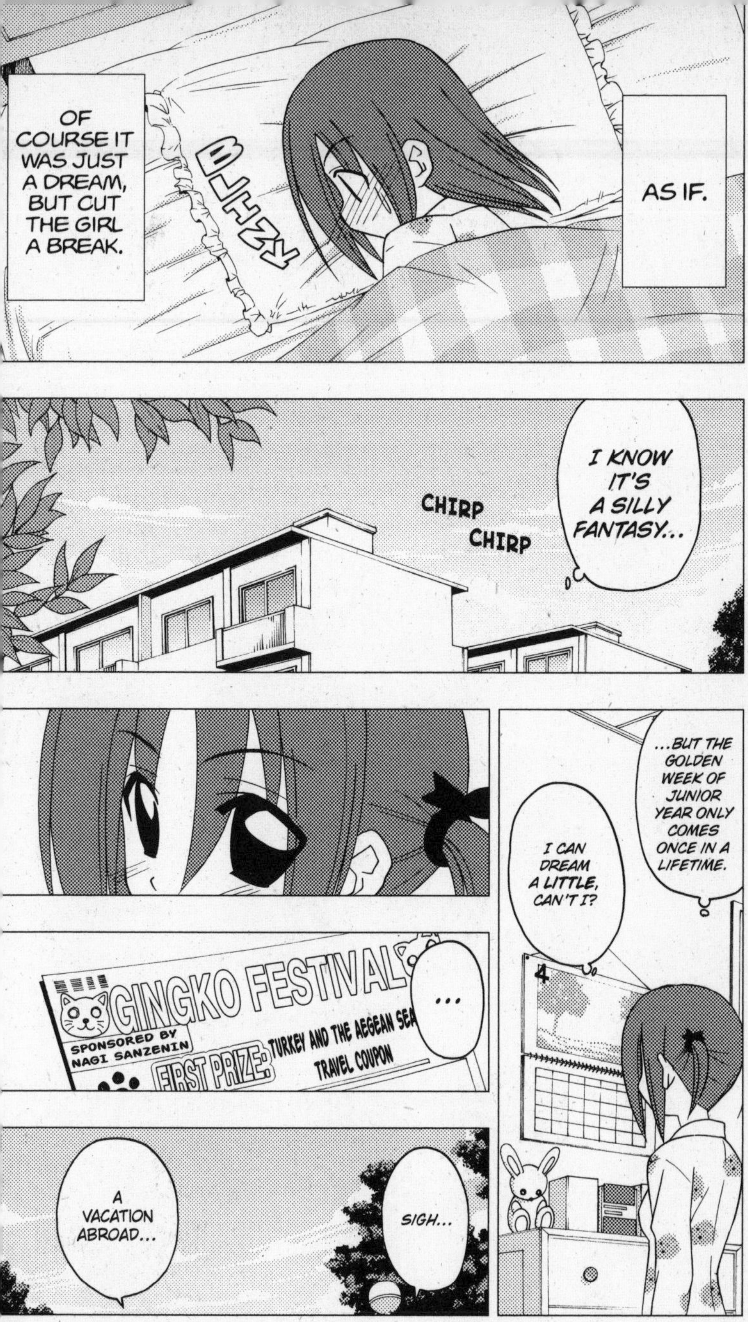
AS IF.
OF COURSE IT WAS JUST A DREAM, BUT CUT THE GIRL A BREAK.
I KNOW IT'S A SILLY FANTASY...
CHIRP
CHIRP
...BUT THE GOLDEN WEEK OF JUNIOR YEAR ONLY COMES ONCE IN A LIFETIME.
I CAN DREAM A LITTLE, CAN'T I?
4
...
GINGKO FESTIVAL
SPONSORED BY NAGI SANZENIN
FIRST PRIZE: TURKEY AND THE AEGEAN SEA TRAVEL COUPON
SIGH...
A VACATION ABROAD...

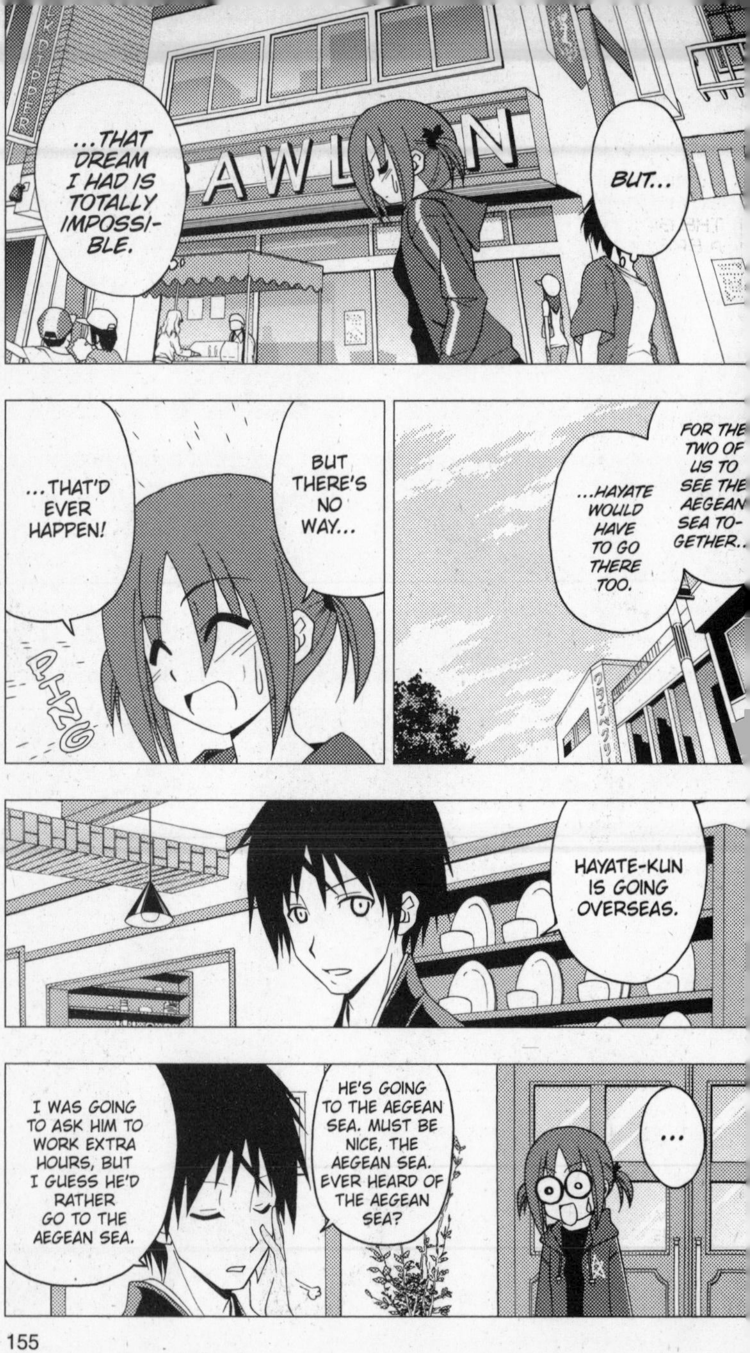
BUT...
...THAT DREAM I HAD IS TOTALLY IMPOSSI-BLE.
FOR THE TWO OF US TO SEE THE AEGEAN SEA TO-GETHER...
...HAYATE WOULD HAVE TO GO THERE TOO.
BUT THERE'S NO WAY...
...THAT'D EVER HAPPEN!
PING
HAYATE-KUN IS GOING OVERSEAS.
...
HE'S GOING TO THE AEGEAN SEA. MUST BE NICE, THE AEGEAN SEA. EVER HEARD OF THE AEGEAN SEA?
I WAS GOING TO ASK HIM TO WORK EXTRA HOURS, BUT I GUESS HE'D RATHER GO TO THE AEGEAN SEA.

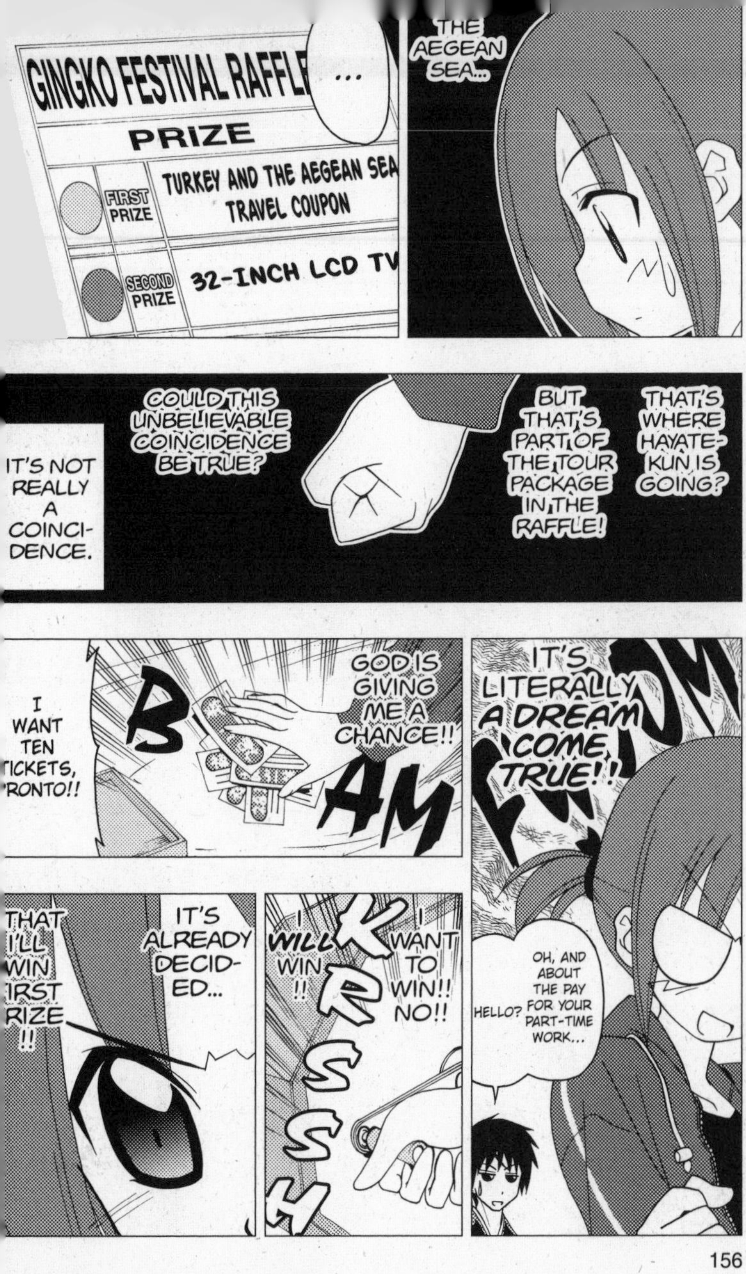
THE AEGEAN SEA...
...
GINGKO FESTIVAL RAFFLE
PRIZE
FIRST PRIZE
TURKEY AND THE AEGEAN SEA TRAVEL COUPON
SECOND PRIZE
32-INCH LCD TV
THAT'S WHERE HAYATE-KUN IS GOING?
BUT THAT'S PART OF THE TOUR PACKAGE IN THE RAFFLE!
COULD THIS UNBELIEVABLE COINCIDENCE BE TRUE?
IT'S NOT REALLY A COINCIDENCE.
IT'S LITERALLY A DREAM COME TRUE!!
OH, AND ABOUT THE PAY FOR YOUR PART-TIME WORK...
HELLO?
GOD IS GIVING ME A CHANCE!!
BAM
I WANT TEN TICKETS, RONTO!!
I WANT TO WIN!! NO!!
I WILL WIN !!
KRSSH
IT'S ALREADY DECIDED...
THAT I'LL WIN IRST RIZE !!

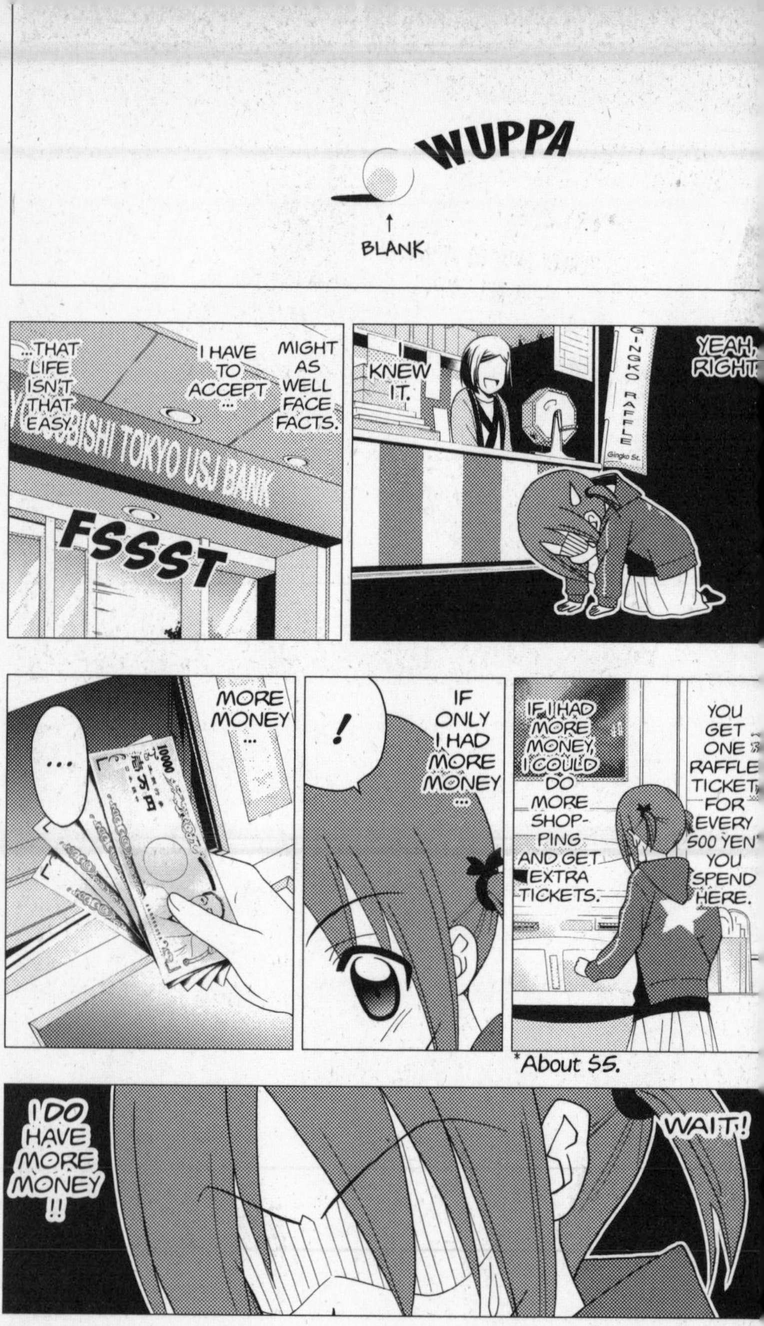
WUPPA
BLANK
YEAH, RIGHT.
I KNEW IT.
GINGKO RAFFLE
Gingko St.
MIGHT AS WELL FACE FACTS.
I HAVE TO ACCEPT...
...THAT LIFE ISN'T THAT EASY.
BISHI TOKYO USJ BANK
FSSST
YOU GET ONE RAFFLE TICKET FOR EVERY 500 YEN* YOU SPEND HERE.
IF I HAD MORE MONEY, I COULD DO MORE SHOP-PING AND GET EXTRA TICKETS.
IF ONLY I HAD MORE MONEY...
!
MORE MONEY...
...
WAIT!
I DO HAVE MORE MONEY!!

*About $5.

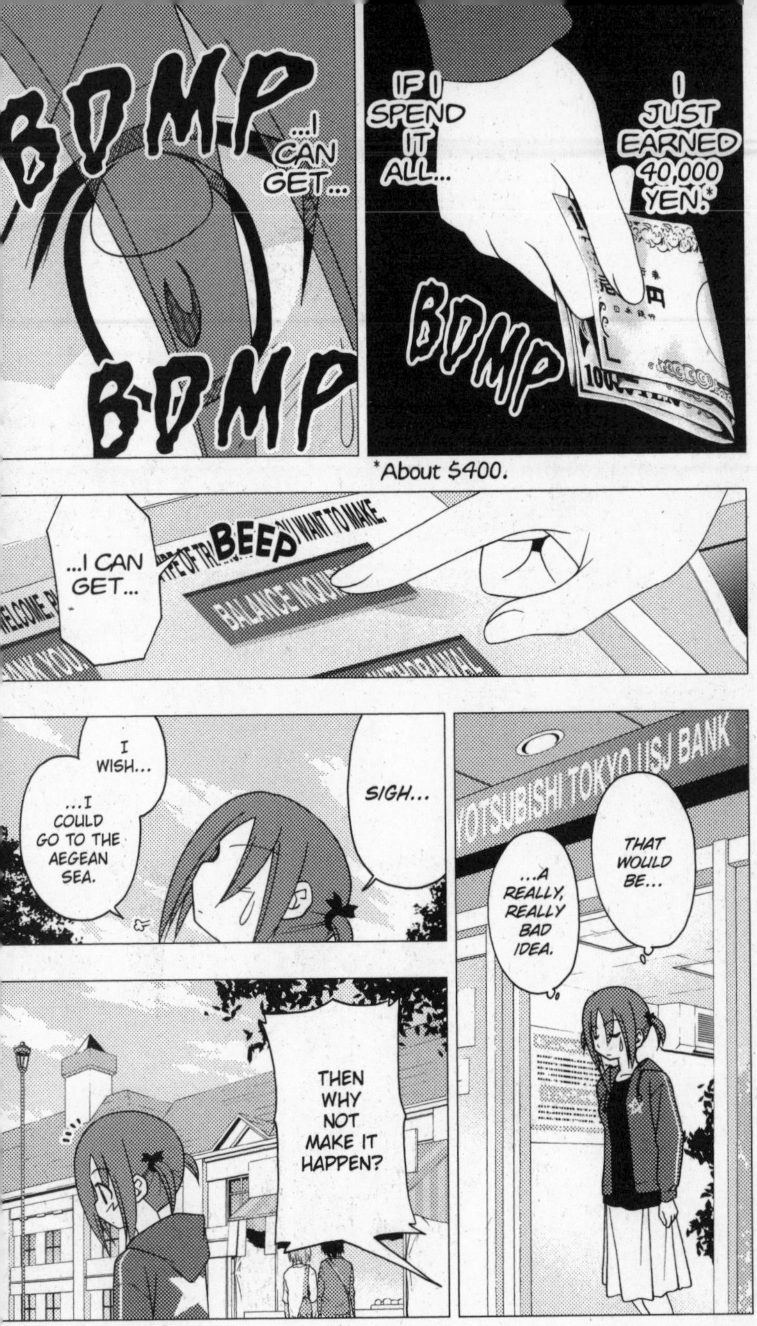
I JUST EARNED 40,000 YEN.*
IF I SPEND IT ALL...
BDMP
...I CAN GET...
BDMP
BDMP
...I CAN GET...
BEEP
YOTSUBISHI TOKYO USJ BANK
THAT WOULD BE...
...A REALLY, REALLY BAD IDEA.
SIGH...
I WISH...
...I COULD GO TO THE AEGEAN SEA.
THEN WHY NOT MAKE IT HAPPEN?

*About $400.

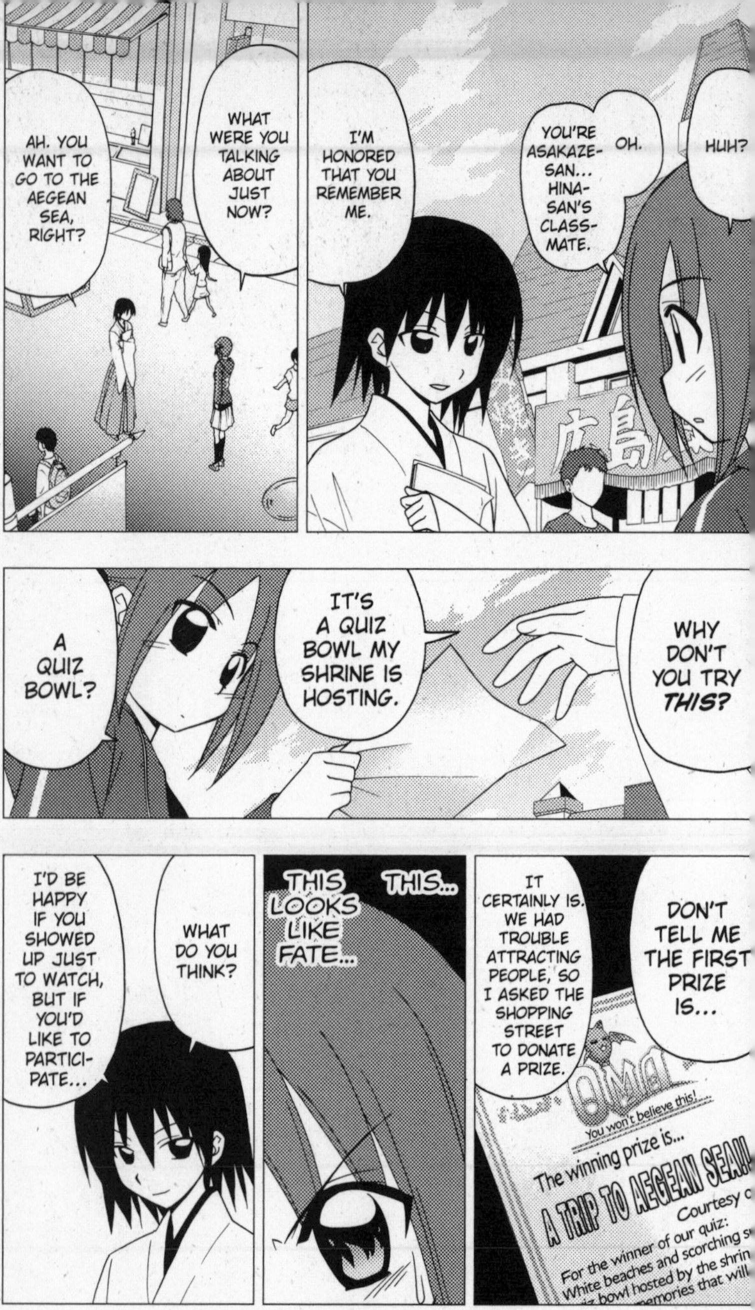
HUH?
OH.
YOU'RE ASAKAZE-SAN... HINA-SAN'S CLASSMATE.
I'M HONORED THAT YOU REMEMBER ME.
WHAT WERE YOU TALKING ABOUT JUST NOW?
AH. YOU WANT TO GO TO THE AEGEAN SEA, RIGHT?
WHY DON'T YOU TRY *THIS?*
IT'S A QUIZ BOWL MY SHRINE IS HOSTING.
A QUIZ BOWL?
DON'T TELL ME THE FIRST PRIZE IS...
IT CERTAINLY IS. WE HAD TROUBLE ATTRACTING PEOPLE, SO I ASKED THE SHOPPING STREET TO DONATE A PRIZE.
OMG
You won't believe this!...
The winning prize is...
A TRIP TO AEGEAN SEA!!
For the winner of our quiz:
THIS... THIS LOOKS LIKE FATE...
WHAT DO YOU THINK?
I'D BE HAPPY IF YOU SHOWED UP JUST TO WATCH, BUT IF YOU'D LIKE TO PARTICIPATE...

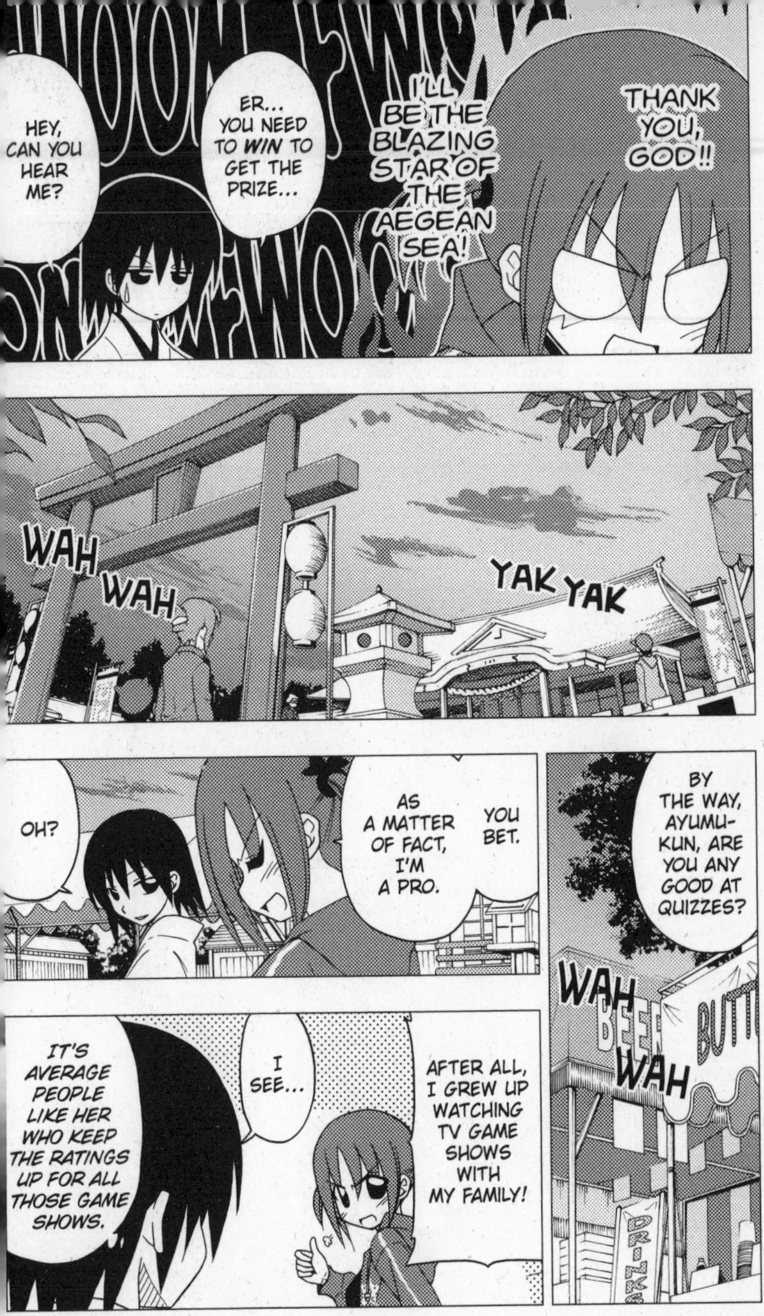
THANK YOU, GOD!!
I'LL BE THE BLAZING STAR OF THE AEGEAN SEA!
ER... YOU NEED TO *WIN* TO GET THE PRIZE...
HEY, CAN YOU HEAR ME?
YAK YAK
WAH WAH
BY THE WAY, AYUMU-KUN, ARE YOU ANY GOOD AT QUIZZES?
WAH WAH
BEER
YOU BET.
AS A MATTER OF FACT, I'M A PRO.
OH?
AFTER ALL, I GREW UP WATCHING TV GAME SHOWS WITH MY FAMILY!
I SEE...
IT'S AVERAGE PEOPLE LIKE HER WHO KEEP THE RATINGS UP FOR ALL THOSE GAME SHOWS.

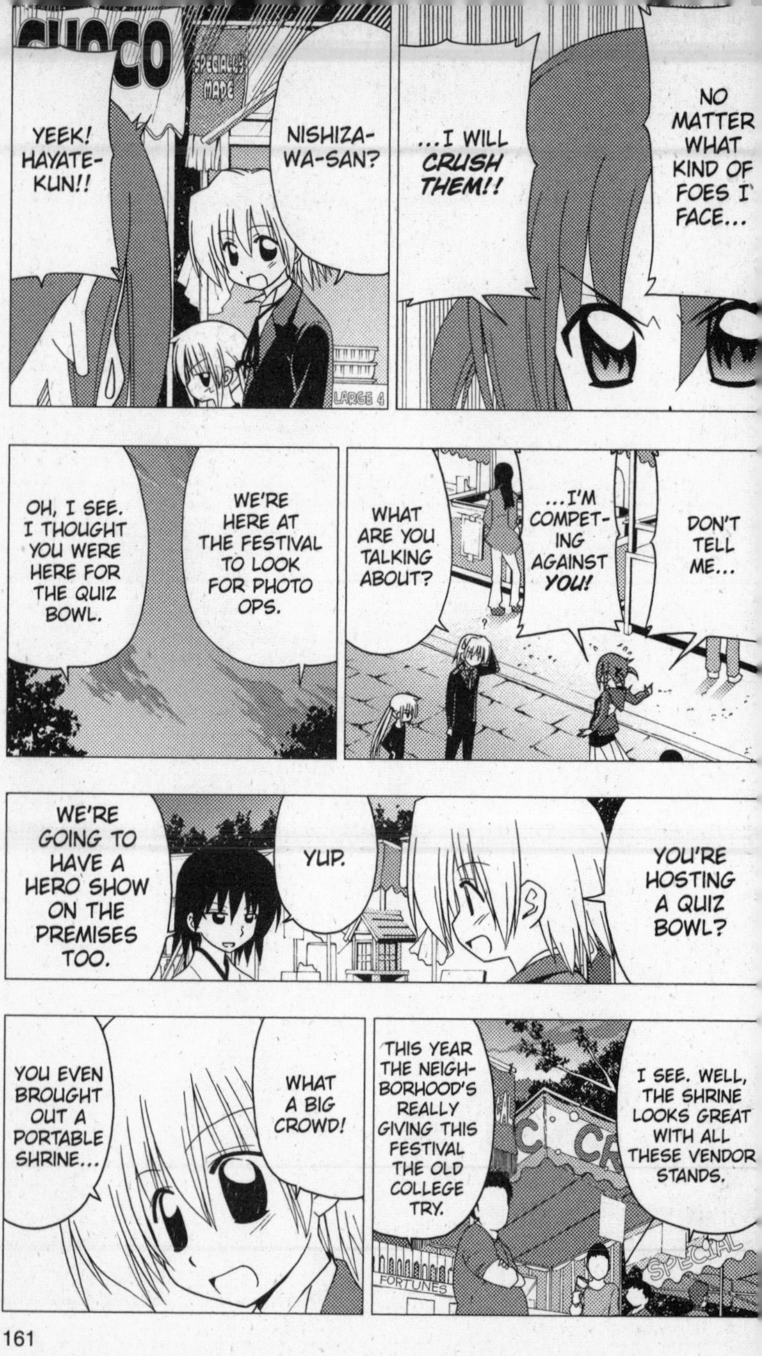
NO MATTER WHAT KIND OF FOES I FACE...
...I WILL CRUSH THEM!!
CHOCO
SPECIALLY MADE
LARGE 4
NISHIZAWA-SAN?
YEEK! HAYATE-KUN!!
DON'T TELL ME...
...I'M COMPETING AGAINST YOU!
WHAT ARE YOU TALKING ABOUT?
WE'RE HERE AT THE FESTIVAL TO LOOK FOR PHOTO OPS.
OH, I SEE. I THOUGHT YOU WERE HERE FOR THE QUIZ BOWL.
YOU'RE HOSTING A QUIZ BOWL?
YUP.
WE'RE GOING TO HAVE A HERO SHOW ON THE PREMISES TOO.
I SEE. WELL, THE SHRINE LOOKS GREAT WITH ALL THESE VENDOR STANDS.
SPECIAL
THIS YEAR THE NEIGHBORHOOD'S REALLY GIVING THIS FESTIVAL THE OLD COLLEGE TRY.
FORTUNES
WHAT A BIG CROWD!
YOU EVEN BROUGHT OUT A PORTABLE SHRINE...

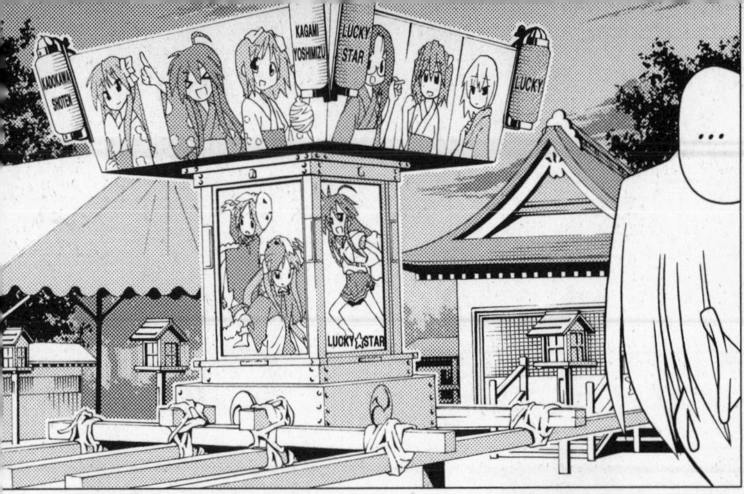
...
KADOKAWA SHOTEN
KAGAMI YOSHIMIZU
LUCKY STAR
LUCKY
LUCKY☆STAR

IN COOPERATION WITH WASHINOMIYA COMMERCE AND INDUSTRY ASSOCIATION/*LUCKY ☆ STAR*

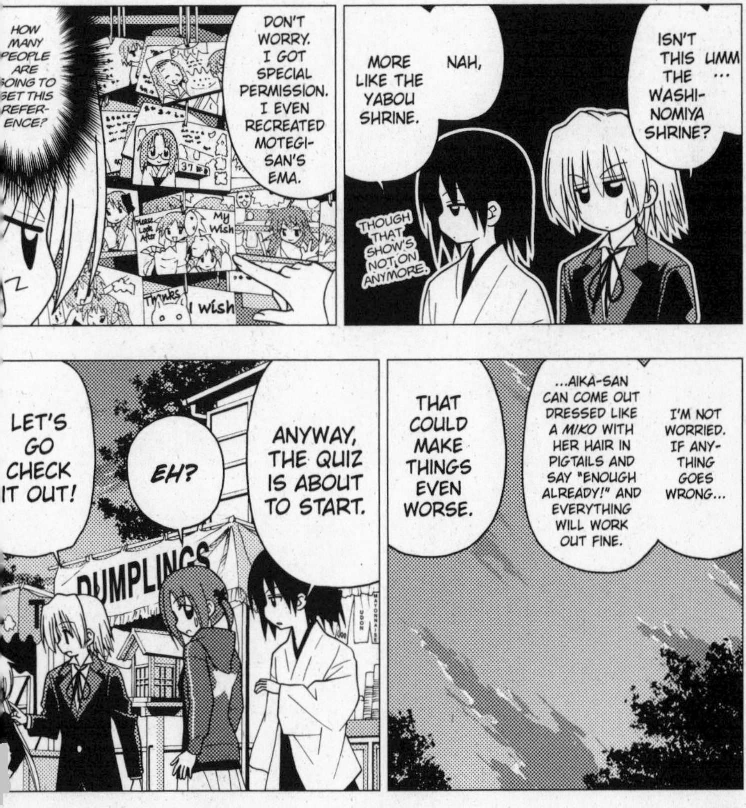
ISN'T THIS THE WASHINOMIYA SHRINE?
UMM ...
NAH, MORE LIKE THE YABOU SHRINE.
THOUGH THAT SHOW'S NOT ON ANYMORE.
DON'T WORRY. I GOT SPECIAL PERMISSION. I EVEN RECREATED MOTEGI-SAN'S EMA.
HOW MANY PEOPLE ARE GOING TO GET THIS REFERENCE?
My Wish
Please Look After
Thanks
I wish
I'M NOT WORRIED. IF ANYTHING GOES WRONG...
...AIKA-SAN CAN COME OUT DRESSED LIKE A *MIKO* WITH HER HAIR IN PIGTAILS AND SAY "ENOUGH ALREADY!" AND EVERYTHING WILL WORK OUT FINE.
THAT COULD MAKE THINGS EVEN WORSE.
ANYWAY, THE QUIZ IS ABOUT TO START.
EH?
LET'S GO CHECK IT OUT!
DUMPLINGS

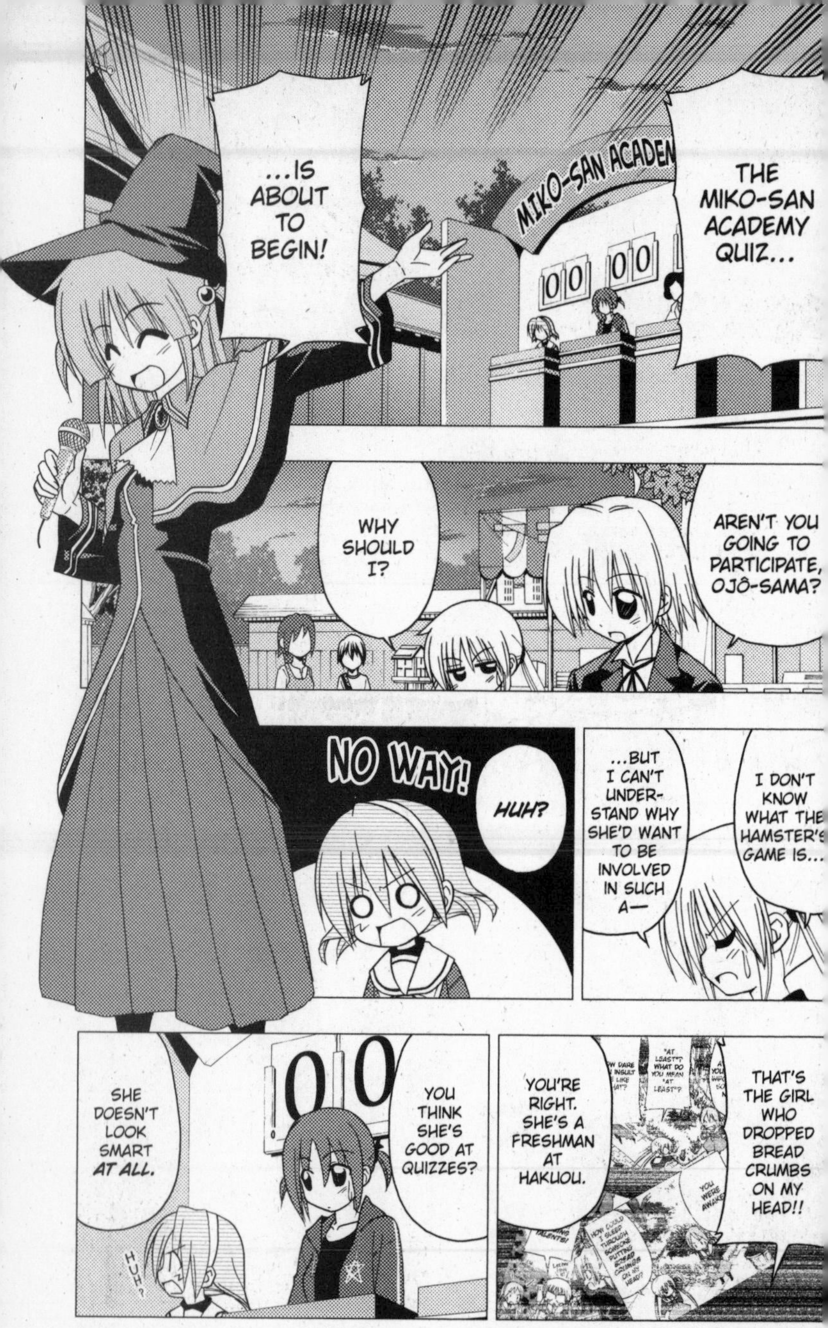

MIKO-SAN ACADEN
THE MIKO-SAN ACADEMY QUIZ...
...IS ABOUT TO BEGIN!
AREN'T YOU GOING TO PARTICIPATE, OJÔ-SAMA?
WHY SHOULD I?
I DON'T KNOW WHAT THE HAMSTER'S GAME IS...
...BUT I CAN'T UNDERSTAND WHY SHE'D WANT TO BE INVOLVED IN SUCH A—
HUH?
NO WAY!
THAT'S THE GIRL WHO DROPPED BREAD CRUMBS ON MY HEAD!!
"AT LEAST"? WHAT DO YOU MEAN "AT LEAST"?
YOU WERE AWAKE
HOW COULD I SLEEP THROUGH SOMEONE PUTTING BREAD CRUMBS ON MY HEAD?
YOU'RE RIGHT. SHE'S A FRESHMAN AT HAKUOU.
YOU THINK SHE'S GOOD AT QUIZZES?
SHE DOESN'T LOOK SMART AT ALL.
HUH?

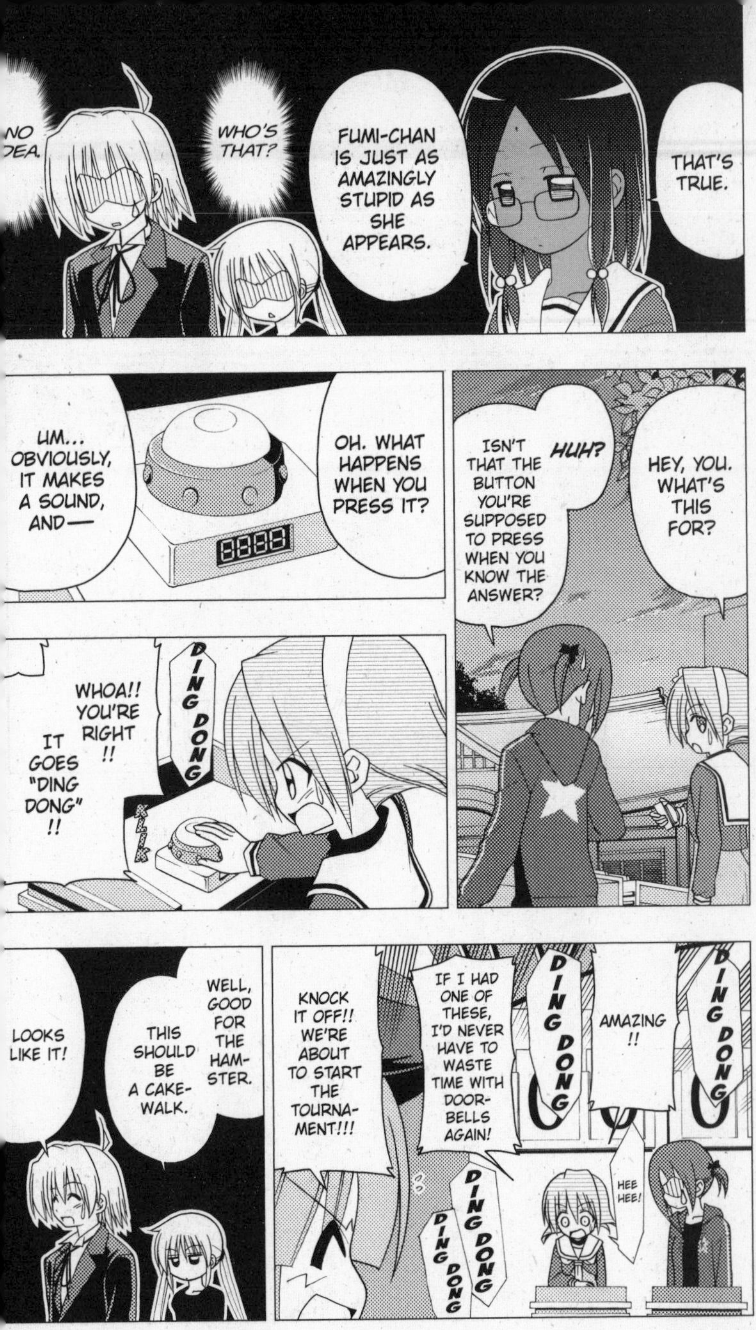
THAT'S TRUE.
FUMI-CHAN IS JUST AS AMAZINGLY STUPID AS SHE APPEARS.
WHO'S THAT?
NO DEA.
HEY, YOU. WHAT'S THIS FOR?
HUH?
ISN'T THAT THE BUTTON YOU'RE SUPPOSED TO PRESS WHEN YOU KNOW THE ANSWER?
OH. WHAT HAPPENS WHEN YOU PRESS IT?
UM... OBVIOUSLY, IT MAKES A SOUND, AND—
DING DONG
KLIK
WHOA!! YOU'RE RIGHT!!
IT GOES "DING DONG"!!
DING DONG
AMAZING!!
DING DONG
IF I HAD ONE OF THESE, I'D NEVER HAVE TO WASTE TIME WITH DOOR-BELLS AGAIN!
HEE HEE!
DING DONG
DING DONG
KNOCK IT OFF!! WE'RE ABOUT TO START THE TOURNA-MENT!!!
WELL, GOOD FOR THE HAM-STER.
THIS SHOULD BE A CAKE-WALK.
LOOKS LIKE IT!

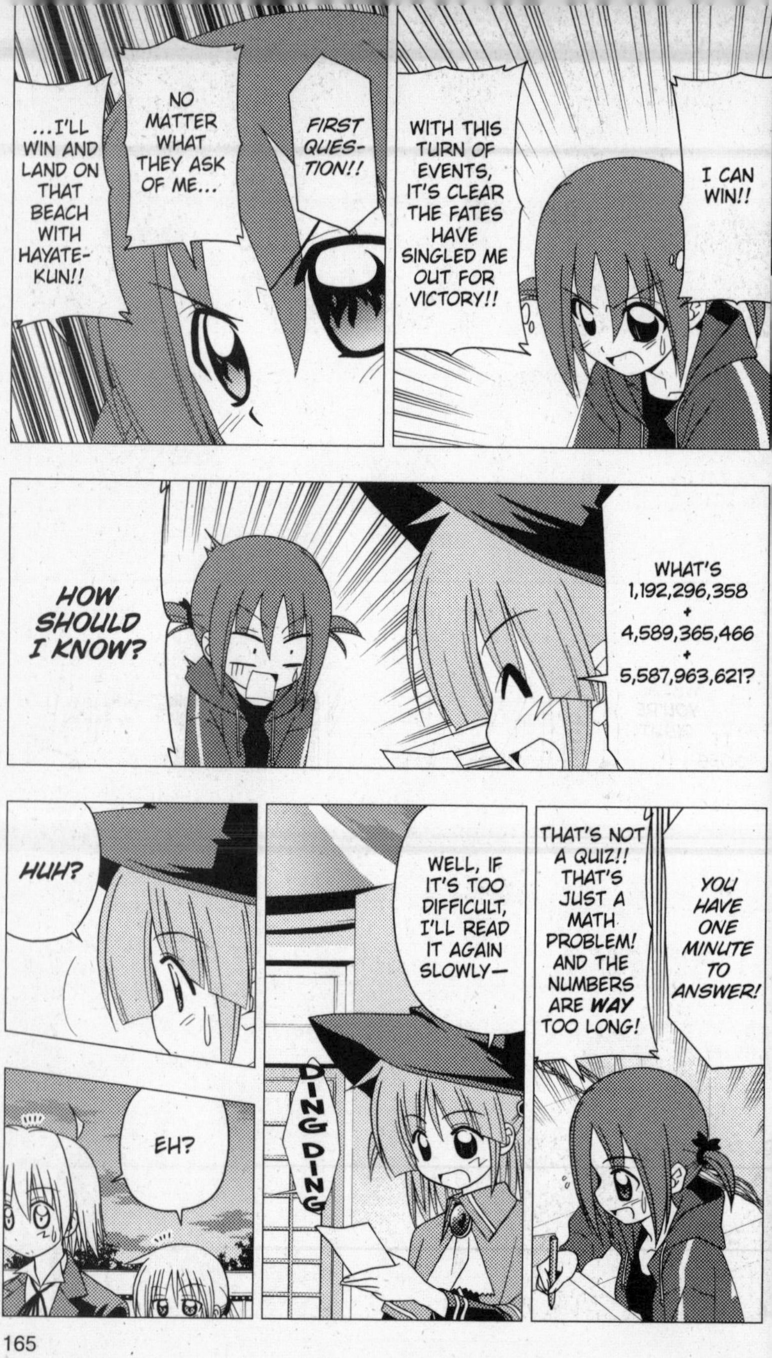
I CAN WIN!!
WITH THIS TURN OF EVENTS, IT'S CLEAR THE FATES HAVE SINGLED ME OUT FOR VICTORY!!
FIRST QUESTION!!
NO MATTER WHAT THEY ASK OF ME...
...I'LL WIN AND LAND ON THAT BEACH WITH HAYATE-KUN!!
WHAT'S 1,192,296,358 + 4,589,365,466 + 5,587,963,621?
HOW SHOULD I KNOW?
YOU HAVE ONE MINUTE TO ANSWER!
THAT'S NOT A QUIZ!! THAT'S JUST A MATH PROBLEM! AND THE NUMBERS ARE WAY TOO LONG!
WELL, IF IT'S TOO DIFFICULT, I'LL READ IT AGAIN SLOWLY—
DING DING
HUH?
EH?

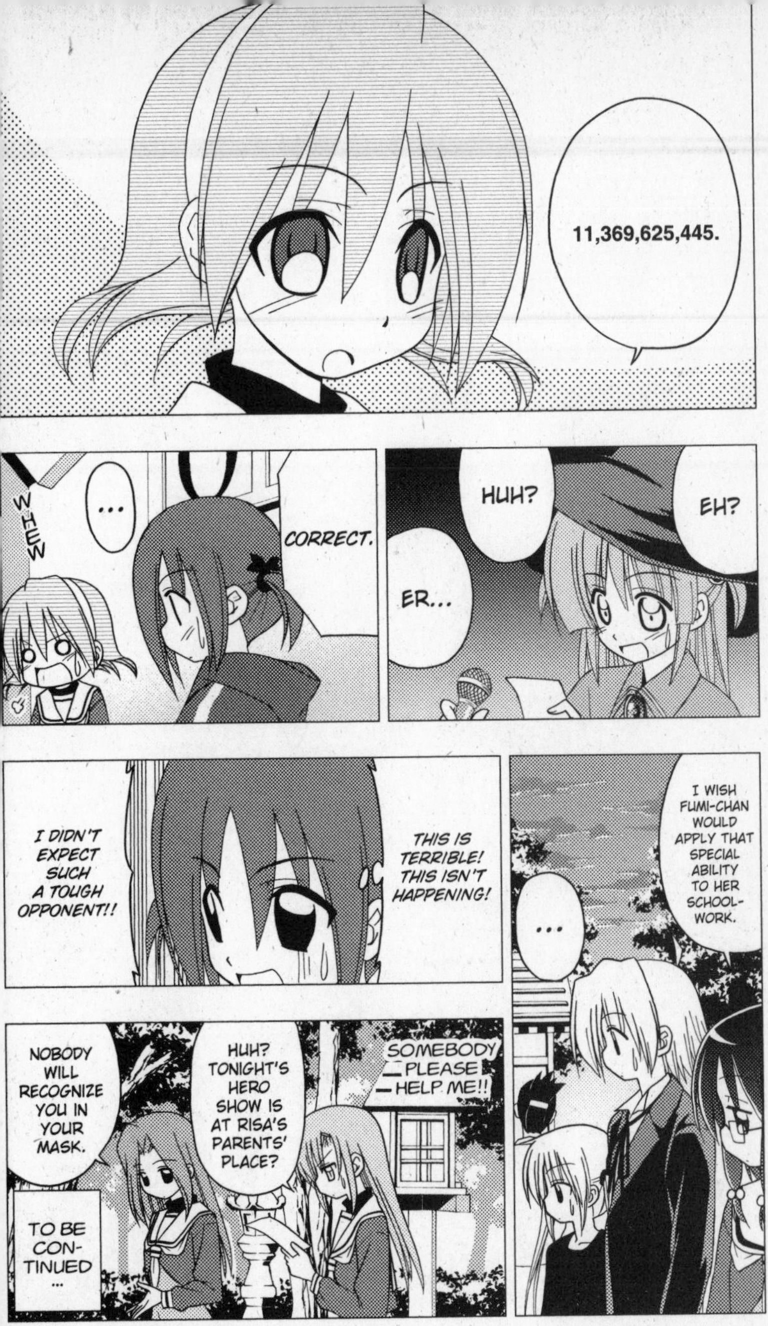
11,369,625,445.
EH?
HUH?
ER...
CORRECT.
...
WHEW
I WISH FUMI-CHAN WOULD APPLY THAT SPECIAL ABILITY TO HER SCHOOL-WORK.
...
THIS IS TERRIBLE! THIS ISN'T HAPPENING!
I DIDN'T EXPECT SUCH A TOUGH OPPONENT!!
SOMEBODY PLEASE HELP ME!!
HUH? TONIGHT'S HERO SHOW IS AT RISA'S PARENTS' PLACE?
NOBODY WILL RECOGNIZE YOU IN YOUR MASK.
TO BE CON-TINUED ...

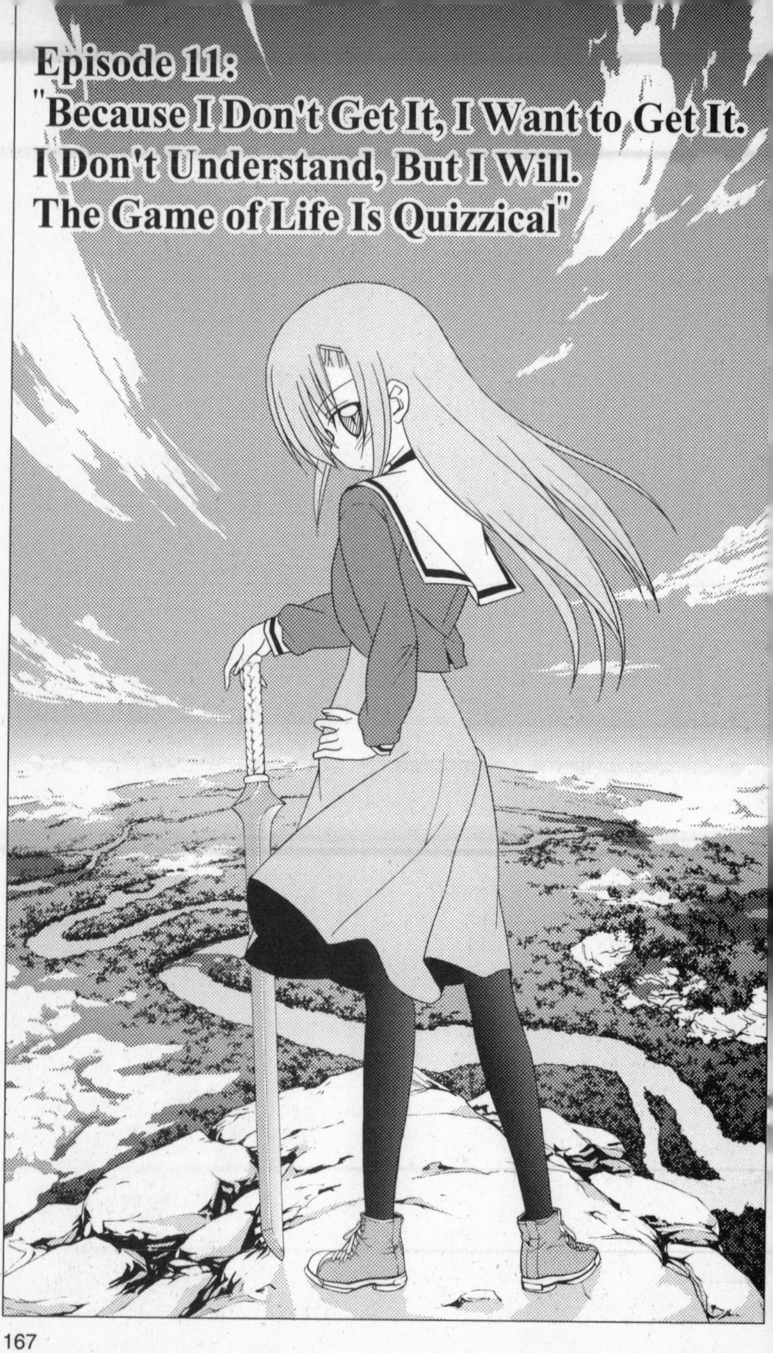
Episode 11:
"Because I Don't Get It, I Want to Get It.
I Don't Understand, But I Will.
The Game of Life Is Quizzical"

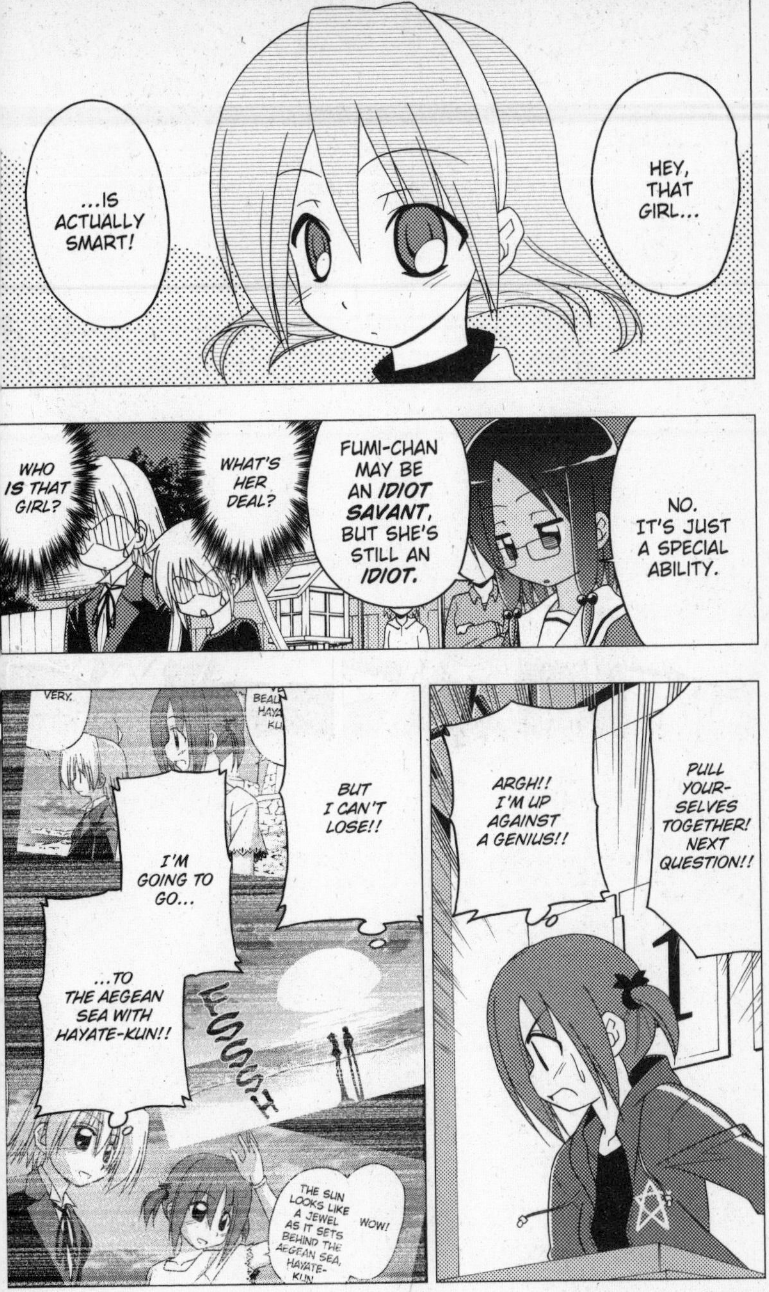
HEY, THAT GIRL...
...IS ACTUALLY SMART!
NO. IT'S JUST A SPECIAL ABILITY.
FUMI-CHAN MAY BE AN *IDIOT SAVANT*, BUT SHE'S STILL AN *IDIOT.*
WHAT'S HER DEAL?
WHO IS THAT GIRL?
PULL YOURSELVES TOGETHER! NEXT QUESTION!!
ARGH!! I'M UP AGAINST A GENIUS!!
BUT I CAN'T LOSE!!
VERY.
I'M GOING TO GO...
...TO THE AEGEAN SEA WITH HAYATE-KUN!!
THE SUN LOOKS LIKE A JEWEL AS IT SETS BEHIND THE AEGEAN SEA, HAYATE-KUN
WOW!

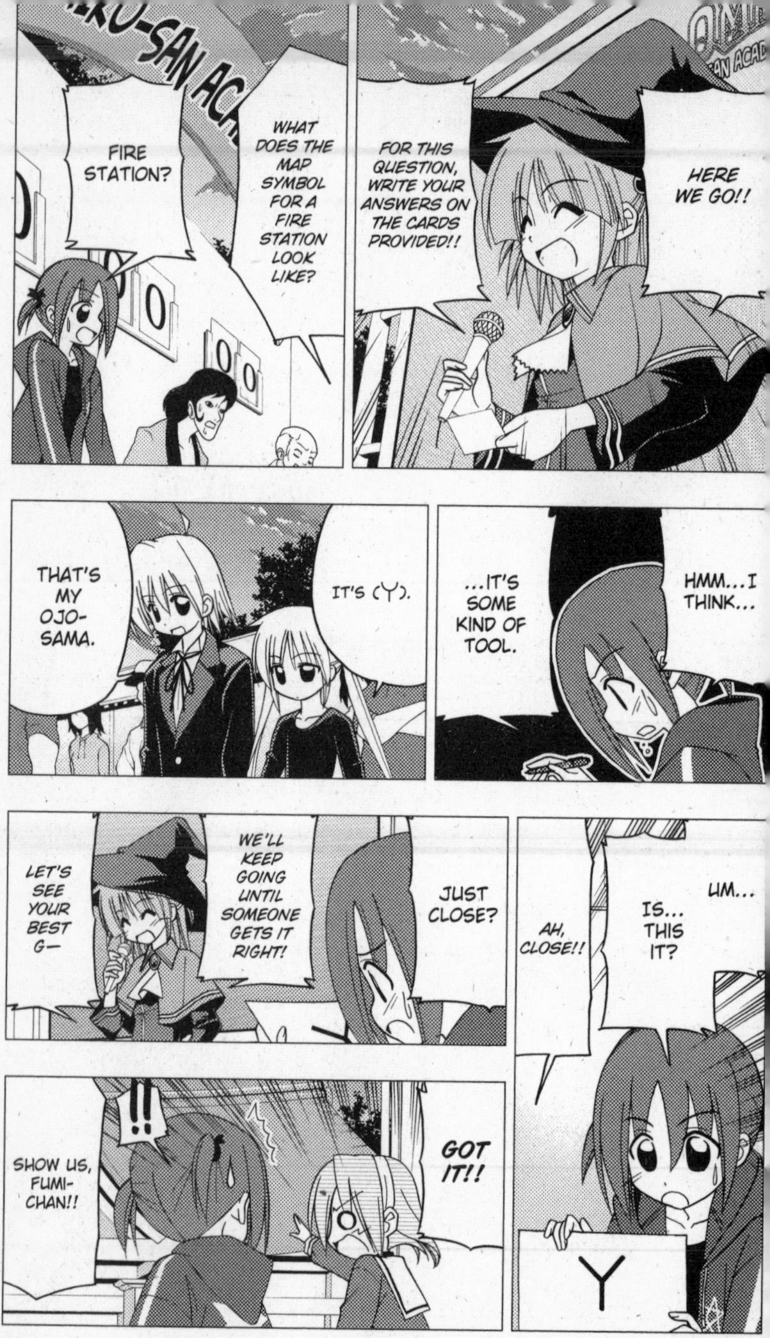
HERE WE GO!!
FOR THIS QUESTION, WRITE YOUR ANSWERS ON THE CARDS PROVIDED!!
WHAT DOES THE MAP SYMBOL FOR A FIRE STATION LOOK LIKE?
FIRE STATION?
HMM...I THINK...
...IT'S SOME KIND OF TOOL.
IT'S (Y).
THAT'S MY OJO-SAMA.
UM...
IS... THIS IT?
AH, CLOSE!!
Y
JUST CLOSE?
WE'LL KEEP GOING UNTIL SOMEONE GETS IT RIGHT!
LET'S SEE YOUR BEST G—
GOT IT!!
!!
SHOW US, FUMI-CHAN!!

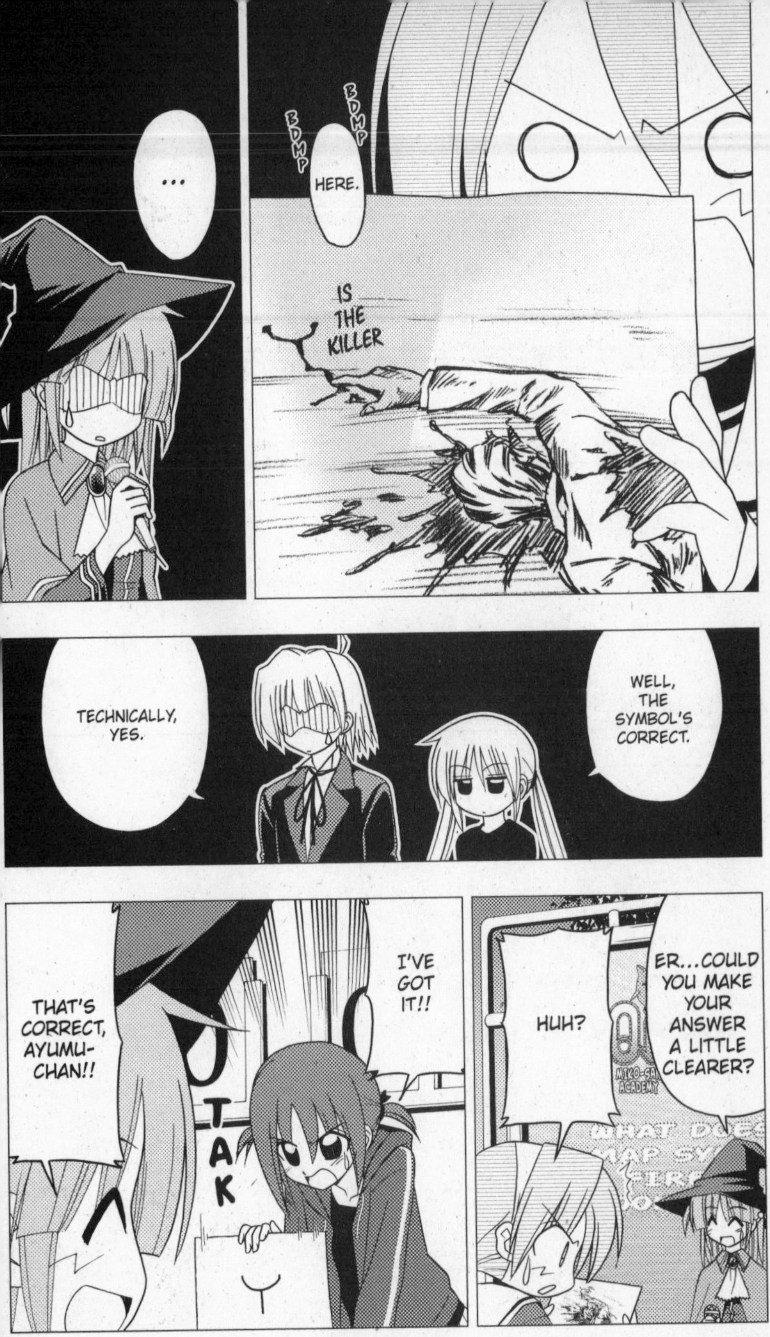
BDMP
BDMP
HERE.
IS THE KILLER
...
WELL, THE SYMBOL'S CORRECT.
TECHNICALLY, YES.
ER...COULD YOU MAKE YOUR ANSWER A LITTLE CLEARER?
HUH?
I'VE GOT IT!!
THAT'S CORRECT, AYUMU-CHAN!!
TAK

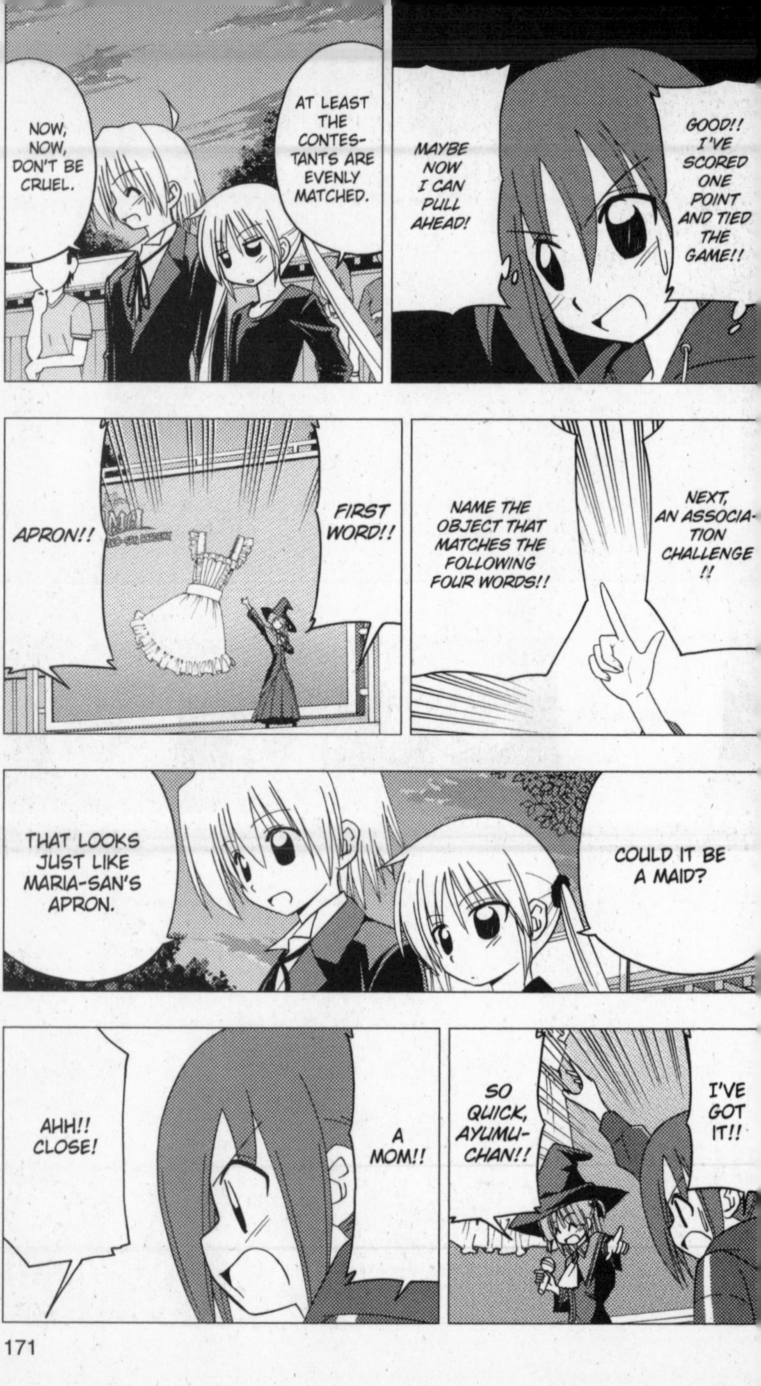
GOOD!! I'VE SCORED ONE POINT AND TIED THE GAME!!
MAYBE NOW I CAN PULL AHEAD!
AT LEAST THE CONTES-TANTS ARE EVENLY MATCHED.
NOW, NOW, DON'T BE CRUEL.
NEXT, AN ASSOCIA-TION CHALLENGE!!
NAME THE OBJECT THAT MATCHES THE FOLLOWING FOUR WORDS!!
FIRST WORD!!
APRON!!
COULD IT BE A MAID?
THAT LOOKS JUST LIKE MARIA-SAN'S APRON.
I'VE GOT IT!!
SO QUICK, AYUMU-CHAN!!
A MOM!!
AHH!! CLOSE!

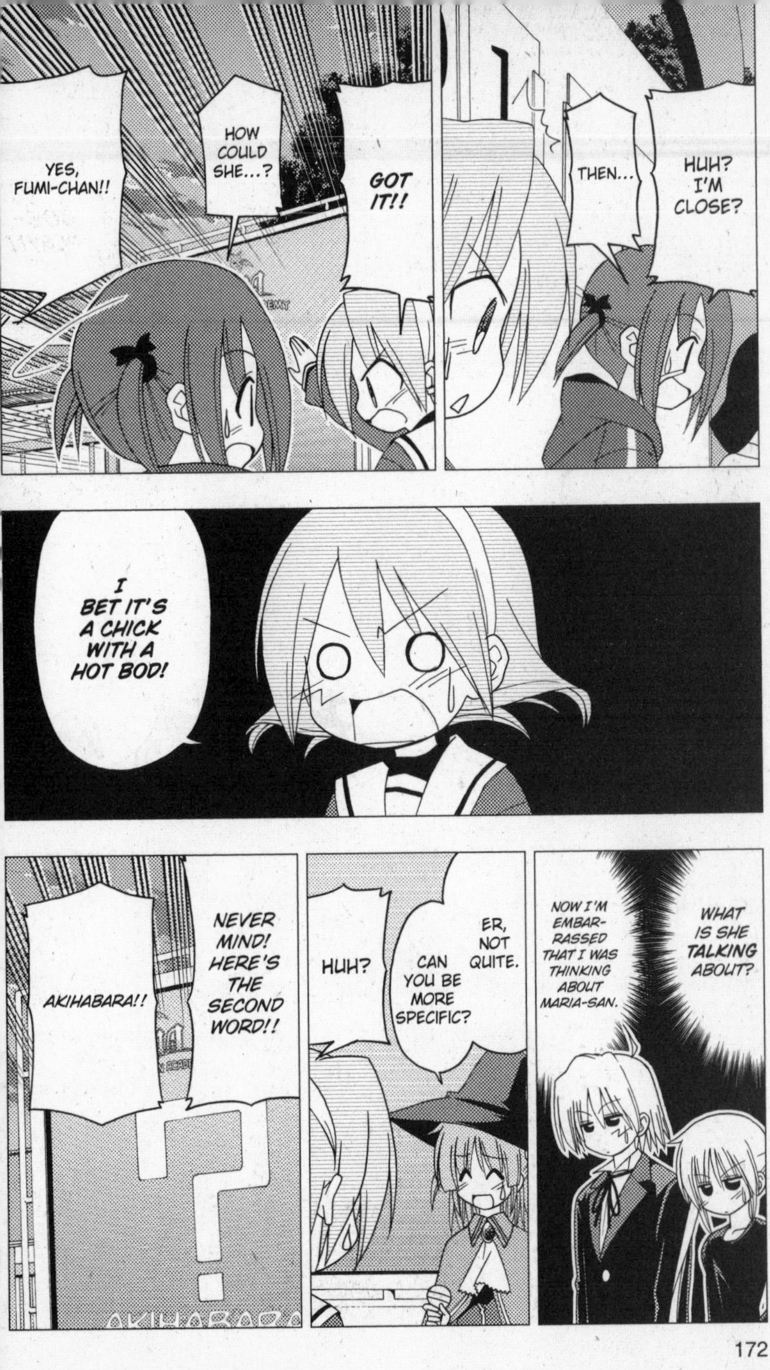
HUH? I'M CLOSE?
THEN...
GOT IT!!
HOW COULD SHE...?
YES, FUMI-CHAN!!
I BET IT'S A CHICK WITH A HOT BOD!
WHAT IS SHE TALKING ABOUT?
NOW I'M EMBAR-RASSED THAT I WAS THINKING ABOUT MARIA-SAN.
ER, NOT QUITE.
CAN YOU BE MORE SPECIFIC?
HUH?
NEVER MIND! HERE'S THE SECOND WORD!!
AKIHABARA!!

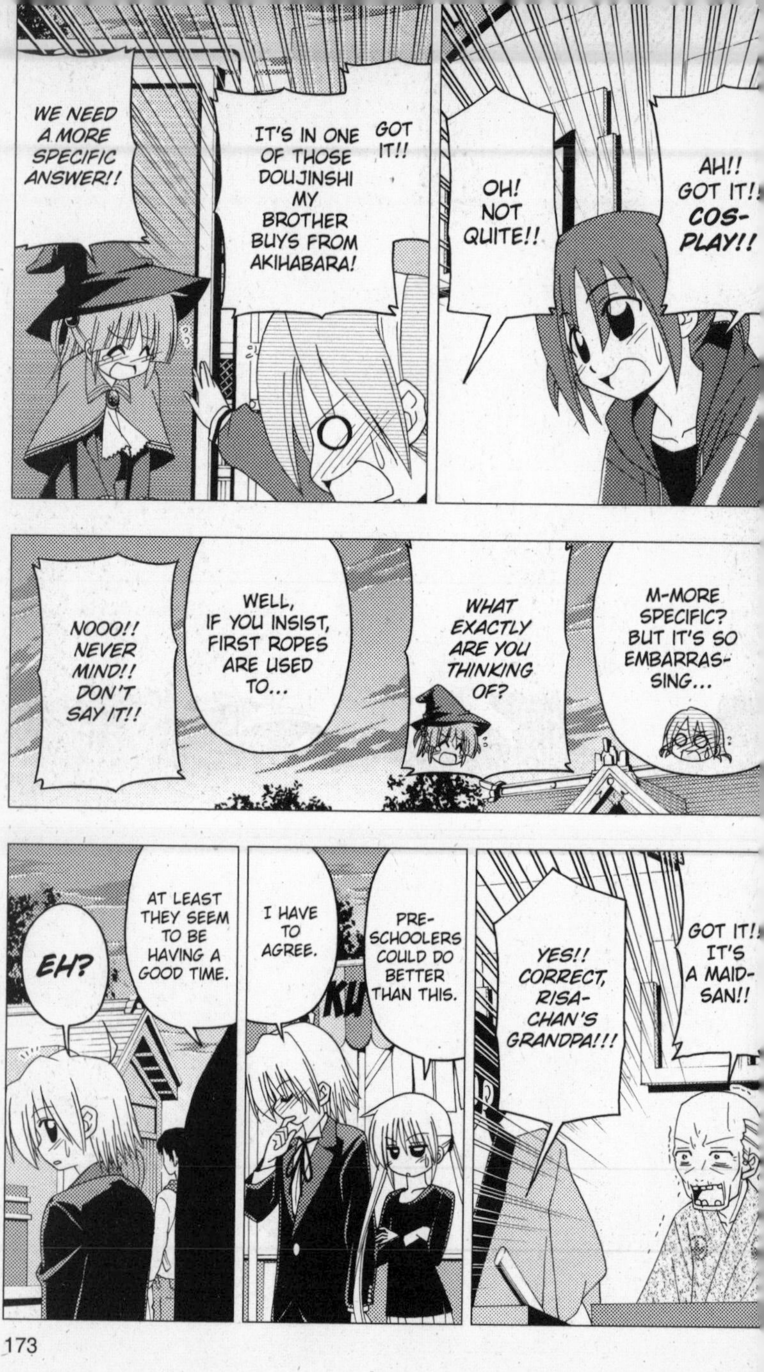
AH!! GOT IT!! COS-PLAY!!
OH! NOT QUITE!!
GOT IT!!
IT'S IN ONE OF THOSE DOUJINSHI MY BROTHER BUYS FROM AKIHABARA!
WE NEED A MORE SPECIFIC ANSWER!!
M-MORE SPECIFIC? BUT IT'S SO EMBARRAS-SING...
WHAT EXACTLY ARE YOU THINKING OF?
WELL, IF YOU INSIST, FIRST ROPES ARE USED TO...
NOOO!! NEVER MIND!! DON'T SAY IT!!
GOT IT!! IT'S A MAID-SAN!!
YES!! CORRECT, RISA-CHAN'S GRANDPA!!!
PRE-SCHOOLERS COULD DO BETTER THAN THIS.
I HAVE TO AGREE.
AT LEAST THEY SEEM TO BE HAVING A GOOD TIME.
EH?

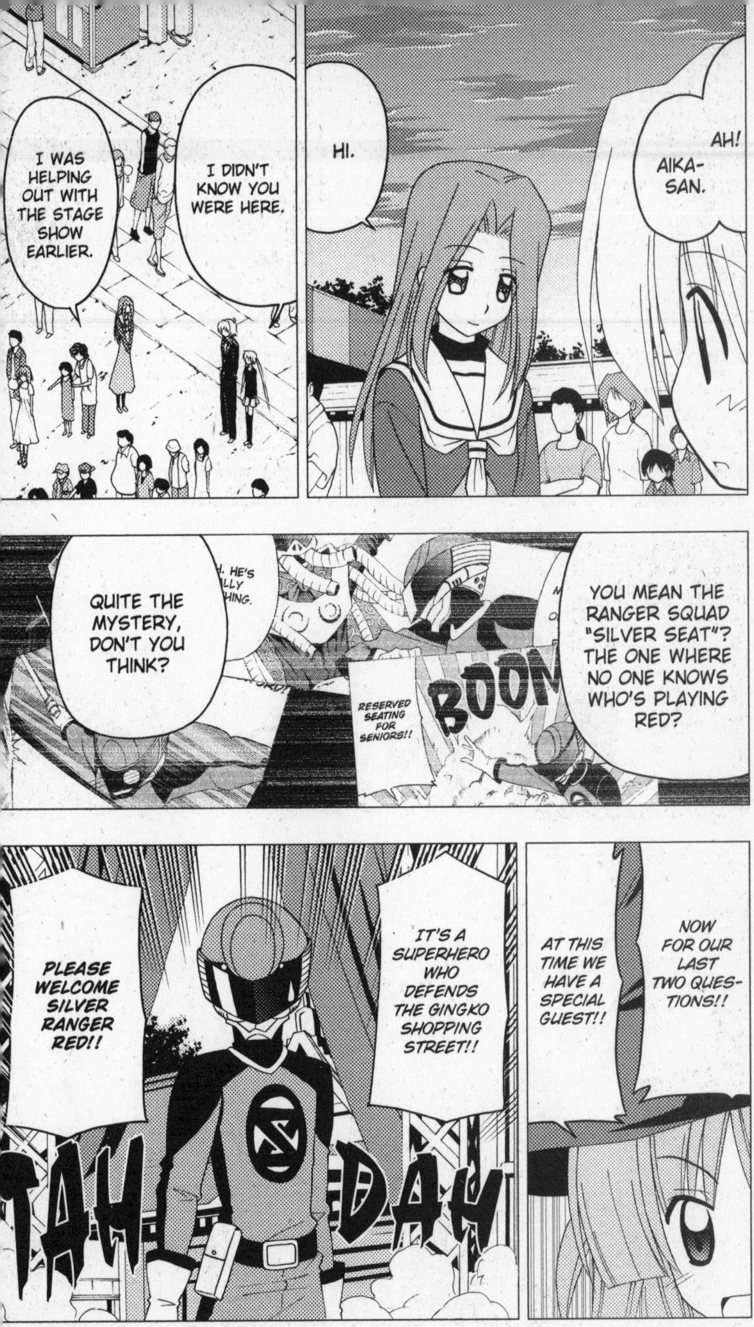
AH! AIKA-SAN.
HI.
I DIDN'T KNOW YOU WERE HERE.
I WAS HELPING OUT WITH THE STAGE SHOW EARLIER.
YOU MEAN THE RANGER SQUAD "SILVER SEAT"? THE ONE WHERE NO ONE KNOWS WHO'S PLAYING RED?
BOOM
RESERVED SEATING FOR SENIORS!!
QUITE THE MYSTERY, DON'T YOU THINK?
NOW FOR OUR LAST TWO QUES-TIONS!!
AT THIS TIME WE HAVE A SPECIAL GUEST!!
IT'S A SUPERHERO WHO DEFENDS THE GINGKO SHOPPING STREET!!
PLEASE WELCOME SILVER RANGER RED!!
TAH DAH

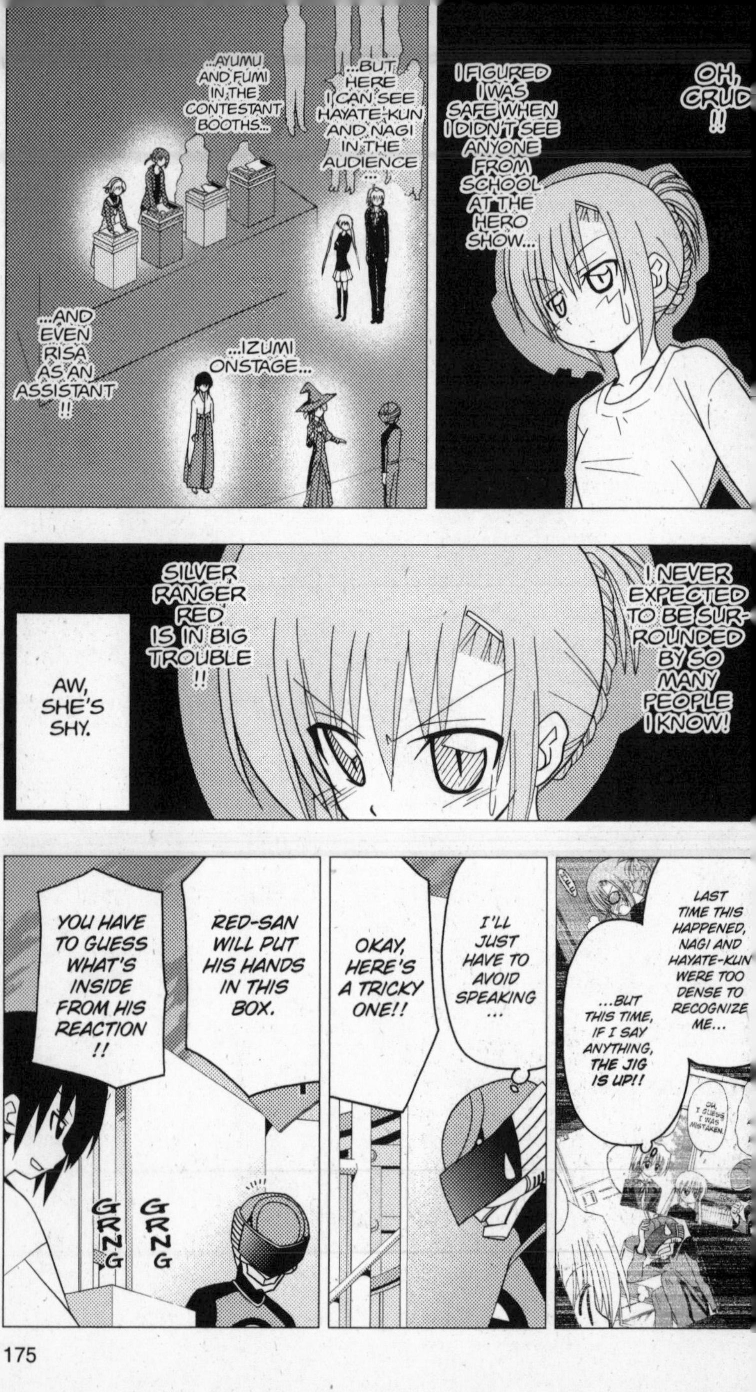
OH, CRUD!!
I FIGURED I WAS SAFE WHEN I DIDN'T SEE ANYONE FROM SCHOOL AT THE HERO SHOW...
...BUT HERE I CAN SEE HAYATE-KUN AND NAGI IN THE AUDIENCE...
...AYUMU AND FUMI IN THE CONTESTANT BOOTHS...
...IZUMI ONSTAGE...
...AND EVEN RISA AS AN ASSISTANT!!
I NEVER EXPECTED TO BE SURROUNDED BY SO MANY PEOPLE I KNOW!
SILVER RANGER RED IS IN BIG TROUBLE!!
AW, SHE'S SHY.
LAST TIME THIS HAPPENED, NAGI AND HAYATE-KUN WERE TOO DENSE TO RECOGNIZE ME...
...BUT THIS TIME, IF I SAY ANYTHING, THE JIG IS UP!!
OH, I GUESS I WAS MISTAKEN.
I'LL JUST HAVE TO AVOID SPEAKING...
OKAY, HERE'S A TRICKY ONE!!
RED-SAN WILL PUT HIS HANDS IN THIS BOX.
YOU HAVE TO GUESS WHAT'S INSIDE FROM HIS REACTION!!
GRNG
GRNG

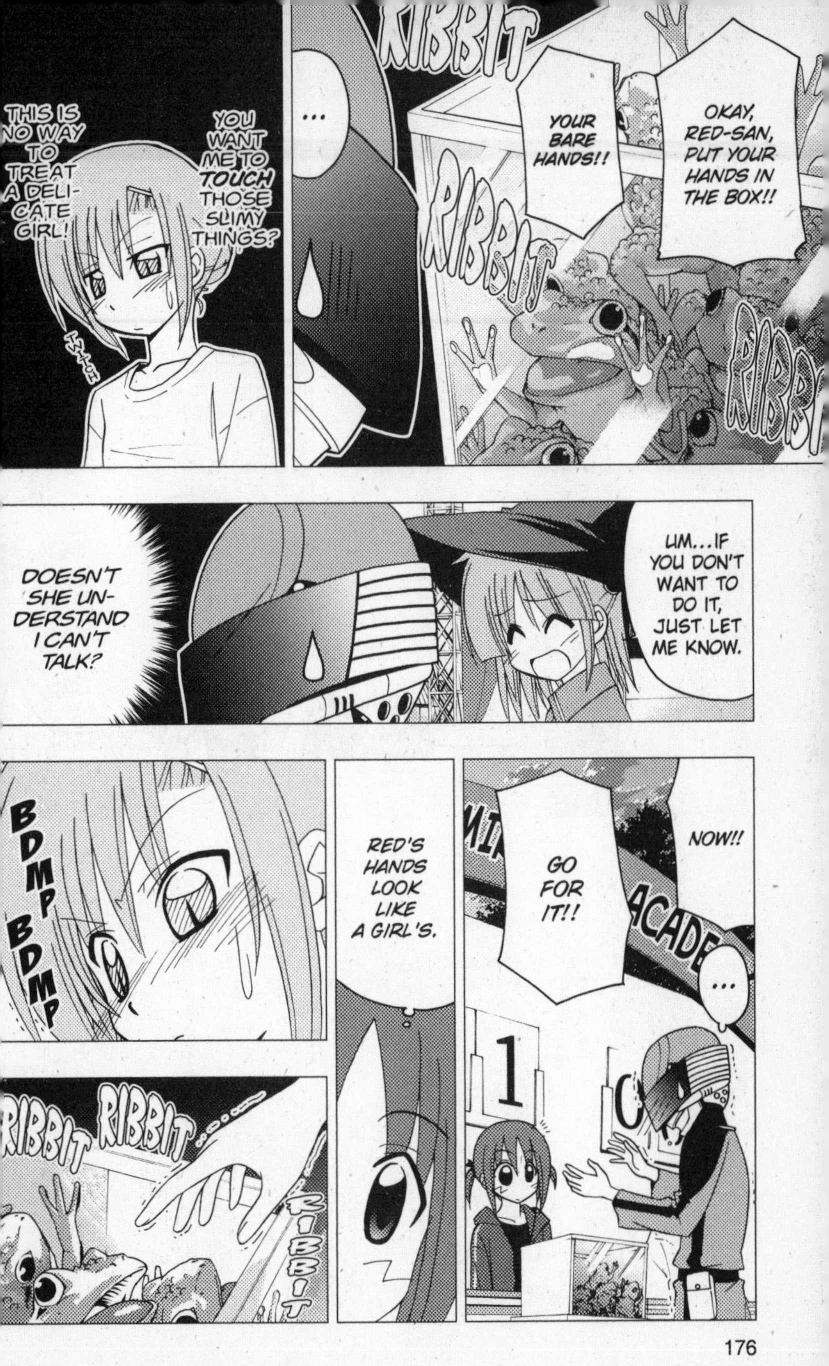
RIBBIT
OKAY, RED-SAN, PUT YOUR HANDS IN THE BOX!!
YOUR BARE HANDS!!
RIBBIT
RIBBIT
...
YOU WANT ME TO TOUCH THOSE SLIMY THINGS?
THIS IS NO WAY TO TREAT A DELI-CATE GIRL!
TWITCH
UM...IF YOU DON'T WANT TO DO IT, JUST LET ME KNOW.
DOESN'T SHE UN-DERSTAND I CAN'T TALK?
NOW!!
GO FOR IT!!
...
RED'S HANDS LOOK LIKE A GIRL'S.
BDMP BDMP
RIBBIT RIBBIT
RIBBIT

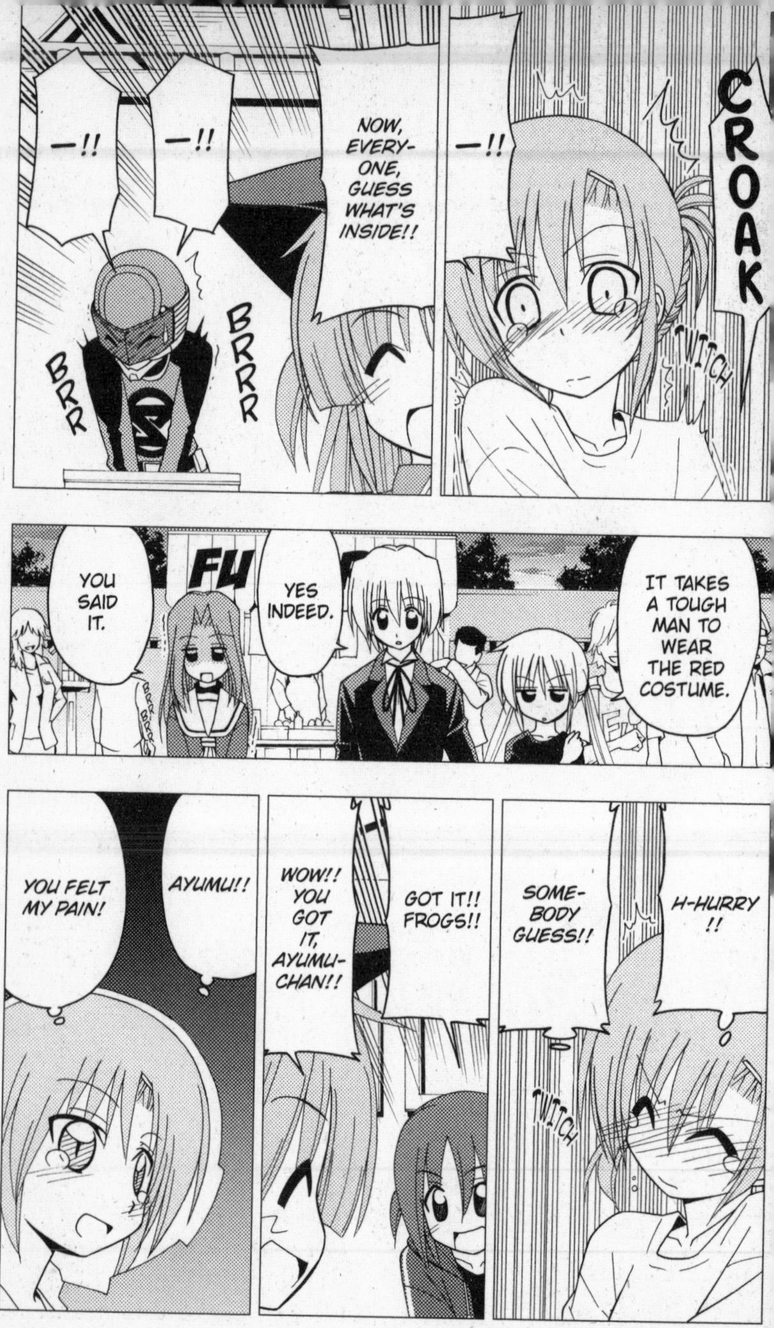
CROAK
—!!
TWITCH
NOW, EVERY-ONE, GUESS WHAT'S INSIDE!!
—!!
—!!
BRRRR
BRR
IT TAKES A TOUGH MAN TO WEAR THE RED COSTUME.
YES INDEED.
YOU SAID IT.
H-HURRY!!
SOME-BODY GUESS!!
TWITCH
GOT IT!! FROGS!!
WOW!! YOU GOT IT, AYUMU-CHAN!!
AYUMU!!
YOU FELT MY PAIN!

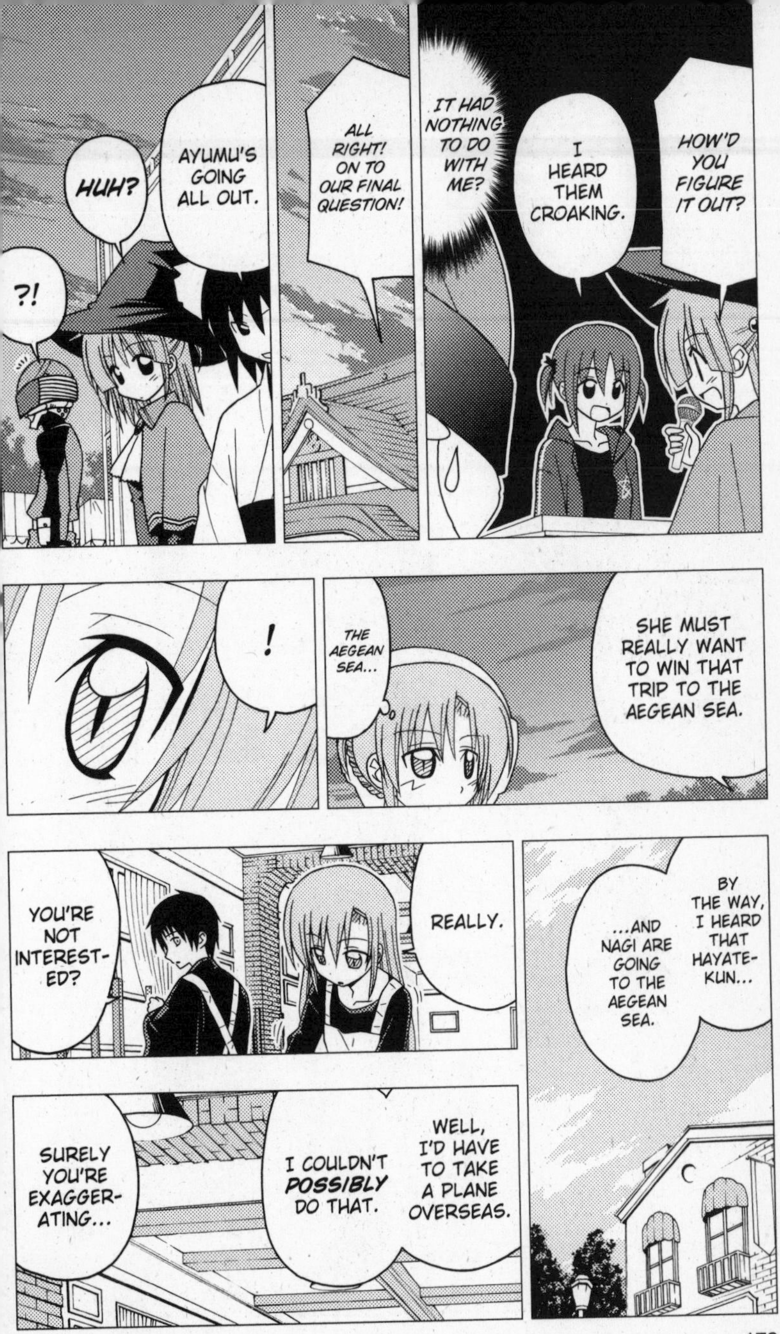
HOW'D YOU FIGURE IT OUT?
I HEARD THEM CROAKING.
IT HAD NOTHING TO DO WITH ME?
ALL RIGHT! ON TO OUR FINAL QUESTION!
AYUMU'S GOING ALL OUT.
HUH?
?!
SHE MUST REALLY WANT TO WIN THAT TRIP TO THE AEGEAN SEA.
THE AEGEAN SEA...
!
BY THE WAY, I HEARD THAT HAYATE-KUN...
...AND NAGI ARE GOING TO THE AEGEAN SEA.
REALLY.
YOU'RE NOT INTERESTED?
WELL, I'D HAVE TO TAKE A PLANE OVERSEAS.
I COULDN'T POSSIBLY DO THAT.
SURELY YOU'RE EXAGGERATING...

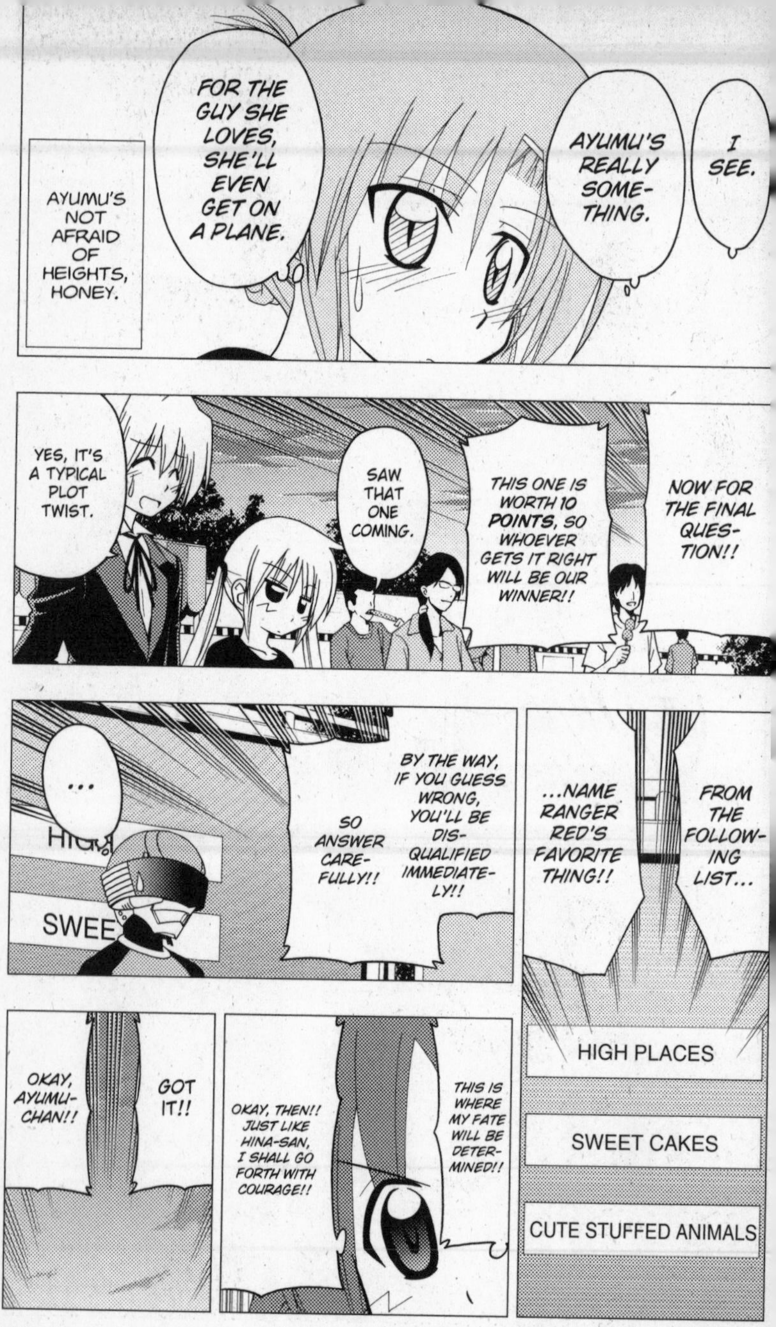
I SEE.
AYUMU'S REALLY SOMETHING.
FOR THE GUY SHE LOVES, SHE'LL EVEN GET ON A PLANE.
AYUMU'S NOT AFRAID OF HEIGHTS, HONEY.
NOW FOR THE FINAL QUESTION!!
THIS ONE IS WORTH 10 POINTS, SO WHOEVER GETS IT RIGHT WILL BE OUR WINNER!!
SAW THAT ONE COMING.
YES, IT'S A TYPICAL PLOT TWIST.
FROM THE FOLLOWING LIST...
...NAME RANGER RED'S FAVORITE THING!!
HIGH PLACES
SWEET CAKES
CUTE STUFFED ANIMALS
BY THE WAY, IF YOU GUESS WRONG, YOU'LL BE DISQUALIFIED IMMEDIATELY!!
SO ANSWER CAREFULLY!!
...
THIS IS WHERE MY FATE WILL BE DETERMINED!!
OKAY, THEN!! JUST LIKE HINA-SAN, I SHALL GO FORTH WITH COURAGE!!
GOT IT!!
OKAY, AYUMU-CHAN!!

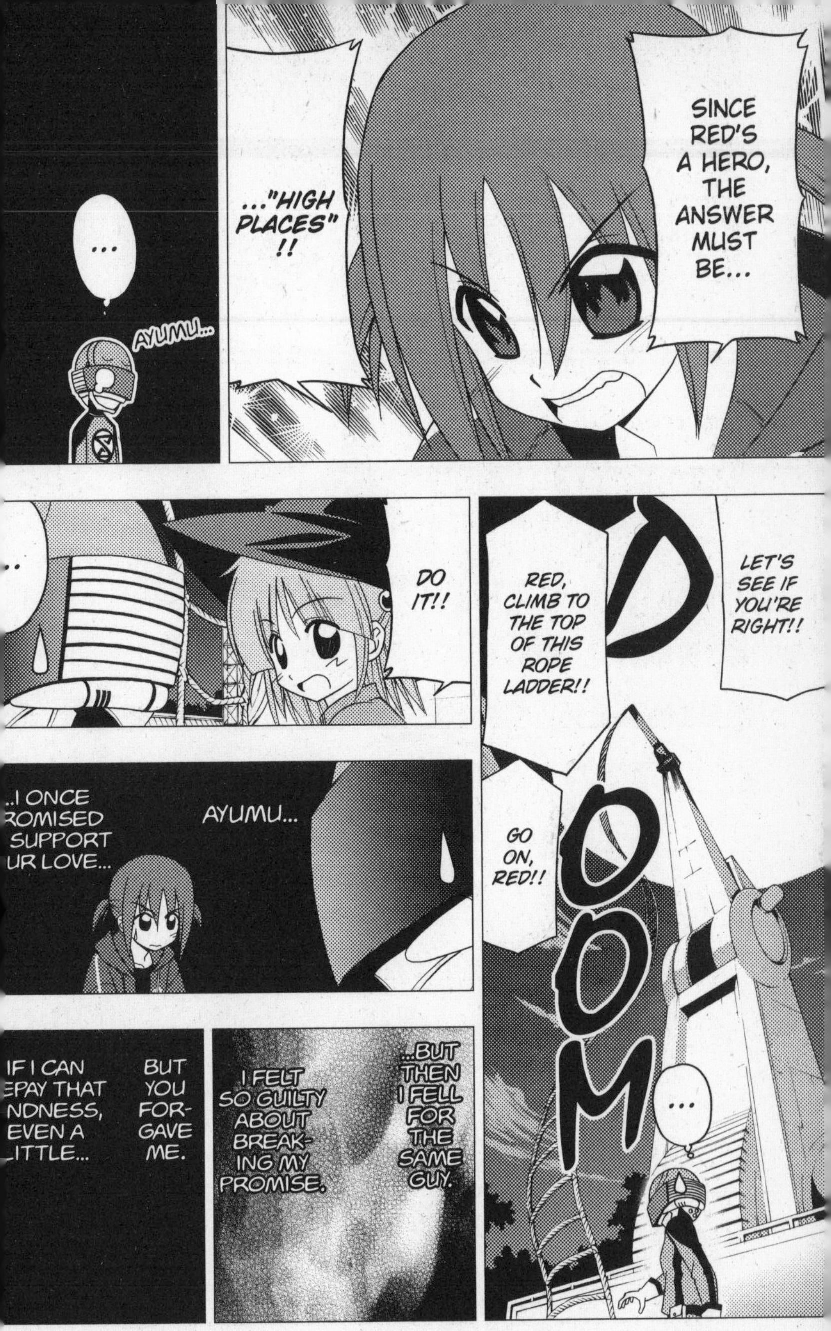
SINCE RED'S A HERO, THE ANSWER MUST BE...
..."HIGH PLACES"!!
...
AYUMU...
LET'S SEE IF YOU'RE RIGHT!!
RED, CLIMB TO THE TOP OF THIS ROPE LADDER!!
DOOM
GO ON, RED!!
...
DO IT!!
..
AYUMU...
..I ONCE ROMISED SUPPORT UR LOVE...
...BUT THEN I FELL FOR THE SAME GUY.
I FELT SO GUILTY ABOUT BREAKING MY PROMISE.
BUT YOU FOR-GAVE ME.
IF I CAN EPAY THAT NDNESS, EVEN A ITTLE...

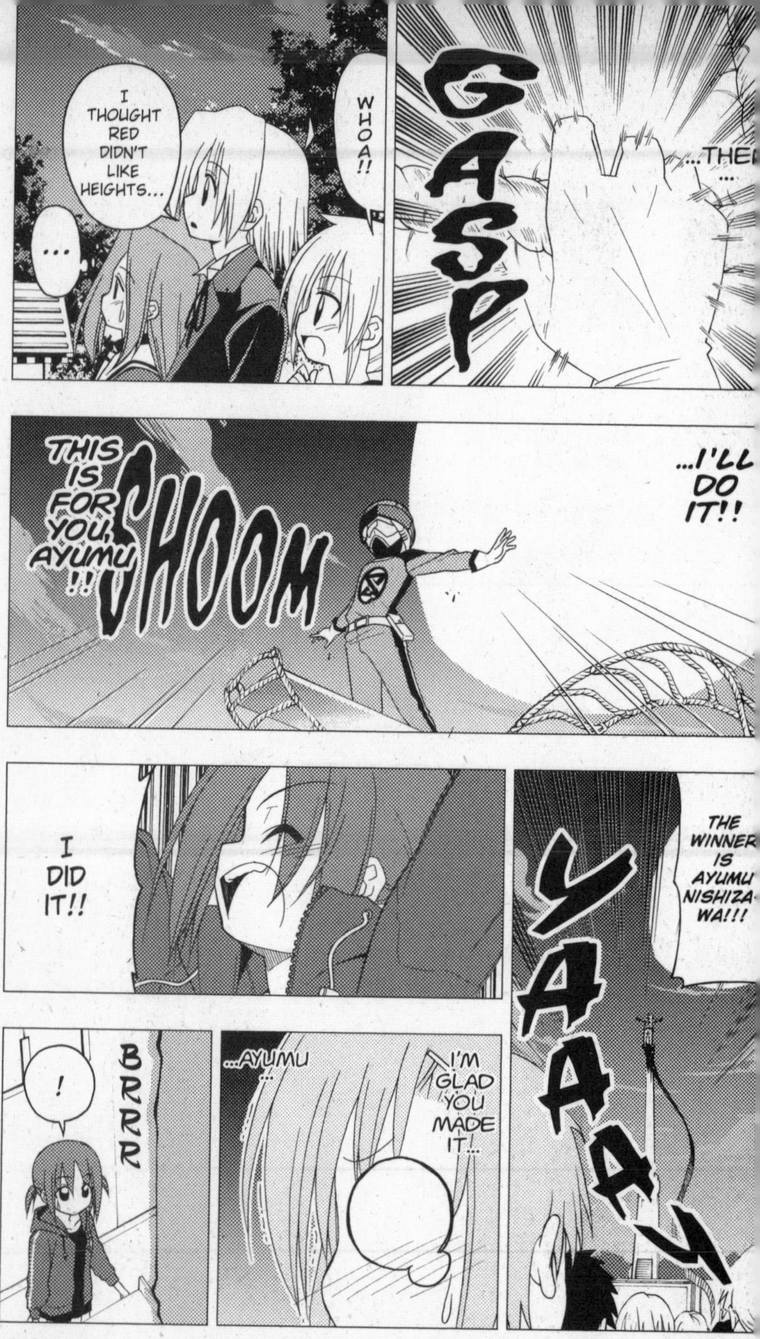

...THE
...
GASP
WHOA!!
I THOUGHT RED DIDN'T LIKE HEIGHTS...
...
...I'LL DO IT!!
THIS IS FOR YOU, AYUMU!!
SHOOM
THE WINNER IS AYUMU NISHIZAWA!!!
YAAAY
I DID IT!!
I'M GLAD YOU MADE IT...
...AYUMU...
BRRR
!

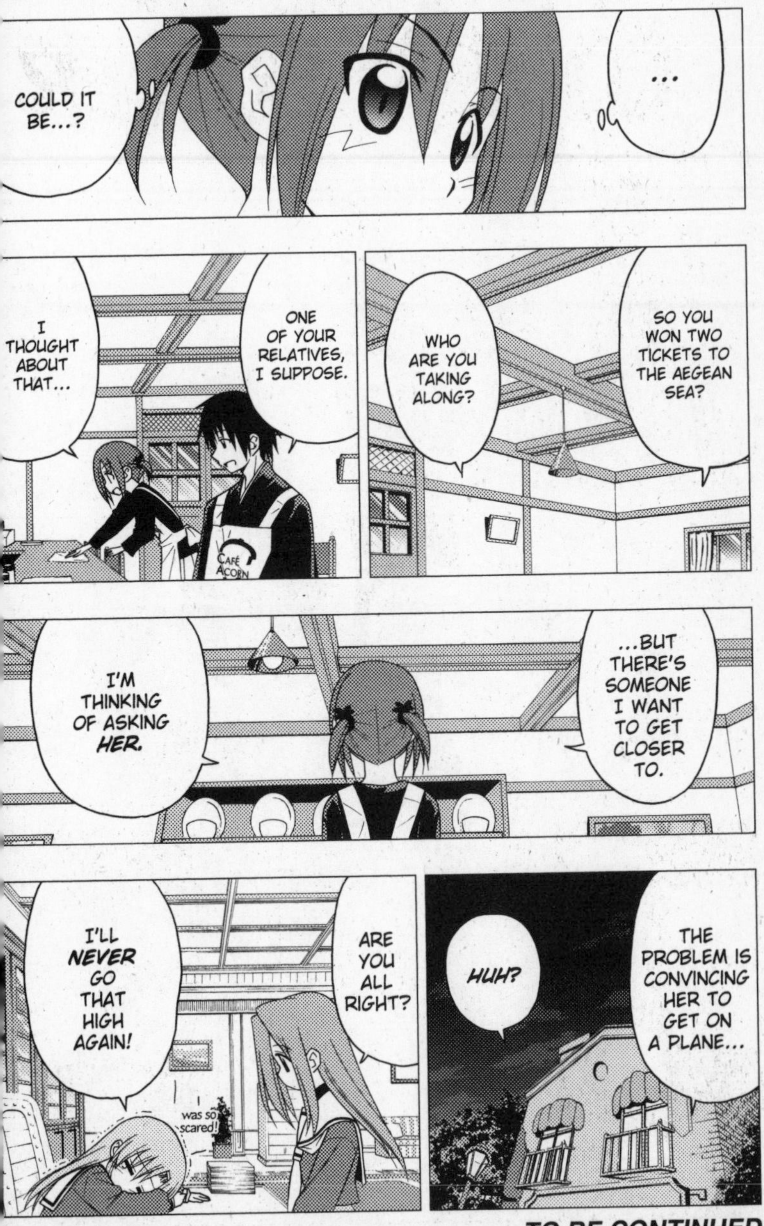
...
COULD IT BE...?
SO YOU WON TWO TICKETS TO THE AEGEAN SEA?
WHO ARE YOU TAKING ALONG?
ONE OF YOUR RELATIVES, I SUPPOSE.
I THOUGHT ABOUT THAT...
CAFÉ ACORN
...BUT THERE'S SOMEONE I WANT TO GET CLOSER TO.
I'M THINKING OF ASKING *HER.*
THE PROBLEM IS CONVINCING HER TO GET ON A PLANE...
HUH?
ARE YOU ALL RIGHT?
I'LL *NEVER* GO THAT HIGH AGAIN!
I was so scared!

TO BE CONTINUED

HAYATE THE COMBAT BUTLER

BONUS PAGE

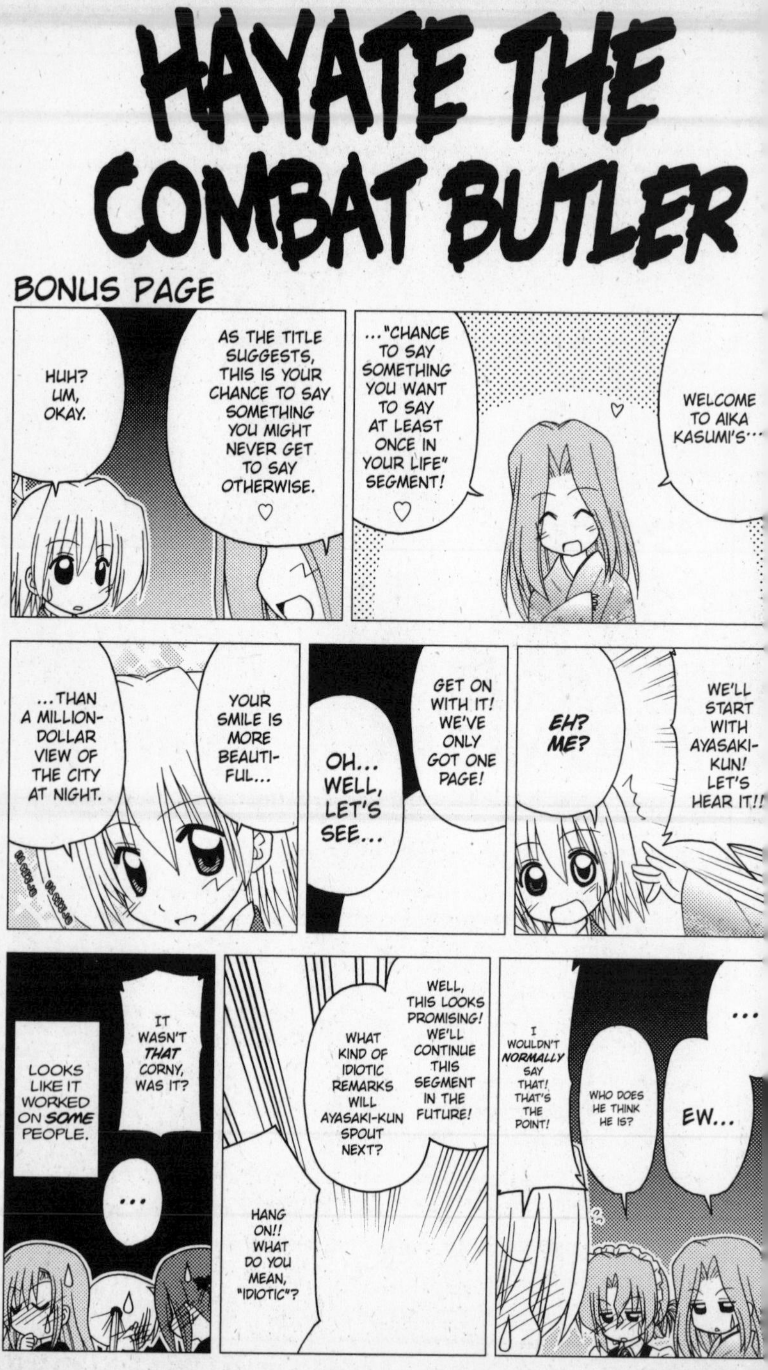
WELCOME TO AIKA KASUMI'S...
..."CHANCE TO SAY SOMETHING YOU WANT TO SAY AT LEAST ONCE IN YOUR LIFE" SEGMENT! ♡
AS THE TITLE SUGGESTS, THIS IS YOUR CHANCE TO SAY SOMETHING YOU MIGHT NEVER GET TO SAY OTHERWISE. ♡
HUH? UM, OKAY.
WE'LL START WITH AYASAKI-KUN! LET'S HEAR IT!!
EH? ME?
GET ON WITH IT! WE'VE ONLY GOT ONE PAGE!
OH... WELL, LET'S SEE...
YOUR SMILE IS MORE BEAUTI-FUL...
...THAN A MILLION-DOLLAR VIEW OF THE CITY AT NIGHT.
...
EW...
WHO DOES HE THINK HE IS?
I WOULDN'T NORMALLY SAY THAT! THAT'S THE POINT!
WELL, THIS LOOKS PROMISING! WE'LL CONTINUE THIS SEGMENT IN THE FUTURE!
WHAT KIND OF IDIOTIC REMARKS WILL AYASAKI-KUN SPOUT NEXT?
HANG ON!! WHAT DO YOU MEAN, "IDIOTIC"?
IT WASN'T THAT CORNY, WAS IT?
LOOKS LIKE IT WORKED ON SOME PEOPLE.
...

PROFILE

[Age]
17 Forever♡

[Birthday]
I don't understand the Christian calendar too well… (^_^;)

[Blood Type]
AB, a bit unusual.

[Family Structure]
Possibly a daughter…

[Height]
About 10 meters?
Shot up a little recently…☆

[Weight]
About 3 apples.☆ Not really.
It's a secret.♪

[Strengths/Likes]
Gold, wealth, military power, tending flowers in the woods.
Really into hats lately.☆

[Weaknesses/Dislikes]
Haircuts, foolish couples.
Weaknesses include careless behavior.

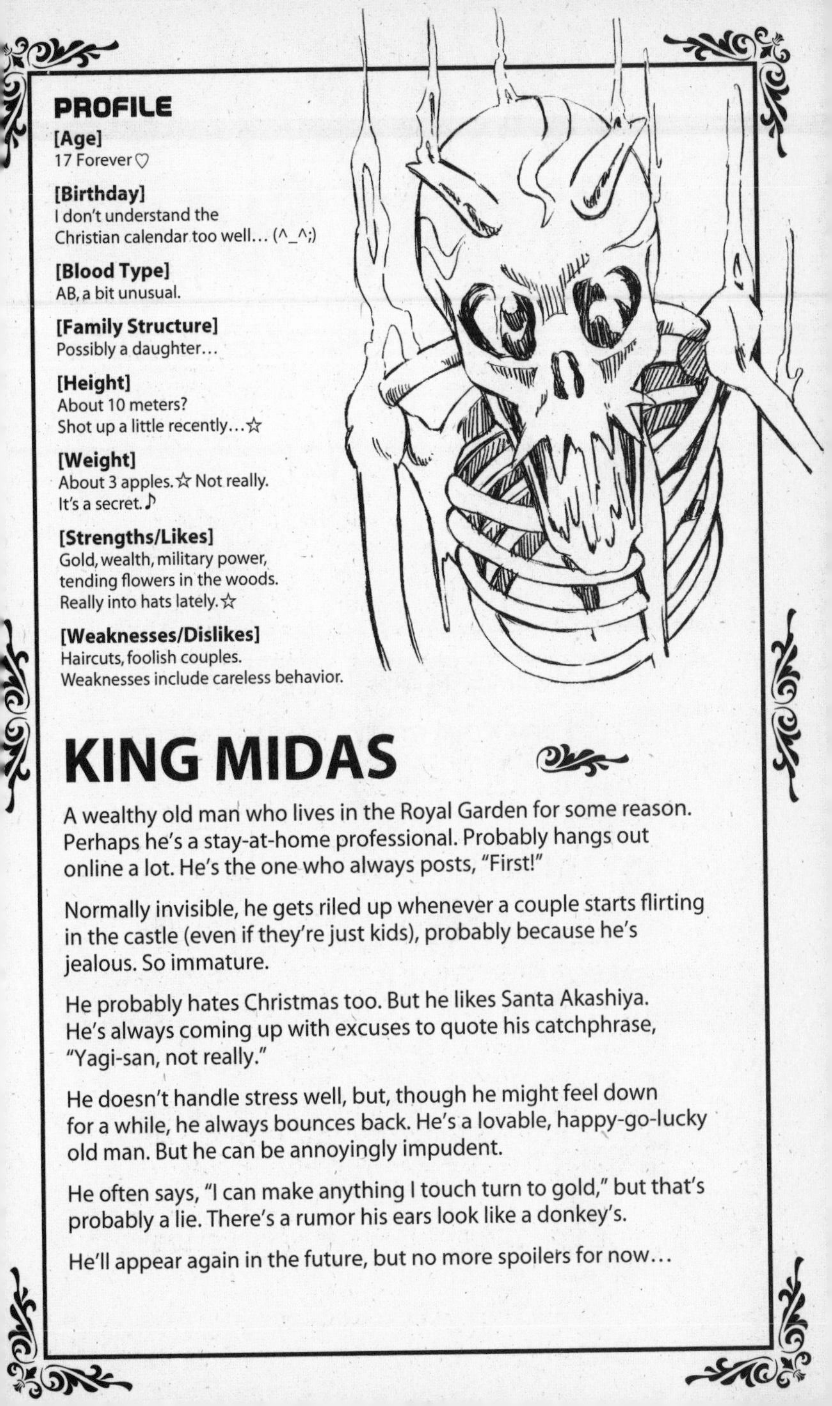

KING MIDAS

A wealthy old man who lives in the Royal Garden for some reason. Perhaps he's a stay-at-home professional. Probably hangs out online a lot. He's the one who always posts, "First!"

Normally invisible, he gets riled up whenever a couple starts flirting in the castle (even if they're just kids), probably because he's jealous. So immature.

He probably hates Christmas too. But he likes Santa Akashiya. He's always coming up with excuses to quote his catchphrase, "Yagi-san, not really."

He doesn't handle stress well, but, though he might feel down for a while, he always bounces back. He's a lovable, happy-go-lucky old man. But he can be annoyingly impudent.

He often says, "I can make anything I touch turn to gold," but that's probably a lie. There's a rumor his ears look like a donkey's.

He'll appear again in the future, but no more spoilers for now…

HATA HERE. WE'RE UP TO VOLUME 18!
HOW HAVE YOU BEEN?

THE SECOND SEASON OF THE *HAYATE* ANIME
WILL BE STARTING SOON. I'VE BEEN SO BUSY
I THOUGHT I'D DIE A FEW TIMES,
BUT I'M OKAY AT THE MOMENT. I CAUGHT
A COLD, BUT I THINK I'M FINE NOW.

IN THIS VOLUME I WRAPPED UP THE
FLASHBACK ARC WITH HAYATE AND ATHENA.
IT TOOK LONGER THAN I EXPECTED.
AS AN AUTHOR, I'M PLEASED I WAS ABLE TO
WRITE SUCH A LONG STORY. I WONDER WHAT
YOU THOUGHT OF IT. IF YOU HAVE ANY
COMMENTS, PLEASE LET ME KNOW.

THE GOLDEN WEEK STORY LINE HAS STARTED
RUNNING IN THE MAGAZINE.
I'M BUSY COLLECTING REFERENCE PHOTOS
FOR THE BACKGROUNDS. MY STAFF IS GOING
TO GO THE EXTRA MILE FOR THIS ONE,
SO PLEASE LOOK FORWARD TO IT!

SPEAKING OF WORKING HARD, I'M DRAWING
A WEEKLY FOUR-PANEL *HAYATE* COMIC STRIP
ON THE WEB (THOUGH IT'S NOT REALLY IN
THE FOUR-PANEL FORMAT ANYMORE). I'VE
BEEN CHURNING OUT STRIPS ONE BY ONE,
SO PLEASE ENJOY THEM. ☆

ALL TOLD, THERE'S A LOT OF NEW STUFF IN
THE WORKS FROM *HAYATE*, SO PLEASE KEEP
READING! I'M BANKING ON YOUR SUPPORT AS
ALWAYS!!!

ONCE AGAIN, SEE YOU IN THE NEXT VOLUME! ☆

HTTP://WEBSUNDAY.NET

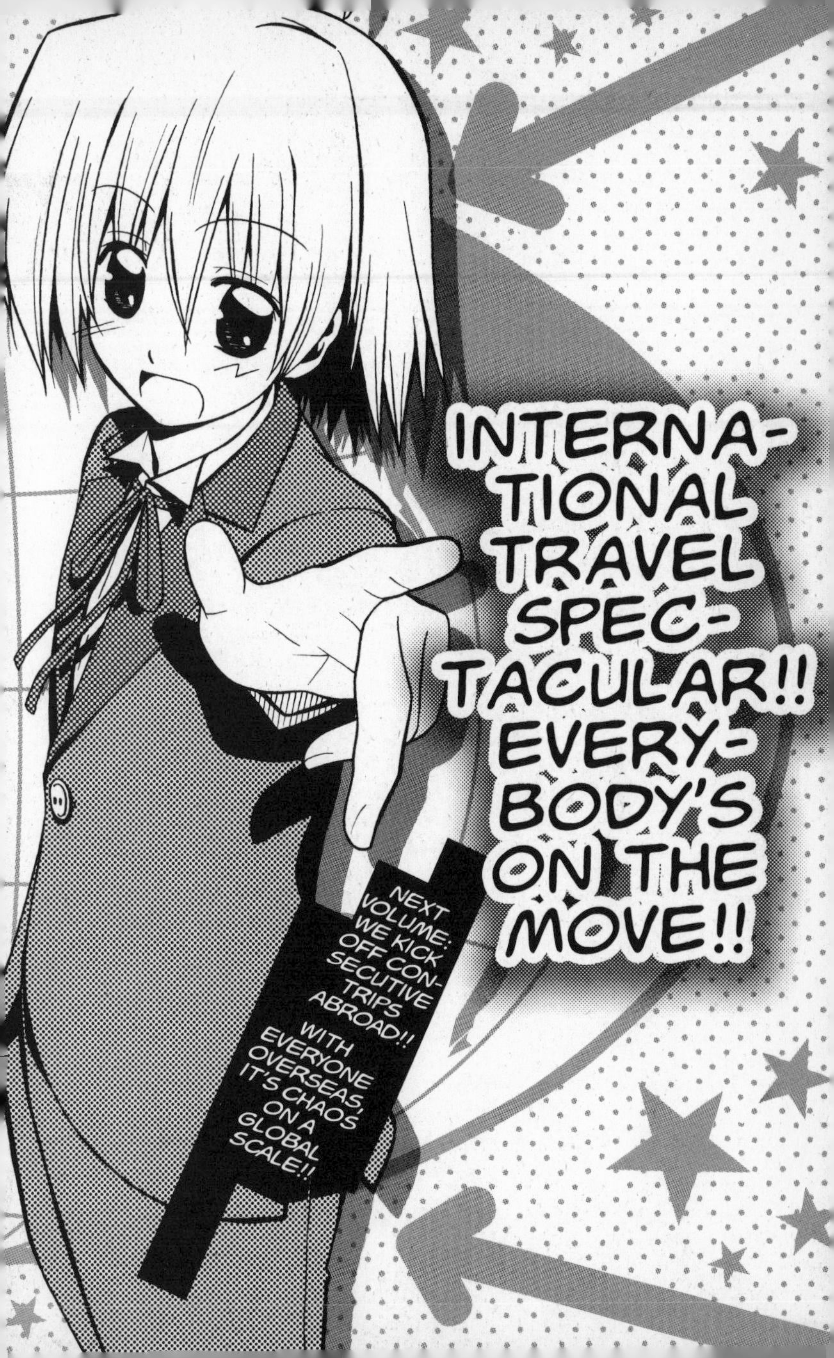
INTERNATIONAL TRAVEL SPECTACULAR!! EVERYBODY'S ON THE MOVE!!
NEXT VOLUME: WE KICK OFF CONSECUTIVE TRIPS ABROAD!!
WITH EVERYONE OVERSEAS, IT'S CHAOS ON A GLOBAL SCALE!!

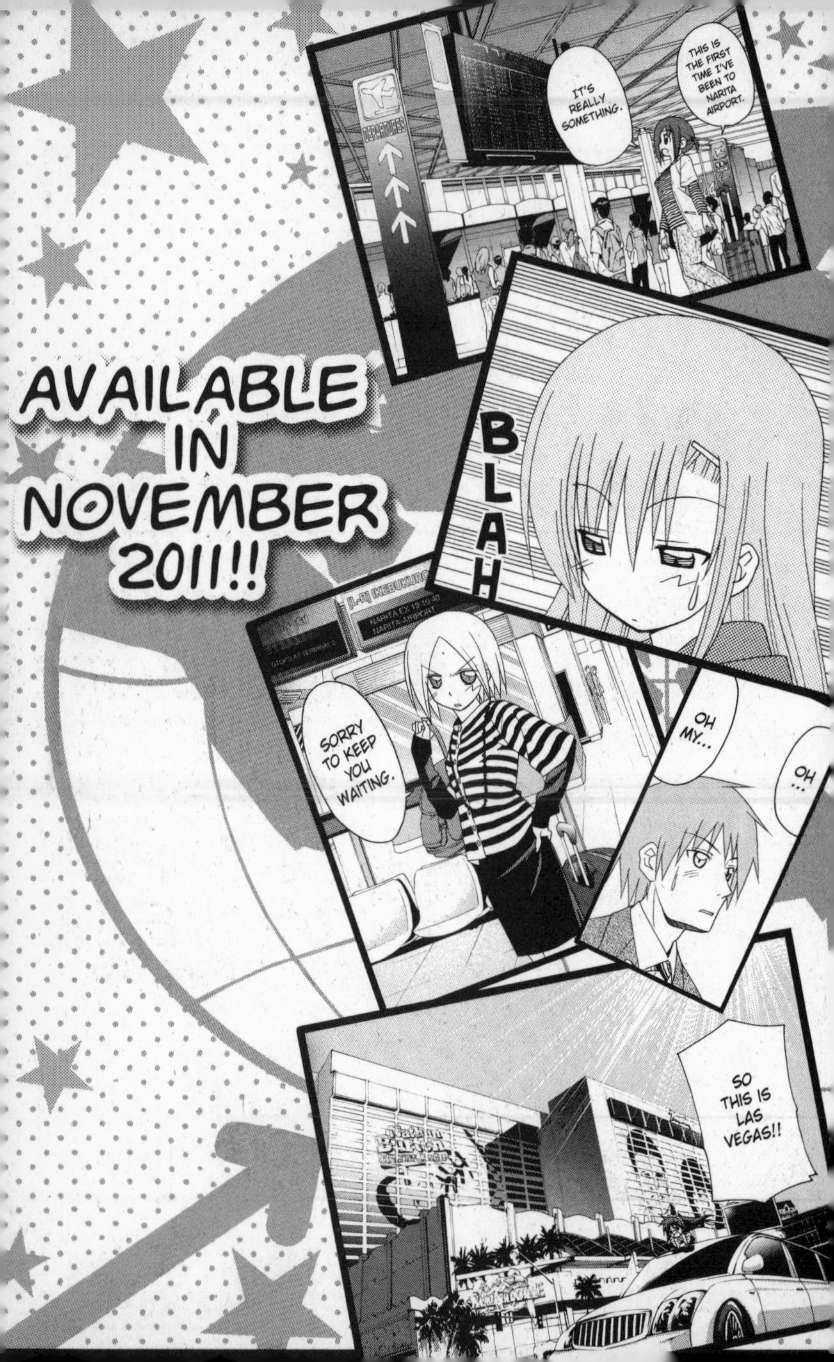
AVAILABLE IN NOVEMBER 2011!!
THIS IS THE FIRST TIME I'VE BEEN TO NARITA AIRPORT.
IT'S REALLY SOMETHING.
DEPARTURES
BLAH
OH MY...
OH...
[L-R] IKEBUKURO
NARITA EX 19 10:40
NARITA-AIRPORT
SORRY TO KEEP YOU WAITING.
SO THIS IS LAS VEGAS!!

Hope for the Future

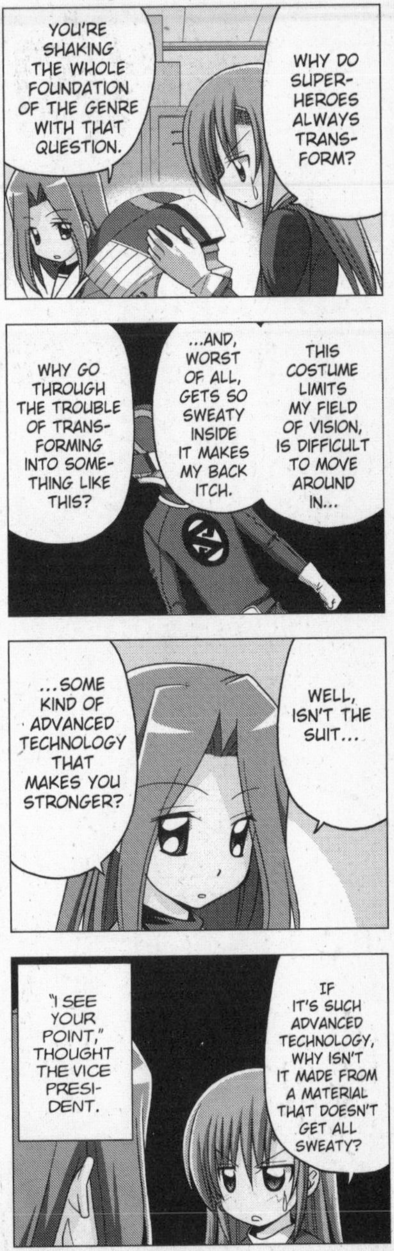
WHY DO SUPER-HEROES ALWAYS TRANS-FORM?
YOU'RE SHAKING THE WHOLE FOUNDATION OF THE GENRE WITH THAT QUESTION.
THIS COSTUME LIMITS MY FIELD OF VISION, IS DIFFICULT TO MOVE AROUND IN...
...AND, WORST OF ALL, GETS SO SWEATY INSIDE IT MAKES MY BACK ITCH.
WHY GO THROUGH THE TROUBLE OF TRANS-FORMING INTO SOME-THING LIKE THIS?
WELL, ISN'T THE SUIT...
...SOME KIND OF ADVANCED TECHNOLOGY THAT MAKES YOU STRONGER?
IF IT'S SUCH ADVANCED TECHNOLOGY, WHY ISN'T IT MADE FROM A MATERIAL THAT DOESN'T GET ALL SWEATY?
"I SEE YOUR POINT," THOUGHT THE VICE PRESI-DENT.

Revenge for the Past

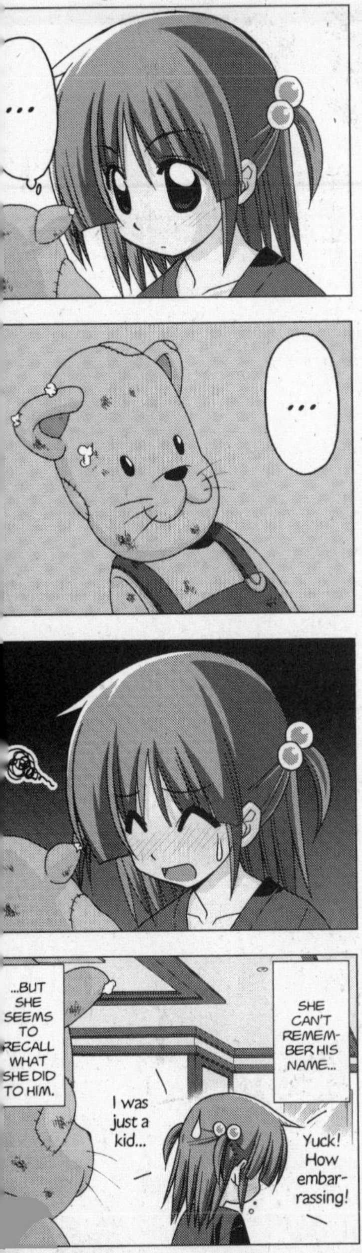
...
...
SHE CAN'T REMEM-BER HIS NAME...
Yuck! How embar-rassing!
...BUT SHE SEEMS TO RECALL WHAT SHE DID TO HIM.
I was just a kid...

HAYATE THE COMBAT BUTLER!

SP EVENT (4)

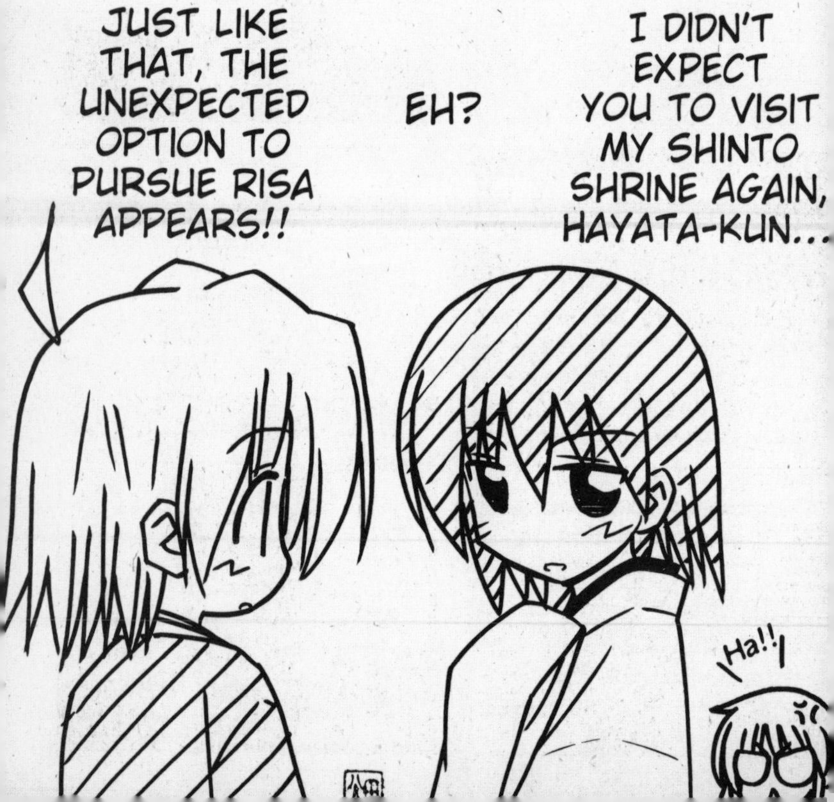
I DIDN'T EXPECT YOU TO VISIT MY SHINTO SHRINE AGAIN, HAYATA-KUN...
EH?
JUST LIKE THAT, THE UNEXPECTED OPTION TO PURSUE RISA APPEARS!!
Ha!!

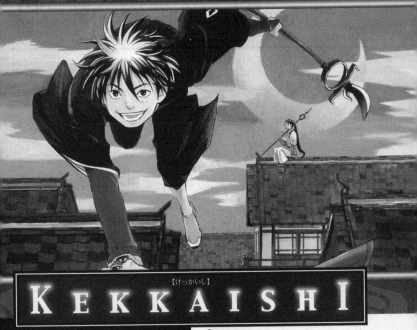
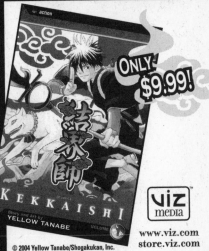

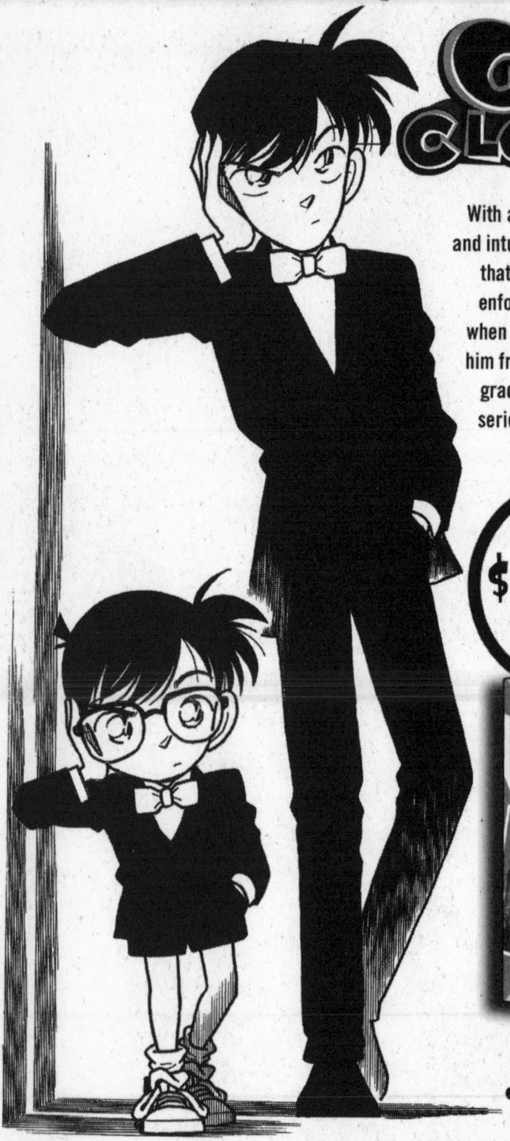

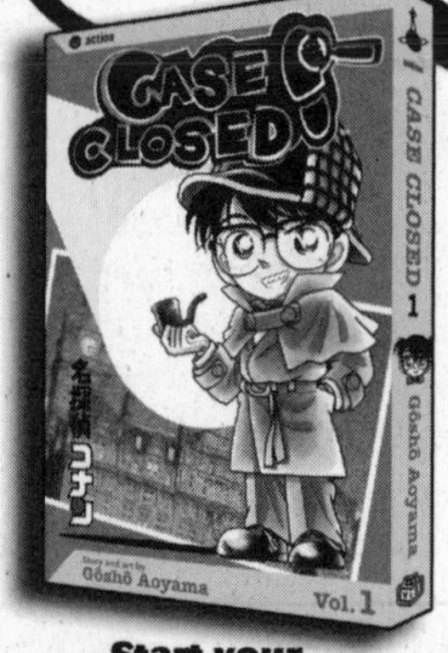

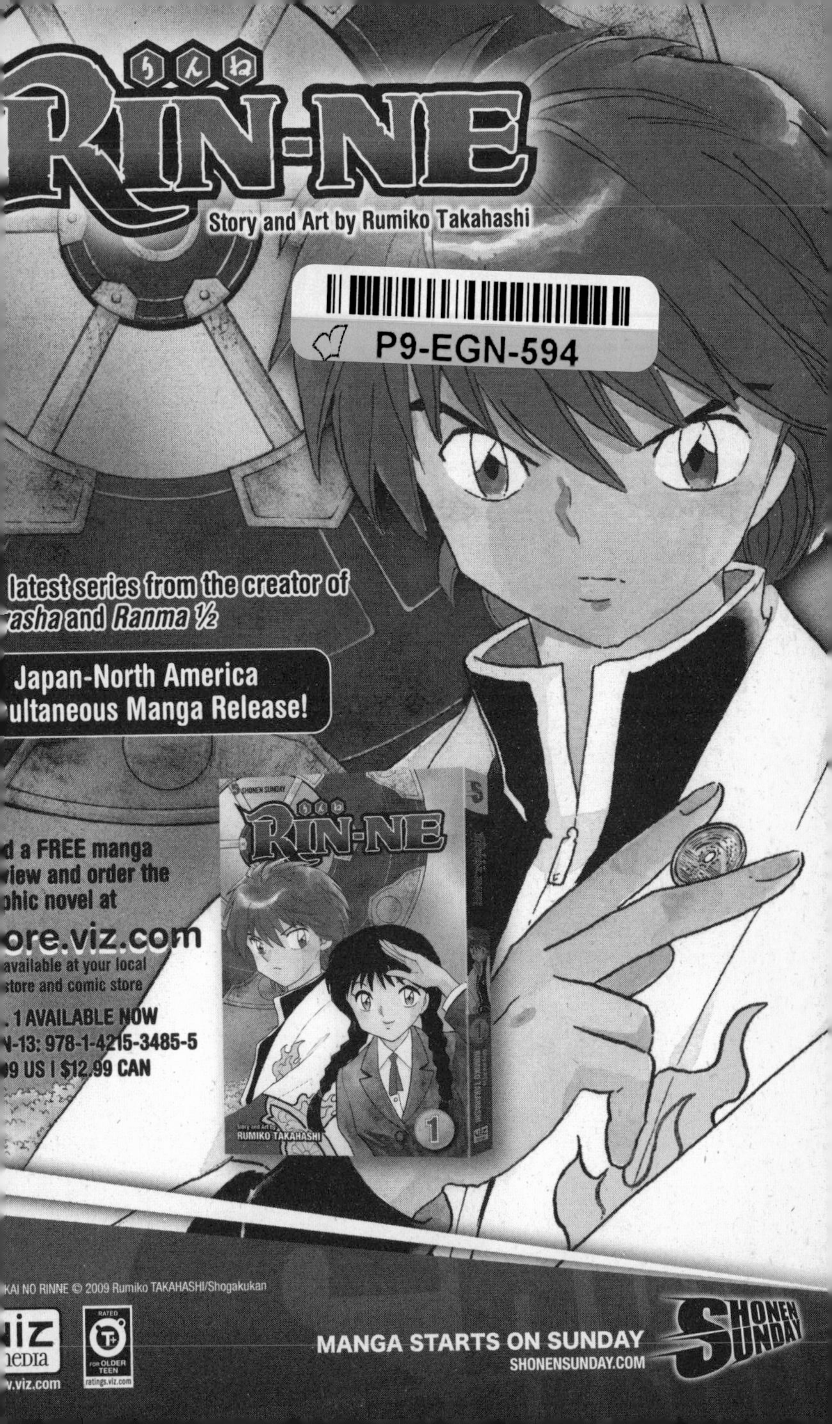
りんね
RIN-NE
Story and Art by Rumiko Takahashi
P9-EGN-594
latest series from the creator of
asha and Ranma ½
Japan-North America
ultaneous Manga Release!
d a FREE manga
iew and order the
phic novel at
ore.viz.com
available at your local
store and comic store
. 1 AVAILABLE NOW
N-13: 978-1-4215-3485-5
9 US | $12.99 CAN
KAI NO RINNE © 2009 Rumiko TAKAHASHI/Shogakukan
iz
media
v.viz.com
RATED
T+
FOR OLDER TEEN
ratings.viz.com
MANGA STARTS ON SUNDAY
SHONENSUNDAY.COM
SHONEN SUNDAY